LIBRARY OF
MONEY AND BANKING
HISTORY

ON FINANCIAL REFORM

ON

FINANCIAL REFORM

BY

SIR HENRY PARNELL

THIRD EDITION

[1831]

REPRINTS OF ECONOMIC CLASSICS

Augustus M. Kelley · Publishers
NEW YORK 1968

First Edition 1830

Third Edition 1831

(London: John Murray, *Albemarle Street*, 1831)

Reprinted 1968 by

AUGUSTUS M. KELLEY · PUBLISHERS

New York   New York   10010

Library of Congress Catalogue Card Number

68 - 56560

PRINTED IN THE UNITED STATES OF AMERICA
by SENTRY PRESS, NEW YORK, N. Y. 10019

ON

FINANCIAL REFORM.

BY

SIR HENRY PARNELL,

BART. M.P.

———

THIRD EDITION.

———

LONDON:

JOHN MURRAY, ALBEMARLE STREET.

———

MDCCCXXXI.

PREFACE

THE THIRD EDITION.

THE numerous Parliamentary accounts and Pamphlets concerning the subjects treated of in this work, which have been published since the first edition of it appeared, have been carefully examined, and such additions have been introduced as are calculated to give a complete exposition of the actual state of the finances.

Additional accounts are inserted in the Appendix, of the Civil List Pensions, and of Salaries exceeding 1000*l.* a year; and also of the comparative state of Ireland with respect to Trade, Manufactures, and Agriculture, immediately before the Union and at the present time. An Index has also been added.

February 1, 1831.

CONTENTS.

[See Index.]

Chapter XII.—Civil Government, p. 188.

Chapter XIII.—Military Expenditure, p. 211.

Chapter XIV.—Slave Trade—Sinking Fund—Dividends, p. 228.

Chapter XV.—Colonies, p. 231.

Chapter XVI.—Ireland, p. 252.

Chapter XVII.—Summary of Retrenchment, p. 257.

Chapter XVIII.—New Taxes, p. 260.

Chapter XIX.—The National Debt, p. 265.

APPENDIX.

FINANCIAL REFORM.

CHAPTER I

TAXATION.

ALTHOUGH it may be impossible to relieve industry
from all those taxes which are injurious to it, no attempt can be made towards accomplishing a partial repeal of them, without producing a great public benefit ; and as, perhaps, the general distaste for close and
accurate reasoning on subjects of this kind may have
led to exaggerated notions of the difficulty attending
the getting rid of taxes producing several millions of
revenue, no one ought to feel discouraged from endeavouring to show,—if, after a full consideration of
the subject, he feels no doubt he can do so,—that
many taxes might be reduced and many repealed,
without any risk with respect to securing a sufficient
revenue for all the services of the state.

But before entering upon a discussion having this
object in view, it is necessary to make some preliminary remarks on Taxation in general, for the purpose
of explaining the circumstances which enable a country
to bear a heavy amount of taxes, without being prevented from progressively becoming more industrious,
more rich, and more powerful.

It would appear that the pressure of the taxes is too commonly estimated with reference only to the total amount of revenue levied by them; and without duly considering the amount of the national income, consisting of the incomes of all the classes of the community, out of which the taxes are paid. But this is a very erroneous way of forming conclusions with respect to the degree in which the taxes affect the public. For, if the income of the country has been going on increasing in a greater proportion than taxation has been increasing, the pressure of taxation will be less now than it formerly was, though the taxes may have been doubled or trebled. So also, if the national income shall continue to go on increasing, taxation may be still considerably increased, beyond what it is now, without any real increase of burden on the community.

There is another circumstance connected with the question of the degree in which the taxes are oppressive, which is seldom noticed, namely, the different effects produced by different kinds of taxes. As it is clear that security and good order are productive of universal advantage, and that without them there would not be any considerable accumulation of wealth, no individual can justly complain, that he is made to contribute, in the same proportion to his means as others, for their attainment; but in selecting the taxes, a great deal of injury may be done to individuals, and to the public at large. If taxes fall on industry, that is, on raw materials, on manufactures, or on trade, they raise prices; by raising prices they diminish the consumption of the productions of industry, and thus diminish the employment of capital and labour, and check the accumulation of new capital.

But if taxes fall on persons not in business, who have incomes derived from rents, tithes, dividends on stock, interest on mortgages, salaries under government, and other such incomes, industry is but little injured by these taxes, in comparison to what it is by those taxes before mentioned; and the country may go on paying them without any great impediment to its becoming richer and richer.   It may be true, that each individual who pays a tax of this kind will spend less on the productions of industry; but as, in point of fact, what he pays is transferred by government in various ways to other individuals, the money paid for the tax is still expended on such productions.   So that, before a correct opinion can be formed of the actual effects of taxation, it is necessary to examine and make a distinction between the portion of taxes which falls on industry and that which does not.

There is still another circumstance to be mentioned, as connected with the pressure of taxation, which also is seldom taken into consideration, namely, the effect of monopolies and protections, in raising the prices of the numerous commodities which are the subjects of them.   These monopolies and protections impose by increased prices burdens on the public, not for any purpose of common utility or national advantage, but for the support of some favoured trades. If the effect of the corn laws be to raise the price of corn five shillings a quarter, this advance on the quantity annually consumed, taken at 50,000,000 quarters, creates a charge on the public of 12,500,000*l*. a year. If the protecting duties on East Indian and foreign sugars advance the price of sugar only one penny a pound, this advance on the quantity annually consumed, namely, 400,000,000 pounds, is a tax on the public of

6,800,000*l.* a year. If the East India Company's monopoly make the price of tea (exclusive of duty) not far short of double what it is at New York and Hamburgh, it imposes a tax of at least 2,000,000*l.* a year in the form of increased price ; and the protection in the timber trade enjoyed by the shipowners and Canada merchants costs the public at least 1,000,000*l.* a year; so that by these monopolies and protections, 17,000,000*l.* a year are taken from the pockets of the people, just as if corn, sugar, tea, and timber, were taxed to that amount, and the produce paid into the Exchequer. The system of monopoly and protection affects almost every branch of industry, and imposes, by increasing prices, many more millions of charge on the public than these 17,000,000*l.*, all which press on the resources of the country exactly in the same way as a similar amount of increased prices arising from taxation, and thus make the taxes appear to be much more burdensome than they really are.

It is because these circumstances are not duly attended to, that so much is heard of the suffering and injury which the taxes produce ; of the ruin which they have brought on our manufactures and commerce, and of its being impossible for this country to embark in a new war, without encountering the greatest financial difficulties, and incurring the risk of bankruptcy. But these notions are only in part well-founded ; for, notwithstanding the very injurious effects of many of the taxes, taxation has not yet been carried to such an extent, as to place this country either in a declining or stationary state with respect to its agriculture, manufactures, and commerce. This is a conclusion come to by reasoning on facts, which show the continued accumulation of wealth in defiance of all impediments. It is a conclusion, in no degree originating in any preconceived theory; nor does it lose any of its claim to have confidence placed in it, by its being directly opposed to the opinion of a number of persons, who maintain that the nation is in a declining state; because these persons wholly omit to sustain that opinion by any reasoning whatever. They merely exclaim, Look at the national debt; the taxes; the distress of agriculture and manufactures;—but they forget that the country was in the highest state of prosperity in the years 1823, 1824, and 1825, with the same debt and taxes which now exist; and that similar distress to what now prevails (February 1830) has been a matter of regular recurrence, and regularly followed by recovery, as soon as the disturbed proportion of supply to demand is restored to its proper ratio,—an event which happens as a matter of course, from the operation of the common rules by which trade is carried on.

The history of this country shows that temporary interruptions have been constantly mistaken for symptoms of habitual decline; and those persons who now maintain that the country is in this state, in ignorance of this historical fact, are committing the same error which has been so often made and so often exposed. It has been remarked, that the English are more inclined than any other nation to view the dark side of the prospect, to fear everything, and hope for nothing. Whenever the manufacturers suffer a reduction in their profits, and landlords find a difficulty in obtaining their rents, distress is universally proclaimed, and every one concludes the country is undone.

Similar desponding apprehensions have been publicly avowed at different times, in works of respectable authority in other respects, in the course of the last hundred and thirty years, during which period the nation has been continually making progress in happiness and prosperity. Dr. Davenant, in describing the state of public affairs in 1699, says, 'our gold and silver will be carried off by degrees; rents will fall; wool will sink in its price; our stock of ships will be diminished; farm-houses will go to ruin; industry will decay; and we shall have upon us all the visible marks of a declining people*.' In 1736 the Craftsman says, ' the vast load of debt under which the nation groans is the source of all those calamities and gloomy prospects of which we have so much reason to complain: to this has been owing that multiplicity of taxes, which have more than doubled the price of the common necessaries of life, and thereby distressed the poor labourer and manufacturer; disabled the farmer to pay his rent; and put even gentlemen of plentiful estates under the greatest difficulty†.' Dr. Chalmers, in describing the state of the country in 1775, says, ' yet prosperous as our affairs had been during the short peace of 1763, they were represented by an analogous spirit to that of 1738, either of designing faction or of interested folly, as in an alarming situation. The state of things, it was said, is approaching to an awful crisis. The navigation and commerce by which we rose to power and opulence are much on the decline; our taxes are numerous and heavy; an enormous national debt threatens the ruin of public credit; our labouring poor are forced by hard necessity to seek

---

* Essay on the Balance of Trade.
† No. 502.   14th Feb. 1736.

that comfortable subsistence in distant colonies which
their industry at home cannot procure them*.'   It
would not be difficult to make many additions to the
above extracts, were it necessary to adduce further
proof that ill-founded apprehensions have led to repeated errors in considering temporary defalcations as
infallible symptoms of a fatal decline†.   But at the
same time it must be confessed that, while there is no
reason for placing any reliance on the predictions
which are now so confidently made of approaching
and inevitable ruin, the preservation of what we have
acquired, and the future progress of public prosperity,
are subjects entitled to inspire deep and constant
anxiety.

With respect to the evils which the taxes occasion,
the true state of the case is, that certain of them,
which fall on raw materials, manufactures, and trade,
and others which are carried to an excess on some of
the principal articles of consumption (together producing a net revenue of about 11,000,000*l*.‡), are as
injurious as it is possible for taxes to be ; but that the
rest of the taxes, which produce about 39,000,000*l*.§,

* Estimate, p. 153.

† See Sir John Sinclair's History of the Revenue, Appendix,
vol. ii. p. 51, in which extracts are given from twenty-two
authors, stating that the nation was wholly ruined and undone
at different periods between 1688 and 1783.

‡ The taxes on raw materials yield 6,000,000*l*. a year; those
on manufactures 2,000,000*l*. ; and that part of the revenue levied
on tobacco and foreign spirits, which may be considered as being
obtained by the duties on those articles being too high, and
injurious to industry and trade, may be estimated at 3,000,000*l*.
(See Appendix, No. I.)

§ The amount of the net ordinary revenue is stated by the
Committee of Finance to have been, in 1827, 49,581,772*l*.—
Fourth Report, p. 113.   The Committee of Finance referred

are paid, for the most part, voluntarily, and out of the
surplus of the incomes of individuals over and above
what is requisite for purchasing the necessaries of life ;
and although these taxes occasion many inconve-
niences and vexations, they are not oppressive and
destructive in the way they are commonly supposed to
be by those persons, who, for want of sufficient examination into their real effect, imagine that all taxes are
equally injurious. So long as a revenue of 50,000,000*l.*
must be raised for the public service, the abovemen-
tioned large portion of it (39,000,000*l.*) is obtained in
a way but little liable to any real objections ; and if
the remainder were provided by taxes of the same
kind, the whole revenue would be paid without any
serious injury ; because, notwithstanding the large
amount of the charge, the stock of national wealth is
so great in proportion to it, as to be fully able to bear

to in this work is the Committee appointed in the Session of
1828.

The following is the account of the ordinary net revenue of
the year 1829, in the return laid before Parliament.

Customs	.	.	.	.	.	£17,211,839	19	6¼
Excise	.	.	.	.	.	19,540,010	19	11¾
Stamps	.	.	.	.	.	7,101,304	13	5
Taxes	.	.	.	.	.	4,896,567	10	6½
Post Office	.	.	.	.		1,481,000	0	0
One Shilling and Sixpence, and Four Shillings on Pensions and Salaries						54,493	1	11¼
Hackney Coaches and Hawkers and Pedlars					.	61,167	1	10
Small Branches of the King's Here-ditary Revenues			.	.	.	6,632	5	0
Surplus Fees of Regulated Public Offices			.	.	.	66,372	15	0¼
Poundage Fees, Pells Fees, &c. in Ireland			.	.	.	8,886	14	8½
						£50,428,275	1	11½

it. It is by reasoning in this manner, with reference to the relation between what is to be paid and the means of paying it, that the true state of the case with respect to the pressure of taxation can be best understood, and those errors avoided which are the grounds of the current opinions that the country is incapable of supporting its burdens, and of the schemes which are proposed for improving the condition of it by some change in the currency, or some other expedient*.

What are called our financial difficulties, and about which so much alarm is felt, are not so much present as prospective difficulties. The Treasury easily finds means for paying all demands upon it ; and we may rest assured, that whatever the difficulties may be

* The administration of Lord Liverpool is entitled to the gratitude of the public for the ability and courage with which it undertook and accomplished the restoration of the currency to its old standard. The fact, proved by Mr. Tooke in his Letter to Lord Grenville, of the paper of the Bank of England having been reduced, before the passing of Mr. Peel's bill, to such a low amount as would have restored the value of the currency if no such bill had passed ; and the flourishing state of the revenue, of trade, of manufactures, and of agriculture, in the years 1823, 1824, and 1825, during which Mr. Peel's bill was in full operation, completely expose the error which those persons have fallen into, who attribute every modern public calamity to that measure. Besides, when it is considered that all the money transactions connected with commerce and manufactures were not at all affected by the restoration of the currency, in consequence of their transitory nature, and that these in point of value comprise a vast many more millions of property than rents and other fixed property, it will appear quite impossible that the passing of Mr. Peel's bill could produce the generally destructive effects commonly attributed to it. The wisdom of rejecting all the schemes proposed in the last session for again altering the currency is now manifest from the disappearance of distress without their aid.

under which the country is at present placed, they may be made to yield to sound principles of legislation.

With respect to prospective difficulties, the notion of them arises from apprehensions of the effects of a new war on our commercial and financial interests. The debt, which has been so little reduced during so long a course of peace, will, according to all that is known of the means by which ministers propose to manage the finances, rapidly accumulate on the recurrence of another war; it is therefore impossible not to feel great uneasiness at the prospect of a very large addition of permanent taxes for the purpose of paying the interest on new loans. But, in point of fact, there would be no ground for anticipating any peculiar degree of embarrassment in the event of a war, if all were now done, that ought to be done, for conducting our financial affairs in a proper manner. If the unfunded debt were reduced to a few millions; if the currency were settled on a sound footing by reforming the banking system; and if a foundation were laid for imposing war taxes whenever a war shall take place, there ought to be no greater difficulty in commencing and carrying on a new war, than has been experienced on former occasions.

But it is by no other means than by applying the most unremitting care and superintendence directed on sound principles to our finances, that they can be preserved from those difficulties in which they are already supposed to be involved. With a skilful management of them, we may trust to the further increase of our productive industry for enabling us to overcome new difficulties, in the same way that it enabled us to provide the expenses of the last war. We have only to remove the impediments with which bad laws still clog the activity and energy of individuals, to render productive industry even still more efficient than heretofore in creating new wealth.

The want of attention to the effect of increasing productive industry in increasing the sources of taxation, has led to much erroneous reasoning on the subject of taxation. For nothing can be more certain, than that the amount of the produce of national industry taken by a government in the shape of taxes, may be regularly increased in every country in which the arts are progressive, without occasioning any additional burden to the people. Every new invention and discovery by which the production of commodities can be facilitated, and their value reduced, enables individuals to spare a larger quantity of them for the use of the state. This shows that governments have precisely the same interest as their subjects in facilitating production. Public wealth is merely a portion of private wealth transferred from individuals to government; and the greater the wealth of individuals, the greater will be the magnitude of the portion they can conveniently spare for public purposes*.

The amount of the income of Great Britain at the revolution has been commonly computed at 43 millions. Mr. Arthur Young, in his work on Political Arithmetic, published in 1776, computed the national income at 100 millions†. Mr. Lowe says, in his work on the State of England, that the *taxable* income amounted, in 1793, to 125 millions; and in 1806, to 170 millions‡. Of late years, the *general* income§ of

* See the Supplement to the Encyclopædia Britannica, vol. vi. p. 689. Article, ' Taxation.'
† Sir John Sinclair's History of the Revenue, vol. i. p. 337.
‡ Appendix, p. 32.   § Sup. Encyc. Brit. vol. vi. p. 643.

Great Britain has been computed at 300 millions
Mr. Ricardo says, in his work on the Principles of
Political Economy, published in 1819, ' Notwithstanding the immense expenditure of the English
government during the last twenty years, there can
be little doubt but that the increased production on
the part of the people has more than compensated for
it. The national capital has not merely been unim-
paired, it has been greatly increased; and the annual
income of the people, even after the payment of their
taxes, is probably greater at the present time than at
any former period of our history. For the proof of
this, we might refer to the increase of population—
to the extension of agriculture—to the increase of
shipping and manufactures—to the building of docks
—to the opening of numerous canals, as well as to
many other expensive undertakings, all denoting an
immense increase both of capital and of annual production*.' As ten years have elapsed since Mr.
Ricardo published these remarks, and as similar proofs
can be referred to, showing a continued increase of
production, it is correct to come to the conclusion,
that the national capital and income are now much
greater than they have been at any former period.

The increase of a million a-year in the rateable income of Lancashire, stated by Sir Robert Peel in the
House of Commons to have taken place between 1815
and 1829, sustains this conclusion†.

The following accounts fully corroborate all that
has been just said with respect to the progressive increase of national wealth:—

* Third Edition, p. 164.
† Mirror of Parliament, June 12, 1829, p. 2099.

An Account of the Quantities of the following Articles imported, or made for Home Consumption, in Great Britain, on an average of three years, to the 5th of Jan. 1781, 1793, 1813 or 1815, and 1830.

	1781.	1793.	1813.	1830.
Cotton Wool } lbs.	6,816,692	30,789,572	78,811,283	218,484,094
Sheep's Wool } „	958,080	3,204,342	7,430,476	27,182,904
Raw Silk „	426,958	827,812	919,162	3,503,289
Indigo „	560,590	884,738	. . .	2,522,311
Tallow, cwts.	99,437	181,887	347,775	1,005,237
Fir Timb. loads,	84,668	222,760	251,690	426,630
			Year 1815.	
Soap lbs.	38,807,408	47,583,591	78,784,075	114,182,804
Candles Tallow } „	51,713,319	58,892,026	77,954,823	115,813,275
Wax do. „	202,079	451,578	817,483	1,002,740

Exports of British and Irish Produce and Manufactures from Great Britain.

Official value.

1792	. . . . .	16,824,007 †
1814	. . . . .	33,200,580 ‡
1829	. . . . .	55,465,723 ‡

An account of the Shipping cleared outwards from Great Britain.

	British, Tons.	Foreign, Tons.
1792	1,563,744	175,556 §
1829	2,063,179	730,250 ‖

As to the future prospects of the nation, there is no reason to doubt that a continued augmentation of capital will take place even in defiance of many obstructions. The same moral, physical, and external·

* Sess. Pap. 1830, No. 545.   † Remarks on Customs, p. 47
          ‡ Sess. Pap. 1830. No. 243.
§ Remarks on Customs, p. 46.   ‖ Sess. Pap. 1830, No. 678.

causes, which have contributed to the existing amount
of national wealth, are still in operation. The free
constitution of the government; the exact administration of the laws; the protection afforded to foreigners;
and the toleration of all religions, will produce the same
effects which they have hitherto produced. The improved manner of conducting business and speculations among the higher mercantile and manufacturing
classes in consequence of more attention being paid
to the science or principles of trade, and the activity,
perseverance, and increased knowledge of the working
class will cause the future efforts of industry to
prosper. Our natural productions of iron, coal, and
other articles of raw materials will preserve our superiority in manufactures over other nations; while a
reformed management of our foreign possessions, and
a more enlarged system of free trade, will extend our
markets. Whatever evils press just now (February
1830) on our manufactures, the more we examine our
situation, the more we shall find it possible to trace
them to causes of a temporary character*.

* The following statement appeared in the *Northampton
Mercury*, early in November, 1829 :—

' In reference to domestic affairs, it gives us infinite satisfaction to be able to report the prospect of the state of trade is become more and more cheering. The crisis of commercial distress is generally considered to be over by competent judges;
and a resumed activity is reported from most of the great
manufacturing districts. From Liverpool, extensive transactions are reported in cotton wool; and, as might be expected,
the accounts for the last few weeks are all confirmatory of
activity in the cotton manufactures. At Manchester, the silk
warehouses have lately been completely cleared of their stock;
at Halifax there is a great demand for woollen cloths; at Leeds
all hands are employed; and at Bradford, the accounts are
equally of a cheering nature.'   The

Improvements, whether in agriculture, manufactures, or foreign trade, are still very far from having

The correctness of these observations is fully borne out by the following extracts from the public papers to a more recent date :—

[From the *Times*, May 10 and 11, 1830.]

' We have great satisfaction in saying, that in consequence of the revival of the glove trade, and other causes, the working classes in this city are much better employed than they have been. *The price of skins has risen* so much in France, that the manufacturers of that country cannot now compete so successfully with English glovers.'—*Worcester Journal.*

State of Trade in Yorkshire.—' It gives us great satisfaction to be able to state, that the improvement which has been experienced for some time past in the trade of this district is not only maintained, but very decidedly increased. During the last fortnight, a greater quantity of woollen cloth has been sold in Leeds than was perhaps ever before disposed of in the same length of time ; and the most encouraging feature in the trade is, that stocks are very low both in the hands of the manufacturers, of the merchants, and of the London dealers. The Huddersfield and Bradford markets this week have been remarkably brisk, as the accounts from those places testify.'— *Leeds Mercury.*

' We understand that work has been given out to the plain silk hose hands, by some of the hosiers of this town, during the past week, at an advance of 3*s.* per dozen; and that the advance is expected to become general this day. The demand for goods is greater now than it has been known for some years. It is a singular circumstance, that there are now seventy-two plain silk frames unoccupied in this town for want of hands.'—*Derby Reporter.*

[From the *Globe* of August 24, 1830.]

' *State of Trade.*—We scarcely ever remember the trade of this town (Manchester) and neighbourhood generally to have been in a more healthy and satisfactory state, than, by common consent, it is admitted to be at this time. The silk manufacture, we are glad to say, participates in the general improvement. The manufacture of bandanas, which the anti-free-traders told us was to be annihilated by the opening of the market for East

arrived at a limit; and no country possesses in its resources greater means of continuing in a career of advancement. If, then, peace continue, it may be expected that the national capital and income will become much greater than they now are. One effect of this will be,—the taxes becoming so productive of revenue, as to allow of some being repealed; but the main and most important effect will be, such increased means of paying taxes as will admit of the expenses of future wars being wholly defrayed by war taxes, so

India goods, has for several months been decidedly more extensive than ever, and very large quantities have been disposed of for foreign markets. There is at present, we are happy to add, less apprehension of the probability of any serious commercial reaction than we have formerly known at similar periods. The business done, generally speaking, is bottomed upon real capital.'—*Manchester Guardian.*

[From the *Globe*, Aug. 28, 1830.]

Huddersfield.—' I have much pleasure in announcing a decided and considerable improvement in the woollen trade of this place. For some description of goods the supply is not at all equal to the demand.'

[*Same Paper.*]

Iron.—' We are happy to hear that the iron trade is in a more flourishing state than it has been. An advance in the price of iron has recently taken place in Staffordshire.'

[From the *Times*, Oct. 26, 1830.]

Wool Trade.—' The markets of Leeds and Huddersfield are still very brisk; the accumulation of wool in the farmers' hands, of which we heard so much two or three years ago, is worked up, and the manufacturers are now at work upon the present year's " clip." The fustian and other weavers in the neighbourhood of Halifax have obtained a very considerable advance of wages; and a similar advance has been made to the woolcombers. This we consider excellent news: as far as the manufacturing parts of the country are concerned, we want only the return of that state of things which will enable the masters to give liberal wages to their workmen.'—*County Chronicle.*

that no addition need be made to the national debt.
If the progress of wealth be not interrupted, this is
the state to which the country would certainly come
by continually growing richer; and as all danger and
difficulty about the national debt would then be got
rid of, the object of all our financial arrangements
ought to be to remove every impediment arising from
taxes on industry and restrictions on trade, in the
way of the most rapid accumulation of capital and
national wealth. No common considerations or apprehensions about the danger of making innovations
ought to be allowed to prevent such a reform in the
táxes, and such alterations in commercial regulations.
Industry would then be relieved from all obstructions,
and those remains of monopoly, which are still so
deeply engrafted in our commercial policy, would be
done away.

The nature of the reform of the taxes which seems
to be required will be explained in the following
pages. The principle that will be held in view in
suggesting each alteration, will be that of levying the
revenue which is wanted for the public service in such
a manner as to occasion the smallest possible loss of
money and enjoyment to the contributors, and the
least possible impediment to the progress of national
industry and national wealth; at the same time, full
consideration will be given to the great importance
of making every change in so gradual a manner, that
nothing may happen which might give a shock to
trade, or reduce the revenue below what is requisite
for all the public services.

Chapter II.

TAXES ON RAW MATERIALS.

It appears, from an account laid before the House of Commons, that the taxes on the materials of manufactures, buildings, ship-building, and other trades, produced in 1827 a net revenue of 6,191,956l.*

Although there is no proposition in finance the truth of which is more readily admitted, than that which affirms the impolicy of taxing the materials of industry, there is, at the same time, so little appearance of a proper effort being made to modify or repeal this class of taxes, that nothing appears to be more wanted than a full explanation of their injurious operation on the employment of capital and labour, the accumulation of capital, and the increase of national wealth.

As the power of the manufacturing capital of a country to purchase raw materials is in proportion to their cheapness, and as the extent of manufactures is in proportion to the quantity of materials that are purchased, every particle of duty laid on them lessens the amount of industry and of annual productions. It consequently lessens the means of adding to the national capital, because these means consist of the surplus of the annual productions of the country. When, therefore, no less a sum is raised, every year, than 6,000,000l. on materials, it is manifest how great

* Par. Pap. Sess. 1829, No. 172; and see Appendix, No. I.

an injury this kind of taxation must do, by limiting manufacturing and every other kind of industry.

These taxes have also a very injurious effect in limiting navigation and foreign commerce ; for if there were no such taxes, the increased quantity of foreign materials that would be imported, and of finished goods that would be exported to pay for these materials, would add considerably to both navigation and foreign commerce.

The levying of so large a sum as 6,000,000*l.* a year on articles that require capital and labour to give them utility and value, must strike every one as being a most serious obstacle in the way of remedying the difficulties which press at this moment the heaviest on the country, namely, the want of employment for capital and labour. The repealing, therefore, of the whole of these taxes, is a measure particularly called for, under the present state of our manufactures, and of the labouring class.

With respect to the foreign market for our manufactures, the taxes on materials produce an evil of the greatest magnitude ; for, by increasing the cost of production, they contribute to lessen the means our manufacturers have of carrying on a successful competition with foreign manufacturers. Whatever may be the difference between one country and another, with respect to soil, climate, capital, wages, and machinery, the circumstance which leads to the exportation of manufactures, and makes it profitable, is the advantage in the smallness of the cost of producing them ; every tax, therefore, on materials, by increasing the price of them, adds to the cost of production, and thus lessens the means of carrying on competition with foreigners. In this way it acts as a

bounty on foreign manufactures, and therefore is a
tax of the most pernicious description.

If all materials were free of duty, the consequence
would be, that our woollens, cottons, silks, hardware,
and other manufactures, might be sent to foreign
markets two or three per cent. cheaper than at present ; and to those persons who have a due sense of
mercantile profit, and of how little a turn one way or
the other secures or loses a market, this will appear
to be of the greatest importance.   What, in point of
fact, under the present circumstances of our manufactures, we have most cause to be alarmed at, is not
the depression of the home market, but foreign competition, in consequence of the progress now making
on the continent of Europe and in America in the
improving and extending of all kinds of manufactures.
We shall do well, therefore, to look into the effects
of taxation ; for if we continue to load our manufacturers as they are now loaded, we may be assured
that taxes will bring upon us the same result that
they brought on Holland, which is thus described in
the work of M. Luzac on the Wealth of Holland :—
' D'autres examineront peut-être si ces taxes ont été
judicieusement placées ; si elles sont perçues avec
l'économie convenable.   Il suffit ici d'observer que
les manufactures de laine, de soie, d'or, et d'argent,
une foule d'autres ont succombé après avoir lutté
longtems contre la progression de l'impôt.   La Hollande n'a sauvé du naufrage de ses manufactures, que
celles qui n'ont pas été exposées à la concurrence des
autres nations *.'

As nothing is more important than to produce a
general conviction of the absolute necessity of repeal-

* La Richesse de la Hollande, vol. ii. p. 73.

ing the taxes on materials, some short remarks will now be made to draw attention to those taxes which are the most particularly inconsistent with sound principles, and the most injurious in their operation.

Hemp being an article of the first necessity for the navy and for the mercantile shipping, and not being produced at home, the duty upon it of 4*l*. 13*s*. 4*d*. a ton is very objectionable. By increasing the prices of sails and cordage, it is quite inconsistent with those numerous legislative regulations which are still in force for protecting and encouraging the shipping interest. It also raises the prices of those kinds of linen which are in general demand, and by thus diminishing the consumption of them, it diminishes the employment of capital and labour.

As the legislature, acting most wisely, has introduced a freer system of navigation, it is bound in common justice to the shipping interest to remove all duties on the materials of ship-building. The permission which has recently been given to British ships to buy foreign cordage, and bring it home free of duty, is an additional reason for taking off the duty on hemp.

The duty on barilla is about 100 per cent., though lately reduced. It produces 79,000*l*. a year. It is used in large quantities in making soap, and raises the prices of the materials of several manufactures. Even in the cases where a drawback is allowed, the obtaining it is attended with much expense and loss of time; while, as is the case with all drawbacks, there is a great waste of public money in the business first of collecting the duty, then in repaying it, and often besides in consequence of more duty being drawn back by fraudulent contrivances than the duty originally paid.   This duty was originally and avowedly imposed as a protection of the manufacture of kelp, for the exclusive benefit of a few families in Scotland.

The duty on thrown silk not only raises the price of the silk imported, but as long as any is imported, of all silk thrown at home ; because the price of the latter will always be as high as the price of the former, in consequence of its being impossible that two prices for the same article can exist in the same market.   If thrown silk were free of duty, the price would be reduced by the amount of the duty ; for our own throwsters, in order to secure a sale for their silk, would be obliged to introduce such improvements as would enable them to go into competition with free foreign thrown silks.   If they could not make such improvements, and lower their prices, then the silk manufacturers would be supplied by foreign silk ; but the progress which has of late been made in silk machinery makes it evident that this is an event by no means likely to happen, if the duty on thrown silk were repealed.

The duty on timber affects and injures industry in a great variety of ways, in consequence of its being so much used in ships, buildings, machinery, &c.   Countries possessing forests in the vicinity of navigable rivers, enjoy great advantages in that respect over our ship-builders ; and to lay a duty upon timber is still further to increase those advantages. Instead of doing this, it would appear as if it were an indispensable preliminary to securing a permanently successful competition with foreign ship-builders, to admit timber to be imported free of all duty.

The present arrangement of the duties, namely, of 10s. a load on North American timber, and of 2l. 15s.

a load on European timber, forces, as it were, the use of the former kind, though of inferior quality. It has already been stated that this arrangement, which has for its object to protect the timber of our North American colonies and our shipping, costs the public 1,000,000*l.* a year ;—many competent judges say 1,500,000*l.* If, in place of the present duties, a duty of 1*l.* 10*s.* a load were imposed on all timber, the prices would be reduced 1*l.* 5*s.* a load, and the revenue would be very considerably increased ; for then nearly the whole of the foreign timber, consumed in the United Kingdom, would pay 1*l.* 10*s.* a load, instead of a small portion of it paying 2*l.* 15*s.* and the remainder paying 10*s.*, in consequence of its being impossible that, with a duty of 1*l.* 10*s.* on all timber, American timber could be imported and sold with profit. In 1809, before the duty on European timber was raised, 428,000 tons of British shipping were employed in this trade[*].

The duty on bricks and tiles falls heavily on industry, in consequence of the number and size of the buildings required for mills, factories, store-houses, &c. It must obviously contribute to diminish the employment of capital and labour.

The duties on coals and culm carried coastwise needs only to be mentioned to obtain a general assent to the inexpediency of continuing it.

The policy of making sea-borne coal a subject of taxation is of vast importance to all classes of persons. Abuses, it appears from the recent parliamentary reports, of the most flagrant description have insinuated themselves into every department of the coal trade. It would seem that the legislature had

[*] Speech of the Right Hon. C. P. Thompson, 26th March, 1830, on the reduction of taxes, p. 22.

forgotten, in laying on this duty, that fuel was indispensable to existence, and also by far the most important of all the instruments of manufacturing industry.
This is proved to be the case by the manufactures of
Manchester, Leeds, Birmingham, Glasgow, &c.

Coal being a very bulky and heavy article, its price
must be greatly increased in London and the southern
parts of England, by the long sea voyage which it
has to be carried; and therefore nothing can be more
unjust and more glaringly oppressive than the levying
on this coal of a duty of 6s. a chaldron. As this duty
does not affect the coals which are consumed near the
mines, every obvious and recognized principle has
been trampled under foot in imposing it. The existing
provisions of the laws are such, that they fall with the
utmost severity upon the southern counties of England; the pressure of them is comparatively light in
Wales; and it does not affect Scotland at all.

The coal duty is not only injurious in the southern
counties by directly advancing the price of coals (to
the amount, with regulations, of a million or twelve
hundred thousand pounds a year in London alone),
but, indirectly, by depriving those subject to it of the
means of giving employment that they would otherwise
have. If the duty and the regulations that grow out
of it were abolished, the expense of carrying coal by
sea would be so much reduced, that many branches of
industry, which cannot at present be carried on except
in the vicinity of the mines, might be carried on at a
distance from the mines, while those which are now
carried on at a distance, might be greatly extended.
The repeal, therefore, of the coal duty would probably
do more in London, and other places in the south of
England, to promote industry, and consequently to in-

crease the demand for labour, than any other measure it is in the power of Parliament to adopt.

The different special charges on coal in the port of London amount to 6s. 4½d. a chaldron. So that, on the whole, between one charge and another, the expenses of the transit of coals from the coal-owner to the consumer in London is 1l. 15s. 5½d. a chaldron, for which chaldron the coal-owner receives 9s. 6d.*

If the duty on coals were repealed, it must not be imagined that it would cause a reduction in the revenue equal to the produce of the duty. The fall in the price of coals, consequent on the reduction of the duty, would give the consumer greater means of purchasing additional quantities of taxed articles, such as sugar, tea, beer, spirits, tobacco, &c. ; and in consequence of a greater demand for coals, the very numerous body of persons that would be required as miners, sailors, &c., in carrying on an increased trade, would have increased means of purchasing these articles.

The practice of selling coals by measure leads to that of screening them, by which not less than 25 per cent. of the coals raised from the pit is destroyed.

The exportation of coals is confined to between three and four hundred thousand tons a year, by the high duty of seventeen shillings a chaldron. If this were reduced, the exportation would be immensely increased, with great advantage to the revenue, and also to the owners of collieries and of ships, and to the labouring class.

It has been said, that by allowing coal to be exported at a low duty, the Belgians and French might advantageously employ it in their manufac-

* See Observations on the Coal Duty. Longman & Co. 1830.

turing establishments ; and to guard against this con-
tingency, a high duty has been laid upon its exportation.   It does not appear that any other reason has
ever been assigned in vindication of the existing
regulations with regard to exported coal ; and yet,
inexplicable as it may seem, *small* coal, or that very
coal which is used in manufactures, is allowed to be
exported at a duty of 4*s*. 6*d*. a chaldron, while *large*
coal, or that which is exclusively used in dwelling-
houses, is burdened with the enormous duty of 17*s*. !

But notwithstanding the low duty on the coal used
in manufactories, the greatest export of it that has
taken place in any one year was only 60,315 chaldrons.
If an equal duty of 4*s*. or 5*s*. a chaldron were imposed
on all coals exported, a check would be given to the
export of that kind of coals which may be used in the
arts, at the same time that a vast additional facility
would be given to the export of that which is used
for domestic purposes only.   Were a measure of this
sort adopted, it may be fairly inferred that the revenue
from exported coal would be at least doubled or trebled.

The duties on tallow and soap are exceedingly injurious to manufactures, and have the same effects that
all the other duties on materials have—namely, that
of deranging the natural course in which capital and
labour would be employed, productions extended, and
the wealth, comforts, and enjoyments of the community increased.

The repeal of the duty on leather, in the last session,
was a measure perfectly in accordance with the principles here laid down ; but the selection of the beer
duty, as one more fit to be repealed than the duties
on materials and manufactures, was a great error. The
giving up of so large a revenue as that received on

beer admitted of the repeal of nearly all those taxes
which are the most injurious to industry.

It is impossible to repeat too often how much good
the repealing of the taxes on materials would do.
The evil of continuing them is so universally pernicious, that the common-place excuse for it should
have no weight; namely, that the circumstances of
the country will not admit of a reduction of the revenue; at least, until those circumstances have been
more fully investigated.   No inquiry has as yet been
made to ascertain whether means may not be found
for securing a sufficient revenue for the public expenditure without the aid of this class of taxes, and
therefore no plea of difficulty, with respect to the
revenue, should be listened to, until it can be shown,
either that the present scale of public expenditure
will not admit of any reduction; or that no other
taxes can be laid on of a less injurious kind than the
existing taxes on materials.

Chapter III.

TAXES ON MANUFACTURES.

Contrary to every sound principle of trade, the manufactures of paper, glass, and printed calicoes have been selected as subjects of taxation.

The following account shows the rates of duty which have been imposed, and the revenue obtained from them :—

An Account of the Net Produce of the Excise Duties in the United Kingdom, as stated in the Finance Accounts for the Year 1827, on Glass, Paper, and Printed Calicoes, and showing the several rates of Duty* :—

ARTICLES, NET PRODUCE.   RATES OF DUTY.

				£ s. d.
			Materials for flint glass	- 0 0 3 per lb.
			Ditto plate -	- 3 0 0
Glass -	613,508 3 9¼		Crown Glass - -	- 3 13 6 } per
			Broad ditto - -	- 1 10 0 } cwt.
			Green ditto - -	- 0 8 2
			First class paper - -	- 0 0 3 } per
			Second ditto - -	- 0 0 1½ } lb.
Paper -	649,779 8 11		Glazed paper, millb. & scaleb. 1	1 0 } per
			Pasteboard, 1st class -	- 1 8 0 } cwt.
			Ditto, 2d ditto -	- 0 14 0
Printed } goods }	662,141 16 1¼		Foreign calicoes - -	- 0 0 7 }
			British calicoes & muslins	0 0 3½ } per
			Stained paper - -	- 0 0 1¾ } yard.

£1,925,429 8 9½   J. EWBANK, General Accomptant.

Excise Office, London, 17th Feb. 1829.

As the extent of the market for these manufactures,

* For the duties on bricks and tiles, soap and starch, see Appendix, No. I:

and consequently the extent of the employment of
capital and labour in producing them, depends on their
cheapness, these duties, by increasing prices, have a
direct effect in limiting the market for them, and
diminishing the employment of capital and labour.
In addition to this, the necessarily severe and vexatious regulations under which these duties are collected, have most injurious consequences.

By the Excise laws prescribing the processes of fabri-
cation, the manufacturer cannot manage his trade in
the way his skill and experience point out as the best;
but he is compelled to conform to such methods of
pursuing his art as he finds taught in Acts of Parliament. Thus the unseen injury arising from Excise
taxation, by its interference with the free course of
manufacture, is much greater than is suspected by the
public. The consequence of the activity and invention of the manufacturers being repressed, is, that the
consumers of their goods pay increased prices, not
only for the duties imposed on them, but for the
additional expense incurred by absurd and vexatious
regulations; and, in addition to this, the goods are
generally very inferior in quality to what they would
be if no duties existed.

The policy of the legislature in laying on the duties
now under consideration, is in direct opposition to that
policy which has been so extensively pursued, of imposing high duties on foreign goods to protect all
other manufactures, and forms a striking instance of
the inconsistency and absurdity for which a great part
of our commercial code is distinguished.

The duty on the paper manufacture varies from 50
to 150 per cent. on the different kinds of paper. The
laws for regulating the collection of it are so scattered
and confused as to render it almost impossible for a

manufacturer to have a perfect knowledge of them. The number and amount of the penalties to which he is subject are quite out of all proportion to the frauds he may, by possibility, be guilty of, while the power of administering these laws and levying these penalties is unlimited.

The duty on paper has an injurious effect on many other trades besides that of the paper-maker. The limited consumption which it occasions injures the makers of machinery, type-founders, ink-makers, printers, engravers, booksellers, bookbinders, stationers, paper-stainers, and several other trades. But the greatest evil of all is the high price of books which it gives rise to. This places a great obstacle in the way of the progress of knowledge, of useful and necessary arts, and of sober and industrious habits. Books carry the productions of the human mind over the whole world, and may be truly called the raw materials of every kind of science and art, and of all social improvement.

The duties on all kinds of glass manufactures are so high, that they necessarily have a most injurious effect in limiting the extent of the market for them, and thereby diminishing the employment of capital and labour. The materials of glass in this country are so abundant, and also the materials for working up the glass materials, that the taking off the duties would lead to an unlimited extension of this manufacture. The use of a great number of articles, which is now confined to the richer classes, would become universal among the lower orders. There is no reason, except the high price which is the consequence of the duty, why every house in the United Kingdom should not be as abundantly furnished with plate glasses as in France. All the information which can be obtained from the best informed travellers goes to show that if the duty were taken off there would be a great exportation of this manufacture to foreign countries. As in the case of the paper manufacture, a great many other trades are injured by the duties on glass besides the glass manufacture. In the Act of Parliament for the collection of these duties there are no less than thirty-two clauses of regulations, penalties and prohibitions; all great obstacles in the way of introducing improvements; vexatious in the highest degree to the manufacturer, and necessarily obliging him to sell his goods at much higher prices than what the mere amount of the duty occasions.

The following statement shows how much the high duties have kept down the consumption of glass.

The quantities which paid duty for home consumption were—

Flint and Plate Glass.   Cwts.
Four years to 1793 - Duty, 21s. 5d. per cwt. - 190,000
      ,, to 1825* - ,, 90s. ,,   }
on Flint, and 60s. per cwt. on Plate - } 167,000

Broad Glass.
Four years to 1793 - Duty, 8s. per cwt. - - 90,000
      ,, to 1825 - ,, 30s. ,, - - 34,000

Glass Bottles.
Four years to 1793 - Duty, 4s. per cwt. - - 881,000
      ,, to 1825 - ,, 8s. ,, - - 697,000

Crown Glass.
Four years to 1793 - Duty, 16s. 1d. per cwt. - 314,000
      ,, to 1825 - Duty, 73s. ,, - - 450,000 †

* This year is taken, because in 1825 the duty on flint glass was reduced to 56s. Since 1825 there has been a considerable increase of flint glass; but the consumption of other kinds is not much altered.

† This statement has been made up from an account of the Excise Office, prepared for Parliament. See Appendix, No. II.

In 1828, 379,365*l.* of the gross duty received on glass (*viz.* 953,257*l.*) was repaid in drawbacks on exportation, being more than one-third of the whole duty. This is in itself a strong reason for repealing the duty; for no system of taxation can be more unwise than that of incurring the expense, and producing the vexation attending the collecting of so much money, with the result to incur the additional expense of paying it back again.

The duty of $3\frac{1}{2}d.$ a square yard on printed calicoes is at the rate of from 80 to 100 per cent. on the description of goods used for garments by the lower orders of society, and only from 5 to 6 per cent. on the fine calicoes worn by the rich. It is calculated that if this duty were repealed, there would be an increased consumption of 600,000 pieces of coarse calicoes, and employment for 4000 additional weavers*. In 1828, the gross revenue received from this duty was 2,019,737*l.*, of which there was repaid 1,420,068*l.*, leaving only 599,669*l.* of net revenue †. If the charge of collecting the sum of 2,019,737*l.* be taken at 5 per cent., which is less than it really is, the cost of collection on the net revenue of 599,669*l.* will be 100,000*l.*, or nearly 20 per cent.; and to this is to be added the cost attending the repaying of 1,420,068*l.*

The duty on hard soap is 3*d.* a pound, or from 110 to 130 per cent., and produces about 1,100,000*l.* a year. This high duty is a powerful check on the consumption of soap; for the poorer classes, who compose the great mass of consumers, are compelled by the high price to dispense with the use of it in any thing like the quantity they would employ it if it were

* See Speeches at Manchester Meeting, Nov. 25, 1830.
† Parliamentary Papers, session 1829, No. 322.

cheaper.   In proportion as this tax deprives the poor
man of the means of cleanliness, it leads to disease,
but particularly to fevers.   The great number of de-
tections amply proves the prevalence of illicit manufacture.   This high duty is therefore fraught with
evil, like every duty which is excessive in its amount,
to all parties, the consumer, the manufacturer, and
the Exchequer.   If this duty were reduced to 1*d.*
a pound, it is probable the soap brought to charge
would increase one-half, that is, from 105,000,000
lbs. to 157,000,000 lbs.   As the present duty yields
1,200,000*l.*, a reduced duty of 1*d.* a lb. on 157,000,000
lbs. would yield 650,000*l.*, making a loss of revenue
by the reduction of about 550,000*l.*

Nothing can be more inconsistent with every sound
principle of taxation than the practice of collecting
this duty by no less than seven different modes*.

In consequence of there not being any duty on
soap in Ireland; of a drawback being given on the
exportation of soap to Ireland; of the drawback being
paid immediately on the exportation; of the duty not
being paid till six weeks after the soap is made, and
of the amount of duty drawn back exceeding the
value of the soap on which it is drawn back, there are
houses in Liverpool which are able to carry on an
extensive business with the capital of the public†.

Large quantities of soap are smuggled from Ireland
into England.

The duty of twenty shillings a quarter on malt is
not one that can be justly objected to as being too
high; but the mode of charging it is conducted under
such severe and vexatious regulations, as to render it

* Speech of the Right Hon. C. P. Thomson, p. 25.
† Ibid.

extremely injurious to agriculture, and to the consumers and manufacturers of malt. " These regulations at one and the same time have the effect of unnecessarily fettering the operations of the maltster—
of deteriorating the quality and adding to the price of
his malt—and of putting him wholly in the power of
the pettiest officer of excise *." In consequence of
this system of collecting the duty, the consumption
of malt has been stationary the last forty years. If
the regulations were simplified, there are the best
reasons for concluding, that the sale of malt would be
so much increased, that a very large additional revenue
would be the result.

The manufacture of machinery is greatly injured
by the prohibition to export it ; at the same time that
the means of raising a considerable revenue, by a
moderate duty upon it when exported, are thrown
away. The superiority that England possesses over
all other countries with respect to the materials of
machinery, and skill in making it, is so great, that
there can be no doubt that a very large quantity
would be exported if the prohibition were taken off.
Such a trade would give rise to increased employment of capital and labour in working collieries and
other mines, as well as in the making of machinery†.

If the government in the last session had adhered
firmly to the principle on which they repealed the
duty on leather, in repealing other duties to the
amount of three millions of annual revenue, instead of

* See Edinburgh Review, vol. xlix. p. 373, for a very full and
able exposition of the evils which arise from the present malt-
laws.

† The value of machinery exported, on an average of three
years to 1830, was 265,000l.   Sess. Pap. 1830. No. 373.

repealing the duty on beer, they would have conferred the greatest benefit on the public.   When it is considered, on the one side, what is the advantage that can in any way be derived from the repeal of this duty, with relation to the employment of capital and labour, and the accumulation of wealth, and also to the relief it will afford in reducing the price of beer; and on the other, what would have been the advantages of repealing taxes on materials and manufactures to the amount of three millions, it is clear that a greater fault could not have been made, under the actual circumstances of the country, than giving a preference to the repealing of the beer duty.

If this course had not been taken, the following duties might have been repealed :—

The duty on ashes and barilla, producing	.	£85,000 a year.
„	glass	.	.	„	.	613,000	„
„	paper	.	.	„	.	.	650,000	„
„	hemp	.	.	„	°	104,000	„
„	thrown silk	.	„	.	.	112,000	„
„	coals	.	.	.	„	.	838,000	„
Two-thirds of the duty on soap (say)	.	.	650,000	„

£3,052,000

The repealing of these duties would have led to an immense extension of all these trades, and to the employment of some hundred thousand more workmen, and also a much larger amount of capital.

Upon closely examining the probable effects of the repealing of the duty on beer, none can be found which at all approach in general usefulness these consequences which would certainly have sprung from the repealing of the duties just mentioned.   The policy of the measure was avowedly declared to be the single object of giving relief to the poor by causing a reduction in the price of beer. But it showed a very slight acquaintance with the circumstances which affect the condition of the poor, to imagine that any real relief from what most injured them would be afforded by a small reduction in the price of beer. What they stood in need of was an increased demand for the employment of their labour, and steadier and higher wages ; increased means of providing the necessaries of life, and not of purchasing a luxury such as beer, for it is a perfect fallacy to consider it as a necessary part of the subsistence of the poor.

Besides, the repealing of the duty on beer cannot be, by any possibility, a benefit to any other portion of the poor but that which is supplied by public breweries ; therefore, by far the greater part of the people of England, and all the people of Ireland and Scotland, derive no advantage from the repeal.

As the error of repealing the duty on beer is not the first great error that has been made in taking off taxes, (for instance, the repeal of the salt tax,) it cannot be too strongly impressed on ministers and parliament to avoid adopting those superficial reasonings upon taxation which first appearances suggest. It is natural and becoming to feel deeply for the sufferings of the poor ; but to overlook all rules of science, and to neglect, in dealing in matters of finance, all established principles ; and to act on feelings and not on reasons, as the groundwork of legislation, will never fail to be followed by great loss of revenue, without any adequate public good. The effort which was made in 1825 to obtain a repeal of the assessed taxes was founded on a total misconception of the comparative effects of different kinds of taxes on the interests of the people—no advantage would have arisen from the repeal of those taxes beyond the mere relief from so much taxation ; while, on the other hand, the repeal of the taxes on raw materials and manufactures, and the reduction of the enormously high duties on tobacco and foreign spirits, would be productive of considerable benefit to the consumer, would put an end to smuggling, and would increase the employment of capital, and labour, and foreign commerce. Lord Goderich is entitled to the greatest praise, for having had the firmness, in 1825, to resist the temptation of sacrificing a sound principle to the acquisition of temporary popularity ; he has the merit of being the first Chancellor of the Exchequer who reduced to practice those principles which are the only secure basis of national prosperity.

CHAPTER IV.

TAXES ON LUXURIES.

IN 1827 the net revenue received from the Customs' duties amounted to 17,894,409*l.*, and from the Excise duties to 18,438,707*l.**, making together the sum of 36,333,116*l.* If from this sum the amount be deducted of the revenue received from the duties on materials, 6,000,000*l.*, and on manufactures, 2,000,000*l.*, and also 800,000*l.* received in 1827 from the duties on corn, making together 8,800,000*l.*, there will remain a revenue of 27,500,000*l.*, nearly all levied on articles of luxury. As these articles are not used by the labouring class but to a limited amount, this revenue is paid by the wealthier classes, and the duties have little influence on wages and profits, and consequently on national industry; and were it not that some of the Customs duties have been raised much too high, there would be no necessity for making any further remarks on this branch of the taxes.

As the effect of these very high duties is in some cases to diminish the revenue, and in all to create smuggling—and further, by greatly diminishing the importation of the articles on which they fall, to diminish the demand for, and the exportation of our own manufactures—these duties are exceedingly injurious, and ought to be reduced.

There is an absolute limit to every duty, beyond which an increase of it necessarily occasions a loss of

* Fourth Report, Committee of Finance, Appendix, p. 113.

revenue. In no instance is an increase of duty followed by an equal increase of revenue; but, on the contrary, the progress of the increase of revenue will be less and less, according as the duty advances, until there is no increase of revenue, but a falling off. Yet, whenever it is proposed to lower any of the excessively high duties, it is immediately said, ' The circumstances of the country are such, that the revenue cannot admit of any reduction.' But this sort of reasoning assumes that a loss of revenue is sure to happen, when, in point of fact, there is no foundation for any such conclusion; on the contrary, there is no difficulty in proving, by reference to experience, that a diminution of taxation is not necessarily followed by a diminution of revenue, or an increase of taxation by an increase of revenue. ' In the case of the commodities which, from the great expense of their production, are necessarily high priced, the consumption of them must be always comparatively limited, and therefore might not be greatly extended by any reduction of the duties with which they are charged; but the reduction of the duties laid on commodities of extensive demand, and whose natural cost is not very considerable, must always be followed by a great increase of consumption: for such a reduction not only enables those who were previously consumers of them to consume a greater quantity, but it brings them within the reach of new and numerous classes of consumers. In this way, it is easy to perceive that such a reduction of the duty or price of any commodity previously used by the higher classes only, as would permit it to be used by those of inferior station, would extend the consumption to a vast amount*.'

* Edinburgh Review, vol. xxvi. p. 518.

The truth of these observations is strongly exemplified by what has taken place with respect to the consumption of cotton goods; it being now at least double what it was a few years ago, in consequence of the low price of those goods, brought about by the reduction in the price of the raw material, and by the aid of machinery.

The following instances of the effects of excessive duties completely confirm all that has ever been said concerning the impolicy of excessive taxation.

The number of gallons of brandy and geneva imported for home consumption on an average for four years to 1807, was 1,820,000*. The duty was then 14s. a gallon (w.m.), and the revenue 1,370,000l. In 1812, the duty was raised to 20s. 7d.; in 1813, to 20s. 11d.; and in 1814 it was fixed at 18s. 10d. a gallon (w.m.); and it has continued at that rate to the present time.

The annual average number of gallons of brandy and geneva imported for home consumption on an average for the four years following 1814, was 742,000 (i.m.), and the revenue 825,000l. So that the revenue was less from a duty of 18s. 10d., by 545,000l. a year, than it was from a duty of 14s. a gallon. Of late years the quantity of foreign spirits imported has increased, but the revenue has in no year amounted to what it was in 1806.

In the case of tea, the raising of the duty from 12 per cent., by successive augmentations, to 96 per cent. in 1806, and afterwards to 100 per cent., has certainly been followed by an increase of revenue. But, though this cannot be disputed, there are the strongest possible reasons for believing that the re-

* Sess. Pap. 1830-1. No. 28. See Appendix, No. II.

venue would have been considerably greater, had the duty not been carried so high. The quantity of tea sold by the East India Company, in 1799, was 24,853,000 lbs. ; and the quantity sold in 1827 was 26,043,223* ; but as the population of the United Kingdom may be taken as having increased from 16,000,000 in 1800, to 25,000,000 in 1829, had there been no diminution of the individual consumption of the Company's tea in the interval between these enumerations, their sales ought plainly to have been increased in the proportion of 16 to 25 ; that is, in the proportion of 25 to 39, instead of in that of 25 millions pounds, in round numbers, to 26 millions pounds.

But the fact is notorious, that no great diminution of individual consumption of tea has taken place, even after making a large allowance for the effect of the increased consumption of coffee in diminishing the consumption of tea ; and therefore we may conclude, that a very large quantity of tea now actually consumed is supplied by adulteration. In proof of this, the numerous convictions of persons having adulterated tea in their possession may be referred to.

The effect of levying so high a duty as 3*s*. a lb. on tobacco in Ireland, is quite conclusive in showing the impolicy of excessive taxation. In four years to 1798, when the duty was 8*d*. a lb., the quantity of tobacco entered for home consumption in Ireland was 32,000,000 lbs., making an annual average of 8,000,000 lbs. But, in four years to 1829, the quantity imported for home consumption in Ireland was only 16,000,000 lbs., making an annual average of 4,000,000 lbs. ; that is, half what it was thirty years ago, when the population was half as numerous

* Fourth Report, Committee of Finance, p. 54.

as it now is. Had the individual consumption of tobacco that paid duty increased according to the increase of the population of Ireland, the annual consumption should now be 16,000,000 lbs. instead of 4,000,000 lbs. As, no doubt, the individual consumption has increased in this ratio, the conclusion to be come to is, that full three-fourths of the tobacco now consumed in Ireland is supplied by smuggling.

It appears by the evidence given last session before the Committee on Irish Tobacco, that there would be a considerable exportation of manufactured tobacco to foreign countries, but for the regulations and restrictions which arise from the high duty on tobacco. The drawback allowed is accompanied with so many vexatious conditions, that it is not a sufficient compensation to the manufacturer for the original duty paid, and he is in consequence obliged to require so high a price as to be unable to meet the foreign manufacturer.

The injurious effects of raising the duties on wine is manifest in the instance of Ireland. In four years to 1796, the quantity of wines imported for home consumption was 6,700,000 gallons, making an annual average of 1,675,000 gallons. The duty was 2s. 7d. a gallon on French wines, and 1s. 7d. a gallon on other wines. The revenue received on an average of the same years was 150,000l. In the four years to 1829, the quantity imported for home consumption was 3,300,000 gallons, making an average of 825,000 gallons ; and the revenue received, from 6s. a gallon on French wines, and 4s. a gallon on other wines, was, on the same average, 130,000l., being less by 20,000l. than the revenue received from the former low duties.

In 1813 the duties on flint and plate glass were
doubled.   In four years to 1813, the average annual
quantity made for home consumption was 66,500
cwt.   In the four years following 1813, the annual
average quantity was only 30,000 cwt.   The duties on
all other kinds of glass were doubled in the same year.
The revenue received in the four years preceding
1813 was, on an average, 340,000*l.* ; that received
in the three years following 1813 was, on an average,
395,000*l.* : so that the doubling of the duties, instead
of producing 340,000*l.*, produced only 55,000*l.*

Subsequent to the year 1808, the duties on bitter
almonds were raised 7*s.* 9*d.* per cwt. ; on Jordan,
16*s.* 3*d.* a cwt. ; and on other sorts, 4*s.* 10*d.* a cwt.,
with the effect of an increase of revenue from 16,319*l.*
in 1808, to 17,991*l.* in 1827.   The duties on currants
were raised 7*s.* 6*d.* a cwt., with the effect of raising
the revenue from 230,259*l.* in 1808, to 265,365*l.* in
1827.   The duties on the different kinds of raisins
were raised, on some kinds, 2*s.* 3*d.*, and on other
kinds 4*s.* 2*d.* a cwt., with the effect of raising the
revenue from 159,000*l.* in 1808, to 160,000*l.* in 1827.

Although the subject under examination is excessive taxation on articles of luxury, it will not be irre-
levant to the general object of this work, to take this
occasion to notice the effects of excessive taxation
in other cases—for instance, on advertisements, insurances, and the postage of letters.

The accounts given in the twenty-third number of
the Westminster Review (p. 10), and in the Scotsman
newspaper of the 14th of March, 1830, remove all
doubts as to the fact of the duty on advertisements
being so excessive as to produce less revenue than a
lower rate of duty would produce.   The effect of the

high duty in diminishing the number of advertisements is made evident by the fact of the yearly number of advertisements in the United States, where there is no duty, amounting to 10,000,000, while the number in the United Kingdom amounts only to 963,000.

The net revenue from marine insurances was, in 1814, 418,000*l.*, and in 1829 it was only 227,973*l.**, notwithstanding a great increase in the number of ships and tonnage since the year 1814. Such an increase should have produced a proportional increase of revenue from insurances; but the fact is, that the high duty has driven merchants to make their policies in the United States or Holland, where they can insure at a cheaper rate.

The revenue of the Post-office has been stationary at about 1,400,000*l.* a year since 1818†. This can be accounted for only by the great duty charged on letters; for with a lower duty the correspondence of the country through the Post-office would have increased in proportion to the increase of population and national wealth.

Nothing can be more unwise than the very high postage on foreign letters. It not only produces a great loss of revenue, but it obstructs foreign commerce, and the spread of science and literature. Foreign newspapers and periodical works should be carried free of postage.

The foregoing statements having shown the effects of increasing duties, the following will explain what the effects have been of reductions of duty:—

In 1745, the duty on tea was reduced from 4*s.* a lb. to 1*s.* and 25 per cent.; but the revenue derived

* Sess. Pap. 1830. No. 230.
† Fourth Report, Committee of Finance, p. 95.

from it increased from 444,659*l.*, the annual average
amount for three years to 1745, to 804,791*l.*, the
annual average amount for three years to 1749*.
The duty on tea was afterwards raised so as to be
119 per cent. in 1784; in that year it was reduced
to 12 per cent. The consequence was, that the sales
of tea at the India House, which in three years to
1784 were 17,164,966 lbs., rose, in three years to
1788, to 48,163,811 lbs. ; and instead of the duties
falling off in the proportion of 119 to 12, that is,
from 700,000*l.*, which they yielded in 1783, to
73,000*l.*, they only fall off in the proportion of 3 to
1, or from 700,000*l.* to 240,000*l.*†

The duty on plantation coffee, previous to 1808,
was 2*s.* per lb., and the annual average produce of it
in three years to 1808, was 144,725*l.* This duty
was afterwards reduced to 6*d.* per lb., and the annual
average produce of it in three years to 1829 has been
378,350*l.*‡ The consumption has increased from
4,069,091 lbs. in 1808, to 18,906,373 lbs., and the
revenue to 484,975*l.* in 1829§.

The duty on spirits made in Ireland was reduced in
1823 from 5*s.* 6*d.* a gallon to 2*s.* (wine measure).
The number of gallons of spirits (imperial measure)
that paid duty in 1822 was 2,328,387, and the revenue received was 797,518*l.* The number of gallons that paid duty in 1828 was 9,937,903, and the
revenue was 1,395,721*l.* ‖

A similar reduction of duty took place at the same
time on spirits made in Scotland. The number of

---

* Hamilton's Principles of Taxation, Appendix, No. XIX.;
and Supp. Encyc. Brit., vol. vi. p. 638.

† Macpherson's Commerce of India, p. 210.

‡ See Appendix, No. II.　　　§ Ibid.　　　‖ Ibid.

gallons have increased from 2,079,556 in 1822, to
5,716,180 in 1828; and the revenue has increased
from 691,136*l.* to 809,559*l.* *

In 1827 the duty on spirits made in England was
reduced from 12*s.* 7*d.* a gallon to 7*s.* The average
consumption for three years to 1827 was 3,677,457
gallons, and the revenue 2,281,526*l.*; in 1829 the
consumption was 7,700,766 gallons, and the revenue
2,695,268*l.* ; being a revenue of greater amount by
413,742*l.*, from a duty of 7*s.* a gallon, than what was
before received from a duty of 12*s.* 7*d.* a gallon†.

The duty on French wines was reduced, in 1825,
from 11*s.* 5*d.* a gallon to 6*s.* (wine measure.) There
were imported in four years to 1825, on an annual
average, 183,000 gallons, that yielded an average
revenue of 106,000*l.* In three years to 1829, the
quantity imported has been, on an average, 382,000
gallons, that yielded an average revenue of 115,000*l.*
So that the reduced duty of 6*s.* has produced at the
rate of 9000*l.* a year more than the former duty of
11*s.* 5*d.* a gallon‡.

The duty on flint glass was reduced in 1825 from
98*s.* to 56*s.* per cwt. The quantity charged with
duty for home consumption, on an average of four
years to 1825, was 30,000 cwt. The quantity on
an average of four years to 1829 has been 47,000
cwt.§.

The Committee of Finance state, in their Fourth
Report on the Revenue and Expenditure, that if the
revenue had fallen off in the five years from 1825 to
1828, in the same proportion that taxes had been

* See Appendix, No. II.
† Sess. Pap. 1830. Nos. 186 and 211; and 1830-1. No. 28.
‡ See Appendix, No. II.   § Ibid.

reduced, the diminution of it would have been 9,000,000*l.*; but that, owing to increased consumption, it had only fallen off about one-third of that sum.

These different facts place it beyond all doubt, that when a tax has been carried to an excessively high point, the reducing of it is not necessarily followed by a reduction of revenue, but may lead to an increase.

The duties which have just been mentioned create the greater part of the smuggling that is still successfully carried on, notwithstanding the enormous expense incurred in attempting to suppress it. Putting together the expense incurred in attempting to prevent it, as given in the examination of Mr. Dean, the Chairman of the Board of Customs, by the Committee of Finance*, and the expense incurred by the Excise in preventing manufacturers from making use of smuggled articles, and the expense of prosecutions and rewards, the whole cannot amount to less than 7 or 800,000*l.* a year. Great, however, as this sum is, the profit that can be gained, in consequence of the excess of duties in proportion to the value of the articles on which they are levied, is so high, that it continues to make smuggling a very flourishing trade. It has already been shown, that three-fourths of the tobacco consumed in Ireland is supplied by smug-

* See Evidence on Smuggling :

Paid by the Customs	.	.	.	.	.	£466,099
„ Excise	.	.	.	.	.	2,223
„ Navy Department	.	.	.	.	157,518

These items are taken from a question asked Mr. Dean by the Committee, p. 18.

181,000*l.* has been expended in building cottages for the coast guard.—See Papers, Committee of Finance, No. cxlii.

glers ; and the statement of Sir Hussey Vivian in the
House of Commons in the session of 1829, pointing
out the severe duty performed by cavalry regiments
on the coast, together with the frequent mention
made in the newspapers of smuggling transactions,
show how extensively this traffic is going on in England.   Mr. Dean was asked the following question,
when before the Committee of Finance.   ' Did you
ever hear that in the ports of Flushing and Ostend,
and in those ports where smuggling is carried on,
it is capable of an insurance, like any other risks ? '
He replied, ' I have no doubt of it.   I have heard of
10 per cent. to 15 per cent.'

The great disproportion of the duty on tobacco to
the natural price of it, the circumstance of its being
almost a necessary to the lowest classes of society, and
the facilities the high duty holds out to illicit trading,
concur in rendering it one of the most objectionable
duties.   As the price of tobacco, exclusive of duty,
cannot be taken at more than 4d. a lb., the tax of 3s.
a lb. is at the rate of 900 per cent. ; and therefore, in
order to withdraw this article from the hands of the
smuggler, a very large reduction ought to be made.
Unless reduction be carried sufficiently far on this
and other articles, smuggling and the expense of
attempting to suppress it will continue, and thus the
principal object in sacrificing revenue will not be
attained.

A reduction of 2s. a lb. on tobacco might perhaps
put a stop to the smuggling of it : if it did not, a
further reduction should be made.   If a reduction of
2s. took place, the loss of revenue could not well be
estimated at less than 1,500,000l.

With respect to smuggling, the duties on brandy

and geneva are not less objectionable than those on tobacco. As the price of these spirits, exclusive of duty, does not exceed 4s. a gallon, the duty of 22s. 6d. (i. m.) a gallon is 550 per cent.

There are four different rates of duty on spirituous liquors. The duty on Irish and Scotch spirits is 3s. 4d. a gallon (i. m.), and experience has fully proved that the illicit distilling of these spirits cannot be kept down, except by having a moderate duty. The complete success of the reduction of the duty in 1823, both with respect to putting a stop to illicit distillation and to the increasing of the revenue, points out the course that should now be taken with regard to the duties on the other kinds of spirits.

The duty on spirits made in England is 7s. 6d. a gallon : the consequence of this duty being so much higher than the duty on Irish and Scotch spirits, is, so large a profit on smuggling the latter into England, that this trade is extensively carried on. Nothing can be more contrary to all sound principles of trade and finance than having different rates of duty on the same article in the same country : this should be got rid of by raising the duties on Irish and Scotch spirits as high as it is possible to raise it without reviving illicit distillation, and by reducing the duty on English spirits to that rate so as to have the same amount of duty on all British corn spirits.

The duty on brandy and geneva is 22s. 6d. a gallon. It is so very high in proportion to the value of these spirits, that it creates an immense extent of smuggling. In point of fact, nearly all the smuggling that is carried on is of foreign spirits and tobacco. The influence of the West-India planters brought about this very preposterous duty, the intent of it

being to exclude all brandy and geneva, and thereby
extend the consumption of rum.

What should be done with respect to this duty, is
to reduce it so as to leave the smuggler no profit
in importing it: nothing short of this will stop his
trade. But as brandy and geneva can be purchased
abroad for about the same price for which British
spirits can be made, it is clear that the duty should at
the utmost be no higher than that on British spirits.

The duty on rum is 9s. a gallon, that is, 1s. 6d.
higher than the duty on English spirits. This additional duty is laid on to give protection to the English
distillers, on the grounds that they are obliged to pay
a higher price for corn than the natural price of it, in
consequence of the corn-laws: so that in this case of
the several spirit duties, there is an example of protection following protection to the manifest loss and
injury in each instance of the public:—first, the
landlords are protected against foreign corn; secondly, the English distillers are protected against the
West-India planters; and thirdly, the West-India
planters are protected against foreign spirits.

As long as the corn-laws continue, there seems to
be a good reason for protecting the English distiller
from this interference of the legislature with his trade;
and therefore, whatever may be the rate of duty fixed
on English spirits, according to the preceding sug-
gestions, the duty on rum should be 1s. 6d. higher;
but there is no reason for giving any protection to the
West-India planter against foreign spirits, because
he can make rum at as low a cost of production as
that for which these spirits can be made.

Whatever might be the effect of such an arrangement of the duties on spirituous liquors as is now

proposed, in promoting the use of one kind of spirits in preference to another, is a matter of indifference to the revenue, because it is the same as to the revenue whether the duty be collected on foreign or home-made spirits. The prosperity of the revenue will depend on whatever extends the consumption of spirits legally imported or legally distilled. The interest of the public at large would be benefited by the proposed arrangement, in consequence of the re-duction of the prices of spirits. If more brandy and rum, and less British spirits, should be consumed, more British goods would be exported to pay for the brandy and rum; and there would be a smaller demand for corn, and consequently the public would have an ad-vantage by its becoming cheaper.

It is not easy to estimate with any accuracy what the loss of revenue would be from such an arrange-ment of the duties; but taking into consideration the increased revenue which would be obtained on Irish and Scotch spirits, and the increased consumption of English and foreign spirits, which the reduction of duty would promote, it would not probably exceed 1,500,000$l.$

The common objection, that the diminishing of the price of spirits will encourage the vice of drunkenness, will not in this case be entitled to much considera-tion. In the first place, the plan goes to raise the price of Irish and Scotch spirits; and in the next, it may be replied to those persons who may urge this objection, that in France, Holland, and the United States, where spirits are much cheaper than they will be in this country with the reduced duty, drunken-ness is comparatively unknown; and it may also be urged that the encouragement which is given to smug-

gling by high duties is far more injurious to the morals
of the people, than the effect of low duties would be in
making the means of intoxication cheaper.

Experience shows how futile it is to attempt to
teach morality by sumptuary laws : the only effectual
mode is by promoting the diffusion of knowledge, and
introducing better habits among the lower classes.

The author of the pamphlet on the Revenue of the
Customs says, ' No material reduction can be made in
the system now in force for preventing smuggling ;'
and the reason he gives is, that without this system
faith could not be kept with the public creditor for
want of a sufficient revenue.   But this reason has no
foundation, because, whatever might be the diminution
of the revenue in consequence of so reducing the
duties on the articles that are smuggled as to take
away the profit of the smuggler and put down his
trade, there are several modes by which the same
amount of revenue might be obtained.   This being
the case, the question is, whether it is more for the
public interest to keep up revenue by means of the
present system of excessive duties with smuggling,
or to get it in some other way without smuggling ?
Supposing the revenue now received from the very
high duties on tobacco and foreign spirits to be
3,000,000*l.* over and above what would be received
from moderate duties,—it cannot be denied that the
raising of this particular portion of the public revenue
3,000,000*l.* produces the following evils.   1. The
prices of the articles taxed are raised so high as to deprive the public, to a great extent, of the use of them.
2. The consumption of them being thus restricted,
foreign trade and navigation are proportionally restricted.   3. Not far short of a million a year is ex-

pended in the collection of these 3,000,000l., in consequence of smuggling, in addition to the ordinary charge of collection.   4. The crime of smuggling is created, and all those collateral crimes which branch from it.   It is, therefore, clearly impossible that 3,000,000l. of revenue could be raised by any more objectionable means than by these high duties on tobacco and foreign spirits.

The lowering of these duties would be attended with another important result besides that of putting down smuggling, namely, the increase of the consumption and importation of the articles subject to them, in consequence of the effect the reduction of the duties would have in reducing prices.   For instance, in the case of tobacco, with a reduced duty, more capital would be employed in buying the additional quantity of tobacco which would be consumed, and more ships and seamen in importing it : in the next place, more raw materials would have to be imported to make the goods which would be required for exportation to pay for the additional quantity of tobacco ; more capital would be employed in buying and manufacturing these materials, more workmen in manufacturing them, and more ships and seamen in importing them, and in exporting the goods made with them.   The reduction of the duty on spirits, and of every other excessive duty, would be followed by similar beneficial results to national industry and wealth.   So that excessive taxation is not only impolitic, from its effect on the revenue and on smuggling, but in consequence of its diminishing the productions of industry and also foreign commerce.

As the sole cause of smuggling being a profitable trade is the high amount of particular duties, and as

all experience proves that every attempt to suppress
it will fail, so long as profit can be made by it, it is
clear that nothing will put it down but reducing the
duties.   It has been well observed, that ' to create,
by means of high duties, an overwhelming temptation
to indulge in crime, and then to punish men for in-
dulging in it, is a proceeding wholly and completely
subversive of every principle of justice. It revolts the
natural feelings of the people, and teaches them to
feel an interest in the worst characters, to espouse
their cause, and to avenge their wrongs.   A punish-
ment which is not apportioned to the offence, and
which does not carry the sanction of society along
with it, can never be productive of any good effect :
the true way to put down smuggling is to render it
unprofitable by reducing the duties on the smuggled
commodities *.'

The statement which has been made to show the
effect of the late reduction of the duty on French
wines, proves that it has been a very successful experiment; and there can be no doubt that an additional advantage would be gained, with respect to the
revenue, the interests of the consumer, and the extension of commerce, if it were still further reduced.
But, considerable as this benefit might be, it is nothing
when compared with the advantage of a less restricted
trade with France, towards which a further reduction
of duty might lead.   ' There are no two countries
better suited for an advantageous commercial intercourse, as well by local situation as by the nature of
their productions, than Great Britain and France.
They may be considered as the two most civilized
nations of the world; they are within a few hours'

* See Edinburgh Review, vol. xxvi. p. 536.

sail of each other; and at the same time the one is
distinguished by peculiar advantages, both natural
and acquired, for the maintenance of manufactures,
whilst the other abounds in all those natural productions for which the extent of its territory, the fertility
of its soil, and the excellence of its climate, eminently
qualify it*.'   As England need no longer be bound
by the Methuen treaty, the duty on French wines
should be lowered below that on stronger wines, so
as to allow the former to be purchased at more
moderate prices.   If the duty were reduced to 2s. 6d.
a gallon, there can be little doubt that the consumption would be treble what it now is.   Forty years
ago, as much claret was consumed in Ireland
(500,000 gallons), when the duty was, 2s. 7d. a
gallon, as is now consumed in the United Kingdom;
so that it is by no means too high an estimate to
take the future consumption at 1,500,000 gallons:
with a duty of 2s. 6d. a gallon, this would yield a
revenue of 187,000l., which would be greater than
the present revenue derived from French wines, by
35,000l.

Although there appear to be some very strong
reasons in favour of reducing the duty on tea, as
this article is not smuggled, it is not advisable to
make any change until the monopoly of the East
India Company be got rid of; for, however low the
duty might be reduced, it does not follow that the
price would fall, because the Company have the
power of keeping it up by limiting, at their pleasure,
the quantity imported and sold.   As the effect of the
monopoly is to make the price of tea at the sales of
the India House nearly double the price of what it is

* Parliamentary Review, 1825, p. 672.

at Hamburgh or New York, it is not impossible but that tea would bear a duty of 100*l*. per cent., if the trade in it were free and the price lowered; the effect of the monopoly, in point of fact, is to make the nominal duty of 100*l*. per cent. a duty of nearly 200*l*. per cent. on the true value of tea.

Notwithstanding it is commonly supposed that the duty on sugar is one of those duties which is excessive in its amount, it would appear that this is a mistake; for the accounts of the quantity imported for consumption, prove that it has increased concurrently with the increase of the duty. The quantity imported for consumption has been as follows:—

In 3 years to	1797,	Duty 15*s*. a cwt.	4,300,000	cwts.
,,	1803,	,, 20*s*. ,,	6,500,000	,,
,,	1829,	,, 27*s*. ,,	10,500,000	,, *

The quantity imported into Ireland:—

In 3 years to	1797,	Duty 15*s*. a cwt.	.	618,000	cwts.
,,	1803,	{ ,, in 1800, 18*s*. } { ,, 20*s*. a cwt. }		982,000	,,
,,	1829,	,, 27*s*. ,,	.	962,000	,,

exclusive of a very large quantity imported from England†.

The fact of the increasing consumption of sugar, notwithstanding the increased duty, shows that the reduction of the duty of 3*s*. a cwt., which took place in the last session, was a great error, and should not

---

* Appendix, No. II.

† No account of the total quantity of sugar imported into Ireland can be given for the period subsequent to 1825: the commercial intercourse between the two countries having, from the termination of that year, been assimilated by law to a coasting traffic, no account has been kept of the trade between them.

have preceded the reduction of those duties which do, beyond all doubt, diminish consumption, and consequently revenue.

The declared object in the last session of lowering the price of sugar, by lowering the duty, might have been secured by other means, and without incurring, according to the statement of the Chancellor of the Exchequer, a loss of revenue to the amount of 450,000*l*.

The price of sugar is raised beyond what it ought to be,—first, by protecting duties on East Indian and foreign sugars; and secondly, by prohibiting the refining of it in the colonies, for importation into the United Kingdom—the removing, therefore, of these restrictions upon the freer use of it, was the measure which ought to have been taken. Such a step would have had the effect of lowering the price, and of allowing the keeping of the duty of 27*s*. a cwt., which is about 100*l*. per cent., with an increasing consumption and an increasing revenue. The reduction of the duties on tea and sugar ought certainly to follow the repeal of the taxes on materials and manufactures, and the reduction of the duties on tobacco and spirits.

The sugar planters, in seeking relief by confining their efforts to a reduction of the duty on sugar, seem to have an imperfect knowledge of the nature of the evil they suffer, and of the proper remedy for it. They seem to overlook the injury from those laws which increase the cost of producing sugar. As every reduction in the cost of production would increase their means of making profit, instead of forcing the government to throw away revenue by reducing the duty on sugar, they should use their influence in securing a repeal of all restrictions upon the supplying

of the West Indies with food and lumber, and with all
the materials necessary for making sugar and rum, and
also in securing the repeal of the other restrictions on
refining sugar in the colonies, and on sending it direct
to foreign markets.

The necessity of raising a revenue of 50,000,000*l.*
makes sugar in every way a fit subject of even high
taxation.   It is a luxury in universal use ; a small
quantity of it goes a great way ; the duty is very
easily collected ; it is an article that is not smuggled ;
and as 27*s.* a cwt. is not a higher rate of duty per
cent. than the duty on the greater part of the coffee,
which is abundantly consumed, there seems to be no
doubt, that if the price of sugar were lowered by
removing restrictions affecting the cost of producing
it, and by allowing the use of foreign sugar, on an
equal duty, the quantity consumed under this rate
of duty would be very much increased, and also the
revenue derived from it.

At present the quantity consumed in the United
Kingdom is 3,600,000 cwts.   If, in consequence of
removing these restrictions and lowering the price,
an additional quantity of 500,000 cwts. were consumed, this, at 27*s.* a cwt., would yield an additional
revenue of 625,000*l.*   There is reason, therefore, for
saying that the maintaining of the restrictions costs
the public this sum annually of 625,000*l.*

In making an estimate of the revenue which would
be lost by reducing duties to the extent proposed in
the preceding pages, nothing should be set down for
repayment of duty on stocks on hand, on the ground
that the holders of such stocks have a just claim
for repayment ; for experience establishes the fact,
that in almost all cases of past reductions of duties,

prices have kept up, and given rise to a good deal of clamour, and much undeserved condemnation of dealers in the articles which have been relieved of duty *.

The practice of repaying duties, if it were regularly adopted, would lead dealers, on finding that a duty was to be reduced, to amass large stocks, for the sake of the profit they would make by prices keeping up, as they always do, in a greater or less degree, for a considerable time after the repeal of the duties actually occurs.

If notice were given of the intention of reducing or repealing a duty on any article some time previous to its being carried into effect, the dealers in it would take care to diminish their stocks; and as, in case of the duty not being repaid, they would all be losers by a sudden reduction of price, they would not enter into competition to undersell each other, but rather combine together to do all in their power to keep up the price until new stock could be brought forward.

* See Speeches in the House of Commons on the last reduction of the wine duties.   In 1824, 460,886*l.* was repaid for duties on the stock of silk goods on hand (An. Fin. Acc. 1825, p. 45); and in 1825, 1,021,044*l.* was repaid for the duty on the stock of wine on hand.—See Appendix, No. II.

Chapter V.

TAXES FOR GIVING PROTECTION TO AGRICULTURE.

It will be seen by the following table of articles of foreign produce, and of the duties to which they are subject, that no opportunity has been lost of endeavouring to promote the interests of the landowners, by excluding foreign competition.

	£.	s.	d.
Bacon, per cwt.	1	8	0
Bark, per ton	0	13	4
Beer, per 32 gallons	2	13	0
Butter, per cwt.	1	0	0
Bristles, not sorted, per lb.	0	0	3
———, sorted ditto	0	0	4
Cider, per ton	21	10	0
Cheese, per cwt.	0	10	6
Copper, per cwt.	1	7	0
Cucumbers, per cent. ad val.	20	0	0
Hay, per load	1	4	0
Hair, cows and oxen, per cwt.	0	2	6
Hair-powder, per cwt.	9	15	0
Hides, per cwt.	2	0	4
Hops, per cwt.	8	11	0
Hemp seed, per quarter	2	0	0
Hemp undressed, per cwt.	0	4	8
Lard, per cwt.	0	8	0
Lead, per ton	2	0	0
Madder, per cwt.	0	6	0
Madder roots, per cwt.	0	1	6
Mules and asses, each	0	10	6
Horses, each	1	0	0
Oil, rape and linseed, per ton	39	18	0

	£.	s.	d.
Ore, copper, per cwt.	0	12	0
—— lead, per ton	1	5	0
—— not otherwise enumerated, per cent.	20	0	0
Peas, per bushel	0	7	6
Perry, per ton	22	13	8
Potatoes, per cwt.	0	2	0
Seeds, clover, hay, &c. &c.	1	0	0
Spirits, foreign, per gallon (I. M.)	1	2	6
Rum, per gallon	0	9	0
Tallow, per cwt.	0	3	2
Tares, per quarter	0	10	0
Timber, per load	2	15	0

Wheat, 1*l.* 5*s.* a quarter to 1*s.*, according as the price rises, from 61*s.* to 70*s.* a quarter.

Barley, 13*s.* 10*d.* a quarter to 1*s.*, according as the price rises, from 32*s.* to 40*s.* a quarter.

Oats, 10*s.* 9*d.* a quarter to 1*s.*, according as the price rises, from 24*s.* to 31*s.* a quarter.

On other grain, flour, and meal, the duties are according to these scales.

Beef, lamb, mutton, pork, sheep, and swine, are prohibited to be imported by 6 Geo. IV. c. 117.

This long list shows with what great zeal those who are invested by the constitution with the power of making laws, have used that power with the view of promoting, by every practicable means, the interests of the owners of landed property. The object of each of these duties is to keep up the rent of land, by preventing the prices of agricultural produce from being lowered by the importation of foreign produce. In whatever degree the duties effect this, they injure those classes which live by industry, because the higher price that is thus maintained is paid either out of the wages of labourers or the profits of capitalists; and they benefit only the proprietors of land and of tithes. Nothing,

therefore, can be more inconsistent with justice than
this scheme of legislation for the advantage of a few,
at the expense of nearly the whole community; and
with respect to the prosperity of the country in industry and wealth, nothing can be more inconsistent with all sound principles. Some reform is clearly
wanted.   The public interest requires that every nation should have full liberty to send us every kind of
food at the lowest possible price.

The duties imposed by the corn-laws being those
which, in this long list, have the greatest influence in
raising the price of food, the following brief observations have been written with the view of contributing
to inculcate a due conviction of the injurious effects of
these laws.   The object of them, namely, to raise the
price of corn, is proved to be effectually secured, by
what are the prices of corn at home and abroad; for
the state of the markets abroad show that, on a moderate calculation, foreign wheat may be imported and
sold at 10s. a quarter, foreign barley at 5s. a quarter,
and foreign oats at 3s. 6d. a quarter less than British
wheat, barley and oats, have been sold for, on an
average of the fifteen years since the passing of the
corn-law of 1815.

The effect of these additional prices (which may be
taken at 5s. a quarter on the three kinds of corn)
upon all the corn consumed in the United Kingdom
(commonly calculated at 50,000,000 quarters), is to
make the public pay 12,500,000l. a year more for the
corn they consume than they would pay if corn-laws
did not exist.

The increased price paid by labourers for corn, or
rather for bread, is a tax on their wages, when this
increased price is not followed by a correspond·

ing increase of wages; and, consequently, in this case nothing can be more objectionable than the restriction on foreign corn. When the effect of the increased price of bread is to raise wages, those writers who are of the highest authority on matters of this kind say, ' it lowers the rate of profit on capital,' while others say, ' it raises the prices of commodities.' But in either of these alternatives a very great public evil arises : if the rise of wages reduce the rate of profit, the return on all the capital of the nation is diminished, consequently its annual income, and the means of accumulating new wealth. If the rise of wages add to prices it diminishes the consumption of commodities, the employment of capital and labour, and likewise the means of accumulating new wealth. All labourers and manufacturers—all persons concerned in trade of any kind—even all farmers *, all,

---

* ' A farmer is as much a capitalist as a shop-keeper or a manufacturer, and the profits of farming capital must, in the end, be lowered by any cause which lowers the profits of other capital. It is the interest of all capitalists to have the necessaries of life, and consequently corn among the rest, cheap; because their labourers will then be contented with lower wages. A farmer's gain cannot be permanently greater than that of other capitalists. Even during the currency of a lease, a rise in the price of corn is not always an advantage to him; for if there be a general rise in the price of all other commodities also at the same time, he must give a corresponding increased price for his coats, hats, horses, sheep, cattle, &c.; and, unless during the currency of a lease, he has no interest whatever in high prices; because competition will effectually prevent him from deriving more than a very temporary advantage from them. He has, however, in common with other capitalists, a very strong interest in high profits; and it is not possible that profits should be high for a long period together, when the necessaries of life are dear. A high price of corn, therefore, not only is not beneficial to the farmer as such, but it is positively injurious to him. He is

in fact, who live by industry, and are not either proprietors of land or of tithes, are injured by the corn-
laws. If the price of corn were reduced 5s. a quarter
by repealing these laws, and the 12,500,000l. which
is now taken from the pockets of the people by these
laws in extra price were left with them, this sum
would be expended, beyond what is now expended by
them, on other necessaries, or on the conveniences
and amusements of human life.

If the whole of these 12,500,000l. were transferred
by the operation of these laws into the pockets of
landlords, so as to enrich this class, and which may
be taken to be one-tenth of the population, at the
cost of nine-tenths of it, the effect of the corn-laws
would be comparatively harmless. But the real effect
of them is to destroy much more wealth than they
transfer, and to give to landlords not more, probably,
than one-fifth of what they take from the pockets of
the consumers by adding to the price of corn; the
other four-fifths are totally lost to the country in consequence of the great additional expense in growing
corn, and do not, therefore, contribute in the smallest
degree to increase the comforts and enjoyments of
any individual whatever.

Landlords, after having suffered so greatly from
those fluctuations in the price of corn which have
taken place since 1815, and which have unquestion-
ably arisen from the corn-laws, and after having found

injured in two ways: first, as a consumer of corn in common
with the rest of the community, by having to consume a dear,
instead of a cheap, commodity; and, secondly, he is injured in
a still greater degree, as an owner of capital, by being compelled
to give high wages to all the labourers he employs.'—Cheap
Corn best for Farmers, p. 23. Second edition.

how injurious they are to all other classes, should now be sensible that they cannot be benefited by any longer continuing these laws. They should at length understand that they would gain largely by their repeal, from the share they would have in the prosperity of manufactures, which would be the certain consequence.

Colonel Torrens says in his ' Treatise on the External Corn Trade,'—' Let not short-sighted avarice destroy the sources of the golden eggs: let not the proprietors of England, by restricting the importation of foreign agricultural produce, artificially raise the value of such produce in our markets, and thus depress the rate of profit, until the seats of manufacture are transferred to France, Holland, or Germany. No proposition, we believe, admits of a more rigid demonstration, than that the highest rents will be paid in countries in which manufacturing industry is carried to its greatest height. But it is obviously impossible that manufactures should continue to flourish in a country where restrictions on the importation of corn raise the value of raw produce in relation to wrought goods, and thereby depress manufacturing profits below the rate prevailing in the neighbouring countries. If we do not freely import foreign produce, our manufacturing superiority cannot be maintained, and, by necessity, our high comparative rents cannot be continued to be paid*.'

As no one can doubt that the fluctuation in the price of corn is what chiefly exposes the poor to misery and famine, and disables them for providing for themselves, it is clear that while the corn-laws continue the pressure of the poor rates can never be effectually diminished. The first step towards the

* Fourth Edition, p. 168.

abolition of all rates levied on account of able-bodied poor can never be effected with facility or security except by abolishing the corn-laws; and if this system of paying able-bodied labourers by the parishes be not soon got rid of, the whole country will be incessantly disturbed by popular contentions between labourers and land-owners, and ultimately all rent will be required for the support of the poor.

What should operate as a further inducement to landlords to repeal the corn-laws is the probability that, if continued, they will, before very long, cease to sustain prices. The stimulus which the high price of corn gives to the growth and consumption of the potatoe, will clearly bring about a reduction in the price of corn. The improvement of tillage in Ireland may also be expected to bring about a similar result. Previously to 1806, when all restrictions on the corn trade between Ireland and Great Britain were abolished, the imports of corn from the former to the latter did not exceed 400,000 quarters; whereas they now amount to 1,600,000 quarters, exclusive of 600,000 cwts. of flour and meal; and there is every reason to expect that Ireland may yet be able to export five or six times this quantity.

The plea set up in favour of the corn-laws, that if foreign corn were imported the employment of labour would be diminished, has no foundation; because as the foreign corn could only be paid for by exporting British productions, there would be a new demand for labour in preparing these productions.

Another plea is equally void of foundation, namely, that the taxes could not be paid without corn-laws. The truth is exactly the contrary, for as the public would have 12,500,000*l.* less to pay annually for corn, they would have this sum to spend beyond what they now can spend in articles of consumption liable to taxes. Besides, it is to be observed, that the makers of the laws have contrived to throw the great burden of taxation, first, by their selection of the taxes imposed, and secondly, by the selection of the taxes repealed, from off their shoulders upon the industrious classes, so that out of the 50,000,000*l.* of annual revenue not more than 6,000,000*l.** falls upon the property of landlords †.

The foregoing observations explain how the duties on corn and other articles of food obstruct the progress of national wealth; but these are not the only obstructions connected with agriculture: tithes are also a great obstruction to national prosperity by their

* See the calculation on which this statement is made in the Parliamentary Review for 1826, p. 669.

† When (in 1813) the author of this work was a party in recommending restrictions on the importation of foreign corn, he was so with the design of ultimately lowering the price of corn. He stated at that time his objects to be, first, to prevent the injury which would arise from peace suddenly opening the ports to foreign corn; and, secondly, to promote such an increased application of capital to tillage in Ireland, as would bring out the powers of that country to supply Great Britain with so large a quantity of corn, as would make the prices as low as if foreign corn were imported. He sees no reason for believing that his expectations were unreasonable, for he is convinced that if the measures of Catholic emancipation and of a commutation of tithes had been passed when the Corn Bill of 1815 was passed, the increase of tillage in Ireland, in consequence of security of property and relief from tithes, would, before this, have reduced the price of corn to what it would be if the ports were open to foreign corn. But, in consequence of so much having of late been written to make the subjects of rents, prices, and profits better understood, he is now fully convinced that the right policy in regard to corn is a perfectly free trade.

influence in preventing the improvement of agriculture, and thus keeping up the prices of corn.   If
the whole effect of tithes be taken into consideration,
it will appear evident that they must have a great
influence in preventing as much capital from being
applied to improved tillage, and consequently as much
corn from being grown as would be the case if they
did not exist.   The giving to the clergy of the tenth
part of that gross produce, which is the result of the
improved cultivation, which arises from large sums of
capital specially applied to expensive improvements,
must operate to a great extent in preventing capital
from being so employed.   This is one way of account-
ing for the fact of the quantity of corn grown in England, where circumstances are so favourable to an
increased growth of it, being so much less than the
quantity required for her consumption.   If more
capital were applied to tillage, there can be no doubt
that more corn could be grown, and, at the same time,
without a diminished return of profit; for in whatever
degree tithes reduce the profit on capital, they have
the same effect as cultivating inferior soils, and they
operate, like the corn laws, in keeping up the price of
corn.   If, therefore, tithes were commuted for a tax
on land, there is every reason to suppose that the
additional capital which would be applied to tillage,
on improved principles of husbandry, would produce
such an additional quantity of corn that the price
would be considerably lowered, and the effect of the
corn-laws greatly counteracted.

Another circumstance that prevents as much capital
and labour from being employed in England in agriculture, and consequently as much wealth being derived
from this source of industry as there might be, is the

custom of not giving farmers sufficiently long leases. In order that land may be made to yield all that it is capable of yielding under the system of artificial grasses and alternate crops, a farmer must employ a very large capital, and a great number of labourers.   But capital so employed will not give a full return for some years, and, therefore, no farmer can make such an outlay of it under a yearly tenure of his farm.   If the custom, as to leases in England, was the same as it is in Scotland, that is, to give them for nineteen years, capital would be employed by farmers to as large an amount as it is in Scotland, the system of husbandry in England would be no longer so inferior as it now is to that in Scotland, and the quantity of corn grown in England would be very much increased.   The circumstance of Scotland being exempt from tithes is, no doubt, one cause of the greater relatively improved husbandry in that country ; but the security a farmer has under his lease of receiving back all he spends on his farm, must clearly be the main cause of his employing all the capital he can command in improving it.   May not the difference in the practice of the two countries, as to leases, be accounted for by the security the Scotch law gives a landlord against his land being sublet by his tenant ; and the want of a similar security in England, arising from the legal construction given by the courts of law to waivers of the covenants of leases?

With respect to a sufficient supply of corn, have not those writers on the corn-laws committed an error in saying that it is impossible the population of the United Kingdom can be fed on produce derived from its own soil without the cultivation of inferior soils, in consequence of their having overlooked the obstacles in the way of employing capital in improv-

ing land, arising, first, from the disturbed state of
Ireland; secondly, from tithes ; and, thirdly, from the
practice in England of not giving leases ?

The landlords of England, instead of bending all
their efforts to secure the continuance of the corn-
laws, should use their influence to obtain the following
measures :—

1st. A commutation of tithes. 2dly. An alteration
of the law of waivers, so as to establish the same
facility in England, as there is in Scotland, in preventing alienation by tenants, and in enforcing other
conditions of leases. 3dly. The restoration of the
poor-law system to what it was in 1790. 4thly. The
establishing a free trade in banking, so that the
farmers may have the advantage of the system of cash
credits and deposits as it exists in Scotland.

Chapter VI.

TAXES FOR GIVING PROTECTION TO BRITISH MANUFACTURES.

Notwithstanding all that has been said of our new system of free trade, with respect to manufactures, little or no change was really made by the alteration of the protecting duties and prohibitions in 1825. Accounts that have been laid before the House of Commons, of foreign manufactures imported in 1824, the year before the alteration, and in each of the years 1826, 1827, 1828, and 1829, the four years which followed it, prove this fact beyond all question[*].

[*] The following Table has been formed out of these accounts:

		1824.	1826.	Imported. 1827.	1828.	1829.
Brass manuf.,	value	£. 740	862	750	1,546	3,864
Carriages,	ditto	927	1,259	1,683	2,257	1,892
China and earthenw. }	ditto	7,418	18,310	18,718	24,727	23,357
Copper manuf., ditto		173	451	818	4,343	3,244
Cotton ditto [ditto		101,840	104,416	109,120		
Gloves . .	pairs		477,107	865,176	1,203,109	865,157
Iron in bars .	tons	12,091	12,820	14,293	15,495	15,739
Leather manuf. value		623	1,672	4,000	13,092	5,852
Silk manufactures, viz.						
Plain lace,	sq. yards	67,526	60,006	122,238	173,259	113,118
Entered by weight } lbs.			48,300	45,278	183,416	132,316
Entered at value }		15,218	26,128	54,179	78,276	81,449
Watches and clocks } value		10,224	15,259	15,599	25,764	27,772
Woollen manufact. } ditto		2,876	24,143	35,157	49,589	53,962

The first three years, from Sess. Paper 1828; No. 322. The last two years, from Sess. Paper 1830-1; No. 28.

With respect to the silk and glove manufactures, this account shows how unfounded the assertions are which are so loudly made, that these manufactures have been utterly ruined by the alteration in the laws in 1825 respecting the admission of foreign manufactures; for the whole amount imported in each year since 1825, forms scarcely a few days' consumption, and a mere nothing in comparison with the quantity of these goods that are annually made in the United Kingdom.

The great increase in the quantity of raw silk imported proves that the depressed state of the silk trade in 1829 was wholly owing to over-production. Whatever doubt may have been felt on this point is now completely removed by the present revival of the trade, notwithstanding that the importation of foreign silk goods is still going on.

As all kid gloves manufactured in England are made with foreign skins, and as none but kid gloves are imported, the great increase which has taken place of late in the quantity of kid skins imported shows that the depression of the glove trade was also owing to over-production. So that, on the whole, it may be stated, in the most unqualified language, that it is a false inference to draw from the distress which did prevail some time ago in these manufactures, that the alteration of the laws in 1825 was instrumental in producing it; and further, it may be stated, in the same unqualified manner, that it is equally false to assert that this alteration has established a free trade in this country in the place of the old system. If free trade be the right policy, the work of introducing it still remains to be done.

In order to leave no possibility of doubt with

respect to the truth of this conclusion, tables are given, in the Appendix, of the protecting duties which are at this moment levied on foreign manufactures. By these it will be seen, 1st, what the protecting duties are for such of our manufactures that cannot be affected by the freest competition ; 2dly, what they are for such of our manufactures that it is commonly supposed would be injured by competition ; 3dly, what they are which fall on manufactures of trivial value ; 4thly, what they are which fall on those manufactures of materials that serve in the first process of manufacture as materials of other manufactures*. These tables fully explain that nothing can be more absurd and unfounded than those statements which attribute all that goes wrong to free trade.

The varieties of climate, situation, and soil, afford to every country some advantages in the employment of industry not possessed by others. By making use of such advantages, a country will contribute its greatest power in the production of wealth. Hence it is that the capital of England is much more productive of wealth if employed in coal, iron, tin, and other natural productions, and in those objects in which these articles contribute to diminish the cost of production, than it is if employed in making those things which a foreign country can make cheaper in consequence of the advantages that are peculiar to it. All protection, therefore, by diverting the industry of the country from those branches of production for which it is best qualified, is mischievous ; and, when once imposed, creates a mass of artificial interests, whose existence, depending on the system from which

* See Appendix, No. III.

they sprang, forms a great obstacle in the way of getting rid of it *.

The history of the protecting system shows it had its origin at a period when nothing was known by statesmen and legislators of sound principles of trade. It seems to have been introduced into European policy by M. Colbert. Before his time Holland supplied all Europe with manufactures, and received in payment for them the raw produce of her poor neighbours. M. Colbert, overlooking the facts, that manufactures cannot be established in a country until it has acquired a considerable capital, and until the people of it have, become rich enough to be able to buy them, sought to force the growth of manufactures in France, merely by issuing his famous tariff of 1667, by which the importation of all manufactures into France was prohibited. The failure of his theory is amply attested by experience. France, ever since that period, has been paying for the manufactures used by her (taking price and quality into consideration) from half to twice as much more as England and Holland have paid for similar articles, and her establishments have continued of the most wretched description till within a few years. They are now, in consequence of the high prices and limited consumption which are the effects of protection, greatly depressed below what they would be if no protection had ever existed, for France is a country possessing great natural advantages for carrying on manufactures.

Immediately after the appearance of the tariff of 1667, the Dutch retaliated by prohibiting the importation of the wines, brandies, and other produc-

* Parliamentary Review, 1825, p. 631.

tions of France*. This commercial warfare produced open hostilities in 1672, and a war that lasted six years ; and it is to commercial prohibition and retaliation that most of the wars in Europe, since 1667, are to be attributed.

England followed the example of Holland in prohibiting French productions ; and from that time has been amongst the foremost of nations in loading her commercial legislation with all kinds of mischievous and erroneous regulations.

As this system of protection has been steadily acted upon by all nations since 1667, on a most mistaken notion, which has been generally entertained, that the protection of trade was a necessary part of the duty of the executive government, when it is considered, on the one hand, what the consequences would have been throughout the world of allowing trade and manufactures to take their natural course in supplying every country with every article of production of the best quality, and at the lowest possible price, and in advancing universal wealth and civilization ; and on the other, what the consequences have been of the numerous wars which the system of protecting trade and manufactures has given rise to, we cannot avoid coming to the conclusion, that those statesmen who invented this system, and who have supported it, and do still support it, deserve to be classed among the greatest enemies to the civilization and happiness of mankind.

The following observations, which are taken from the admirable work of Mr. M'Culloch on the Principles of Political Economy, are so applicable to the subject now under consideration, that no apo-

* Richesse de la Hollande, vol. i. p. 345.

logy will be made for inserting them at length.   Mr.
M'Culloch says :—

' It is easy to see that foreign trade, or the territorial division of labour between different and independent countries, contributes to increase their
wealth in precisely the same manner that the inter-
nal trade contributes to increase the wealth of the
different provinces of the same kingdom.   There
being a far greater variety in the productive powers
with which nature has endowed different and distant
countries than there is in those of the provinces of
any one country, it would seem that a free intercourse
between them must be proportionally more advantageous.   It would, it is evident, cost infinitely more
to raise the wines of France, the fruits of Spain, or
the sugars of Jamaica, in England, than to make
Yorkshire yield the same products as Devonshire.
Indeed, there are myriads of products, and some of
them of the greatest utility, that cannot be raised
except in particular countries.   Were it not for
foreign commerce, we should be wholly destitute of
tea, coffee, raw cotton, raw silk, spices, gold bullion,
and a thousand other equally useful and valuable
commodities.   Providence, by giving different soils,
climates, and natural productions to different countries, has evidently intended that they should be mu-
tually serviceable to each other.   If no artificial obstacles were thrown in the way of their intercourse,
each people would naturally engage, in preference,
in those employments in which it has a superiority,
exchanging such parts of its produce as it could spare
for the productions it could more advantageously
bring from others.   And thus, by exciting industry,
rewarding ingenuity, and using most efficaciously the
peculiar powers bestowed by nature, commerce dis-

tributes labour as best suits the genius and capacities
of every country.   By making us acquainted with
various productions to which we should otherwise
have been entire strangers, it gives us new tastes and
new appetites, at the same time that it affords the
means and excites the desire of gratifying them.   It
enables each particular people to profit by the inventions and discoveries of all the rest; while, by bringing
the home producers into competition with foreigners,
it stimulates their industry and invention, and forces
routine to give way to emulation.   The division of
labour is carried to its farthest extent, the mass of
necessary and useful products is vastly augmented,
and opulence generally diffused.   Nor is the influence
of commerce, in other points of view, less powerful
and salutary : it is the grand engine by which the
blessings of civilization are diffused, and the treasures
of knowledge and of science conveyed to the remotest
corners of the habitable globe ; while, by making the
inhabitants of each country dependent on the assistance of those of others for a large share of their
comforts and enjoyments, it forms a powerful principle of union, and binds together the universal
society of nations by the common and powerful ties
of mutual interest and reciprocal obligation.'

' Combien,' to use the words of a late French
writer*, ' le spectacle de tous les travaux concourant
à la production de la richesse, sans autre preéminence
ni distinction que celle que leur assure l'échange de
leurs produits, est encourageant pour les classes labo-
rieuses, stimulant pour les peuples, favorable à la

* Ganilh, des Systêmes d'Economie Politique.   Tome i.
p. 173 ; ed. 1821.   Principles of Political Economy, by J. R.
M'Culloch.   Second Edition, p. 143.

civilisation, honorable pour l'humanitié! Dans ce système tous les hommes suivent leur penchant, développent, perfectionnent, leurs facultés, s'encouragent par une noble émulation, sont avertis à chaque instant du besoin qu'ils ont des uns les autres, se lient entre eux par des rapports habituels, s'attachent par leurs intérêts réciproques, et renouent les liens de la grande famille du genre humain que la séparation des familles nationales avoit brisés. Ces familles, éparses sur le globe, ne sont plus étrangères entre elles, travaillent l'une pour l'autre, et correspondent ensemble malgré les gouffres des mers et l'aspérité des climats, les montagnes inaccessibles, et les déserts inhospitaliers. Grâces au génie du commerce, et aux inépuisables ressources de l'industrie, tous les périls sont bravés, toutes les difficultés sont vaincues, tous les obstacles sont surmontés, et les bienfaits du travail général circulent dans le monde entier.'

As there are still many persons who imagine the system of protection is right, the explaining of the various evils which it occasions cannot be too often repeated.

When protections are introduced, and foreign cheap goods are shut out, and the same kind of goods are made or grown at home, but at a greater cost of production, then the capital and labour of the country that excludes foreign goods cease to produce the greatest possible quantity of productions; the country is consequently poorer than it otherwise would be; for when a country consumes an article made at home, which could be got cheaper from another country, it employs a certain number of men's labour, in providing that article, more than it would be necessary to employ if it imported that article. The country is therefore poorer, by the whole value of these men's labour*.

When the labour required to produce, or the money required to purchase, a sufficient supply of any commodity is diminished, it is clear that more labour or money must remain to produce or purchase other commodities, and that the sum of national wealth and comforts must be proportionally augmented. As the general advance of prices, which is the consequence of protecting all trades, is clearly a great public evil, it would seem that the principle on which the advocates of protection have founded their theory, is, that public evil is the fountain of private good. The theory of free trade is founded on the opposite principle—that private good is the fountain of public good; and that private good is best promoted by leaving every individual to employ his capital and labour in the way he judges best, rather than by inter-

---

* ' The fundamental principle, that it is only through the agency of labour that the various articles and conveniences required for the use and accommodation of man can be obtained, being thus established, it necessarily follows, that the great practical problem involved in that part of the science which treats of the *production* of wealth, must resolve itself into a discussion of the means by which labour may be rendered most efficient, or by which *the greatest amount of necessary, useful, and desirable products may be obtained with the least possible outlay of labour.* Every measure that has any tendency to add to the power of labour, or, which is the same thing, to reduce the cost of commodities, must add proportionally to our means of obtaining wealth and riches ; while every measure or regulation that has any tendency to waste labour, or to raise the cost of commodities, must equally lessen these means. This then is the simple and decisive test by which we are to judge of the expediency of all measures affecting the wealth of the country.' —*Principles of Political Economy*, p. 75.

fering with legislative regulations, bounties, monopolies, protections, and restrictions.

This system of protection, by preventing the importation of foreign goods, diminishes the demand for the exportation of British goods of home production.

All commerce being bottomed on a fair principle of reciprocal dealings, a country that refuses to import must cease to export. By excluding foreign goods, a country does all in its power to drive the merchants of foreign countries from her markets. The necessary and inevitable effect, indeed, in all cases of the protecting system, is to lessen exportation to the same extent that it lessens importation. Every protection that seems to benefit one trade by excluding importation, injures another by excluding exportation: so that the cost paid by the public for protection is always the loss of some branch of trade, and increased price of the goods protected. In this way foreign commerce is diminished, also the employment of ships and seamen, and universally the employment of capital and labour in advancing national wealth.

The present state of the commerce between England and France affords a decisive proof of the impolicy of the protecting system. In the natural course of things, two such countries, so contiguous o each other, and each having so many productions eculiar to itself, would carry on a trade to the amount of many millions; but according to the accounts laid before Parliament, the whole of the trade in exports and imports does not exceed 3,000,000*l.* a year.

Another evil of the protecting system is the increased prices of a number of articles, which are the result of it. These prices take immense sums of

money from the pockets of the consumers of the protected commodities, who are not aware how large a
proportion of price is caused by this kind of tax.

Prices are, in fact, so generally and so much increased by protecting duties, that it is by no means
clear that they do not bear as heavily on the national
resources and on the productiveness of capital and
labour, as the taxes themselves; and therefore, the
reducing of these prices, by taking off protecting
duties, would afford all classes of the community the
greatest possible relief.

There can be no greater mistake than supposing
that manufacturers derive any benefit from protections; for if, in the first instance, they raise profits,
this leads to immediate competition, (in consequence
of the protections being only against foreign goods,
and of there being nothing to exclude new manufacturers from entering into the protected trades,) and
profits are soon brought down to their ordinary level.
But, in truth, the persons who carry on the protected
trades are more exposed to suffer than any other
class of manufacturers; for since the goods that are
made under the influence of protection are necessarily
dearer than foreign goods of the same kind, whenever competition in the home market leads to a glut
of them (a circumstance which is continually occur-
ring), there is then no means of relieving the market
by exportation.   In addition to this, the protected
manufacturers are always exposed to suffer great
injury from smuggling.

Another injurious effect of protection is, that it
checks inventions, and enables manufacturers to keep
the public supplied with commodities of inferior
quality; for no manufacturer will incur the loss of

laying aside old and imperfect machinery, and of reforming the processes of his trade, until he is forced
to do so by the necessity of keeping on equal terms
with his competitors.

Another evil of protection is the encouragement it
gives to smuggling. It also occasions a great loss
of revenue; for if the protecting duties were so reduced as to be moderate duties, that is, to about 12
per cent., for the sole object of obtaining revenue,
the increased consumption of foreign goods, which
would be the result, would yield a very considerable
revenue.

The history of the protected trades of this country
furnishes an abundance of facts in illustration of the
accuracy of all the foregoing reasoning, and shows
that nothing can be more opposite to the truth than
the statement in the Report of the late French Commission of Inquiry, that 'England has only arrived at
the summit of prosperity by persisting for centuries
in the system of protection and prohibition.' In
France, where this system has been universally and
most rigidly acted upon during the last fifteen years,
every protected trade (and every trade is protected)
is in great distress. Dijon and Bordeaux cannot
sell their wines, nor Lyons its silks, nor Louvaine its
cloth, nor Tarrare its muslins, nor Rouen its cottons,
nor Charenton its iron—all in consequence of the
encouragement given by protection to over-production;
and while the trades are thus distressed, the people at
large as consumers suffer by being obliged to pay
higher prices than they would have to pay if the legislature had not interfered. They pay at least 1,500,000*l.*
a year in the increased price of iron, as the direct cost
for the protection given to native iron-masters; full

as much for the cost of the protection given to the growers and makers of beet-root sugar ; and more or less, in the same way, as the cost of every other protection*.

There is not the slightest foundation for the commonplace argument, that, if British manufacturers were not protected, the low price of labour in foreign countries would enable them to supply our markets. For it is not necessarily true, that, because labour is dear in England, as compared with other countries in Europe, those countries would be able to compete with us in manufactures. The argument is built on a wrong notion of what determines us to export.   Exportation takes place from England rather than from France, not because wages are lower (for in fact they are higher), but because the whole cost of production of the exported commodities in England is less than the whole cost in France. Of the cost of production, wages are only a part ; but they seem to be considered the whole by those who insist upon the argument in question†.

The support that is still too generally given to the protecting system, can only be accounted for by the habit of indolence with which the strongest minds sometimes receive without examination those opinions which have been long established. It is, however, satisfactory to observe that there are appearances, of late, of a more correct knowledge of the subject, and of a great change in the public mind.

In 1820 a measure took place, which has been well described as forming an important era in the commercial history of this country ; namely, the pre-

* Edinburgh Review, No. XCIX., Article ii.
† Par. Review, 1825, p. 703.

senting of a petition to the House of Commons by the merchants of London, in which the principle of a perfectly free trade is proposed, and supported by un-answerable reasoning. The petitioners say, with reference to the system of protections, ' That unfortunately a practice, the very reverse of freedom from restraint, has been, and is more or less adopted and acted upon by the governments of this and almost every other country ; each trying to exclude the productions of other countries, with the specious and well-meant design of encouraging its own productions: thus inflicting on the bulk of its subjects who are consumers, the necessity of submitting to privations in the quantity and quality of commodities ; and thus rendering what ought to be the source of mutual benefit and harmony amongst states, a constantly-recurring source of jealousy and hostility. That the prevailing prejudices in favour of the protective or restrictive system may be traced to the erroneous supposition, that every importation of foreign commodities occasions a diminution or discouragement of our own productions to the same extent; whereas, it may be clearly shown, that although the particular description of production which could not stand against unrestrained foreign competition would be discouraged, yet, as no importation could be continued for any length of time, without a corresponding exportation, direct or indirect, there would be an encouragement for the purpose of that exportation of some other production to which our situation might be better suited ; thus affording at least an equal, or probably a greater, and certainly a more beneficial employment to our own capital and labour.'

Similar petitions were presented at the same time

from Glasgow, and all the great trading and manufacturing towns.

The following extract is taken from the petition of
the merchants of Bristol, against the renewal of the
Charter of the East India Company, presented on the
12th of May, 1829, to the House of Commons.   It
affords the best practical authority in favour of what
has been so often stated in the preceding pages, of
the advantage of extended importation in increasing
the demand for British productions.   The petitioners
say, ' That the extension of this most important
branch of commerce (our exports) with so many
millions of our fellow-subjects, is prevented by the
deficiency of suitable returns; for the production of
which the soil, climate, and population of India are
peculiarly adapted, and which need only the due
application of British skill and capital.   The removal
of the existing restrictions will necessarily create
increased demand for British goods, the increased
employment of British artisans, encouragement to
British agriculture, augmented and improved imports
of East India produce, extended employment of British
shipping, and increase of national revenue.'

The Committee of Ways and Means of the Congress of the United States say, in their Report of the
12th of March, 1828, ' In all cases where high
duties are imposed to afford protection, foreign commerce must, in the nature of things, be diminished to
a greater extent than domestic industry is en-
couraged;' and they add, ' In closing this brief and
imperfect review of the destroying operation of the
proposed prohibitory policy, denominated, with singular unappropriateness of language, a protecting
policy, they cannot but pause to make a remark,

obviously suggested by the occasion, that it is much easier to destroy than to create wealth by legislation *.'

The Committee of the citizens of Boston and its vicinity, in their Report, dated Nov. 30, 1827, on the new American Tariff, make the following remarks:—
' That dear goods made at home are better than cheap ones from abroad;—that capital and labour cannot be employed in this country without prohibitory duties;—that it is patriotic to tax the many for the benefit of the few;—that it is just to aid by legislation manufactures which do not succeed without it;—that we ought to sell to other nations, but never to buy from them,—are, we have long since known, fundamental principles among the advocates of the American system. It is, however, extraordinary that these ancient and memorable maxims, sprung from the darkest ages of ignorance and barbarism, should take their last refuge here, and find a statesman of great experience and knowledge willing to risk his reputation in their defence †.'

But the most complete proof of the impolicy of the protecting system has recently been presented to the public in Mr. Camberleng's Report of the Committee of Congress on Commerce, dated Feb. 8, 1830. The following are only a few of the most striking parts of this report, every sentence of which is highly valuable, and deserving of being studied with care, as a most important publication on foreign commerce.

' The Tariff of 1816 laid the foundation of all our subsequent errors. We have wasted millions of our ancient profits of commerce in a visionary experiment

* Parliamentary Paper, 1828; No. 178.
† Report, p. 35.

of increasing our national wealth. Whatever may have been the honest intentions of those who framed our laws (of restriction), they can have no other tendency than to increase our taxes, diminish consumption, and destroy trade. The millions invested under the act of 1816 were swept away in 1818 and 1819; those under the act of 1824, by the revulsions of 1825 and 1826; and the investments under the act of 1828 by the tremendous shock of 1829. It is a common opinion that, in consequence of high duties, our manufacturers are actually in a more prosperous condition than they would have been had our laws never been altered. This is altogether a mistake. Taking a view of the whole Union, we are at this day as much an agricultural and as little a manufacturing people as we were at the adoption of the constitution.

' We are evidently sacrificing the rich resources of a young country in an attempt to force manufactures against all the rules which regulate and control industry. Since our new system has been in full operation, the change is becoming annually and rapidly more unfavourable to our navigation. The proportion of foreign to American tonnage was, in 1824, 9—in 1825, 10—in 1826, 11—in 1827, 14—in 1828, 15 per cent. While such is the retrograding condition of our navigation, England is beating all her competitors, and adding millions to her tonnage.'

The Committee, in support of the measures in favour of getting rid of the American restrictive system, quote the following passage from a Report to Congress by Mr. Jefferson :—' Instead of embarrassing commerce under piles of regulations, duties, and prohibitions, could it be relieved from all shackles, in all parts of the world ; could every country be employed in producing that which nature has best fitted it to produce; and each be free to exchange with others mutual surpluses for mutual wants, the greatest mass possible would then be produced of those things which contribute to human life and human happiness: the numbers of mankind would be increased, and their condition bettered.'

The petition of the proprietors of vineyards in the department of the Gironde, presented to the French Chambers in 1828, and signed by 12,563 individuals, also places in a clear point of view the great evils of the prohibitory system, and strikingly demonstrates, that if it confer on one or more branches of industry any advantage, this must be obtained by the infliction of an equal or greater loss to others that are naturally more advantageous. The petitioners say, ' Considérè en lui-même, le système prohibitif est le plus déplorable des erreurs. La Nature, dans sa variété infinie, a départi à chaque contrée ses attributs particuliers; elle a imprimé sur chaque sol sa véritable destination; et c'est par la diversité des produits et des besoins qu'elle a voulu unir les hommes par un lien universel, et opérer entre eux ces rapprochements qui ont produit le commerce et la civilisation.

' Quelle est la base du système prohibitif? Une véritable chimère, qui consiste à essayer de vendre à l'étranger sans acheter de lui.

' Quelle est donc la conséquence la plus immédiate du système prohibitif, ou, en d'autres termes, du monopole? C'est que le pays qui est placé sous son empire ne peut vendre ses produits à l'étranger. Le voilà donc refoulé dans lui-même; et à l'impossibilité de vendre ce qu'il a de trop, vient se joindre la nécessité de payer plus cher ce qui lui manque.

' Notre industrie ne demandoit, pour fructifier, ni la faveur d'un monopole, ni cette foule d'artifices et de secours dont bien d'autres ont inposé le fardeau au pays. Une sage liberté commerciale, une économie politique fondée sur la nature, en rapport avec la civilisation, en harmonie avec tous les intérêts véritables—telle étoit son seul besoin. Livrée à son essor naturel, elle se seroit étendue d'elle-même sur la France de 1814, comme sur celle de 1789 ; elle auroit formé la plus riche branche de son agriculture ; elle auroit fait circuler, et dans son sol natal, et dans tout le sol du royaume, une sève de vie et de richesse ; elle auroit encore attiré sur nos plages le commerce du monde ; et la France, at lieu de s'ériger avec effort en pays manufacturier, auroit reconquis, par la force des choses, une supériorité incontestable comme pays agricole.

' Le système contraire a prévalu.

' La ruine d'un des plus importantes départements de la France ; le détresse des départements circumvoisins ; le dépérissement général du Midi ; une immense population attaquée dans ses moyens d'existence ; un capital énorme compromis ; la perspective de ne pouvoir prélever l'impôt sur notre sol appauvri et dépouillé ; un préjudice immense pour tous les départements dont nous sommes tributaires ; un décroissement rapide dans celles de nos consommations qui profitent au Nord ; la stagnation générale du commerce, avec tous les dèsastres qu'elle entraîne ; toutes les pertes qu'elle produit, et tous les dommages en matériels, en politiques, en moraux, qui en sont l'inévitable suite ; enfin l'anéantissement de plus en plus irréparable de tous nos anciens rapports commerciaux ; les autres peuples s'enrichissant de nos

pertes, et developpant leur système commerciale sur
le débris du notre.

'Tels sont les fruits amers du système dont nous
avons été les principales victimes.'

Such, then, are the consequences of the protective
system ; a system which prevents those countries
which are subject to its influence from enjoying the
full measure of productiveness which their separate
advantages might be made to yield; which divides
the community of each country into two classes, the
consumers and the monopolists, each interested in
each other's loss; a system which bolsters up a bad
principle with an infinitely vexatious detail of duties,
drawbacks, and prohibitions ; and, what is worst of
all, which is established to the advantage of nobody,
and the disadvantage of all the world. The public
interest, therefore, requires the total abrogation of it ;
but this should be brought about by degrees, for it
must be admitted that those who are now protected
by restrictions have a right to demand that they
should not be suddenly repealed, and that a reasonable time should be allowed them to prepare themselves for meeting foreign competition, or to withdraw from their present employments. This much
they have a right to ask, and ought to obtain, and no
more ; for if more be granted, the interests of the
majority of the public will be sacrificed to those of a
very small part of the community *.

One point only remains to be noticed belonging to
the protecting system, namely, the opinion which
some persons hold, that we ought not to remove the
restrictions on the importation of foreign goods, unless foreign countries agree to allow our goods to be

* Foreign Quarterly Review, No. vi., p. 649.

imported.   But the true grounds on which it is expedient for us to remove these restrictions, are the
numerous injuries we suffer from them in the several
ways already described ; if, therefore, we postpone
the removal of them till we can persuade other countries to make an arrangement for a reciprocal removal,
we postpone taking advantage of the power that is in
our own hands of relieving ourselves.

The petition of the merchants of London, before
referred to, contains the following paragraph on this
point :—

' That although, as a matter of mere diplomacy, it
may sometimes answer to hold out the removal of
particular prohibitions or high duties, as depending
upon corresponding concessions by other states in our
favour, it does not follow that we should maintain our
restrictions in cases where the desired concessions on
their part cannot be obtained. Our restrictions would
not be less prejudicial to our own capital and industry,
because other governments persisted in preserving
impolitic regulations.'

As exports cannot go on without imports, the progress of industry and the increase of capital are
greatly promoted by everything that adds to the annual amount of imports ; the right policy, therefore,
is to remove all obstructions in the way of importation,
without the slightest reference to what course foreign
governments think proper to adopt.

Everything has now been stated that seems necessary to be urged in favour of a revision of the taxes
on materials, manufactures, and luxuries, and also
on the taxes for giving protection to agriculture and
manufactures.   The explanations which have been
given of their effects on industry should leave no

doubt as to how much the wealth of the nation
would be increased if they were to undergo such a
revision that the means of paying the charges for
the public services might be provided with as little
injury as practicable to the improvement of the
country.

If such a thing were possible as taking off all taxes
that the promoting of industry and national wealth
require to be taken off, the following ought to be
wholly abolished or greatly reduced :—

Estimate of Taxes to be Abolished or Reduced.

Customs—Duties on materials, producing £4,153,000
Excise duties—

On bricks and tiles . .	368,000
On starch	84,000
On glass	613,000
On paper	649,000
On printed calicoes . . .	662,000
Two-thirds of the duty on hard soap; as this reduction would increase the consumption, the loss of revenue may be set down at not more than . .	600,000
Reduction of duty on spirits and tobacco	3,000,000

£10,129,000

Although a general notion prevails, that no means
exist for making good so large an amount of revenue
as would, in the first instance, be given up by repealing the taxes here mentioned, this is a mere con-
jecture, and not deserving of any weight; because
no proper efforts have as yet been made to trace in
sufficient detail the sources from which new revenue
might be derived, or the savings by which the present

scale of expenditure might be diminished. If the repealing of duties in the last session had not been
applied to the beer and sugar duties, but to those in
the foregoing table, more than a third of the amount
of them would have been got rid of. If, also, on
the one hand, the country has been going on, as
would appear to be the case from what has already
been said, in a progressive course of accumulating
new wealth, and thus adding to the resources of new
taxation; and, on the other, a system of great profusion has been engrafted on the administration of the
public expenditure, there is a strong *primâ facie* case
to justify the conclusion, that, if proper measures
were taken, there would be no great difficulty in providing by new methods a sufficient revenue for the
public service.

It is, no doubt, the duty of ministers to act with the
greatest circumspection with respect to every plan of
reform, which, by possibility, might place the Treasury in a situation not to be able to meet the current
demands upon it, and keep faith with the public
creditor. But all hazard of this kind would be avoided
by proceeding in the business of reducing or repealing taxes by degrees, and by making the measures
for supplying new funds for the public expenditure
take precedence.

If it were thought expedient to make so considerable a reduction in the taxes affecting industry as
is now proposed, the revenue might be rendered sufficient for all the public services in the following ways:
1st. By the increased revenue which would arise from
increased expenditure on taxed commodities, in consequence of repealing taxes and taking off protecting
duties. 2dly. By retrenchment of the public expenditure. 3dly. By new taxes.

Chapter VII.

EFFECT OF REPEALING TAXES AND TAKING OFF PROTECTING DUTIES IN MAKING THE REMAINING TAXES MORE PRODUCTIVE.

The extraordinary effect of reducing taxes in increasing consumption and producing new revenue, is completely established in the Fourth Report of the Committee of Finance. The Committee refer to the accounts showing the actual produce of the duties under the Customs, Excise, Stamps, and Assessed Taxes, compared with what the produce would have been, if the reduction of taxes which took effect after 1823 had diminished those revenues in the exact proportion which they bore to the produce of that year ; and say, ' It will be seen by this abstract, that the abatement of the revenue by taxes remitted would have been, in 1827, as compared with 1823, no less than 9,182,571*l.*, and that it proved to be only 3,308,316*l.* ; the difference of 5,874,255*l.* being the increase of revenue from increased consumption *.'

The fact that is here so completely established, of the immense influence of reducing taxes in increasing the revenue derived from those which remain, is of the highest importance. It fully exposes the futility of the plea, that the financial circumstances of the nation do not admit of taking off any more taxes ; and it gives to those persons who now argue in favour of the revision of the taxes a right to say, that

* Page 10.

a very large proportion of the revenue, which might appear on a strict calculation likely to be lost, would be made good by the increased productiveness of the taxes which would remain. According to the case stated by the Committee of Finance, if all the taxes were repealed which fall on industry, the loss of revenue would amount to but a few millions.

Some of the measures which have been proposed for reforming the taxes will lead to the production of revenue, and therefore should be taken into the account in showing how lost revenue may be made good. For instance, if the restrictions on the sugar trade were taken off, four or five hundred thousand pounds of revenue would be the probable result. If prohibitions and duties on corn and other agricultural productions must be kept, but were altered to a duty of 12 per cent., such a duty would, in all probability, produce a revenue of six or seven hundred thousand pounds a year on corn, and of three or four hundred thousand pounds a year on other productions of land.

If, as has been proposed, all the protecting duties were reduced to 12 per cent., so as no longer to be duties for protection, but only for revenue, such large quantities of various kinds of foreign articles would be imported, that a revenue of some millions a year may reasonably be calculated upon as the result of such an arrangement. If the duties on coals exported to foreign countries were reduced, an additional revenue of three or four hundred thousand pounds would probably be received; and if machinery were allowed to be exported under a duty of about 12 per cent., so great would, no doubt, be the demand for it, in all parts of the world, that a similar amount, at least, of revenue would be obtained in this way.

If those monopolies and protections which have been mentioned as having the effect of taking many millions annually out of the pockets of the people, by the high prices they occasion, were removed, these millions would be expended on taxed commodities, and thus augment the revenue. What has been already said on the subject of the malt duty, shows that a proper revision and reform of the regulations by which it is collected would, to a certainty, be accompanied with a considerable increase in the revenue derived from this duty. If the duty on European timber were reduced to 1*l.* 10*s.* a load, there can be no doubt that the revenue would be increased three or four hundred thousand pounds a year. So that, on the whole, when the effects which would ultimately be produced on the public revenue, by a proper revision and modification of the taxes, are duly examined, it is clear that, although several millions might be given up in the first instance, in order to give new force to national industry, the measure itself, with the other reforms of duties which it is proposed to accompany it, would reproduce a very large portion of the former revenue.

Chapter VIII.

RETRENCHMENT.

In the following pages the public expenditure will be examined in detail, in order to point out where retrenchment may be introduced; but before going into this inquiry, some general observations will be made to explain—First, the necessity of it; secondly, the practicability of it; thirdly, the principles on which it ought to be conducted ; fourthly, the difficulties in the way of accomplishing it.

First—Retrenchment is necessary as one of the principal means of relieving industry from a large part of those taxes which press the heaviest upon it. Sufficient has already been said to explain in what manner taxation restrains the progress of industry and of national wealth.

Retrenchment is also necessary as a preparation, in order to protect the finances of the country from the destructive effects of the funding system, whenever a new war shall take place ; for in proportion as our peace establishment is low, the difficulty of procuring the additional funds which a war will require by war taxes will be less.

No one can deny, that if we have to begin a new war with a peace expenditure of 55,000,000*l.*,* the

---

* The following is the amount of the public expenditure in 1827, as given in the Fourth Report of the Committee of Finance.

1. Charges of collection £3,868,761

Carried over, £3,868,761

prospect will be most frightful; nor can any one take a comprehensive view of the state of public affairs, and feel satisfied in observing, that while the most expensive preparations for war are making in all the military departments, none are made for placing the Treasury in a state to provide for those demands upon it which a war will occasion.

If war should take place under these circumstances, recourse will probably be had to borrowing to a great amount, and to new permanent taxes—measures which will expose the country to suffer the loss of its manufactures, and finally to undergo all the evils of a national bankruptcy.   For these reasons, it is the

Brought over,	£3,868,761
2. Payments for bounties, and other services charged on the gross revenue . . .	1,339,725
3. Payments for interest, &c., on the funded and unfunded debt, including the Russian loan raised in Holland	28,940,701
4. Permanent civil services, including the civil list	2,103,105
5. Occasional expenditure and advances under Acts of Parliament	363,511
6. Civil services, voted under the head of Miscellaneous	2,863,248
7. Military and naval services, annually voted,	16,205,812
	£55,744,863

Of this sum, the Committee of Finance say, (p. 14,) that 35,952,830*l.* is not susceptible of diminution. Thus, according to their authority, the balance, or 19,792,033*l.*, admits of reduction.   And to this sum may be added the sinking fund, estimated by the Committee at 3,000,000*l.*

All the calculations in the following pages, of the sums that may be retrenched, are made with reference to this expenditure of 1827.

bounden duty of ministers to make every possible retrenchment, and to confine the public expense within
the narrowest limit within which it can be compressed,
consistently with the maintenance of the tranquillity
and independence of the country.

Secondly, as to the practicability of retrenchment,
the zeal with which all existing expenses are defended
throws a considerable difficulty in the way of proving
it. Each public department stands prepared to give
the most confident reasons why it is absolutely necessary to keep up the scale of its expenditure to
the exact point at which it now is. Every kind of
sophism, insinuation, and assertion is worked up with
vast ingenuity into a case to resist any attempt at
effective retrenchment; and not only government and
parliament, but also the public, suffer themselves, in
this way, to have their judgment influenced rather by
the personal authority of official men, who are always
endeavouring to keep their respective services in the
highest possible state of equipment and show, than
by those principles of a sound system of finance,
which require that that portion of the public expense
which is incurred for military preparation and protection, should be regulated by the quantity and measure of the danger to be guarded against.

It is almost impossible for persons, not themselves
in office, to have sufficient knowledge of details, to
be able to expose the fallacies on which the pleas for
expense are enforced; and the absence of such an
exposure produces too often a belief, that the expense
is necessary. The only mode, therefore, that is left
for making out a case to establish the practicability
of retrenchment, is by reasoning on probabilities,
founded on those facts which are within the observa-

tion of every one. Although this is necessarily an imperfect kind of proof, the facts of profusion which can be adduced, when combined together and patiently examined, will be quite sufficient to lead to conclusions that will leave no doubt on any unprejudiced and disinterested mind.

1. When we see how great the expense of the army, navy, and ordnance services is, in comparison with what it was in the peace preceding the war of 1793, we have a right to infer, *primâ facie*, that the present expense is much too great; and the *onus probandi* rests, clearly, with those in authority, to point out what the circumstances are which can justify so great an additional charge on the public. It may be seen, by referring to the evidence taken before the Committee of Finance of 1828, that they concurred in this opinion: for they commenced the examination into each of the above-mentioned departments by quoting a similar opinion of the Committee of Finance of 1817; and by calling on the witnesses for an explanation of the causes which had led to so expensive a peace establishment as the present one.

After beginning their labours on such a principle, there can be little doubt that if they had been re-appointed in the session of 1829, they would have recommended considerable reductions in our military and naval forces to have been made, as soon as the war in Turkey and the affairs of Greece were settled.

It is customary for the advocates of the present scale of expenditure to assume that Mr. Pitt was guilty of very unstatesman-like conduct, in having fixed so low an establishment in the peace preceding the war of 1793. But the defence which was made by Lord Grenville of Mr. Pitt in the House of Lords,

on the 14th of February, 1816, should be attentively
examined, before this assumption of persons interested in the present scale of the expenditure is
allowed to have much influence. Lord Grenville on
that occasion said, ' He wished to call their Lord-
ships' attention to the state of our establishment in a
former period of peace—he meant the period between
1783 and 1793. The establishment of that period
was now to be not only doubled or trebled, but
quadrupled, quintupled. He well remembered that
at that period there was considerable doubt whether
the establishment was not larger than the circumstances called for. The subject was much discussed,
and the propriety of so large an establishment rested
on the peculiar circumstances of Europe at that
period. He had heard it said, that the great man
who was then minister had changed his opinion, and
had observed that in acting to the best of his judgment in requiring only 1,800,000l. for the army, and
2,000,000l. for the navy, he thought, on reflection,
he had ill discharged his duty. But he did most positively declare that he had not the smallest recollec-
tion, that he had no belief that Mr. Pitt ever expressed himself otherwise on that subject than in
terms of self-congratulation and conscious satisfaction, that he had, by the most scrupulous economy,
at that time enabled the country to meet that dreadful
period of trial which it had afterwards to encounter.
He was convinced that, if Mr. Pitt were now alive,
he would have anxiously enforced the propriety of a
low military expenditure at this period of peace ; and
it was only by following the plan of that great man,
and bringing the expenditure of the army and navy
to the very lowest practicable point, that any hope

remained of extricating the country from those difficulties in which it was involved*.'

It is by no means sufficient to say, in order to meet
the charge of profusion in the military expenditure,
that the services are in a very high state of efficiency;
for this charge can be properly met, only by showing
that preparation and equipment have not been carried
beyond the point which manifest grounds of public
necessity prescribe.   Unless this condition of necessity be taken into consideration, the expense to be
incurred for the public service would be a mere matter
of fancy, and might be made twice what it is without
any blame, provided that efficiency and equipment
were doubled at the same time.   Although this principle of necessity appears to be so evident as almost
to make it unnecessary to point it out, every one must
be sensible, who has closely watched the reasoning
of those military authorities according to which our
establishments are regulated, that it can have had
but little consideration in their minds.

Referring, therefore, to the fact of the very great
present amount of the peace establishment in comparison with what the establishment was prior to
1793 ; and no satisfactory reasons having been given,
grounded on a proper exposition of the danger to be
apprehended, to prove that a public necessity exists
for fixing it at treble the former amount, we come to
the conclusion, that a case can be made out to show
that retrenchment is practicable in our military and
naval expenditure†.

2. The spirit of profusion which is admitted to have

* Hansard's Debates, vol. xxxii. p. 514.
† This conclusion is further established in the following pages,
under the heads of Army and Navy Expenditure.

prevailed during the last war, coupled with the fact of nothing having since been effectually done to control it, suggests another argument for its being possible to make a considerable reduction in the expenditure. The nature, character, and extent of the war destroyed all previously established systems of control and economy. The facility of getting money by loans, through the help of inconvertible bank paper and of the sinking fund, led to that boundless expenditure in subsidies, expeditions, fortifications, military pensions, civil superannuations, and increased salaries, which consumed so many millions, and of which we are now feeling the effects. Now, though the war is over, the spirit of this profusion survives; for it is not possible to point out any measure, or system of measures, which has produced any general and decided change in it; and therefore there can be no doubt that if a strict spirit of economy were substituted instead of this spirit of profusion, a great deal of the present expenditure might be reduced*.

3. The fact which is admitted on all sides, that the Treasury has for many years ceased to exercise the control that constitutionally belongs to it over the public expenditure, makes it even more than probable, that if it resume and rigorously enforce its rights over the departments, a great deal of useless expenditure would be put a stop to. Before Mr. Pitt's administration, the Treasury exercised an active control over the public expenditure; but under his administration it would appear, from the following extract from a

* Although the late administration evinced, in several instances, a disposition to be economical, nothing was done in a way to make an impression on a so long-established evil as the profusion of several preceding governments.

speech of the late Lord Lansdowne, on the 28th of February, 1797, that it had then ceased to do so. ' Every office,' said Lord Lansdowne, ' seemed to be the lord of its own will, and every office seemed to have unlimited power over the purse of the nation, instead of their being, as the spirit of the constitution directed, under the constant check of the Treasury. It used to be the distinguishing feature of the British administration, that the Treasury was its heart; it distributed the necessary nourishment to the other parts, and everything flowed from it as the commanding centre; the other departments were necessarily subordinate. In point of fact, in former times the heads of the great departments for the management of the expenditure, attended the Board of Treasury with their annual estimates, for the purpose of examination and of explanation previously to their being submitted to Parliament. The estimates were fully considered in all their details; and the officers who attended were questioned and heard previously to the final decision and approbation of the Board being entered on its minutes. This was all consistent with the ancient, and constant, and uniform system of check and control which had been invariably exercised by the Treasury over the expenditure of all the departments, in all their branches, and in all their details*.'

If this system of check and control were again brought fully into practice, there can be no doubt that retrenchment to a large amount would be found to be practicable.

4. The numerous reports on the public depart-

* From MS. Treasury Document on the Ordnance Department, No. 2, referring to precedents from 1755.

ments for the management of the public expenditure, which have been made by Commissions of Inquiry and Select Committees of the House of Commons, show that there is not one of these departments, of which the constitution and organization is not extremely defective. Every department has more branches, and every branch more officers and clerks, than would be necessary if a proper principle of consolidation were adopted for the despatch of public business, and for the control of the individuals entrusted with it. In addition to this, the forms of doing business are ancient and cumbersome ; reformation, which has made such universal inroads into ancient institutions, and with such universal advantage, has been successfully excluded from the public offices ; returns are required of what is doing to a useless extent; checks are heaped upon checks of no real use ; correspondence is carried on between office and office, and between the offices and individuals, in a manner quite uncalled for by any public object; salaries have been immensely increased ; pensions and superannuations have been lavishly regulated, and very large sums of money have been squandered on official residences*.

With proofs upon proofs of the existence of these facts, the conclusion cannot be shaken, that a great saving of expense would be the consequence of such a revision of all the departments, as would introduce modern improvements, instead of a system of organization and regulation, of which the origin may be traced back to centuries from the present time.

5. The complicated and multifarious methods of

* There was paid, in five years to 1828, 125,688*l.* for expenses incurred in official residences.—Pap. Com. Fin. No. 124.

keeping accounts in all the public offices; the numerous and dilatory methods of auditing them; and
the almost incredible fact, that there is not made up
in any office such a document as an account of the
actual annual expenditure of the public money, show
that there is reason for presuming, that if all this
were changed, and a simple, uniform, and accurate
system of public accounts introduced in its stead, a
great retrenchment might be made in all the official
establishments; at the same time that the public
money would be under a more secure custody. ' The
annual accounts that are laid before parliament are
confined to the exchequer receipts and issues: they
leave millions unexplained and unaccounted for in
detail.   They state, for instance, the expenditure of
the army, navy, and ordnance, no further than the
gross amount of the issues for each of these services*.'

Thirdly—With respect to the principles on which
retrenchment should be conducted, it is of the greatest
importance that these should be well considered, and,
when decided upon, most severely adhered to.   No
person can have his mind in a perfectly fit state to
form a judgment on any question of retrenchment,
without having acquired the habit by previous study of
referring to what the uses and object of government
are, and the grounds on which taxes can justly be
required to be paid.   The great error which is commonly committed is taking the utility of an expenditure as a sufficient justification of it; whereas, however useful it may be, if it cannot be shown to be
absolutely necessary for securing some public object
that could not be had by any other means, it is super-

* Report on Public Accounts of Messrs. Brooksbank and
Beltz, p. 6.

fluous, and ought to be discontinued. It is not an uncommon opinion among those persons who are in situations to have considerable influence in matters of finance, that we ought first to secure all the revenue we can, and then regulate the expenditure according to it. Others allow themselves to be guided by their feelings and their passions, and not having formed, by proper researches, any fixed principles of the science of legislation, are continually favouring expense, and resisting economy, when cases of apparent individual hardship come before them : not recollecting what those persons suffer, who pay the taxes for providing for the effects of their mistaken compassion and unjustifiable liberality with the public money. If right principles were referred to, they would suggest that taxation is the price we pay for government ; and that every particle of expense that is incurred beyond what necessity absolutely requires for the preservation of social order, and for protection against foreign attack, is waste, and an unjust and oppressive imposition upon the public. Every minister, and every member of parliament, who has the power to spend or to save the public money, should do his best to prevent the wants of the state from depriving the people of the means of providing for their wants ; and, therefore, economy and frugality, which are virtues in a private station, from their vast influence upon national happiness in a public station, become the most pressing of duties.

Fourthly—the difficulties of carrying into effect a complete system of retrenchment are extremely great. The first is to get ministers sufficiently well educated to comprehend the necessity of it, and to understand the means by which it may be accomplished.

The distaste for abstruse reasoning, and the prejudice against the science of political economy, confine
the numbers among those who take a lead in public
affairs to but a few who possess an extensive acquaintance with trade and finance, and with the principles which ought to govern these branches of
political science. It has been observed by Mr. Hume,
that ' the more simple ideas of order and equity are
sufficient to guide a legislator in a great part of his
duties ; but that principles, like those of commerce,
are much more complicated, and require long experience and deep reflection to be well understood,
because real consequences are often contrary to first
appearances.'

But if the first difficulty be overcome, of having a
government sufficiently informed as really to comprehend the necessity of retrenchment, and sincerely
willing to retrench, another great difficulty presents
itself, namely, the opposition which is sure to be made
to their plans of economy, even by their own friends,
in both Houses of Parliament.   When measures of
economy have been proposed by government, the
House of Commons has so frequently been anything
but faithful in its representative character, that government cannot but fear the consequences of attempting to carry into effect such a system of reform as
the circumstances of the country require. The remedy
for this, is for government, instead of exaggerating
every trifling appearance of prosperity, to explain,
fully and without reserve, all the facts of suffering
and injury which show the propriety and necessity of
retrenchment, so as to excite the public to interfere
and control their representatives.   This is perhaps
the only way by which the opposition to retrenchment,

which is the consequence of the interest which peers
and members of parliament have in continuing a profuse scale of expenditure, can be successfully resisted.
If the public were made thoroughly acquainted with
the causes which keep it up at its present amount, they
would very soon load the tables of parliament with
such remonstrances, as would enable government to
carry their measures, without being exposed to be
defeated, as they were in the Session of 1828, on
the Superannuation Bill, by members holding offices
taking a lead in opposing it.

In order that nothing may be omitted that can be
urged in support of the foregoing general reasoning
respecting the practicability of retrenchment, the
public expenditure will be examined in detail under
the heads of,

1. The collection of the revenue. 2. Bounties. 3.
The control and management of the expenditure.
4. Civil government. 5. Military expenditure. 6. The
slave trade. 7. The sinking fund. 8. Colonies. 9.
Ireland.

Chapter IX.

THE COLLECTION OF THE REVENUE.

In the following short statement there seems to be a strong case in favour of the practicability of making a very considerable reduction in the charge for collecting the revenue.

In the year 1806, the gross receipt of the revenue of the United Kingdom was 58,255,175*l.*, and the charge for collecting it was 2,797,722*l.*

In the year 1826, the gross receipt was 54,839,685*l.*, and the charge for collecting it was 4,030,337*l.*

Hence it appears that 58,255,175*l.* was collected in 1806, at a less charge by 1,232,615*l.*, than 54,839,685*l.* was collected in 1826 *.

The accuracy of this statement cannot be disputed, because the dates and figures are taken from accounts which were prepared by the Treasury for the Committee of Finance, with the view of supplying the place of the annual accounts, which cannot be relied on †.

* There is no account made up since 1826, on the same plan as that here quoted.

† These accounts are entitled ' *Accounts of the ordinary revenue of the United Kingdom from* 1802 *to* 1827 (*after deducting the repayments, allowances, discounts, drawbacks, and bounties of the nature of drawbacks*): *stating the amount paid in each of the said years for charges of management,*' &c. No notice is taken in them of the abolition of fees and patent offices in 1812, by the Act of 51 Geo. 3, c. 71. The author of the pamphlet on the Customs' Revenue says, ' The additional salaries granted

The charge of nearly 4,000,000*l.* a year for collecting 54,000,000*l.* is 7½ per cent. ; if by any means it could be reduced to 5 per cent., the saving under the head of collection would be 1,300,000*l.*

The circumstance of the charge of collection continuing so high, is a proof that there must be great fault somewhere, because much of late has been done for the purpose of diminishing it. This subject has been examined into by three Select Committees of Finance, and at least three different Commissions of Inquiry ; and numerous improvements have been adopted at their suggestion ; the principal of which are, the abolishing of the patent offices, and of the several revenue boards in Ireland and Scotland ; the consolidation of the duties and of the laws *, and the introducing of a great many regulations for promoting the despatch of business. As the result of the whole of the attempt to economise is an increase in the charge of collection, it is clear the spirit of profusion still holds the master-hand.

Management of the Collection of the Revenue.—It is possible that the cause of this evil may be the principle on which the management of the taxes is administered, namely, that of having a separate and completely independent board of management for each branch of the taxes. These boards, although nominally under the control of the Treasury, are practically, and necessarily, nearly altogether exempt

under this arrangement amounted to about 200,000*l.*, and the temporary compensation allowances to be about 40,000*l.*' (p.11.)

* Too much praise cannot be given to those who originated, and successfully carried into execution in 1825, the plan of consolidating the revenue laws.

from it, and possessed of powers, either direct or indirect, of incurring any expense they please. Whatever may be the intentions of the Treasury, the superior knowledge which these boards have of details, and the various means they can employ to influence the opinions and conduct of the Chancellor of the Exchequer, enable them in practice not only to get rid of the control of the Treasury, but to put it under their control.

The proper remedy to be applied to correct this source of profuse expenditure is to abolish these numerous independent governments, and form one board of Commissioners, to be Commissioners of the Treasury, acting with the first Lord of the Treasury and the Chancellor of the Exchequer for the general administration of all the taxes. This board of Commissioners to be composed of the present chairmen of the customs, excise, stamps, woods and forests, the Postmaster-General, the First Lord of the Treasury, and the Chancellor of the Exchequer. Each of these chairmen to continue to act as the head of the department he now belongs to, and to have a small board of sub-commissioners to assist him :* the duties of the sub-commissioners to be confined to carrying into execution the orders of the general board. The members of the general board, excepting the First Lord of the Treasury and the Chancellor of the. Exchequer, not to sit in parliament.

If the whole taxation of the country were revised and simplified, and also the various methods for administering the management of it, the business of management might be so much diminished, that one

---

* The assessed taxes to be under the Excise branch.

or two meetings a week of the general board would be sufficient. The presence of the first Lord of the Treasury and of the Chancellor of the Exchequer at the board would enable them effectually to control the expense of management, and at the same time render them responsible in their places in parliament for every item of expense belonging to it.

In order further to simplify the managing of the collection of the revenue, the business of receiving the money for the taxes from the persons who have to pay them, should be wholly separated from the business of the administration of the taxes. The latter business should be confined to what is necessary for charging or assessing the taxes to be paid, and the former business to the operation of receiving the money to be received for the taxes; and it should be placed in the hands of officers having no connexion with the revenue board, but acting under another board of Commissioners of the Treasury to be appointed for this branch of service, and also, as will hereafter be proposed, for managing all payments of public money: so that the business of receiving all money and paying all money, belonging to the public, may be under one board of management, and the accounts of the receipt and expenditure of the public money kept on one clear, consistent, and uniform plan.

It should also be provided, that the whole money received from the taxes should be paid into the Exchequer, without any deduction for paying the charges of management; and that all such charges should be paid and stated in the public accounts, as items of the general annual expenditure.

If the changes here proposed were made, a great

expense would be saved. The great sums now spent in maintaining the office establishments belonging to the several boards of revenue might be greatly reduced: also the number of commissioners; and one set of law agents, collectors, receivers, comptrollers, inspectors, and accountants, would be sufficient, instead of the separate sets now employed by the separate departments.

That nothing may be omitted that can serve to give full information to the public concerning the taxes, they should be laid annually before parliament by the Chancellor of the Exchequer in a printed budget of revenue, showing the estimated produce of each tax; and they should be annually voted for the year, commencing on the following first of January.

Customs' Duties.—It appears, from accounts laid before the Committee of Finance, that the revenue collected in 1827 from the customs' duties, was received from 566 duties on as many different articles :—

18	articles produced £100,000 and upwards, making . .		£17,683,445	8 8
9	articles produced 50,000 to 100,000		784,415	18 6
9	do. do. 25,000 to 50,000		370,066	17 1
20	do. do. 10,000 to 25,000		370,402	5 1
510	do. do. less than 10,000		585,072	6 0
	Miscellaneous articles		20,903	7 7
566	Gross Revenue		£19,815,206	3 1½*

This sweeping system of taxation shows the customs' duties laws have been framed by persons but little acquainted with the principles of trade and

* Paper of Com. No. 173, p. 11.

finance, and who had not the slightest consideration for the feelings and conveniences of individuals, or for the interests of foreign commerce. The effect of it is to render the accounts complex, and to generate smugglers. Prices are enhanced with little or no advantage to the revenue; the comforts and enjoyments of the people are uselessly abridged; and a great deal of delay, vexation, and loss, must attend the collecting of duties on so many hundred commodities. Each of the duties on the 510 articles, which produce less than 10,000*l.*, should be repealed. If this were done, the imports of foreign goods, and, as a necessary consequence, the exports of British, would be greatly increased; the business of collection would then be confined to 56 articles, and the saving of expense in management would, in all probability, be greater than the revenue (585,000*l.*) which would be lost by repealing these duties.

Excise Duties.—The circumstance of the excise revenue being collected at a low rate of charge per cent. is not a conclusive proof that there is less profusion in this department than in the others; for a large proportion of this revenue is paid by a few individuals, on operations carried on upon a large scale, and requiring the attendance of few officers in proportion to the sums derived from the duties of which they have the charge.

The regulations for collecting the duty on malt are carried to such an extent of unnecessary, and, with respect to the trade, destructive details, that they afford direct testimony of the practicability of diminishing the number of officers employed, by simpli-

fying the system of collection.   In this case the zeal
for securing revenue has so kept down the trade of
malting, as to have made the consumption stationary
for the last forty years; whereas there can be no
doubt, that if the trade had not been so harassed by
excise rules, checks, and penalties, the consumption
would have increased with increased population and
wealth, and, consequently, the revenue derived from
it. So that, in point of fact, it is clear that the mistaken
zeal with which the excise department has sought to
benefit the revenue, has incurred a loss of a great
annual amount on the article of malt alone.   The
stationary state of the glass manufacture, for a number of years, and of other trades subject to the excise
laws, is to be accounted for, in a great degree, by
ignorant and harassing regulations.   Excise legislation, in consequence of having been under the direction of inferior officers, has been grounded on the
narrow principle of grasping, by force of penalties,
at the capital of manufacturers, in direct opposition
to enlarged and sound principles.   These would have
pointed out the way of making laws consistent both
with the interests of the trade of the country and
those of the revenue.

As no inquiry has been made into this department
for a great many years, it is impossible to know
whether it be well or ill managed : some circumstances have transpired, particularly with respect to
the distilleries, which afford reason to suppose that, if
an inquiry were instituted, occasions would be found
for making many improvements, and saving a great
deal of expense.

Some of the duties of excise yield so little revenue,

that there can be no good reason for continuing
them.   The net revenue received in 1828 was as
follows :—

On starch	.	.	.	£87,348
Stone bottles	.	.	.	3,405
Sweets and mead		.	.	2,606
Vinegar	.	.	.	24,500

These duties are liable to the same objections as
those just made to the customs' duties, which produce
little revenue, and ought to be repealed.

The repeal in 1825 of those parts of the assessed
taxes which were productive of a comparatively
trifling profit to the revenue, forms a good precedent
for repealing this class both of customs and excise
duties.

Post Office.—The twenty-second Report of the
Commissioners of Revenue Inquiry, recently presented to Parliament, exposes an immense loss of
public money, occasioned by the Post-office becoming
builders and managers of steam-packets for the home
packet service, instead of accepting offers made to
them by private companies, which, in the opinion of
the commissioners, ought to have been accepted.
With respect to the consequences to the public as
to expense, of the Post-office not having adopted this
course, the commissioners say,—' The annual excess
above stated, amounting in a period of nine years to
about 300,000*l.*, must be considered a total loss*.'

With regard to the station at Holyhead, the commissioners recommend, ' that as soon as the vessels
now employed to carry the correspondence can be

* p. 6.

satisfactorily disposed of, the whole packet establishment, the property, or maintained at the charge, of
the crown, in all its branches, should be dispensed
with.' They add,—' The vast increase in the number of steam vessels, the offers formerly made at this
station, and the present competition for employment,
leave, we think, no doubt of the practicability of providing satisfactorily for the conveyance of correspondence between Holyhead and Dublin by hired vessels
of this description*.

With respect to the Liverpool station, the commissioners say,—' The arrangement which still sub-
sists should be no longer permitted ; and his Majesty's
Postmaster-General should be instructed to provide
for the transmission of the correspondence between
Liverpool and Dublin in the manner prescribed in
the Report of the Committee of Finance of 1798,
already quoted :' namely, ' to contract publicly for
the conveyance of mails by packets, with such individuals or *companies* as would undertake it at the
lowest prices, for a term of years, upon different
stations, so as to open this lucrative department to
public competition †.'

The Commission of Inquiry have recommended in
other reports very extensive reforms in the Post-
office establishments in England and Scotland, and
the abolition of the separate department in Ireland.
The reasons on which these reforms are founded
leave no doubt that, if they were adopted, a great
improvement would be made in the mode of carrying
on the business of this branch of the public service
and that a considerable saving of expense would take
place.

* p. 23.   † pp. 30—40.

Stamp Duties.—Although the raising of revenue
by stamp duties is perhaps a less objectionable mode
than any other, many of the present duties are exceedingly vexatious, and some of those which are the most
vexatious produce so little revenue, that they should
be at once repealed. Such, for instance, as the duty
on pamphlets, soda-water bottles, quack medicines,
and horses let to hire by the day. The plan of charging
some of the duties on horses as assessed taxes, and
others as stamp duties, should be changed. The tax
on horses let to hire by the day should be repealed,
in consequence of there being, perhaps, no tax which
so much interferes with the comfort and amusement of
the public.

The net revenue from hackney coaches and pedlars
paid, in 1828, into the Exchequer, was only 55,000*l.*,
and the charge for collecting the gross revenue of
77,437*l.* was at the rate of 13*l.* 18*s.* 7*d.* per cent.
The small amount of revenue, and large expense of
collection, are good reasons for repealing these duties.
There is no justice in selecting the inhabitants of
London as the only part of the public to be taxed for
hackney coaches. The tax on hawkers and pedlars
has its origin in an ancient notion, that the public
interest is benefited by protecting shopkeepers against
the competition of itinerant dealers. As the trade
carried on by them is particularly convenient and
beneficial to the public, this penalty on industry should
be removed.

Chapter X.

BOUNTIES AND DRAWBACKS.

AMONG the numerous instances of waste of public money, there is none more flagrant than that which consists in giving bounties on linen and sail-cloth exported, amounting, for a number of years, to 300,000*l*. a year. What makes the continuing of these bounties the more to be condemned, is, that the chief part of the linen-manufacturers themselves called on the Treasury some years ago to abolish them. Some manufacturers in Scotland have derived all the advantage of them, and their influence has been allowed to put the country to this great loss. When a saving of the public money could have been effected to the amount of 300,000*l*. so easily as this saving might have been, it is quite clear, that whatever may have been the professions of Government to economize, they have not been influenced by any strong or sincere desire to do so, but have always been ready to keep up useless expense, rather than come into collision with any of those private interests which benefit by it. In this case, they have at length been driven to abolish these bounties; but by fixing for the period of their extinction the 1st of January, 1832, at least 200,000*l*. more will be lost.

It is no longer necessary to continue the remarks contained in the last edition of this work, on the bounties on the fisheries. It certainly was the intention of Government to renew them in the last session ;

and it may therefore be possible that those remarks had some influence in saving the public from this most useless expenditure. There is still, however, an annual expense incurred on the fisheries, of 15,600*l.*, in maintaining establishments of Irish and Scotch Commissioners. The meddling of these commissioners with the trade of fishing, cannot fail to be a vexatious and mischievous impediment in the way of private enterprise, and the natural extension of the trade.

In consequence of the reduction in the duty on sugar of 3*s.* a cwt., the bounty on refined sugar, exported since the 5th of October last, is fixed as follows:—

	£.	s.	d.
On bastard sugar, per cwt. . . .	1	4	0
Single-refined ditto	2	6	0
Double-refined ditto, and single, equal in quality to double	2	14	0

with a deduction of one-fifth on the total amount.— This makes the rate of bounty exactly what it was before the reduction of the duty.

It is forcibly insisted upon by many persons conversant with this subject, that this rate of bounty exceeds the duty paid, and that it is a gratuitous bounty to the exporter of refined sugar to the amount of 5*s.* 3*d.* a cwt. To support this conclusion, a speech is referred to of the then Secretary of the Treasury, in which it is said he distinctly admitted that the act of 1826, for lowering the bounty, left half of it remaining. A letter is also quoted of Mr. Hibbert, written in 1824, in which he says, ' the drawback upon the export of refined sugar is little, if at all short of a gratuitous bounty of six shillings per hundred weight.' The persons above referred to contend, that at that time the drawback was a gratuitous bounty of 8s. 4d., and that since the act of 1826, if the estimated quantity of refined sugar obtained from a cwt. of raw be taken at 74lb. to 75lb., there is now a gratuitous bounty of 5s. 3d. a cwt. These persons say, in answer to those who assert that there is no such bounty, ' How does it happen that though the West Indians are now at liberty to export their surplus directly from the plantations to the continent, they prefer sending it first to England, and then from England to the continent, though it thus becomes loaded with double freight, insurance, commission, and shipping and landing charges? The fact is, that the drawback on the refined sugar exported from this country is so regulated, as not only to compensate to the West Indian planter the heavy extra charges just mentioned, but to afford him a considerable profit besides, all which must obviously come out of the pockets of the people of this country *." If it be true that there is a bounty of 5s. 3d. over and above the duty paid, this on 456,000 cwts. of refined sugar annually exported, will make a charge on the public of 120,000l. a year.

In contradiction to these arguments, it is said that the bounty should not be considered more than equal to the duty paid on the raw sugar, and that it is only a drawback.

The author of the pamphlet on the Customs' Revenue states, that, many years ago, a large quantity of Muscovado sugar, selected as of average qualities, to the satisfaction of government, was refined in a par-

* See Nos. 24 and 57 of the Anti-Slavery Reporter.

ticular refinery, under inspection, which was also satisfactory to government, in order to ascertain the produce ; and that all subsequent calculations of drawback have been founded upon this trial *.'   The fact here mentioned of this trial having been made several years ago, suggests some degree of suspicion of the bounty being now more than equivalent to the duty.   For, supposing even that those persons who acted for Government in making this trial, sufficiently understood the trade of refining as not to have been in any way deceived by the refiners, the long period which has elapsed has afforded an opportunity to introduce improvements in the manner of conducting the process of refining, which the refiners no doubt have taken advantage of.   It cannot be imagined, that in such a trade as this is, no improvements have been practicable in converting raw into refined sugar. The uniform success of the Scotch distillers in increasing the power of working off their stills faster and faster by many degrees than the Government increased the charges on them, shows that the greatest precautions on the part of Government cannot in all cases counteract the ingenuity of the traders they have to deal with.

In the same way, all drawbacks of duty, so numerous in our present system of taxation, must necessarily become bounties, in consequence of its being quite certain, that notwithstanding the calculations on which they were fixed in the first instance may have been made with greatest care, the introduction of improvements, or the practising of fraud, will be employed successfully in favour of the trades to which they apply.

* Page 33.

The drawbacks also occupy much of the labour and time of the officers, and add to expense of management in recording a number of particulars and checking accounts. The abolishing, therefore, of all drawbacks, is a most desirable object. It seems to be one that might be attained without any very great difficulty, partly by the total repeal of some duties, partly by the facilities afforded by the warehousing system, and in allowing the fullest opportunity of exportation from the warehouses free from all restraint, and at a small expense.

The sum paid annually for various drawbacks amounts to 3,300,000*l.**

* Paper Com. Fin. No. 43.

CHAPTER XI.

THE MANAGEMENT OF THE PUBLIC EXPEN-DITURE.

The following is a list of the several departments that are intrusted with the business of expending the public money pursuant to the general appropriation of it by Parliament. The sums which are paid for their establishments are here stated as accurately as the documents respecting them will admit.

	£.
1. The Treasury, including the Commissariat Department, in 1827	80,542*
2. The Exchequer	48,000†
3. The Audit Office, in 1828	32,977‡
4. The Bank of England, do.	267,597§
5. The Commissioners of the Sinking Fund, do.	10,350‖
6. The Civil Departments of the Army, do.	108,837¶
7. Ditto of the Navy, do.	179,647**
8. Ditto of the Ordnance (the Tower and Pall-mall), do.	57,961††
	£779,911

This account shows only the expense of the civil establishments in London, and therefore falls very far short of the total expense of the civil establishments of the military departments.

* Paper of Com. of Fin. No. 102.   Acc. No. 27, and Par. Pap. 1822, No. 110.   ‡ An. Fin.   † Ib. 1828, p. 137.
§ Ib. p. 134.   ‖ Ib. 134.   ¶ Army Estimates, 1828.
** Navy Estimates, 1828.   †† Ordnance Estimates, 1828.

The Treasury.—It appears, by a paper laid before the Committee of Finance, that the expense of this department, which is now 80,542*l.*, was, in 1797, 44,066*l.*—so that it has nearly doubled since that time : although the income and expenditure (the superintending of which constitutes the chief business of the Treasury) of 1797 was as great as the income and expenditure of 1827.

As the Treasury exercises the same powers, and discharges nearly the same duties now as it did in 1797, this immense increase of expense in the establishment of a department whose duty it is to control the other departments, is alone sufficient evidence of the profusion with which salaries must have been increased and officers multiplied. There are no fewer than fifteen clerks in the Treasury, who receive salaries amounting to 1000*l.* ; five of these fifteen receive 1500*l.* a year 'each, and upwards *.

Nothing can more fully prove the want of system and uniformity on the part of those persons by whom public business was originally regulated, and the necessity of revision and reform, than the mode by which the Treasury establishment is paid—for intance, some of the salaries are paid out of the Civil List ; some from the consolidated fund ; some out of a fee-fund ; some out of the Customs' revenue, and some by annual grants of Parliament. Such kind of complication must lead to great perplexity and confusion of accounts, and to frustrate all efforts to keep down the expense of official establishments.

The Exchequer.—It is so generally acknowledged that the forms by which business is carried on in this

‡ Paper, Committee of Finance, No. 102.

office are antiquated and absurd, that it would be
wasting time to give any description of them; and
since there seems to be but one opinion with respect
to the expediency of abolishing this office, as an expensive and inconvenient mode of doing business, what
deserves most to be attended to, is the consideration
of the sort of office which should be substituted in its
stead. As the chief duty of the Exchequer, so far as
the public money is concerned, is to take care that
no issues of it are made by the Treasury without their
being in conformity with the authority specially
enacted by Parliament, this duty ought to be easily
and effectually performed by a small department, consisting of a few officers, and occupying only a few
rooms.

The Audit Office.—Little need be said here concerning this office; for if a proper system be adopted
for controlling and keeping the public accounts, it will
be necessary to make a total change with respect to
its present functions.

Management of the Debt.—The Bank of England
annually receives about 270,000*l.* for its trouble in
paying the dividends. This is a very extravagant
misapplication of the public money; for had the
Government made a proper bargain with the Bank,
on granting or renewing the charter, they would not
have allowed it the benefit of exclusive privileges in
carrying on the trade of banking, and also of holding
several millions of balances of public money free of
interest, without at least having required, as a condition of these advantages, the paying of the dividends without any charge. In the numerous dis-

cussions which have taken place on this subject in the House of Commons, the extravagance of the arrangement has been but little disputed; but it has been suffered to continue on the ill-supported plea, that it was binding on the public so long as the present charter had to run. As this is now so near its close, the advantage the Bank derives from holding the balances of the public money should be taken into account, in making any new arrangement with it respecting the dividends, so that the whole of the sum now paid for the management of the debt may be saved.

THE CIVIL DEPARTMENTS OF THE ARMY.

Paymaster of the Forces.—The office of the Paymaster of the Forces may be considered as being almost a sinecure, in consequence of nearly the whole of the business of it being performed by a deputy and three cashiers. As each of these persons has a power of drawing money out of the Bank of England on his own order, the effect of this office being a sinecure is to diminish considerably the security of the public. It is also attended with this further inconvenience, that it multiplies the number of imprest accountants, and thus adds to the difficulty of establishing a proper system of keeping the public accounts.

The true remedy for these evils is, to introduce an entirely new principle for the management of all payments of public money. How this should be carried into effect will be explained after examining the offices of the treasurers of the navy and ordnance, and of other pay offices.

Comptrollers of the Army Accounts.—Strange as it may seem, the office of Comptrollers of Army Accounts has nothing to do with the accounts arising out of the money voted in the army estimates ; these are under the War Office. The Comptrollers' office ought to be called that of Auditors of a portion of the Accounts of the Army Extraordinaries.

Army Extraordinaries.—Nothing can be more opposed to every principle of simplification and consolidation in conducting public business than the account which is called the army extraordinaries. The best informed official men admit that it leads to a great confusion of accounts, and can only be intelligible to persons who are in office, or to those who bestow a great deal of time in unravelling it.

The vote of parliament for the army extraordinaries is explained, as ' not being matter of previous estimate or specific grant,' such as is contained in the army estimates *. It includes, among other items, the pay, clothing, allowances, recruiting, &c., for the forces serving in India ; and, although the sum annually voted is no more than 800,000*l.* or 900,000*l.*, the payments that are made and stated in the annual account, which the paymaster of the forces lays before parliament, commonly amount to 3,000,000*l*†. This arises, in part, from payments made nominally for army extraordinaries during the year, comprehending a considerable number which do not belong to that head of service, but which are of the nature of temporary advances for other services provided for by parliament, and which it is convenient to pay, in the

* Report of Messrs. Brooksbank and Beltz on Public Accounts, p. 55.　　　† Ib. 53.

first instance, under the name of army extraordinaries, and afterwards to adjust, by repayments from specific grants*. The consequence of thus making the paymaster of the forces pay for those services that do not belong to the army, is the producing annually to parliament of an account with a false title. This scheme of army extraordinaries serves to conceal from parliament and the public a great deal of wasteful and illegal expenditure : for instance, the sums paid at home to colonial agents, and the sums drawn from abroad for colonial expenses, although they are wholly for civil colonial purposes, are paid as army extraordinaries, and without any previous vote of parliament : in point of fact, as what constitutes, in reality, the vote of the army extraordinaries, is the balance of the account of every expense called by this name, and as any expense may be so called, there is no kind of expense that may not be covered by this sort of parliamentary sanction.

There is no reason for not putting into the army estimates the expenses to be incurred for the forces serving in India : these and all other military expenses that can be specified, which are now voted in the mass, and without being named in the army extraordinaries, should be put into the army estimates ; and also such a sum as might be wanted for other military expenses which could not be specified, but the heads of which may be stated. In this way the vote for the army extraordinaries might be got rid of, and the whole of the army expenditure brought into the War Office, under a uniform and systematic control with the rest of the military expenses. A further advantage

---

* Report of Messrs. Brooksbank and Beltz, p. 3.

would be gained by this arrangement,—namely, the getting rid of all pretext for continuing to keep up the office of comptrollers of army accounts.

The payments for other services, under the name of army extraordinaries, should be made in some new way, so that the use of the military chests under the care of the commissaries abroad may be continued, and so that the several branches of the public services may be furnished with the same kind of banking facilities and conveniences which they now have.

The Commissariat.—There are some circumstances belonging to the Commissariat which call for observation. The first is, that of the business of providing bread, meat, forage, fuel, and candles for the army and artillery in the United Kingdom, and fuel and candles for the troops on foreign stations, being under the management of the Treasury ; for so it is, in consequence of the Commissariat department being a part of the Treasury. Government wished to transfer this business to the Ordnance in 1822, when the providing of other military stores was transferred to it ; but the then master-general objected to it. The peculiar unfitness of the Treasury to transact this kind of business, and the fitness of the Ordnance, require that the transfer of it should not be longer delayed.

The next circumstance to be noticed relates to the accounts of the commissaries, who are both cash and store accountants. Those accounts which relate to pecuniary expenditure are audited by the Audit Board, while the store and provision accounts are committed to the exclusive investigation of the comptrollers of army accounts. This course of examining and auditing these accounts shows with what negli-

gence the modes of doing public business have originally been arranged.

So many obvious considerations lead to the conclusion, that the entire accounts, whether cash or
stores, of a public accountant ought to be simulta-
neously examined by one and the same department,
that an alteration in the present system should be
immediately made*.

The employing of Commissaries of Accounts
abroad was suggested in consequence of the great
accumulation of accounts during the war; but since
the conclusion of it, the motives which originated
the plan have gradually ceased to have any force, and
therefore the public may be saved the expense of
keeping up any of these officers †.

Army Agents..—It would appear that there is no
necessity for incurring the expense of Army Agents.
The accounts of the paymasters of regiments are examined at the War Office, and not by the agents;
all that the agents do for the public, is to receive
money from the Paymaster of the Forces, and to pay
with it the drafts of the regimental paymasters: their
other duties are private, and for the benefit of the
officers of the army‡.

The measure which would the most contribute to
diminish useless expense, and secure an efficient performance of duty in the civil departments of the army
and Ordnance, is the constituting of an Army Board
for both services, to be composed of the heads of each

---

* Report of Messrs. Brooksbank and Beltz, p. 107.
† Ibid. p. 107.
‡ Evidence of Lord Palmerston, before Committee of Finance,
p. 234 and 219.

chief branch, on the plan of the Ordnance Board. By doing this, a more concentrated direction would be established, and the whole control of the army and Ordnance expenditure would be rendered more effectual. A precedent for such an arrangement conducting military affairs, is afforded by the Army Board which presides over and manages the East India Company's army. This Board is composed of the Commander-in-Chief, as President; the General Officer commanding the Presidency Division of the army, as Vice-President; the Chief Engineer, the Commandant of the Artillery, the Quarter-Master-General, the Adjutant-General, the Commissary-General, and the Military Auditor-General. In this board, as in the English Ordnance Board, there is an individual responsibility and duty, superintended by the general control of the individuals themselves, in their capacities as members of the board*.

Army Accounts†.—It would appear from the Report of Messrs. Brooksbank and Beltz on the Public Accounts, that the mode of examining the regimental accounts answers every purpose; and that but some slight improvements are wanted, to make the mode

* Paper, Committee of Finance, No. CLI. Answers of Mr. Brownrigg.

† The Committee of Finance, soon after they were appointed, suggested to government the expediency of having an inquiry made into the methods employed in keeping accounts in the public offices. Accordingly, Messrs. Brooksbank, Beltz, and Abbott were appointed commissioners for this purpose. It appears that the two first-named gentlemen have not acted with Mr. Abbott; in consequence of which, they have presented one Report on the Accounts to the Treasury, and Mr. Abbott has presented another. Both have been laid before parliament, and printed.

of keeping the accounts of the Pay-Office efficient.
They say, ' That the books neither of the Navy-Office,
of the Victualling, nor of the Ordnance, will enable
those departments to furnish an account of receipt
and expenditure, according to the heads of the estimates, with the like facility as the books of the Pay-
Office.' Mr. Abbott, the Third Commissioner of
Accounts, did not make a Report on the Army Accounts. There are persons who have some acquaintance with them, who say, that they are as imperfect
as the accounts of the other departments.

THE CIVIL DEPARTMENT OF THE NAVY.

Treasurer of the Navy.—Some reformation has
of late been made in this department, but on much
too narrow a principle to put the business of paying
the expenses of the Navy and of keeping the accounts
on a perfect system.

Nothing can more conclusively shew the stubborn-
ness with which public offices cling to antiquated
and absurd practices, and how far they will go in
shutting out improvements, than the circumstance of
continuing to send money in waggons, under officers
called conductors, and with military escorts, from
the Navy Pay-Office in London to the sub-cashiers
at the ports*.

The Navy Board.—According to the evidence
given before the Committee of Finance, by Sir
George Cockburn, Sir George Clerk, Mr. Douglas,
and Mr. Barrow, it appears, that of late years the
Admiralty have made various efforts to reduce the

* Evidence Com. Fin. p. 63.

civil expenditure of the navy. It seems, however, that they were so much opposed, as to be able to accomplish in this department only some trifling reductions; but that, with respect to the Victualling Office, in consequence of the Commissioners having zealously co-operated with them, a very great reformation and saving of expense has been effected.

In the session of 1829, the old Navy Board was abolished, and a new one formed, according to the suggestion of the Committee of Finance, on the model of the Ordnance Board. As the evidence just referred to explains the practicability of making some considerable reductions in this department, this change should lead to a large saving of the public money.

Dock-yards at Home.—The evidence given before the Committee of Finance makes it quite clear that a considerable reduction of expense might be secured, if a proper change of system were introduced in this branch.

The following is an abstract of the evidence referred to :—

Mr. Douglas says, ' It has occurred very strongly to myself, and to other persons who have visited the yards, that the returns which are made from them daily, weekly, monthly, quarterly, and annually, are much more voluminous than are necessary for any practical use[*].'

Sir George Cockburn says, ' In the present good state of our Navy, a still further reduction of workmen in our yards might be permitted[†].'

Mr. Barrow says, as to the dock-yards, ' With

[*] Evidence Com. Fin. p. 100.   [†] p. 15.

respect to superintending officers, perhaps we might
be able to reduce some of the principal officers.   The
inferior officers may certainly be reduced considerably, mostly among those, I should say, below the
situation of foreman of the yard; such, for instance,
as the masters of trades.   There is not a single
trade, I believe, carried on in the dock-yard which
has not a master.   There is a master smith, bricklayer, sail-maker, rigger, rope-maker, painter, and
others.   They have each 250*l.* a year, and many of
them have not above four or five men under their
superintendence *.'

'In Sheerness the master bricklayer is receiving
250*l.* a year for superintending five common brick-
layers.'

Mr. Barrow, in further speaking of these masters,
says, he prefers giving pay to giving salaries, on
many accounts; and adds, ' It is one of the greatest
evils of our dock-yards, that the Commissioners of
Naval Revision thought it necessary to bring forward
so many working people, as the inferior officers all
were, and to make them at once salaried officers;
the consequence of which is, that they have not
only large salaries, but are all of them entitled to
large superannuations.'   ' Of this,' he adds, ' there
is a striking instance in the estimates: a measurer,
originally taken from the working shipwrights,
where he had only about 60*l.* or 70*l.* a year as his day
pay, the moment he became a measurer, had a salary
of 180*l.* a-year: he now stands upon the superannuated list with a retirement of 165*l.* a year; and
if his place is filled up, the public is paying 345*l.*
a year for the labour of one measurer.'   Mr. Barrow,

* Evidence Com. Fin. p. 116.

after repeating, ' It is in the number of inferior officers that very considerable reductions can be expected to be made,' says, ' of the measurers I find we have seventy-four; their employment is that of ascertaining the earnings of the workmen; and they are attended by twenty-five clerks, who calculate those earnings. The measurers merely give in a certain number of figures, which the clerks understand, and from them they calculate the earnings. The amount of the salaries of these measurers and clerks is about 17,000l. a year.'

The excuse that is made for employing so many measurers and clerks is, the quantity of detail of measurement which is required in consequence of the Commissioners of Naval Revision having substituted a new plan of building by task-work in place of the old one. Mr. Barrow says, ' The Commissioners of Naval Revision altered the old plan greatly for the worse. The practice was, to divide a ship into a certain number of sections, which I believe was twenty-five; each of these sections had a price affixed to it, according to the size of the ship; to each section was a gang or more of shipwrights, as might be necessary, according to their numbers, to complete the work of those separate sections.' In place of dividing a ship in that manner into sections, ' we have upwards of 1000 separate articles, into which our measurers must go, and some of which, ridiculous as it may appear, are not valued at more than three-farthings.' Mr. Barrow stated the following comparison between the management of a private yard and one of our dock-yards. ' I have an account of the establishment of a private builder; he has two hundred and fifty shipwrights. In Woolwich yard, which comes the nearest, we have two hundred and forty-eight shipwrights, eighteen clerks, six masters of trades, eight foremen, eight measurers, eleven cabin-keepers; besides surgeon, boatswain, and warders, and other people.

‘ In the private yard, where I said there are two hundred and fifty shipwrights, there are one foreman, one measurer, two clerks, and ten labourers.’

Mr. Barrow says, ‘ If I wanted a ship built of 500 tons, a private builder would estimate the workmanship at 48s. per ton, though he might charge me more.’ On Mr. Barrow being asked, ‘ At how much per ton is a ship of 500 tons in the King’s yards built ?’ he answered, ‘ A great deal more than that; for it takes in the whole expense of superintendence as well as labour. I must observe, that it is not quite fair to compare the two yards together, because we have all the trades working in our yards ; the private proprietor goes to others. I mention this to show the simplicity of one proceeding, and the complexity of the other. The Actæon sloop of war, 455 tons, is estimated to cost 5l. a ton in our yard ; but then there is no doubt that our ships of war are much better built than those in private yards.’

Mr. Barrow further states, that the building of thirty-two ships in Pembroke yard cost 25l. a ton, including workmanship and materials, and every expense of the establishment.

On the general subject of the great cost of our establishments for providing the superintendence of labour in the dock-yards, Mr. Barrow gives the following evidence :—

‘ To give the Committee some idea of the quantity of superintendence exercised by those officers, and of the quantity of work performed by the artificers, I have drawn out a few of the proportions from the last year's estimate. The whole establishment of the officers and clerks, and other salaried persons, at the dock-yards at home, amounts to about 155,000*l*.; and the amount of wages paid for work done by artificers, labourers, &c., was 502,000*l*. These sums will give the price paid for superintendence, &c., to that for labour, or unproductive to productive labour, as 1 to about 3 and $\frac{1}{4}$; that is to say, for every three pounds and a quarter paid to the men, there is one pound paid for superintendence and other expenses of the yard, which is certainly enormous. I do not mean to give this as a strictly accurate statement, but it will come pretty near to the truth. In Deptford dock-yard, the proportion thus taken was as 1 to 1 and $\frac{8}{10}$; in Woolwich, as 1 to 2 and $\frac{3}{10}$; in Sheerness, as 1 to 1 and $\frac{3}{4}$; in Chatham, as 1 to 3 and $\frac{5}{10}$; in Portsmouth, as 1 to 3 and $\frac{7}{10}$; in Plymouth, 1 to 4 and $\frac{7}{10}$; and Pembroke, 1 to 4 and $\frac{2}{10}$. It is fair to say, that in the amount of each establishment are included watchmen, warders, and those inferior persons whose salaries amount to a considerable sum—I believe to somewhat about 15,000*l*. a year in the whole; but that will not make much difference in the proportions: but, deducting the expense of the duties performed by the clerks, and some other contingencies, the superintendence to the earnings will be generally about 1 to 6. I believe there is no private establishment, and certainly no public one, in any foreign country, in which the superintendence and the labour bear anything like that proportion. In one of the principal dock-yards of France, the superintendence bears a proportion to the labour of 1 to $22\frac{1}{2}$;

but there I think it also right to observe, their mere labourers are all convicts, which will make a considerable difference; they are superintended by a military guard, placed round the naval yard.'

In 1830, the sum voted for the dock-yards at home was 458,720*l.,* so that it would appear that no great change in the system has yet taken place.

Navy Accounts.—According to Mr. Abbott's report on the Accounts of the Navy and Navy Pay Offices, there is a want of a clear distinction between the duties of the account branches in the Navy Office and those of the Treasurer of the Navy; the operations of one run perpetually into the other*; and great labour is unnecessarily expended in filling up, on printed forms, cash orders to be attached to original bills and other documents, as warrants for payments by the treasurer †.

The present system of Navy accounts is described by Mr. Abbott as altogether disjointed, made up of many elaborate branches, but without a trunk to which to unite them. The abstracts, which are formed at the expense of much labour, do not carry with them any such criteria for the proving of their correctness as would satisfy any professional mercantile accountant ‡.

Mr. Abbott shows, in the clearest and most satisfactory manner, that if the accounts of the Navy Office and Navy Pay Office were kept according to

---

* p. 4.　　　　　† p. 5.

‡ The observations on the public accounts in this edition, refer to what the practice was of keeping them in 1828. No such change has since been introduced as to require that they should be omitted.

the Italian or common mercantile method of book-keeping, great savings of expense in officers, clerks, and stationery, would be the result.

In the Navy Pay Office, where the payments made by the treasurer now employ three cashiers and about thirty clerks, three sub-cashiers and three sub-ordinate clerks would be sufficient *.

When a claim is made for a payment, after it has been examined in the branch of the department to which it belongs, it is sent to the office of bills and treasurer's accounts, and then to the board, where a bill is made out on the treasurer : he keeps this bill, and gives in its place a check on the Bank.   Mr. Abbott proposes to avoid this multifarious course of useless operations, by having the claim for a payment made by a bill drawn on the board by the person who makes the claim : by the board accepting it on the certificate of the first examiner's office, and then by the treasurer countersigning it, so that the bill shall be the order on the Bank for payment †.   Mr. Abbott says, that in the wages branch of the Navy Office, twelve books, which are now kept to check the treasurer's payments, might be discontinued.   He proposes the consolidation of the wages branch with the ticket and allotment branches ; and says, that the advantages to be derived from it would be the simplification of the accounts, and the reduction of labour, by keeping one copy of many accounts instead of two ‡.

Mr. Abbott proposes that the officers' and seamen's wages should be paid by the pursers ; and says, if

* Page 7. Since Mr. Abbott made his report, the duties of Greenwich Hospital, in paying prize-money and out-pensioners, have been transferred to the Navy Pay Office.

          † p. 7.   ‡ p. 9.

this plan was adopted, more than one-third of sixty-one books in the wages office, and a yet larger proportion of about ninety books in the ticket office, would no longer be required*.

Mr. Abbott recommends that the office for foreign and home accounts should take charge of the promiscuous and imprest registers, now kept in the office for bills and treasurer's accounts; that the contract and store departments should be consolidated; and that the business of condensing accounts relating to cash payments, now done in the office of bills and treasurer's accounts, should be conducted in an accountant's department. He says, that the bulky and unsatisfactory abstracts now prepared in this department would be superseded by the more accurate and comprehensive balance-sheet to be obtained from the ledger and journal, when properly kept in the accountant's office †.

Mr. Abbott observes generally on the present system of navy accounts, that there is a great variation of record, without a distinction of purpose; that the whole of the business of the accountant's department is so entirely devoid of system, that no sound repairs can be made of it; and he adds, the annual payments are at present so limited in number and amount, that there would be no difficulty in uniting them all in one cash-book, and transferring every item in detail to the journal, preparatory to forming the ledger.

Messrs. Brooksbank and Beltz, in their joint report on the public accounts, agree in several of the statements made by Mr. Abbott upon the navy accounts. They say, ' Upon our examination of the accounts of the Navy Office, it appeared to us that they had been

* p. 16.   † p. 11.

modelled more for the purpose of checking the accounts of the treasurer of the navy, than for affording any explanatory detail of the naval expenditure*; that the expenditure is scattered and distributed in different books, and the process of preparing any detailed account from them has been done by means of a large and broad sheet of paper, divided into partitions and squares, in which the sums are entered from the registers, according to the items of expenditure required. This is the substitute for a regular ledger; and the great defect of the old system of account is the want of a good general cash-book and a proper ledger †.'

Paymaster of Marines.—The duties which are performed by this office have such a close connexion with those of the Navy Office, that it would appear to be advisable to abolish their separate character. The Treasury minute of 1822, for putting the Army Stores and Barracks under the Ordnance Department, lays down so strongly the policy of consolidating offices, that it will be the height of inconsistency, on the part of government, not to transfer the business of the office in question to the Navy Board.

Mr. Abbott says, in his report on this office, the accounts partake of the fault common to all the government offices, in having a great variety of books, an evil arising from the want of a well-arranged plan of account. Each description of expenditure has its distinct set of books, making thirty-three in all; but in a department of such limited extent this cannot be necessary. Books are also made up for each separate branch of expenditure at a great expense in clerks, all of which would be super-

* p. 18.   † p. 19.

seded by as many separate heads of accounts in a
general ledger *.   Besides the books just mentioned,
a great number of unnecessary books are kept of the
accounts of the sub-accountants†.

The Victualling Office.—It has already been stated,
that of late a great reform has been made in the
Victualling Office.   What is still wanted is to abolish
the separate Board of Commissioners, and instead of it
to add one or two Commissioners to the Navy Board.

In this department, as well as in that of the Navy
Board, it is the practice to manufacture a variety of
articles, instead of providing them by contract‡.

With respect to the method of keeping the accounts of the Victualling Office, Mr. Abbott says,
' Considerable attention has been paid by the heads
of the department to the plan now in operation; and
it has been purified by much labour from a far more
objectionable state : still so differently is it con-
structed from any systematic plan of account, that,
at first sight, it is unintelligible, even to one intimate
with accounts ; and no man, not officially educated
in the existing plan, would know how to set about
the detection in it of an error or fraud §.'   After
describing the great number of books that are kept,
he says, ' I feel quite confident that the introduction
of a connected and well-arranged plan of account
would, in the end, tend greatly to diminish the quan-

---

* p. 83.   † p. 86.
‡ The following articles are manufactured by the Navy
Board, viz. sheet lead, lead pipes, solder, paint, cables and
cordage; copper sheathing, boltstaves, rings and spikes; brass
mixed metal and cast iron articles; blocks and blockmakers
wanes. (Papers, Com. Fin., Nos. 114, 222, and 223.)   The
following are manufactured by the Victualling Board, viz.
bread, beer, and flour; and cattle are bought and salted.
§ p. 93.

tum of labour (consequently of expense) required for all purposes of account *.'

Civil Departments of the Ordnance.—The Committee of Finance, in their Second Report, in noticing some of the civil services of the Ordnance, say, ' that, notwithstanding so much has been done in diminishing the expense of the Ordnance establishment below what it has been of late, it still is a much greater charge on the public than it was some years ago, and that government ought to institute an inquiry to ascertain whether it might not be further reduced †.' They recommend, that the office of Lieutenant-general of the Ordnance should be abolished; and say, that if the duties of the board and of master-general could be brought more together, the charge for clerks in the office of the master-general might be considerably reduced ‡. They also recommend, that the whole establishment of the Tower should be removed to Pall Mall, except that part of it which is concerned with the stores §; that the medical department of the Ordnance should be united with that of the Army; and that the medical stores for the Army and Ordnance should be bought by contract, as is the case in the Navy ‖. They strongly condemn the practice of providing residences for public officers ¶; and they express a very decided opinion in favour of constructing all buildings by one contract for a whole work, instead of by several contracts for the several parts of it **.

The following articles are manufactured by the

* p. 99.   † p. 18.   ‡ p. 13.   § p. 20.
‖ p. 24.   ¶ p. 23.   ** p. 25.

Ordnance, viz., charcoal, gunpowder, gun-carriages, gun-sights, and swords.

It is attempted to defend the practice of carrying on manufactures by the Naval and Ordnance departments, on the ground that the articles which they make are provided cheaper and better than they could be provided by contract; but such a defence rests upon what is morally impossible; because private manufacturers can buy materials cheaper, and take better care of them; and they can get labour cheaper, make it go further, and superintend it better, and at a less expense than any public office. The success of a public office in manufacturing depends on what it is impossible it can accomplish, namely, to find numbers of officers willing to work with the same zeal and integrity for the public as they would work for themselves.

It is obvious that the slightest deficiency in skill, activity, and integrity, on the part of the public officers, in performing the various operations, from their going to market to buy a stock of raw materials, to the storing of the goods made with them, will be taken advantage of by numbers of persons in numberless ways. Materials will be bought in too dear; they will be wasted in working them up; they will be liable to be stolen or damaged; and the finished articles will be more exposed to be wasted and stolen than when purchased by contract, from the difficulty of keeping equally exact accounts of the quantities received and delivered.

Although the Ordnance, Victualling, and other offices that carry on manufactures, produce accounts with the view of making it appear that they have them cheaper in this way than they can be bought by contract, this does nothing towards supporting their case, because these accounts are all kept in so imperfect a manner, that they cannot be relied on.

With respect to contracts, it may be confidently maintained, that everything may be had by them, with proper management, of the best possible quality, and at the lowest possible price. The contract prices of the best articles, under a system of free competition, cannot exceed, on an average, what is just sufficient to pay, first, the cost of materials, when purchased at their lowest price; secondly, the labour of working them up, managed with the greatest skill and economy; thirdly, the ordinary rate of profit on capital employed in trade. To suppose that contractors can, by any means, force public offices to pay prices beyond what can be justified by these three component parts of the prices of commodities, is to show a great want of acquaintance with the principles which govern prices—a fault, however, very common with many official men; many of whom, however, have great weight with higher authorities, under a wrong impression of their possessing superior means, derived from official practice, of forming correct opinions on these matters. The fact, therefore, of contract prices being always kept by competition as low as the combination of manufacturing skill, perfect economy, and a very low ordinary rate of profit can keep them, it follows that it is impossible that public offices can themselves manufacture any article at as low a price as it can be bought by a contract. With respect to the quality of contract goods, this may be secured without the slightest risk of fraud or disappointment, by having proper specifications and deeds of contract, and by enforcing a strict inspection. The Committee of

subject, in their Second Report,
e not disposed to place implicit
ments which have been urged by
ients against contracts by com-
our of the superintendence and
y themselves. The latter plan
occasions the employment of a great many officers,
clerks, artificers, and workmen, and not only adds to
the patronage, but to the appearance of the importance of a department. Nor can the Committee
suffer themselves to feel any prejudice against the
contract system, by references to some instances of
failure.   They believe that most cases of failure may
be attributed to negligence or ignorance in the management of contracts, rather than to the system
itself*.'

Mr. Burke's opinion on contracts is given in the
following terms in his speech on Economical Reform:
' The principles of trade have so pervaded every
species of dealing, from the highest to the lowest
objects; all transactions are got so much into system,
that we may, at a moment's warning, and to a
farthing value, be informed at what rate any service
may be supplied. No dealing is exempt from the
possibility of fraud. But by a contract on a matter
certain, you have this advantage : you are sure to
know the utmost *extent* of the fraud to which you are
subject. By a contract with a person in his own trade,
you are sure you shall not suffer by want of skill †.'

In the calculations of the prices of the articles
which are manufactured by the public departments, the

---

* Second Report, p. 23.

† Burke's Works, vol. iii. p. 305.

charges for residences, superannuation allowances, and other items, to the advantage of master millers, brewers, bakers, butchers, and a great many other officers, are never taken into account. If they were, and they certainly ought to be, the case would be so clearly against all office manufactures, as to justify the most decided prohibition of them.

In the evidence given by Sir Henry Torrens and Mr. Sarjent, before the Committee of Finance, it appears, that the Commissariat Department do not find the least difficulty in providing bread, and other articles of food, of the best quality, and on reasonable and proper prices, by contract: so that there is not the slightest reason for the Victualling Office continuing to be manufacturers of flour, bread, &c.; and it is equally clear, that the great sums of money which have been expended of late in building flour-mills have been completely thrown away *.

The foregoing observations having, as it was to be expected, produced several attempts to show they are incorrect, it is necessary to examine, in this edition, how far this charge is made out. The question,— whether it is for the public advantage than government should be manufacturers, is of such a nature that none can be qualified to discuss it without being acquainted with the elements, at least, of that part of the science of political economy which explain cost of production, prices, and profit. The first remark, therefore, which every argument which has been

* Evidence of Sir H. Torrens, p. 205.—Q. The bread and meat are supplied by contract?—A. Yes. Q. Is it found by experience that good provisions are obtained in that way?— A. They are so watched, that, generally speaking, very good provisions are received; and it is quite impossible that any attempt to give inferior provisions can be persevered in.

advanced against the contract system suggests, is that those who use them are very imperfectly informed on these subjects. Instead of meeting directly the explanation of the proposition which traces the question by a series of reasons founded on self-evident truths, to the conclusion that it is morally impossible that goods can be provided cheaper and better by government manufacturers than they can be provided by well managed contracts, they go on continually referring to failures of contracts, although these failures have wholly arisen from ignorance, or negligence, or fraud, in managing them; and also referring to accounts that do not carry with them a single circumstance that exhibits anything like a proof of the conclusion they are produced to establish. Sir Samuel Bentham expresses surprise that the late Committee of Finance doubted the reiterated assertions of Sir Henry Hardinge of savings having arisen from the ordnance manufactures*. The doubts of the committee arose from their having compared these assertions with the reasons advanced by Sir Henry Hardinge, and from their seeing nothing in them with relation to general principles, facts, or accounts, which satisfied their judgment that the conclusion he sought to establish, namely, that a government department could do work cheaper than a private manufacturer, was well founded.

The defect which runs through all the argument in favour of Government manufactures, is that it is not conducted on any established rule of sound reasoning. Sir Samuel Bentham says, ' It can be proved

* ' Financial Reform Scrutinized,' by Sir Samuel Bentham, K.S.G., p. 82.

that a variety of articles have been manufactured in his Majesty's naval arsenals both cheaper and better than articles provided about the same time by con-tract*'. But although proof may be brought of this fact, this proof does not show that a conclusion can be logically drawn from it against the contract system, because *at that time* every kind of negligence, igno-rance, and fraud, was to be found in the management of contracts, as Sir Samuel Bentham himself admits to have been the case. Sir Samuel also says, ' Long experience has shown that manufacturing contractors find means of evading specifications†.' But this again proves nothing against the principle of contracts: all it proves is ignorance, negligence, and fraud, in managing them. Sir Samuel mentions many instances of ships built by contract in private yards being badly built, but he exposes the incorrectness of the conclu-sion he draws from these instances, and at the same time proves the correctness of all that has been said in favour of contracts by what he further says about the building of the Bellerophon‡. Sir Samuel says, that this ship was built by contract, and commissioned in 1786; that ' she is still (1830) lying at Ports-mouth, after an existence of forty-four years; that up to 1790, although always in commission, she had no works whatever done to her but common fittings; that she had still required no repairs, nor had she, as I have been since informed, had any considerable re-pairs from the first building to the time, when, being twenty-nine years old, she carried Napoleon to St. Helena.' ' In this instance,' continues Sir Samuel, ' I have little doubt that the goodness of that ship depended on the uncommon degree of firmness and

* p. 51.   † p. 71.   ‡ p. 71.

steady incorruptibility of a single government ship-
wright officer, of an inferior rank and low pay.' Now
this statement is in itself everything that can be desired to illustrate the superiority of the contract system.
The Bellerophon is probably the best built ship that
was ever in the public service. And the reason of it is
that she was built under a contract superintended by
a firm and incorruptible officer. As there would be
no difficulty in finding hundreds of such officers in
every department of the public service, even of low
rank and low pay, there really is nothing wanted but
good management in order to apply the principle of
contracts universally in providing everything, as in
the case of the Bellerophon, to the best advantage
for the public service.

But Sir Samuel Bentham goes still farther in furnishing the advocates of the contract system with the
means of defending it; for he shows, by his own can-
did statements, that there has been, at least for the
last thirty years, every kind of defect in the management of them. What he says is so valuable, as con-
firming the accuracy of the opinion, that the failures
of contracts are owing to mismanagement, and not to
anything in the system itself, that the whole of his
statement is well worthy of being quoted *.

' It is true that the present mode in which purchases are made by contract are in many respects ill
suited to the obtainment of any article at a just price.
For these thirty years past I have, on various occasions, called the attention of the superior authority to
these defects, and suggested such measures as appeared applicable to the obviating them. I have proposed, for example: First,—A mode of advertising

* p. 55.

for contracts, and receiving tenders, less repugnant to competition than the present one. Secondly,—Simplicity in the mode of expressing the price of articles, instead of the present additions and subtractions of per centages on former prices, and other complications, which render the real price offered or paid scarcely intelligible to many who are thus deterred from becoming competitors. The obscurity as to the real sum contracted for is further increased by delays in making out bills, by payment by bills at a future period instead of ready money, by fees of office, and other circumstances, which can only be fairly taken into account by the few who are long accustomed to this mode of contracting. Thirdly,—Taking off all unnecessary restraints on contractors, which, without ensuring either quality or timeliness of delivery, require to be compensated by an increase of price. Fourthly,—Requiring the fixing the delivery of the articles at such a period as may enable contractors, who have not the advantage of previous intimation, to enter into competition for the supply. Fifthly,—The fixing the time of delivery of certain portions of the whole quantity by certain days, instead of, as under the present system of contracting, for the delivery of the whole by a certain day, by which the contractor, when the article happens to be at a low price, loads the public with an anticipated supply, for which he obtains immediate payment, thus entailing a considerable loss in useless interest ; and on the contrary, when the articles are dear, delays the supply, so as either to cause works to be retarded for want of the requisite materials, or to make it necessary to substitute less appropriate materials. Sixthly,—The not contracting at prices at which the article

evidently cannot possibly be supplied; for the consequence of this practice is a need for allowing a
subsequent advance upon the contract price, which is
often so great as to far exceed the value of the article.'

If it had been a premeditated scheme in the public
departments to deprive the public of the benefit of the
contract system, in order to increase their patronage
and importance, it is scarcely possible that human
ingenuity could have invented modes of managing
contracts so well calculated to secure this object.
What is here stated about advertising and complicated
forms, is quite repugnant to all competition. The
delays in making out and paying bills, and the
numerous restraints and inconvenient regulations,
must lead to the necessity of giving high prices
to compensate the contractors; and the modes of
management, as to tenders, must have driven away
all respectable tradesmen, and kept the contracts in
the hands of a few persons accustomed to the vexatious intricacies of bad official management.

In consequence of this system of management, the
public has been deprived of the benefits of a sound
contract system, and millions of money have been
squandered on bad and high-priced contract goods, or
on wasteful schemes of government manufactures.

To have a proper system of contracts, they should
be made on the following principles :—

1. To have all specifications drawn in the fullest
and clearest manner.

2. To have all minor conditions arranged for the
convenience of contractors, so as to put them to the
least possible expense, and to take up the smallest
possible portion of their time.

3. To covenant to pay such prices as will be

sufficient to enable contractors to furnish goods of the best quality, and do works in the best manner, with a fair rate of profit.

4. To pay monthly for what is furnished or executed, according to the conditions of the contract; reserving 10 per cent. to be paid on the fulfilment of it.

5. To select with the most scrupulous care, firm, honest, and sober inspectors, and to have the inspection constantly going on over the various operations of the contractors.

6. To make the contracts, when practicable, to continue from time to time for providing each article till notice be given of their discontinuance.

7. To advertise very generally every contract.

Papers were laid before the House of Commons, in the last session, under the title of ' Accounts showing the profit or loss on Manufactures in the Dock-yards and Ordnance Departments.' These may serve to satisfy those members who are incompetent to understand them, but no others ; because, from the method in which these accounts are kept and made up, they do not contain anything like proofs of profit or loss: they really prove nothing else but the total want of everything like correct notions upon the subjects of manufactures and of accounts in the departments which furnished them.

Royal Woolwich Academy.—In 1828 the sum of 4,046*l*. was voted for the Royal Woolwich Academy. The clerk of the Ordnance, in giving his evidence before the Committee of Finance, defended this institution by showing how good an education the cadets received at it. But the utility of it, however great, is not a sufficient justification for continuing it; the necessity of it should be established by proving that good artillery and engineer officers could not be had without it. But this cannot be done, because what is taught at the Academy is quite elementary, and what can be learned just as well at private military schools. If instruction were made to begin at the Academy just where it stops at present, that is, when the cadets are seventeen or eighteen years old, then there might be some reason for keeping it up; because the instruction afforded to officers might be of such a description in the higher branches of military knowledge as could not be attained elsewhere *. The whole of that elementary knowledge which a cadet now acquires at Woolwich at the public expense, might be completely secured by a proper examination of each individual, wishing to be an artillery officer, prior to his being appointed to a commission.

Ordnance Accounts.—Mr. Abbott begins his report on the Ordnance Accounts with the following paragraph:—' It appears from the acknowledgment of all parties in this department, that the accounts were, some years back, truly complex and unsatisfactory. They have since been pruned with an unsparing hand, prompted no doubt by an anxious desire to simplify; but, like most attempts to repair an ancient establishment, these efforts have tended more to disjoint the fabric than connect and strengthen it. The projectors of the alterations in the accounts, to which

* See Evidence of Sir H. Hardinge on the Senior branch of the Academy of Sandhurst.

alone this observation applies (for a man must be more than blind who does not admire the beneficial arrangements introduced by his Grace the Duke of Wellington and Sir Henry Hardinge), do not appear to have been *men of account;* they seem, so to speak, to have been altogether unconscious of the following *established principles* in book-keeping :—

'1st. To record nothing but facts.

'2dly. To record them in the manner they occur.

'3dly. To record them under the precise date of occurrence.

'Indeed, the very names given to the different books prove a total absence of all acquaintance with book-keeping. The terms ledger, journal, cash-book, are not applied to books of any similarity to those which accountants have so designated. In all their alterations the projectors have lost sight of that continued connexion between one book and another, until the whole centre in one condensing book; an arrangement so essential in every good system, it being the very end and object of accounts *.'

Mr. Abbott proceeds to say, the Store branches will admit of considerable simplification, at the same time that they require a fundamental improvement, by the introduction of the value of stores, in addition to the present records, which are confined to quality and quantity †. He says the business transacted between the offices of the Clerk of the Ordnance and the Surveyor-General is circuitous and dilatory, and consequently expensive; that there is unnecessary labour in making the Clerk of the Ordnance dependent on the Surveyor-General; that the Clerk of the Ordnance, who is the accountant of the department,

* p. 117.　　　　　　† Ibid.

is never able to show its liabilities or engagements, from the control of the accounts for purchases not being under his authority* ; and that the Surveyor-General keeps fifty-seven books, of which the greater part could be dispensed with, if the examination of accounts was attached to the office of the Clerk of the Ordnance†.

It appears from Mr. Abbott's report, that the Treasurer of the Ordnance has a power over the public money, which ought not to be vested in any public officer. If, for instance, he wishes to have the use of money for a few days, he may draw a check for any sum he pleases. He may draw the amount of debentures in his hands, for which the payees have not demanded payment, without the Clerk of the Ordnance being cognizant of the fact ; and as the Treasurer gets credit in the books of the Clerk of the Ordnance for the total amount of a quarter-book the instant it is sent forward to him, and as the demands for payments often leave a large balance in his hands, he can use this balance as he pleases‡.

Mr. Abbott shows in what manner all personal power over the public money might be taken from the Treasurer ; and that if he kept proper books, two would serve the purpose of twenty-five now kept§.

Mr. Abbott states that the books of the Ordnance Department, kept by the Clerk of the Ordnance, are not founded on the Treasurer's half-monthly statements, which are the only current cash account of the Ordnance ; but in the imprest and cash journals, which are fallacious as to dates, and liable to great variations from fact ‖.

* p. 118.   † p. 120.   ‡ p. 124.
          § p. 132.   ‖ p. 125.

In the Barrack Branch of the Ordnance Department, an originally perfect system of accounts has
been changed into an imperfect one: which proves,
Mr. Abbott says, that ' *men of account*' are not frequently to be found in the government offices *. Yet
still enough of the good system is left to make the
accounts superior to those of the Ordnance. ' There
is the power and habit of balancing the books annually, to prove their correctness.' ' The books themselves are, generally speaking, connected with each
other, and not disjointed masses of accounts, like
those of the Ordnance†.'

Messrs. Brooksbank and Beltz, in their report on
the Ordnance Accounts, find little or no fault with
them. They notice the changes which have been
made, but do not follow Mr. Abbott's example in explaining their imperfections.

Public Accounts.—It is of so much importance
that a proper system of accounts should be generally
established, not only for the security of the public
money, but as a means of making a great retrenchment in official establishments, that it may be of
use to examine this question more at length.

With respect to the present system, it appears by
the report of Messrs. Brooksbank and Beltz to be
various, complicated, and expensive; without fixed
rules clearly defined, and not generally applicable;
a system framed in accommodation to the transactions of times remote from the present, and under
circumstances which have since undergone considerable alteration‡. Mr. Abbott says, every govern-

* p. 125.   † p. 128.   ‡ p. 88.

ment office has its peculiar system; and that if he were employed professionally to test the accuracy of any of the accounts, he would put aside every book in use, and, taking up the original documents, throw them into a totally new shape*. He adds, ' As to the construction of a balance sheet, for the purpose of proving the correctness of the books, nothing of the kind has been attempted; neither could the most diligent exertions accomplish that desirable object while the general system remains as at present†.'

It further appears from these reports, that there is no uniformity in the constitution and organization of the great departments that conduct the public expenditure, nor any uniformity of classification of business in the several branches of these departments. The Crown, even in exercising its prerogative in regard to the issues of money by the Exchequer does so according to no uniform rule—sometimes an issue is made by privy seal, sometimes by warrants; and these have effect,—some for issuing at once the whole sum voted by Parliament, some for a part of it, some for the period of a year, and some for a whole reign.

For want of a proper system of accounts, a great redundancy of unnecessary books are kept; forms and checks are so multiplied as to occasion an infinity of useless copying, repetition, perplexity, and confusion; business which ought to be done in one branch of a department is divided among several; so that the result of the whole is the failure of accomplishing what are the only objects of public accounts, in order that they may be of any use: namely, first, the providing of security against the negligence or dishonesty of accountants; and secondly, the affording of

* p. 73.   † p. 73.

the means of giving, with correctness, facility, and promptness, information upon the several parts of the receipt and expenditure of the public money.

The public accounts, under a proper system, might be made available to much financial and commercial instruction. As a merchant's books show the result of every speculation, so the public accounts ought to give full information on every tax with respect to the quantity of the articles made, or imported, or exported, on which it is imposed; the places where it is levied, and the expense attending the collection of it. With the aid of this information, the Minister of Finance would be able to estimate the comparative burthensomeness of different imposts, and to introduce improvement in those cases where taxes are found to be at variance with the four maxims laid down by Dr. Adam Smith, with regard to taxes in general[*].

The public accounts ought also to show the quantities of the principal articles imported and exported; and more particularly the quantities of the principal articles of foreign raw materials imported. Quar-

[*] The following are Dr. Smith's maxims:—

I. The subjects of every state ought to contribute towards the support of the Government, as nearly as possible in proportion to their respective abilities.

II. The tax which each individual ought to pay ought to be certain and not arbitrary.

III. Every tax ought to be levied at the time, or in the manner in which it is most likely to be convenient for the contributor to pay it.

IV. Every tax ought to be so contrived as both to take out and to keep out of the pockets of the people as little as possible, over and above what it brings into the public treasury of the state.—*Wealth of Nations*, vol. iii., p. 368. *Mr. M'Culloch's edition.*

terly returns of these transactions should be made up and published in the Gazette, to afford the means to all classes of persons in trade to conduct their speculations on correct information.

In selecting the principle on which a reform of the present system of accounts should be grounded, it is necessary to take a much more extended view of the subject than the commissioners, whose reports have been referred to, were empowered to take ; for unless the constitution and organization of the great departments, and the classification of business in the several branches of them, are, in the first instance, revised and new modelled, according to some uniform and simple principle, no attempt can succeed that may be made to establish an uniform, accurate, and perspicuous system of public accounts.

In observing upon the office of the Treasurer of the Ordnance, the Committee of Finance say, they are induced to think the public has not that complete security against possible loss which it ought to have ; and that they postpone recommending any alteration until they can have an opportunity of proposing some general system for regulating the payment of money in other departments—alluding to a similar want of complete security in the offices of Treasurer of the Navy, Paymaster of the Forces, and several other pay offices which had come under their notice.

It appears, from a statement laid before the Committee of Finance*, that besides the pay offices just mentioned, there are a number of paymasters who receive money from the Exchequer, and have the power of drawing money out of the Bank of England

* Paper, No. 252.

by their own drafts. The evidence given by Mr. Sarjent before the Committee, shows that besides being a paymaster to a very large amount, as Agent of Commissariat Supplies, he is also Paymaster for the Civil Contingencies, for the repairs of Windsor Castle, for emigration to Canada, and for the Ecclesiastical Establishment in the West Indies, although nominally an Officer of the Treasury. The several sums of money which he receives for these services are placed to his account at the Bank of England, as Agent of Commissariat Supplies. In 1827, the sum which was at the disposal of Mr. Sarjent amounted to 2,000,000*l.* : he has sometimes a balance of 250,000*l.* at the Bank. He can draw, by his own draft, for any sum he pleases : his clerk has the same power ; and they do not give security*.

According to the evidence of Mr. Spearman, it appears that he and three other officers of the Treasury are paymasters of the public money to a considerable amount ; that they keep the money they receive from the Exchequer at their private bankers', and that they do not give security.

These statements make it evident, that some great change is necessary in the whole system of paymasters of public money, as a preparatory measure for settling a proper system of public accounts. But to make such a change effectual, it should not be confined to reforming the defects in each office, but should be founded on a general principle of uniformity and security, to be applied to all kinds of payments of public money.

The facts which have just been stated with respect to the several Paymasters and Treasurers, and those

* Evidence Com. Fin., April 21, 1828.

which have before been noticed with respect to the Exchequer and Audit Offices, and also with respect to the various modes of keeping accounts in the public departments, establish a case which proves the necessity of making a general reform of the whole system of managing the business of making payments, and of keeping the accounts of them.

There is also another material circumstance connected with the public expenditure, which should be changed, namely, the practice of voting the estimates, that is, granting the money wanted for the expenses of a year some months after the commencement of the year.

The following is an outline of the kind of plan that seems to be required to correct the defects now pointed out.

1. To have, instead of the present estimates of a part of the expenses, the whole of the public expenses stated in a printed budget for the year beginning on the following 1st of January. The Civil List, charges of management, and everything else of the nature of public expenditure, including what is granted permanently as well as what is voted annually, to be comprised in the budget; and also to have attached to the general statement of the expenditure in the budget full explanations of the particulars of each head of expense.

2. As the chief cause of the defects in the present system of managing and making payments is the combining together, in each of the principal departments, of the business of the administration of the public expense, that is, of contracting debts with the business of paying debts, these functions should be separated; and no department engaged in the ad-

ministration of the public expenditure should receive any money, and become in any way an accountant department. Each department should have only a credit to enable it to incur expense according to the votes in the annual budget; and its business should be, with respect to payments, to fix what is due to the individuals who have claims upon it, and to give orders for payment upon a distinct department, to be established as the general pay office of all payments for the public service. This department should also be the general office for managing the receiving of all the revenue, so as to form one controlling account department, prescribing forms to all other departments, and bringing all matters belonging to the receiving and the paying of money under one system of harmony, simplicity, clearness, and accuracy. By providing proper regulations, so that every order shall have on the face of it proper proofs of correctness, and so that a due examination shall be made of it before the discharging of it, the business of paying the public money will be rendered, to a considerable extent, an efficient control over that of spending it.

If such a plan as this were adopted, everything about the payment of the public money would be so much simplified, that the controlling and auditing of the public expenditure, and the keeping of the accounts of it, would be matters of no great difficulty. There would also be a great saving of expense by getting rid of the offices of the Paymaster of the Forces, Treasurer of the Navy, Treasurer of the Ordnance, Paymaster of Marines, and twenty or thirty other paymasters, with their deputies, cashiers, sub-cashiers, and clerks.

After determining to revise and new-model the constitution and organization of the several departments in the manner suggested in the preceding pages, it will not be difficult to determine what plan of accounts ought to be established.

Mr. Abbott's proposal to establish the Italian or mercantile system in all the public offices, deserves to have great weight with Government and Parliament. As a professional mercantile accountant, he holds the highest rank; and he has acquired a full knowledge of official accounts by diligently making use of the powers vested in him for ascertaining the nature, description, and purpose of the several books used in each office. He has stated in a memorandum submitted by him to the Treasury, of the 28th of February, 1829, that for every hour passed by his colleagues Messrs. Brooksbank and Beltz in the offices in examining the books of accounts, he had passed twenty; and this statement was not contradicted in the observations of these gentlemen on this memorandum. To those persons who are practically acquainted with the mercantile system of accounts, the reasoning on which Mr. Abbott founds his opinion of its being applicable to all official accounts cannot fail to be completely satisfactory. The contrary opinion of Messrs. Brooksbank and Beltz, however respectable it be, is connected with circumstances which justify some suspicion of its soundness. In the first place, they evidently have had to form a plan of accounts for a most defective official system of transacting business; and having this defective system constantly before them, they were led to conceive a notion of an official system of accounts as contradistinguished from the mercantile system. This is a fundamental error that pervades all their views and all their plans ; for if the official system of doing business were new-modelled, and all the payments of money vested in a distinct department, there could be nothing necessarily in an office system of accounts that should differ, in any respect, from the common mercantile system.

Messrs. Brooksbank and Beltz cannot be blamed for not having proposed the new-modelling of offices as a necessary element of a proper system of accounts. Their commission did not require them to do so; and no one could expect that they would take upon themselves to propose to abolish sinecure treasurerships, and to recommend other great official changes.

There are no grounds for the objection of Messrs. Brooksbank and Beltz to that part of the Italian or mercantile system which requires the entries in the waste and cash books to be transcribed into a journal, and afterwards into a ledger, wherein nothing more is shown than the titles to the accounts and references to details in the journal *. The objects of a perfect plan of accounts are correctness, and security that those who are entrusted with money shall not be able to misapply it without a facility of detection. The Italian system provides for the attaining of these objects in so complete a manner, that it has been adopted universally in all commercial countries. But Messrs. Brooksbank and Beltz seek to do more than secure their objects ; they want, not only to provide this security, but, by one and the same operation, to obtain the means of making out returns to orders of Parliament for special accounts, merely by taking

* p. 89.

copies of the ledger. They say, ' a public office, which is continually called upon for information upon a variety of subjects, should possess the readiest possible means of furnishing that information ; and to this end, the ledger should be made to contain a condensed, but more circumstantial detailed account of proceedings than is usually effected under the mercantile system*,' and they, therefore, propose to dispense with keeping a journal. But a ledger so formed from the cash book, without a journal, would bear no substantial similitude to a mercantile ledger, because the whole principle of utility and security belonging to the mercantile system, consists in the manner in which the journal is kept ; so that Messrs. Brooksbank and Beltz propose a plan which sacrifices the security of the pure Italian system to the minor object of saving the trouble of referring to a regularly kept journal in making out accounts for Parliament. As to these accounts, if the public annual accounts were laid before Parliament in a proper form, they would alone furnish all the information that could be wanted ; and the practice of calling for special accounts would be got rid of.

What makes the journal of such great importance, is the guarantee it affords against errors. Two main objects should be constantly kept in view in a good plan of accounts, one of them extreme correctness in making the first entry of each transaction; the other the placing of each transaction, or each part of each transaction, under a proper heading, in order that branches of business, or articles of the same kind, may be collected together in distinct accounts.

* p. 8.

In the mercantile system of accounts, the use of the day-book is to secure the first object, and the use of the ledger is to secure the second. But as errors might be made in consequence of its not being always practicable to take sufficient time for carefully writing the first entries in the day-book, and also as errors might be made in classifying these general entries under the proper headings in the ledger, directly from the day-book, the journal is employed as an intermediate book, to prevent both these kinds of errors.

By transferring without much delay the entries from the first book of record, whether that book be called a Day-book, Bill-book, a Register, or by any other name, into the journal, an opportunity is given of quickly correcting any error that may have been made in the day-book; and by transferring the entries from the journal into the ledger, at stated periods, an opportunity is given of correcting any error that may have been made in classifying the entries in the journal: so that the use of the journal is essentially necessary in order to secure correctness in keeping accounts of extensive and complicated transactions.

Although the keeping of the journal may, in appearance, consist merely in copying the entries in the day-book, and of putting them into a technical form, it is accompanied with such great advantages, that all persons, thoroughly conversant with accounts, have at all times, and in all countries, considered the journal indispensable in a perfect system of keeping accounts.

The mercantile system of accounts has been objected to, because it employs unintelligible locutions;

and is not, therefore, intelligible to all alike*. But if accounts were stated in the language employed in ordinary discourse, the matter would swell to such a bulk, that before the result could be obtained, the minds of writers and readers would be bewildered and put to a stand—' the conceptive faculty not being able to grasp at once the whole quantity necessary to the attainment of the result.' Hence arises the necessity of compression ; and this compression can only be obtained by employing technical language and forms, as is the case in everything which is not altogether a common simple matter, but an art or science, and, therefore, more or less, *ex necessitate rei*, under the government of rules of science. The technical modes employed in book-keeping are very few and very simple. Perhaps the terms ' Debit' and ' Sundries ' are the only two requiring any particular explanation.

The mercantile system of accounts is nothing more than a reduction to practice of the algebraical simple equation. Quantities equal to each other are placed on the *Dr.* and *Cr.* sides of the ledger, and the balance is merely the result, after having reduced those quantities to the lowest number of terms. By this application of geometry, the science of book-keeping may be said to be founded. The terms Dr. and Cr. are the signs of equality, combined with the positive or negative ; and as to the term ' Sundries,' it is merely a ' vinculum.' Thus, if so much wine or corn be exchanged for so much cloth, the ' Sundries ' forms the vinculum ; and the term ' Creditor ' shows that

---

* Constitutional Code. By Jeremy Bentham, Esq., c. ix, p. 340.

the quantity of wine and corn is equal in value to the corresponding quantity of cloth, which is ' Debtor.'

The terms Dr. and Cr. are neither useless nor misrepresentative; they are strictly applicable to accounts of property, as well as of persons, and equally so to the third class of accounts, namely, ' nominal accounts.' That these terms are appropriate to ' personal accounts,' is acknowledged; and an accountant may correctly say, ' If a person be a debtor to me for property which I have transferred to him, why should not the account of that property be said to have credit for the debt become due to me by the transfer of that property? Cloth, wine, and corn are so many component parts of my property: if I sell these, my property, in debts due to me, is increased, and in merchandise diminished. If it be not irrational to charge these articles, at the moment of their acquisition, for their cost, as absorbents of so much of my property, in cash or otherwise, ought I not to diminish that cost by stating what sum I receive for any portion of them? And the words Dr. and Cr. are the most applicable and brief which language supplies, as signs to indicate whether the property to which they are applied has been acquired or parted with. These two actions—of acquisition and disbursement—are, in fact, the only first causes of record in accounts.'

The technicalities of book-keeping are used as indices to point out heads, under which the arrangement of receipt and expenditure is to be placed; but the narration of each transaction is given in ordinary language, for which there can be no need of abbreviation.

The opinion of Messrs. Brooksbank and Beltz,

that the office system of doing business requires an
office system of accounts, different from the mercantile system of double entry, is proved to be altogether
untenable by the practice of the East-India Company,
the governments of France, Holland, Prussia, the
Hanse Towns, and, in fact, of every country where
the public business is conducted with a view to the
public good.   In France, the mercantile system is
acted upon, in all the public departments, and all
persons who are acquainted with the government
accounts are ready to attest the great advantages
of it.

By the Ordonnance of 1822, title 4, section 18, the
different departments are required to keep their accounts on one uniform principle, and to adopt the
same regulations and forms ; and for this purpose it
is ordered that each department shall keep a general
journal, and a ledger, in which books they are to
record immediately, and according to their date, all
operations concerning credits, incurring expenses,
orders for payment, and payments.   These operations
they are further to record in auxiliary books, the
number and forms of them to be determined upon by
the nature of the different public services*.

* ' Titre IV.   Des Comptes.—Nos ministres établiront leur
comptabilité respective d'après les mêmes principes, les mêmes
procédés, et les mêmes formes.

' A cet effet, il sera tenu dans chaque ministère un *journal
général* et un *grand livre* en parties doubles, dans lesquels seront
consignées sommairement et à leur date toutes les opérations
concernant la fixation des crédits, la liquidation des dépenses,
l'ordonnance et le paiement.

' Ces mêmes opérations seront décrites en outre et avec détail
sur des livres auxiliaires, dont le nombre et la forme seront
déterminés suivant la nature des services.'

In a former chapter it has been said that the Exchequer ought to be newly modelled, and also that the Audit Office required extensive reformation. As the object of these offices is to establish a control over the crown and its ministers, and other public servants, perhaps the best course to pursue would be to form one board of commissioners to hold their offices for life, to do the duties of guarding against the issuing of money from the Exchequer, but with the authority of Parliament, and of auditing the public accounts.

If such a board were established, it should be provided by law, that an annual account of the money received, and money paid in each year by the Government, should be closed within a few days after the end of the year; that this account should be examined and reported upon, as to its general correctness in form and substance, by the board, and presented to Parliament in each session, before the voting of the budgets. If a proper system of accounts were established in all the departments, the board would find no difficulty in making such a report.

These several reforms, as well as others which have been proposed in the preceding pages of this work —namely, first, the consolidating of the boards of revenue ; secondly, the separating the business of collecting taxes from that of the general administration of the revenue ; thirdly, the separating of the business of making payments from that of the general administration of the expenditure fourthly, the laying of regular accounts before Parliament; and, fifthly, the voting of all the taxes and of all the public expenses in annual budgets—cannot be objected to on account of their being speculative and impracticable projects, as some persons attached to ancient customs may possibly be disposed to say they are, because all that is here recommended under the five foregoing heads is in full operation in France, where the amount of the annual revenue and expenditure is no less than eighty millions, with great ease and satisfaction to all the public departments, and with great advantage to the public*.

* The following is a statement of the public income and expenditure of France for 1828 :—

(In 1829 the public income and expenditure amounted to 80,000,000*l.*)

	REVENUE.	£.
Enregistrement, Stamps, and Crown Lands	.	7,612,000
Woods and Forests	.	904,000
Customs and Salt Duty . . .	.	5,920,000
Land Tax, Personal Tax, Windows, Patents	.	11,578,000
Excise, Wine, Brandy, Tobacco, &c. .	.	8,526,000
Post Office	.	1,244,000
Lottery	.	620,000
Miscellaneous	.	759,680
Gross total of ordinary Revenue . .	.	37,163,680
Deficiency to be supplied by Bons Royaux	.	1,340,000
Total of the Receipts		£38,503,680

EXPENDITURE.

Consolidated Debt.			£.
Annual interest on 5 per cent.	.	£6,612,000	
on 4½ ,, .	.	40,000	
on 3 ,, .	.	1,400,000	
Total .	.	8,052,000	8,052,000
Annual grant of Sinking Fund . . .			1,600,000

Besides the annual interest on the 1,500,000*l.*,

I. The whole management of the collection of the taxes in France is immediately under the authority of the Minister of Finance.   M. Villèle, in his Report of 1826, as Minister of Finance, ' Sur le Controle des Comptes des Ministres,' expresses himself as follows on this subject:—' The public revenues were under

		£
5 per cent. and 3 per cent. redeemed and included in the 8,052,000*l.* above mentioned, and paid annually by the Treasury to the Board of Commissioners for the Sinking Fund.		
Civil List for the King and Royal Family	.	1,280,000
Justice Department	.	784,000
Foreign Affairs	.	360,000
Home Department	.	3,708,000
Catholic Clergy	.	1,324,000
Public Education	.	72,000
War Department	.	7,840,000
Navy	.	2,280,000

Treasury.		
Annuities	£308,000	
Pensions	2,320,000	
Miscellaneous	808,000	
		3,436,000
House of Peers		80,000
House of Deputies		32,000
Miscellaneous		815,680

	£
Total of the various heads of expenditure for ordinary services	31,663,680
Extraordinary expenses according to the Report of the Minister of Finance, 22d March, 1828, being chiefly for the War and Navy Department	1,340,000
Charges of Management and Expenses for collecting the various heads of Revenue included in the gross total of the receipt	5,500,000
Total public Expenditure	£38,503,680

the management, before the restoration, of departments not belonging to the department of the Minister of Finance. The independence of their po-
sition was not at all reconcileable with the duties
which the responsibility of the minister made to de-
volve upon him. The necessity was soon perceived
of bringing together, under one common moving
principle, all the scattered parts of this branch of the
public service*.' There are bureaux in the department
of the Minister of Finance, for the several branches
of taxes, each consisting of a Director-General and
two or three Administrateurs. These several bureaux
perform, under the general and immediate government of the Minister, all the business belonging to
the administration of the taxes : that is, what belongs
to bringing them to charge against the individuals
who have to pay them; but they do not collect, or
in any wise receive or pay money.

II. The business of the collection of the taxes, and of
the paying of all the expenses attending it, is performed
by another department of the Minister of Finance,
called the Trésor Royal. The expenses of collection
are charged in the public accounts like any other
expenses, and are not paid, as in England, out of the
revenue, in what is called anticipation. There is, in
every *territorial department* of France, a Receiver-
general belonging to the Trésor Royal, who receives
from other receivers and collectors the produce of all
the taxes collected in the department. The Receiver-
general applies the money he receives according to
the orders given to him by the Trésor Royal; and he
transmits to the Trésor Royal an account every month
of all his receipts and payments.

* Report, p. 9.

III. The expenditure of France is administered by nine departments or *ministères*. Their business is to do all that is necessary in the way of the administration, or applying of the public money in providing for the public services; but it is not in any respect their business to receive or pay money. The business of making payments is performed in the following manner :—First, there are officers in each department called ordonnateurs, who draw up, according to fixed regulations and forms, orders for the payment of all sums of money due for debts incurred by the department. Secondly, other officers, called payeurs, receive and pay these orders. These officers belong to the Trésor Royal; for, by the French ordonnance of the 14th Sept. 1822, it is declared that ' Les fonctions d'ordonnateur et d'administrateur sont incompatibles avec celles de comptables.'

The forms according to which the orders for payments are drawn up and attested, and the examination they undergo by the payeurs before they are paid, establish an audit in the first instance, and are perfectly effective in preventing frauds. Monthly accounts are transmitted to the Trésor Royal of all orders issued, and of all payments made pursuant to them ; so that all payments of public money, and all receipts of revenue, come under this department. The several monthly accounts that are transmitted to this office of the taxes, and of the payments, serve as the elements for making up in each year a general journal and a general ledger on the mercantile system of book-keeping.

IV. The law of the 25th of March, 1817, requires that, in every session, before voting the budgets, the following accounts be laid before the chambers :—

1. An account of each of the nine departments, or *ministères*, employed in managing the public expenditure.

2. An account of the public debt.

3. A general account of the budgets.

4. An account of the Trésor Royal.

5. An account of the gross produce of all the taxes.

Each account of the nine *ministères* contains very detailed explanations of all the particulars relating to each item in the account.

The general account of the Minister of Finance for the year 1829, consists of 394 closely printed quarto pages, and contains—

1. A report of this minister on the state of the finances in 1829.

2. A general statement of the financial operations in 1829.

3. An account of the public revenue in each of the years 1828 and 1829.

4. An account of the public expenditure in each of the years 1828 and 1829.

5. An account of the Trésor Royal.

6. An account of the budgets, and of extraordinary funds, and of arrears.

7. A summary account of the situation of the finances on the 1st of Jan. 1830.

8. Documents and vouchers in support of the several parts of the preceding accounts.

9. The declarations of the Cour des Comptes with respect to the accuracy of the accounts of the Minister of Finance in the years 1827 and 1828.

10. Details of receipts and payments in each territorial department of France.

11. Details of the produce of the taxes in each department.

12. Accounts of divers public services.

Pursuant to the ordonnance of the 10th of Dec. 1820, the king appoints, at the end of each year, a commission, composed of one Conseiller d'état, two Maîtres des requêtes, one Maître des comptes, and three Référendaires, whose duty it is to examine the general journal and ledger of the ' *comptabilité gé- nérale des finances*' for that year. The certificate of the commission for 1829, relating to the accounts of that year, is given in the general account of the Minister of Finance, and is dated 15th March, 1830*. The following is a copy of it:—' La commission nommée à procéder aux vérifications prescrites s'était fait représenter les livres de la comptabilité générale des finances, les élémens des écritures, le compte rendu pour l'année 1829, et les trois documens justi- catifs dont il est appuyé.'

' CERTIFIE, 1. Qu'il y a concordance entre le grand livre et le journal général des finances ; que chacun de ces deux regîstres présente les mêmes détails, et le même·total, et que la balance imprimée, qui en reproduit les articles munis par ordre de matières, est le résumé exact des faits consignés dans les dits regîstres.

' 2. Que le développement que présente par classe de comptables, les recettes et les paiemens effectivés pendant l'année 1829, est établi d'après les écritures et les pièces justificatives que ces préposés ont adressées au ministère, et dont les résultats sont reproduits dans les comptes d'année parvenus à la comptabilité géné- rale, et qui vont être soumis à la Cour des Comptes.

' 3. Que le bilan de l'administration des finances

* The certificate has commonly been signed much earlier in former years.

est le résumé complet des comptes ouverts au grand livre, et qu'il concorde avec les résultats du compte général de cette administration.

' 4. Que le compte de l'administration des finances pour l'année 1829, offre des résultats fidèlement extraits des différens livres officiels qui ont servi de base à ce compte. Ce 15 Mars. 1830*.'

By the ordonnance of the 9th July, 1826, the Cour des Comptes is required to make two declarations at the beginning of each year, upon the accounts of the two years preceding the last year. These declarations must be printed and presented to the Chambers before voting the budgets †.

In the declaration made on the 9th of March, 1830, on the accounts of the year 1828, the Cour des Comptes ' DECLARE, que les recettes, dépenses, valeurs en caisse et en portefeuille, comprises au compte général des finances publié pour l'année 1828, et qui forment les élémens des comptes des budgets, et du service de trésorerie, sont d'accord avec les arrêts rendus sur les comptes présentés par les

---

* Compte Général de l'Administration des Finances pour l'année 1829, p. 192.

† ' A chaque session législative, une première *Déclaration générale* de la Cour de Comptes, prononcée en séance solennelle, établira la conformité de ses arrêts avec les comptes ministériels publiés pour l'année précédente ; et par une seconde *Déclaration*, cette cour certifiera, sous la foi des mêmes garanties, la concordance des résultats de ses jugemens avec ceux du règlement légal du dernier exercice expiré. Les Chambres pourront ainsi procéder, avec une entière confiance, à la discussion de comptes généraux dont l'exactitude leur sera si authentiquement démontrée, et faire reposer les bases définitives de chaque loi de finances sur des résultats irrécusables et à l'abri de toute critique.'—Report of M. Villèle, p. 7.

agens comptables pour la même année, ainsi qu'il résulte des deux états ci-annexés*.'

In the second declaration of the same date, on the ' Situation définitive de l'exercice 1827,' the Cour des Comptes ' DECLARE, que la recette et la dépense comprises dans les comptes des ministères pour l'exercice 1827, et définitivenent arrêtées par la loi du 26 Juillet 1829, sont conformes aux résultats des arrêts rendus sur les opérations dudit exercice portées dans les comptes des années 1826, 1827, et 1828, des receveurs et payeurs des finances, et appuyées des pièces justicatives qui leur servent de preuves, ainsi qu'il résulte de l'état ci-annexé†.'

V. Two laws are passed at the commencement of each session of the French Chambers, one entitled ' La loi relative à la fixation du budget des *dépenses ;*' the other, ' La loi relative à la fixation du budget des *récettes.*' To these laws are attached schedules containing estimates of all the expenses, and of the probable produce of all the taxes.

Since the year 1823, the vote of the budgets of money to be paid for the public services, and to be received from taxes, is, for services to be performed, and for taxes to be collected, in the year commencing on the following 1st of January.

Each of the departments, or *ministères*, is required by law to make up two annual accounts immediately after the close of the year: the first, an account called ' la situation provisoire' for the year ending 31st of December just passed ; secondly, a definitive account for the year preceding the last year.

The law of the 16th September, 1807, established a

* Compte générale pour l'année 1829, p. 196.
† Ibid. p. 202.

Cour des Comptes, composed of a first president, three presidents, eighteen maîtres de comptes, and eighty référendaires, who hold their offices for life. The duty of this court is to examine and pronounce judgment upon the accounts of the receipts and expenses of the state, and of all public accountants. Some opinion may be formed of the efficiency of this institution, from the following extract from the report of M. Villèle already referred to :—' All the accounts of the persons employed in the receipt and expenditure of the public money are presented to the Cour des Comptes on the 1st of July of the year following the year to which they belong. The Cour des Comptes has been able to pronounce its judgment upon them before the 31st of December,—a remarkable example of a vast system of public accounts constantly in operation, in which everything is proved by written vouchers before the expiration of the second year, and which does not leave the least doubt as to the regularity of the whole of the proceedings, with regard to the acts of a single department, or with regard to the conduct of a single accountant*.'

By an ordonnance of 1st September, 1823, all the expenditure of the money voted for a particular year, in the budget of that year, ought to be applied, and orders given for the payment of it, within the nine months which follow the end of that year, in such a manner that a definitive account may be closed and settled within twelve months, that is, by the 31st of December. If it be found that any part of the money so voted for a year's expenditure has not been applied, and accordingly that orders for the payment of it have not been made before the closing of the account

* Report, p. 11,

within the nine months, this part of the expenditure cannot be discharged but by means of a royal ordonnance, to authorize its being charged in the budget of the current year.

In each session of the Chambers, a law is passed for the definitive settlement of the budget for the last year but one.

The following extracts taken from the official reports on the Finances of France, place beyond all doubt the success of the system of ' Compatibilité,' which has now been for some years established.

From the Report of the Commission of Accounts, dated 25th April, 1828.

' One of the numerous advantages of applying the system of double entry to all the accounts of the public money, is the facility which this method affords to obtain quickly a complete guarantee of the correctness of all the results which are shown by the several balances. All these balances grow one from the other and control each other; as they always appear under two opposite statements, their union should give the same sums; so that after this general proof of the correctness of the whole, a slight examination of the details is sufficient to secure complete satisfaction as to the correctness of all the parts *.'

' We cannot but repeat the praises bestowed by former commissions on the system of public accounts †.'

' The Journal General of 1827 contained a complete exposé of the operations of all the finance departments for that year ‡.'

* p. 12.   † p. 13.   ‡ p. 15.

From the Report of the Commission of Accounts, dated 29th May, 1830.

' This essential regularity of the documents and of the accounts is the natural effect of the strict method of public accounts which has been introduced into the public departments *.'

From the Report of M. Villèle, Minister of Finance, dated 26th July, 1826.

' It is from this first return to better principles of administration that may be dated the introduction of the system of accounts of double entry in the Treasury and its dependent branches,—an important improvement, which exposed a number of frauds, and which has preserved the public money from being subject to them in future †.'

From the Report of M. Chabrol, Minister of Finance, dated 15th March, 1830.

' The ordonnances of the 14th September and 11th December, 1822, laid the foundation of the new system of accounts. They established accounts in the different public departments according to the strict rules of double entry. The Minister of Finance can now control the application of every grant of money made by the Chambers for the public service. Reciprocal communications are established between those public offices which incur expenses (qui liquident les créances) and those which pay the expenses (qui les acquittent). The accounts of the different public departments, as well as those of the persons who hold offices in them, are drawn up at the end of each year

* p. 3.   † p. 8.

with a clearness and readiness which add considerably to the facility of verifying and auditing them.'

' Six months of examination of the Cour des Comptes is scarcely required to secure a regular quietus to every public accountant *.'

' The business of keeping public accounts has taken a course the most simple and most rapid; everything has become clear and regular in the results; accounts that were incomplete and in arrear have been replaced by a system of accounts always open for inspection, and calculated to produce its balances at the end of each month; and which system of accounts is controlled at the end of each year by the public declarations of the Cour des Comptes†.'

The Minister of War says, in the report on his department, dated 25th February, 1830, ' Finally, I ought not to omit to draw attention to the fact, that of the sum of 8,960,000l., forming the total amount of the expenses of the War Department in 1828, there remains only the trifling sum of 1,070l. not paid. Such a result confers the highest honour to the War Department, and, at the same time, affords the strongest testimony of the excellence of the system of accounts established in it ‡.

Notwithstanding, however, the seeming perfection to which the mode of keeping the public accounts of France has been brought, the defects in her financial system are very numerous and very injurious. The taxing of all raw materials of industry, the tobacco monopoly, the octrois duties, and several other taxes, are contrary to every sound principle of taxation, and very great obstructions to the prosperity of France. The charges for collecting the revenue,

* p. 2.   † p. 5.   ‡ p. 52.

although of late years considerably reduced, are still 12½ per cent.* But the great defect of all, is the want of a sufficient legislative control over the Crown, similar to that which is exercised in this country by the Exchequer. The law now allows the King to incur, by ordonnances, what are called extraordinary and urgent expenses, beyond what are voted in the budget by the Chambers, on the condition that these ordonnances are to be converted into laws at the next session of the Chamber †. What the consequence is of this power in increasing the public expenses may be judged of by the following extract from the speech of M. Barbé Marbois, the first president of the Cour des Comptes, on opening the session of it on the 3d of November, 1830 :—' It was after having raised the taxes to 40,000,000*l.* a year, that these ill advised persons (the ministers of Charles X.) declared their insufficiency ; and it was then that they had recourse to provisional and supplementary credits, and such a number of false expedients, that the budget was rendered nothing better than a chimerical and delusive compilation of figures.'

Notwithstanding, therefore, the various legislative regulations for securing a sound system of accounts in France, unless the King and his Ministers be effectually prohibited from spending the smallest sum of money without a previous legislative authority, there can be no real security against irregularity and extravagance.

The financial accounts which are annually laid before the House of Commons, and everything connected with the keeping of accounts in the offices, and the voting of public money in Parliament, stand

* Report of M. Chabrol, p. 117.   † Loi, 25th March, 1817.

so much in need of reformation, that it would be a very wise measure to make use of the French system of accounts as a model for substituting an entirely new system in this country, instead of the present one. Some improvement of it could no doubt be introduced, particularly by making use of the assistance of our banking system. Such a measure would not only produce the same advantages here in securing generally public economy and control as it produces in France, but it would likewise lead to the saving of an immense expense in making up and printing Parliamentary papers, because a proper system of annual financial accounts would furnish all the information which is now sought to be obtained by calling for special accounts.

CHAPTER XII.

CIVIL GOVERNMENT.

THE next head of expenditure to be examined, with the view of ascertaining what retrenchment may be made, is that incurred for conducting the Civil Government of the country. It has proved quite impossible, with all the pains that could be taken, to make out what this expenditure amounts to. Every public account, that could contribute to assist in discovering it, has been examined, and the result is, that no sum can be set down to show the expense of any branch of this expenditure with a certainty of its being correct. There are no less than five different ways of paying the office establishments connected with the civil government of the country, namely, 1st. The Civil List; 2d. The Consolidated Fund; 3d. Fees; 4th. Annual Grants; 5th. Payments out of the gross produce of the Revenue. So that, after labouring through and selecting the sums paid by two, three, or more of these ways, and imagining that the whole of them have been discovered, there is always a risk incurred of having overlooked some payment in the fourth or fifth of them; and, if this occur, then every public office proclaims a triumph over the individual who has thus failed in unravelling the mystification of the system. In the Fourth Report of the Committee of Finance, the total expense of permanent civil services, including the Civil List, is stated to be 2,103,105*l.*, but no details are given of this expenditure *.

The following statement of some of the annual charges for the civil government has been prepared from official documents, such errors to be excepted as have just been alluded to :—

	£:
The Civil Lists of England and Ireland	1,057,000
The Three Secretaries of State	137,000
The Privy Council Office	9,000
The Board of Trade	11,400
The Mint	32,450
The Civil Government of Scotland	132,000
The Judicial Establishment of England partly paid out of the Civil List }	150,000
Ditto of Ireland ditto	147,000
Ditto of Scotland	187,000
Annual Grants for Civil Contingencies	160,000

The progressive increase of expenditure has been, in some of these offices, as follows :—

Secretary of State for the Home Department	1829	£31,916
	1796	14,423
Increase		£17,493

Secretary of State for the Foreign Department	1829	£65,681
	1796	34,495
Increase		£30,186

Secretary of State for the Colonies	1829	£39,624
	1796	9,111
Increase		£30,513†

The Committee of Finance, in their second report, point out, as one of the principal objects of econo-

* See note, p. 97.
† Papers, Com. Fin., Nos. 103, 104, and 105.

mical reform, the revision of every office, in order to introduce a principle of simplification and consolidation for transacting public business ; and there can be no doubt that, if this principle were effectually and universally adopted in every office employed in the civil government of the country, the business of the public might be performed by a much smaller number of officers and clerks, and, at the same time, with lower salaries.

Civil List.—With respect to the Civil List, from the restoration to the accession of George III., the practice was to grant to each King, on his coming to the throne, certain taxes and duties, called the Hereditary or Civil List Revenues for life, as the fund for defraying the whole of the expenses of the civil government. These revenues were obtained from the following imposts :—Hereditary Excise, Subsidy of Tonnage and Poundage, Post Office, Fines of Alienation Office, Post Fines, Wine Licenses, Sheriffs Profers, Compositions in the Exchequer, Seizure of Prohibited and Unaccustomed Goods, Rents of Lands, Fines of Leases, and Sale of Lands*. The revenue received from these sources amounted, on an average of three years to 1815, to 1,300,000*l.* † When this fund proved insufficient for the whole civil government, sums of money were voted by parliament in aid of it.

On the accession of George III., a new plan was introduced, namely, that of giving the King, for life, a fixed sum in lieu of the Civil List revenues, which were paid with the other revenues of the country into

‡ 1 Geo. I. c. 1.   See marginal note of this statute for the acts granting these taxes.   † Report Com. Civil List, 1815.

the Exchequer. The annual sum given to George III. was 800,000*l.* During his reign various additions were made to it, and some millions of Civil List debt were incurred and paid by the nation.

On the accession of George IV., 255,000*l.* of annual charge was transferred from the Civil List to other funds, and the annual sum of 850,000*l.* was given to him as the Civil List for England. 84,000*l.* of annual charge had been transferred in 1804, so that the allowance to George IV. was at least 400,000*l.* a year greater than that given to George III.—the confusion of the accounts make it impossible to give the exact sum.

The following copy of the schedule of the act of 1 Geo. IV. c. 1. shows how the sum of 850,000*l.* was appropriated.

		£.
1st Class.	His Majesty's Privy Purse	60,000
2d Ditto.	Allowances to the Lord Chancellor, Judges, and Speaker of the House of Commons	32,956
3d Ditto.	Salaries, &c. of his Majesty's Ambassadors and other Ministers ; Salaries to Consuls and Pensions to retired Ambassadors and Ministers	226,950
4th Ditto.	Expenses (except Salaries) of his Majesty's Household, in the Departments of the Lord Steward, Lord Chamberlain, Master of the Horse, Master of the Robes, and Surveyor-General of Works	209,000
5th Ditto.	Salaries in the above Departments	140,700
6th Ditto.	Pensions limited by the act 22 Geo. III. c. 82	95,000
7th Ditto.	Salaries to certain Offices of State and various other allowances	41,306
8th Ditto.	Salaries to the Commissioners of the Treasury and Chancellor of the Exchequer	13,822
	Occasional payments not comprised in any of the aforesaid classes	26,000
		£845,727

The sum of 850,000*l*., which was granted to his late Majesty, corresponds with the estimate of a new Civil List, made by the Select Committee of the House of Commons, in the year 1815. This estimate was founded on the actual expenditure of the Civil List in the years 1812, 1813, and 1814 ; and that expenditure was of the most extravagant description. These circumstances, together with the fact of the sum of 850,000*l*. having been sufficient, without incurring any debt, to defray all the expenses of the Civil List during the last reign, prove, beyond all doubt, that the Civil List of 1820 was a very extravagant arrangement.

With respect to the Civil List of Scotland, it has been the practice, on the accession of each King, to grant him the hereditary revenues of Scotland on the old plan.

By the Act of the 1 Geo. IV. c. 1., (the Civil List Act) it is declared, that ' the several respective duties and revenues which were payable to his late Majesty King George the Third in Scotland, shall be continued, raised, levied, and paid, during the life of his present Majesty (George the Fourth), in the same manner only, and subject to the same or the like charges thereon, as the same were liable or subject to during the life of his said late Majesty.' In consequence of this clause, the hereditary revenues of Scotland have been levied and applied in the old way. Some special charges have been made on them by Acts of Parliament, but a great part of them has been expended according to the pleasure of the Crown, and without any authority of Parliament*.

* See Sir J. Sinclair's History of the Revenue, vol. iii. p. 119, for a description of the Hereditary Revenues of Scotland.

It is enacted, by the 9th section of the last-mentioned Act, that ' every surplus or balance which may remain after defraying the whole of the charges upon or incident to the said fund, shall go and be carried to the account of the consolidated fund of the United Kingdom.' It appears from a Parliamentary account of the Income and Expenditure of the King's hereditary revenues of Scotland, that during the last reign the sum received was 844,253*l.* 17*s.* 6*d.* ; and that of this sum there was paid to the consolidated fund only the small sum of 20,000*l.**

There does not appear to be any good reason for not having extended the same rule to Scotland with respect to these revenues as was introduced in England on the accession of George III. In consequence of this not having been done, a very large portion of them has been given in pensions, and no small amount has been applied to local purposes. In 1761, the sum paid for pensions was 5,940*l.*† ; in 1829, it was 33,030*l.*

The following is an account of the Income and Expenditure of the Hereditary Revenues in 1829 :—

Year from 5th January 1829, to 5th January 1830 :—

	£.	s.	d.
RECEIPTS　．　．　．　．	109,132	12	$10_{\frac{1}{2}}$

DISBURSEMENTS.

Permanent Charges :

King's Household and Officers
　on Civil Establishment　　£10,940　18　　7

　　　Carried forward,　£10,940　18　　7

* Parliamentary Paper, Sess. 1830-1. No. 18.
† Third Report of Committee on Public Expenditure, 1808.

Brought forward, £10,940	18	7	
Pensions on Civil List .	33,050	5	8
His Majesty's Commissioner to General Assembly .	2,085	10	0
Procurator to Church for Itinerant Preachers .	2,098	10	0
Crown Agent for Criminal Prosecutions . .	11,300	0	0
Annual Salary to Solicitor of Tithes . . .	100	0	0
Agents before the Court of Session relative to Tithes	998	16	$2\frac{6}{12}$
Agent for Officers of State	495	7	$2\frac{6}{12}$
Alexander Mundell, Esq. for preparing Public Bills, and for attending to Scotch Peerage Business, &c. .	648	15	6
Annual Expense of Botanic Garden . . .	419	3	0
Ditto of Edinburgh Museum	100	0	0
Annual Salary to Chamberlain of Ettrick Forest .	300	0	0
Annual Allowance for Coachhouse and Stables to Barons	48	0	0
King's Plate to be run for at Musselburgh . .	105	0	0
Ditto to Royal Company of Archers . . .	20	0	0
Ditto to Caledonian Hunt	105	0	0
His Majesty's Almoner for Alms and Beedsmen's Gowns ' . . .	108	6	8
Annual Allowance to Clerks in Chancery . .	35	0	0
Deputy Keeper of Regalia, Balance on his Accounts	120	2	7
Stipend to Minister of Hallyards . . .	5	11	$7\frac{8}{12}$
Three-fifths of Contingent Expenses of the Office of Works in Scotland, from Jan. 1827 to Jan. 1829	92	4	5

63,176 11 $5\frac{8}{12}$

		£.	s.	d.
Brought forward,		63,176	11	$5\frac{8}{12}$

CASUAL AND TEMPORARY CHARGES :

Alexander Mundell, Esq. Expenses of Appeal; the Directors of Bible Societies against his Majesty's Printers	169	6	2	
Repairs on Palace of Holyrood House	4,010	10	0	
Repayment of Penalty on Bail-bond	50	0	0	
For restoring & embellishing the external Walls of St. Giles' Cathedral, and Fees	2,010	17	6	
Expense of Mineralogical Survey of Scotland	3,124	9	$7\frac{6}{12}$	
Grant for the benefit of the Daughters of Scottish Clergy	1,000	0	0	
Repairs on Windows of the Cathedral of Glasgow	44	8	0	

	£.	s.	d.
	10,409	11	$3\frac{6}{12}$
	£73,586	2	$9\frac{2}{12}$

Charges in course of Payment in 1830 :

	£.	s.	d.
Repairs to the exterior Walls of St. Giles' Cathedral, in Edinburgh	6,000	0	0
Expenses of Building for the Royal Academy of Exercises of Edinburgh	5,000	0	0
Expenses of fitting up the interior as a place for Meeting for the General Assembly of the Church of Scotland	3,000	0	0
Sheriffs' Expenses in the several Counties in Scotland	25,000	0	0
Expenses of the Commission for Inquiry into the State of the Scottish Universities	1,000	0	0
Expenses of the Mineralogical Society of Scotland	3,000	0	0

A Civil List for Ireland was first settled by the Irish Act of 33 Geo. III. c. 34. By this act, 145,000*l.* a-year was granted to the King in lieu of the hereditary revenues of Ireland ; and this sum was appropriated to pay the following charges :—

1. Pensions to the Royal Family, and the salaries of the Lord Lieutenant and his Chief Secretary.

2. The salaries of the Lord Chancellor and the Judges.

3. The bills of all tradesmen, artificers, and labourers, for every article supplied, or work done in the Castle of Dublin, or in any other houses of the Lord Lieutenant, the Chief Secretary, or the Under Secretary.

5. Pensions.

By the Civil List Act of 1 Geo. IV. c. 1, the sum settled for the Civil List of Ireland was 207,000*l.*

The accession of his present Majesty to the throne affords an opportunity of making a very valuable reformation in all matters connected with the hereditary revenues, and the charge on the public for the Civil List, or rather Civil Government expenditure. There seems to be no longer any reason for not abolishing the distinction between hereditary and other revenues. Every right of the crown may be effectually secured in a more simple and convenient manner ; and now that the Civil List cannot be what it formerly was intended to be—the fund for paying the whole of the expenses of the Civil Government—there is no reason for preserving any part of the public expenditure under a distinct head bearing this denomination. The better way would be to provide for the expenses of the King and Royal Family without mixing them

with any other expenses ; and to provide for the
expenses of the Civil Government by themselves, so
that the whole of them may be paid out of the same
fund, and appear in the same account.

With regard to the expenses to be in future incurred for maintaining the dignity, and providing for
the comfort of the King and Royal Family, and for
the Civil Government, they ought to be very much
reduced below what they were in the last reign.   In
the fifth class of the late Civil List a considerable
saving should be made, as 140,700l. is much too
large a sum to be paid merely for the salaries of the
servants of the household.   Each salary should be
revised, and settled with reference to the services to
be performed, and to the financial circumstances of
the country.   If the salaries were wholly abolished
of the Lord Steward, Lord Chamberlain, Master of
the Horse, and Master of the Robes, and if the
salaries of the Lords of the Bedchamber, and of the
other principal officers, were reduced, there can be no
doubt, that well-qualified individuals could be found
to fill these offices : the distinction and rank which
they confer should be a sufficient remuneration for
the duties of them.

In the fourth class it would also appear that there
was room for reduction ; for if 209,000l. a-year was
sufficient to pay the tradesmen's bills in 1815, when
this sum was settled, a smaller sum should now be
given in consequence of the great fall which has since
taken place in prices, and the system of profusion
which prevailed at that period.

In the third class, namely, Foreign Ministers, a
much larger saving should be made than that proposed

by the late administration : and considering how heavy
the charge now is on the public (6,152,702*l.**) for
pensions, superannuations, and half-pay, the whole of
the pensions on the late Civil List should be revised
and put on a more economical plan.

Every item in the late Civil List expenditure in
each part of the United Kingdom should be strictly
examined, and, where practicable, reduced or suppressed ; and the whole charge for the civil government should be brought annually under the view of
Parliament in the budget of expenses, which has
already been proposed.

The following extracts from Mr. Burke's speech
on economical reform, concerning the Duchies of
Lancaster, Cornwall, &c., are well worthy of consideration, preparatory to the new settlement of the
Civil List. He said—' As in the Saxon times this
country was an heptarchy, it is now a strange sort of
pentarchy. It is divided into five distinct principalities, besides the supreme. . . . In every one of
these five principalities, duchies, palatines, there is a
regular establishment, of considerable expense and
most domineering influence. . . . Thus every one of
those principalities has the apparatus of a kingdom,
for the jurisdiction over a few private estates ; and
the formality and charge of the exchequer of Great
Britain, for collecting the rents of a country squire.
. . . This revenue exists for the sole purpose of
multiplying offices and extending influence. . . This
duchy (of Lancaster), which is not worth 4000*l.* a
year at best, to revenue, is worth 40,000*l.* or 50,000*l.*
to influence. . . . Indeed, the whole of the estates

* See note in page 209, infra.

which support these minor principalities is made up, not of revenues, and rents, and profitable fines, but of claims, of pretensions, of vexations, of litigations. . . . For what plausible reason are these principalities suffered to exist? . . . Do they answer any purpose to the king? . . . I propose, therefore, to unite all the five principalities to the crown and to its ordinary jurisdiction—to abolish all those offices that produce an useless and chargeable separation from the body of the people—to compensate those who do not hold their offices (if any such there are) at the pleasure of the crown—to extinguish vexatious titles by an act of short limitation—to sell those unprofitable estates which support useless jurisdictions ; and to turn the tenant right into a fee, on such moderate terms as will be better for the state than its present right, and which it is impossible for any rational tenant to refuse*.'

On the 14th of February, 1780, leave was given, on the motion of Mr. Burke, without opposition, to bring in, 1st, A bill for the sale of the forest and other Crown lands. 2d, A bill for the more perfectly uniting to the Crown the Principality of Wales, and the County Palatine of Chester.   3d, A bill for uniting to the Crown the Duchy and County Palatine of Lancaster.   4th, A bill for uniting the Duchy of Cornwall to the Crown†.

With respect to the landed property of the crown, there is the opinion of Mr. Huskisson, as given in his speech of the 18th March, 1830, in the House of Commons, to the following purport :—' I think that the control of Parliament may be most properly exer-

* Burke's Works, vol. iii. pp. 257—270.
† Ibid., p. 350.

cised over those revenues which are managed under the Office of Woods and Forests. They might be placed under a system of less laxity, and of more effectual control. With respect to these revenues, they do not form part of the Civil List, but are part of the funds that have been commuted for the Civil List. And although I think that the proportion of the revenue, left for the gratification of the sovereign, is properly left, yet a further check and a further system of control ought to be placed over other branches of receipt and expenditure in the Woods and Forests' department*.'

Lord Lieutenant of Ireland.—The Catholic Question having been settled, there is not the least excuse for keeping up the office of Lord Lieutenant of Ireland. What has been said of other viceroys is fully applicable to the office in Ireland. ' It seldom happens that viceroys can exercise their charge with advantage to the country over which they are temporary sovereigns. The instability of their power, and, too frequently, the desire to improve their own fortune, tend to withdraw them from any attention to their duties, beyond what is necessary to keep all quiet. All measures tending materially to amelioration must be necessarily slow ; the unpopularity which attaches to all wholesome innovations falls on the viceroy who introduces them—while the merit which follows from them is given to his successors. On the whole, it is generally fortunate when a viceroy is contented to be merely passive in his office, and is negatively a clog on the improvement of the state. The situation being frequently given to some noble-

* Mirror of Parliament, Sess. 1830, p. 884.

man embarrassed with debts, or overwhelmed with a large family or numerous dependants, it has often happened that he has considered the country over which he is the ruler, less as a country to be fostered and rendered happy, than as a mine from which to extract for himself and his followers, within the shortest possible space of time, the greatest possible quantity of wealth*.'

The saving of expense from abolishing this office would be the least of the benefits of such a measure ; for the laws will never be administered in Ireland in the true spirit of the British Constitution, or the constitution be enjoyed fully as it ought to be in every other respect, until the intermediate authority of a local government be removed, and the King's Cabinet become responsible, personally, to both Houses of Parliament for every act of Government in Ireland. The management of the army, navy, ordnance, revenue, and trade, has been already taken away from the Lord Lieutenant ; and in each case many vices of administration have been suppressed. In truth, what is best done in Ireland is that with which the local government have no connexion. The establishing of lords-lieutenant of counties would make the county system of government much more efficient than it is at present ; and the few hours now required for communicating between London and Dublin removes all apprehensions with respect to being able to contend with any sudden difficulty or danger, with immediate and full effect.

As a great part of the sums granted for Irish miscellaneous services relate to matters of civil government, this is the proper place to say, that if His

* For. Quart. Rev., vol. iv. p. 358.

Majesty's Ministers carry into execution the recommendations of the Committee of the House of Commons with respect to them, a considerable saving of expense will be the consequence.

There are several items which will admit of still greater reductions than the Committee have proposed; so that if all were done that might be done, at least 150,000*l.* a year might be saved.

Judges' Salaries.—The present expenditure of so large a sum annually as 484,000*l.* on the judicial establishments of the United Kingdom, should admit of some considerable reduction. The salaries of the judges, raised, as they professedly were, on account of the high prices of all articles of consumption, should be lowered. The following Parliamentary account shows what these salaries were in England in 1792, and what they now are* :—

KING'S BENCH.

	1792.	1829.
Chief Justice	£4,000	£10,000
Puisne Judges, each	2,400	5,500

COMMON PLEAS.

Chief Justice	3,500	8,000
Puisne Judges, each	2,400	5,500

EXCHEQUER.

Chief Baron	3,500	7,000
Barons, each	2,400	5,500

In addition to the above salaries and allowances paid in 1792, the Judges of the several courts were remunerated also by fees, the amount of which, received by each, is not known. The Judges derive no emolument from this source at present.

* Sess. Paper, 1830, No. 532.

The Mint.—The establishment of the Mint costs the public 32,450*l.* a year *. Mr. Burke proposed, in his speech in 1780 on economical reform, to abolish this department, and to require the Bank of England, in compensation for the use of the balances of the public money, to take charge of the business of it †. He said, ' The mint, Sir, is a manufacture, and it is nothing else; and it ought to be undertaken upon the principles of a manufacture: that is, for the best and cheapest execution, by a contract upon proper securities, and under proper regulations ‡.'

By a recent regulation, which allows bullion to be exchanged at the mint for sovereigns, without waiting, as formerly, for its conversion into coin, a large expense is likely to be incurred to the public; for there can be no doubt that this plan will induce the importers of bullion to convert the whole into coin, and which coin will be exported and melted whenever the bullion trade gives a profit on exportation : so that there will be going on a constant coining and receiving of the same gold, according to the fluctuations in the trade of exporting and importing gold, and consequently there will be a great loss in the expense of coinage. The old plan of giving a higher value to coin than to bullion, not by a seigniorage but by delay in coining the bullion deposited at the mint, should be reverted to, as the best way of securing a sufficient supply of coin at the lowest charge to the public.

By an act passed in Scotland in 1686, duties were imposed for defraying the expenses of a mint in that country. These duties were made perpetual by 9 Geo. III., c. 25; and although every species of the

* Parliamentary Paper, Sess. 1822, No. 64.
† Works, vol. iii. p. 301.   ‡ Ib. p. 291.

money of Great Britain is now coined in London, the establishment of a mint is retained in Scotland. The expense of it in 1804 was 1200*l.* The pretext for putting the public to this charge for a relict of the ancient independence of Scotland, is a provision in the Act of Union, that a Scotch mint should be maintained*.

Office of King's Printer.—All Acts of Parliament, Proclamations, Orders in Council, Bibles, Testaments, and Prayer Books, and various other works, have been printed for a long period under a patent of the Crown. In this way a most extravagant monopoly has been given to a few individuals, who have received immense sums of money from monopoly prices, with great detriment to the trade of printing, and with the absolute loss of so much money to the public. There exists, perhaps, among the numerous cases of government prodigality, no instance of a more wanton waste of public money.

For the Acts of Parliament, the patentees have been allowed to charge 2½*d.* a sheet, while, according to the prices of the trade, less than a penny a sheet would have afforded a liberal rate of profit. But this is not all; for, notwithstanding there is not a word in the patent giving the patentees a right to sell what they print, they do sell, at very exorbitant prices, large numbers of Acts of Parliament to lawyers, magistrates, companies, and many other persons all over the country; and, in consequence of this assumption of the authority to sell as well as to print, they put into their pockets a sum which has been calculated to amount to from thirty to forty thousand pounds a year. If

* Sir John Sinclair's History of the Revenue, vol. iii., p. 125.

due regard had been paid to the public interests, after incurring the expense of printing, the sale of the Acts of Parliament ought to have been so conducted as, at least, to have produced a sum equivalent to the expenses.

The patent that was granted in 1799 expired in 1829, and thus gave an opportunity of correcting this abuse. But, notwithstanding the glaring violation of all principles of trade and economy, and notwithstanding the Committee of the House of Commons of 1810, on the Public Expenditure, had condemned the principle of this patent, and had recommended the separation of the two branches of printer and bookseller ; and notwithstanding another Committee, which sat in 1829 on the Irish Miscellaneous Services, had recommended the getting rid of a similar patent in Ireland, the Government, in defiance of all these most powerful reasons against renewing the patent, did renew it for thirty years in favour of the old patentees !!! It is difficult to express what must be the extent of injury, in one shape or other, which the public sustains by such deviations from sound principles. Those who are at the head of the administration of affairs, in consequence of not being well acquainted with the subjects which come under their government, and of seldom referring to any general principle to assist their judgment, are too frequently led to do things very injurious to the public interests. There can be no doubt that, if this patent had not been renewed, and if the business had been transferred to the Stationery Office, the difference to the public would have been the profit now made by the patentees to the amount, according to the calculation referred to, of from 30,000*l.* to 40,000*l.* a year.

There surely must be some mode of getting rid
of this patent; but if there be not, in such a case as
this, Parliament should interfere by an express law to
abolish it, as no claim can justly be set up of private
loss against so great a public evil.

If it were possible to collect together all that the
public pay for printing to the king's printer, for
printing for the Houses of Parliament, for printing
for the public offices, and for printing in Ireland, it
would probably amount to something not far short of
150,000*l.* a year—possibly to 200,000*l.* ; and, more-
over, as the printing work for the Houses of Parliament is on a much more expensive plan than
is necessary for any useful purpose, the revising of
the whole business, and establishing it on such principles as would secure to the public good and plain
work, and, at the same time, a fair profit to the persons employed, would certainly be attended with very
great advantages *

Salaries and Superannuations.—Having noticed,
in a general way, nearly all the civil official establishments, it is now time to say something concerning
the rates of salaries in them. The Committee of
Finance, in their Second Report, point out the general
principles on which they ought to be regulated.
They say the proper question with respect to them is,

* It appears from a Parliamentary Paper ordered to be
printed on the 2nd December, 1830 (No. 49), that there was paid
to the patentees, Messrs. Reeves, Eyre, and Strahan, for goods
delivered and work performed by them, in 1826, 10,706*l.*; in
1827, 11,384*l.*; and in 1828, 11,275*l.*; and that they were paid
for each sheet of Public General Acts, in folio, 2¼*d.*; of Public
General Acts, in quarto, 4½*d.*; and of Local and Private Acts,
in folio, 3*d.*

what course will best secure a perfectly efficient performance of the services of the public at the smallest expense?—They lay it down that the principle of competition is as applicable to the remuneration given to clerks in the public offices for their time and trouble, as it is to the price paid for the time and trouble of other persons who live by the wages of labour: and they add, that, as it is by this principle the salaries of clerks in commercial establishments are determined, the salaries of clerks in the public offices should be regulated by the salaries given to the former; and that every exception in favour of a higher rate should be grounded on a clear case being made out of more talent and trust being required.

The present rates of official salaries are stated by the Committee to rank higher than those in commercial houses. Some of the witnesses examined by the Committee seem, according to their evidence, to have attempted to justify this, by assuming that in every public situation more talent and trustworthiness are required than in mercantile situations; but this is not so, as by far the greatest part of the office clerks have nothing but common clerks' work to do. It is perfectly well known that, in those offices where the salaries are the lowest, namely, in the Commissariat, and the office of the Paymaster of the Marines, the work is best done. The clerks in the Commissariat are real clerks, not the sons of persons of the higher ranks, but of an humble description; they are perfectly satisfied with what they receive, and do their work remarkably well. The Paymaster of Marines says, in his evidence, that the salaries in his office are lower than in any other; that he can place full confidence in his clerks, and has to place a great deal in them.

The more the question of salaries is examined, the more fully it can be shown that high salaries are not only the source of a great burden on the public, but also that they actually contribute to make the clerks less efficient, and, consequently, to the employing of a great number of them.   There cannot be a greater mistake than the notion generally entertained, that fitness will follow in proportion as the amount of the salary is high.   Those persons who are willing to work for a small remuneration always have the greatest relish for work ; and, therefore, giving low salaries will secure the filling of the offices with the most efficient clerks.   On the other hand, when a clerk has a high salary, the less is his activity, and he is wholly adverse to anything like the drudgery of office.   He possesses a greater facility for enjoying pleasurable and other trivial occupations.   He has a greater facility of obtaining accomplices in his trans-gressions, and in finding supporters to shield him against being displaced, and against having his con-duct thought disreputable.

The present rates of salaries of officers and clerks place them in a much better situation than the remu-neration given to that part of the clergy who per-form the laborious part of the church duties, and to officers of high rank in the army and navy.

As the pretext for raising salaries to their present rates was the depreciation of money, now that the value of it is restored, the public have a right to require a reduction to be generally made on a large scale.   It appears from a Parliamentary ' Return of the number of persons employed, and of the pay or salaries granted to such persons, in all public offices and departments in 1797 and 1827,' that the number and salaries were as follows :—

In 1797 ...... number 16,267...... salaries £1,374,561
In 1827 ...... number 22,912...... salaries £2,788,907*

The number, it seems, has increased about one-third, and the salaries have doubled. It is not easy to discover any good reason for such an increase; for, in 1797, war was actively going on, and the effective expenditure of that year was much more than double what it was in 1827. If these salaries were brought back to what they were in 1797, this alone would be a saving to the country of 1,400,000*l*. a year.

The account recently presented to Parliament of officers with salaries of 1,000*l*. a year and upwards†, gives a total of nearly one thousand persons who enjoy among them 2,066,574*l*. sterling. Of these there are 216 persons whose salaries average 4,429*l*. It certainly must be possible to make a very large diminution in this enormously extravagant use of the public money.

The Committee of Finance, in their Third Report, have pointed out the practicability of making a considerable retrenchment by means of a reform in the existing system of superannuation allowances. Since 1810, when the present law was passed, the charge for civil superannuations has increased from 94,550*l*. to 480,081*l*.‡ The Committee say this increase is enormous, and represent it as an evil that calls loudly for a remedy. They state that several abuses have arisen under the law as it now is, particularly from the disposition of the superior authorities to favour the retirement of efficient clerks; they say they have been informed, that the cases are not few, in which

* Sess. Paper, 1828, No. 552.
† See Appendix, No. VII. for this Parliamentary Account.
‡ Third Report Com. Fin., Appendix, No. 13.

persons superannuated as unfit for public service, have
enjoyed health and strength long afterwards, and
have discharged active duties in other public offices,
and in private business ; and they recommend that
there should be a per centage reduction of all salaries,
to form a fund for paying the superannuation allowances.

Nothing can be more extravagant, and inconsistent
with a proper guardianship of the public money, than
the system of salaries and superannuations now in
operation. The salaries are so much higher than
they ought to be, that every officer and clerk has
sufficient means of making a provision for infirmity
and old age. But notwithstanding this fact, as to the
sufficiency of salary, in the true spirit of profusion, a
great superannuation allowance has been added. If
the Committee of Finance had recommended what
was most proper to be done in the case, they would
have proposed the abolition of all such allowances on
future appointments to office: for, although it might
be difficult for Government to resist the claims of
hardship and real sufferings, which would, in that
event, be made upon them, it may be considered as
quite certain, that in their hands, the sums which
would be granted would never amount to what is now
paid under the compulsory plan of giving to every
officer a regulated allowance. It is quite impossible
to explain why we are to have a privileged class in
society, who, because they have once touched public
money, are to be supported all their lives at the
public expense ; why they are to be put into a more
fortunate case than clerks in mercantile and banking
houses, and than many of our clergy, and of our
military and naval officers.

CHAPTER XIII.

MILITARY EXPENDITURE.

The next head of expenditure, namely, the military part of the service of the Army and Navy, affords the means of retrenchment on a large scale.

In the report of Messrs. Brooksbank and Beltz, on the public accounts, the estimates of the Army, Navy, and Ordnance for 1828 are stated in a manner to show what part of them was for effective, and what for non-effective expenditure. The following account has been made up from their statements.

	Effective Expenditure.	*Non-Effective Expenditure.*
Army	£5,067,793	£2,982,146
Navy	4,576,730	1,557,132
Ordnance	1,419,975	365,221
	£11,064,498	£4,904,499

Twelve millions having been about the average annual effective expenditure, no less than 180 millions have been expended on soldiers, sailors, ships, and artillery, since 1815, exclusive of the non-effective expenditure, although we have been all the time in a state of profound peace.

The only ground on which it is attempted to justify this expenditure, so enormously great in comparison with that of any former peace establishment, is the expediency of being at all times prepared for war. But, during the last fifteen years, there has been less likelihood of war than at any former period, in consequence of the exhausted condition of all the powers of Europe, after the last war, and of the triumphant display of military and naval force which England was able to make at the conclusion of it. If, in 1816, a peace expenditure had been arranged on a principle of sound economy, having relation only to the real wants of the nation, a very large portion of the 180 millions would have been saved.

Although it is right to be prepared for war, it should be borne in mind that several of the most popular and substantial grounds of war have ceased to exist. The barren nature of military trophies, and the substantial advantages of peace, have been fully exhibited in the last forty years. The laws most offensive to foreign trade have been expunged from our statute book; every country now sees the wisdom of seeking commercial prosperity in concurrence with that of its neighbours; the discovery of the real sources of wealth has shown the folly of wasting lives and treasure about colonial possessions; and nothing is now more universally acknowledged than the fallacy of expecting any national advantage from war.

The Committee of Finance, in their Second Report, state it to have been one of the principal objects of their attention to secure ' a strict adjustment of the numbers of the military and naval forces, so as not to exceed what is really necessary for the peace and security of the empire *.' They say, ' this principle ought not, on any account, to be given up to speculative apprehensions;' that, ' as the army and navy are the great sources of expense, it is only by keeping them within proper limits that any great saving can be effected;' and they add, ' it is particularly necessary carefully to examine the reasonings and state-

* Second Report, p. 5.

ments of those individuals, who, being qualified from their official stations to give full information on these subjects, are liable to be led by professional feelings to recommend a higher standard of preparation for war, than a less biassed view of circumstances might suggest.'

Military and naval officers connected with government have had their own way so much in fixing the amount of the forces to be kept up, that it would be strange if it had not been carried beyond its proper limit. Many motives of a personal and professional kind serve to warp their judgments in forming just conclusions with respect to what that limit ought to be. Every officer feels a natural and just pride in the perfection of his own department, and at the same time he has no great inducement to care much about what it costs; and therefore it is by no means right to consult professional men alone, and leave it to them to decide what the number of the forces should be of our peace establishment.

According to every rational consideration of the subject, it is clear that the preparation for defence should always be kept down to the lowest possible, rather than always raised to the highest possible point. At the highest, it produces a great share of the evils of war. A moderate preparation, strictly proportioned to the occasion, and not allowed to go beyond it, will save more evil than it risks ; all beyond this infallibly produces more evil than it prevents; it impoverishes the nation, and renders it more easily injured by a powerful enemy, than if it had been allowed to save expense, and gather strength in peace *. Our large and well-equipped fleets, and numerous well-dressed

* See Supp. En. Br., vol. iii. p. 276.

troops, give, to be sure, an air of magnificence ; but those who furnish out this show should remember the claims of the industrious class for a reduction of taxation.

At the same time, the public who pay the taxes which are levied to defray the immense expense which is incurred by maintaining the Army and Navy on a footing much beyond what the necessity of the case requires, are not only to blame for the readiness, but even the eagerness, with which they listen to every pretext for increasing it. To judge from experience, it may be truly said, that nothing seems to have any influence in attracting public attention to measures of economy, but a positive deficiency of the revenue. While, in 1827, and in the beginning of 1828, the revenue was deficient, the necessity of retrenchment was heard on all sides, and a Committee of Finance was appointed. But as soon as the April quarter's account of 1828 showed that the revenue was recovering, not a word more was said on the subject, and the Committee of Finance was got rid of by ministers without any public expression of disapprobation. Seeing, therefore, that such is the result of just having revenue enough to go on with from year to year, and that there is no regard to the consequences of postponing the revision of our financial system, it would, perhaps, in the end, be for the public good, if the revenue should not only be again deficient, but continue so for some time.

The state of the finances just at this time, and also of our foreign and domestic affairs, makes it necessary to introduce some further observations in addition to those in the last edition of this work, on the military establishments and expenditure. The following estimate of what will be the balance of revenue and expenditure at the end of the year 1831, if the taxes be not more productive than they have been, will, it is hoped, make the public see the absolute necessity of reducing these establishments :

REVENUE of 1829, according to the Parliamentary Paper called the Balance-sheet * . . £50,786,000
Add produce of new Duties on Spirits in 1831 . 600,000

                                                                    51,386,000

DEDUCTIONS TO BE MADE IN 1831.

Beer Duty repealed . . . £3,000,000
Leather Duty ditto 400,000
Duty on Cider and Perry ditto . 25,000
Sugar Duty reduced . . . 450,000
                                           ——— 3,875,000

                           Revenue for 1831, £47,511,000

EXPENDITURE of 1829, by Balance-sheet £49,075,000

DEDUCTIONS TO BE MADE IN 1831.

Reduced vote for the Army in 1830 £453,000
Ditto, ditto, Navy . . 273,000
Ditto, ditto, Ordnance . 29,000
Ditto, ditto, Miscellaneous services 276,000 -
Reduction of Interest on 4 per cent. Stock 750,000
Ditto on Exchequer Bills . 180,000
                                           ——— 1,961,000

               Expenditure for 1831 . . . 47,114,000
               Revenue for 1831 47,511,000

Surplus of Revenue on the 5th January, 1832 £397,000

As every item in this estimate is taken from statements made in the House of Commons in the last

* Session 1830, No. 11.

session, and as nothing has been added or omitted by way of making the balance less favourable than it probably will be, the result which is produced shows, that instead of having a surplus of 3,000,000*l.* as there ought to be according to the calculations of the Committee of Finance in 1828, for a sinking fund, there will be one of only 397,000*l.*, making the state of the balance, on the 5th January, 1832, worse than it ought to be by the sum of 2,603,000*l.*

As the revenue of Great Britain, arising wholly from the taxes for the year ending the 10th of October 1830, was less than the revenue for the year ending the 10th of October 1829, by the sum of 648,000*l.*, and as the revenue of the United Kingdom for 1829 was less than the revenue of 1828, by the sum of 1,237,000*l.*, there is no want of reasons to establish the necessity of diminishing the military establishments *.

But there is already opposed to this view of the question, some supposed want of even an increase of the army, in consequence of the revolutions in France, Belgium, and Poland, and of the disturbed state of some of the counties in England.   This may, and very probably will, appear to most people a good

---

* Produce of the taxes in Great Britain in the

year to Oct. 1829	.	.	.	£47,054,000
Ditto ditto ditto			1830,	46,406,000

Decrease	.	.	648,000

Produce of the taxes in United Kingdom in the

year to Jan. 1829	.	.	.	51,665,000
Ditto ditto ditto ditto			1830,	50,428,000

Decrease	.	.	£1,237,000

See Balance Sheets for 1829 and 1830.

reason for increasing the sum of 15,000,000l. voted last year for the military expenses ; but if it do so, it will be because most people take very little trouble to examine whether or not pleas of this kind in favour of increased expense are well founded.

With respect to the revolution of France, the truth is, that the early recognition by the Government and people of this country of the new King of France, and the rule of non-intervention which the new Government of France has determined to act upon, have established so good an understanding between the two countries, that the revolution should be considered as extremely favourable to the continuance of peace ; for while France and England are in amity with each other, and act together on the principles of maintaining civil liberty, and of respecting the independence of other states, the other powers of Europe will not venture to make war. But should this conclusion prove to be ill founded as to making war against France, there is no English interest that can be pointed out to show that this country ought to become in any way a party to it.

The revolution of Belgium, by establishing a new independent state, removes one of the principal grounds for apprehending war, namely, the supposed design of France to regain possession of Belgium. The revolution of Poland, by providing employment for the armies of Russia, Austria, and Prussia, connected at the same time with the probability of popular movements in these countries, diminishes also the chance of war.

With respect to the disturbed state of the interior of England, if proper measures be taken for reforming abuses, if the law be duly administered, and if the civil constabulary force be improved and rendered more effective, as circumstances may seem to require, there can be little doubt that tranquillity will be restored without the aid of the army.

If, however, it shall be decided by Government and Parliament that the military expenditure shall be increased, then it is clear, from the foregoing estimate of the probable condition of the finances at the end of this year, that the expectation of the public to see a large reduction of taxes cannot be realized without imposing a property-tax; so that it is evident that those who will have to pay this tax can have no chance of preventing its being laid on, but by opposing every increase, and promoting every reduction, of the military expenditure.

But if it should so happen that Parliament should refuse to impose a property-tax, and if, at the same time, the public should insist on a reduction of some millions of taxes, then the means of paying the dividends may be shaken; so that all owners of property in the funds have also the greatest possible interest in opposing the increase and promoting the reduction of the military expenditure.

The great amount of the non-effective expenditure in the Army, Navy, and Ordnance, shows the profusion and the want of due consideration for the public interests with which everything in the nature of pensions, half-pay, and retired allowances, has been regulated. Those persons who were the authors of these schemes ought to have known that ' liberality, exercised at the expense of the public, is but another name for waste and a vice, and that all praise bestowed upon it is false and hypocritical.'

In order to protect the public, for the future, from

this system of making provision out of the public purse for so many thousand persons who, while in active service, receive full remuneration for their time and trouble, it may be well to consider whether any individual not now in public service, who shall be hereafter appointed to any civil or military employment, should be allowed to receive any pension, half-pay, or superannuation allowance, except in special cases, and under the responsibility of Government*.

Army Expenditure.—It appears, from papers laid before the Committee of Finance, that in 1792 the number of all ranks in the Army was 57,251, and that they were distributed as follows :—

	Officers and Men.
Great Britain	17,007
Ireland	11,901
East Indies	10,700
Canada, Nova Scotia, and Bermuda	6,061
Gibraltar	4,221
West-India Islands	6,886
New South Wales	475
	57,251

* The following account shows to what an extent the principle has been carried of granting pensions and similar allowances.

	Per Annum.
Military Pensioners, Half-pay, &c.	£4970,349
Pensions (a)	772,702
Superannuation allowance (b)	485,990
	£6,229,041

(a) Paper, Com. Fin., 234.   (b) Paper, Com. Fin., No. 89.

In 1828 the number of all ranks was 116,738, who were distributed as follows :—

Great Britain	29,616
Ireland	23,969
Colonies	37,037
East Indies	26,116
	116,738*

The chief part of the increase was thus accounted for :—

Rank and File.

Increase in the New Colonies	17,112
in the Old Colonies	849
in Great Britain	9,096
in Ireland	10,363
in the East Indies	14,287
	51,707

The following statement was laid before the Committee of Finance by the Secretary at War, to explain what number of troops are necessary for our foreign possessions :—

Rank and File.

' There are in the Colonies (exclusive of India, and supposing the troops to have evacuated Portugal) 52 battalions, each at 516 rank and file, that make . . . } 26,829

There are in the East Indies . . . 22,560

Making together . 49,392

' One-tenth of this force would have to go out every year (supposing a regiment to be abroad ten years, and to remain at home four years), that is, 4939 rank and file.   There ought to be at home four times 4939, that is 19,756 ; and there ought to be,

* Pap. Com. Fin., No. 79.

besides, a depôt (say) of 120 men for each regiment
of the 52 battalions abroad (52 × 120), making 6240
men *.'

According to this statement of the Secretary at
War, the total force required for our foreign possessions is 75,388 rank and file, namely,

			Rank and File.
Number abroad	•	•	49,392
Depôts at home	•	•	25,996
			75,388

This explanation of the number of troops which is
said to be requisite for foreign service makes it evident that the colonies are the main source of the
great expense incurred on the army; and that no very
considerable reduction can be made in it until the
whole colonial system of management be altered.

The number of rank and file voted for the army in
1830 was 78,282. The means of diminishing this
number are the following :—

1. The reducing of the number of troops in each
foreign garrison and in each colony.   In 1828, there
were 1100 men in the Mediterranean, 5580 in North
America, 3479 in Jamaica, and so on; that is to say,
much larger numbers than the public service now
requires.

2. The substituting militia and police for regular
soldiers in the West Indies. A witness of the highest
authority in these matters stated in his evidence
before the Committee of Finance, that the duty of
soldiers in the West Indies was that of a police.
Surely it must be possible to find a sufficiently fit
police force without sacrificing English money, and

* Evidence of Lord Palmerston.

the lives of English soldiers, in this sort of local service.   The interior protection of our colonies should be left to a militia, as is the case in Cuba, to be paid by the colonies, while the external defence of them from foreign attack should be provided for by our naval squadrons.

3. Another mode of reducing the army is by the getting rid of some of our foreign possessions.   This would be the most effectual way; and there ought to be no hesitation about transferring some of them to other countries, and placing others under the East India Company.   If this were done in a complete and perfect manner, and if also what has been before suggested, with respect to reducing the number of troops in most of our foreign possessions, and substituting a local police in the West Indies for soldiers, the number of troops that would be required for foreign service need not exceed 30,000 ; which number, with half as many more for reliefs and depôts, would make the whole force to be kept up for our foreign possessions 45,000.   As the reliefs and depôts would be at home, and amount to 15,000, a further number of 15,000 would make 30,000 for home service, which ought to be fully sufficient : so that the total number of rank and file to be voted annually for the army would on this plan be 60,000, instead of 78,000.

Navy Expenditure.—The following sums were voted for 1830 :—

For 29,000 Seamen's wages . . .	£980,200
Ditto ditto victuals . . .	603,200
Artificers and Labourers in the Dock-yards .	458,720
Timber, and other materials . . .	784,000

In 1828 the number of ships was as follows :—

Building . . .	41
In Ordinary . . .	151
In Commission . .	182

374*

Of these 94 are ships of the line.

It appears from the Report of the Committee of Finance of 1817, that in 1792 it was considered likely that the number of seamen might be reduced to 16,000; and the examination of Sir George Cockburn by the last Committee shows that they considered this fact of so much importance, as to induce them to require him to go into a very minute explanation to account for keeping up more seamen at the present time. As the justification made by Sir George Cockburn rested on the state of affairs in Greece and Turkey, and on the piracy then going on in Greece and in the West Indies, the public have now a right to expect a very large reduction in the number of seamen, and generally in the Navy expenditure.

If the expenditure in the Navy, since the war, had been regulated with reference to the naval forces of other countries, it could never have amounted to what it has; and, therefore, many millions of money have been wholly thrown away. Our efforts to increase our naval power could not have been greater, had other nations continued to keep up as large fleets as they did in former times. According to the evidence of Sir George Cockburn, France had, in 1793, eighty efficient ships of the line, and a large number capable of being made efficient. Now she keeps forty in

* Paper, Com. Fin., No. 68.

good order, and has only twenty more*.   In 1792,
Holland had so large and efficient a fleet, that she
was enabled to fight the battle of Camperdown.   Sir
George Cockburn says, she has now no navy of any
importance†.   In 1793, Spain had seventy-six sail of
the line‡; but her navy was so completely destroyed
in the battles of St. Vincent and Trafalgar, and on
other occasions during the war, that, according to
Sir George Cockburn's evidence, she has a very small
one now.   On the other hand, Russia and the United
States have more ships than they had in 1792; but
the increase of their ships is very small in comparison
with the numbers lost by France, Spain, and Holland,
and in a comparison with the present effective number
of the fleet of England.

In alluding to the great success of the British
Navy in diminishing the naval power of other nations,
Sir T. B. Martin stated, in his evidence before the
Committee of Finance, ' the glorious fact, that England seemed to have swept from the face of the ocean
the fleets of her enemies, by the capture or destruction
of 156 sail of the line, 382 large frigates, 662 cor-
vettes, with other vessels, making, in all, 2,506 sail of
vessels of war§.'   Notwithstanding, however, this
fact, no less than 67,000,000l. have been granted by
Parliament, since 1815, for the effective naval service,
just as if the whole of these 2,506 sail of vessels had
never been taken or destroyed, and were all ready to
be employed against us.

But this is not all; for, after having spent so many
millions, it would appear by the sums voted this year

* p. 12.   † Ibid.
‡ James's History, vol. i., p. 80.
§ Evidence, p. 20.

for artificers, timber, &c., that the time for reducing the Navy expenditure is not even yet arrived. Sir T. B. Martin says, ' Respecting the force now employed, it may be said, if contrasted with former periods of peace, that we have a fleet in commission approaching more to a war than a peace establishment*.'

If those persons who, by virtue of their offices, have the ordering of what is proper to be done for maintaining a suitable naval force, could lay aside their prejudices, and reason correctly on the duty they have to perform, they would see that no well-founded necessity exists for burdening the nation, in the present state of its relation to other naval nations, with an annual charge of 4,576,000l. for the effective expenditure on the navy. Such a rate of expenditure should be resisted in every possible way, as being demanded on apprehensions and calculations wholly erroneous. A firm Minister of Finance should fix on a much smaller sum, and tell the Naval Departments that they must make it answer.

Ordnance Expenditure.—The Committee of Finance, in their Second Report, observe, that in the estimates there are no less than 92 stations kept up in the Ordnance service; namely, 46 in Great Britain, 17 in Ireland, and 35 abroad; and they say that this number appears very great. They suggest that a strict examination should be made into the necessity of keeping up so many.

The Committee state the numbers and expense of the Ordnance military corps as follows:—

In 1792, 4846 Officers and Men, £151,606 expense.
    1828, 8682   ditto   471,543 ditto.

* p. 19.

The Committee say, that, in referring to the year 1792 as a year with which to compare the expense of the Ordnance military corps in 1828, they have followed the example of the Select Committee of 1817, who particularly called the attention of the House to the low establishments of that year, by stating, ' That as near an approximation to that low scale of establishment and expense, as might be found consistent with our more extended possessions, would be highly advantageous in relieving the burdens and supporting the credit of the country*.'

The Committee proceed to say they have examined into the cause of the increase of the numbers and expense of the military corps, but that their inquiries were attended with the difficulty of having to rely on the evidence of those persons who, being qualified by official stations to give information, are liable to be influenced by professional feelings. They further say, that when they see the sum required is no less than 471,543*l.*, it may be a matter of doubt whether this corps be not on a larger scale than is necessary to secure the keeping up a sufficient extent of military knowledge, or consistent with a fit and prudent degree of preparation for war when the country is in a state of peace.

This report of the Committee contains the following important general observation on our military expenditure:—' Towards the conclusion of the late war, circumstances obliged this country to have a larger army in the field, and to maintain establishments, much beyond what can, on any reasonable calculation, be requisite on a future occasion. The Committee, therefore, are of opinion, that the establish-

* Second Rep. Com. Fin., p. 20.

ments of the country should be regulated, not with
reference to the unusual circumstances of that war,
or to the probability of being again called upon to
make a similar exertion, but rather with reference to
the policy of depending mainly on our navy for protection against foreign invasion, and for the means of
attacking our enemies*.'

* p. 20.

CHAPTER XIV.

SLAVE TRADE.—SINKING FUND.—DIVIDENDS.

The Slave Trade.—THE great sum of five millions seven hundred thousand pounds has already been expended in carrying into effect the measures of government for co-operating with other nations in putting down the slave trade; and the annual current expense amounts to near 400,000*l.** But the attempt appears to have altogether failed. The governments of France, Spain, and Portugal, according to the Parliamentary Papers, make no efforts whatever to enforce the laws for putting down the traffic; and the persons in authority in Cuba and Brazil not only neglect to execute the laws, but, in some cases, have been engaged in it themselves: so that our treaties and laws, where such parties are concerned, are so much waste paper; and spending money to try to give effect to them is a perfect folly. The African Institution say, in their twentieth Report, ' The slave trade has increased during the last year; and, notwithstanding the number of prizes taken, it continues to rage with unabated fury.' Surely these are sufficient reasons for saving the 400,000*l.* a year now expended to so little purpose.

* This is the amount expended up to the year 1828.—Pap. Com. Fin., No. 176. In the last session, the bounty on each captured slave was reduced to 5*l.*

The Sinking Fund.—Our present arrangement of
the Revenue and Expenditure, by which a revenue of
58,700,000*l.* was calculated upon as requisite for the
public service, is formed on the plan of providing
55,700,000*l.* for the public expenses, with a surplus
of 3,000,000*l.* a year, to be applied in redeeming
debt *; so that, if the Sinking Fund were abandoned,
and the revenue continued to be as large as it was in
1828, three millions of taxes might be repealed.   It
is obvious, from what has been said in these pages
respecting the injurious effects of many of the taxes,
that the public cannot possibly derive any kind of
advantage from reducing 800,000,000*l.* of debt at
the rate of 3,000,000*l.* a year, which can be set
against the certain good that will follow from reducing taxes to the amount of 3,000,000*l.* There should
therefore be no hesitation about suspending the Sinking Fund, till funds could be got for it, without doing
so much injury to industry.

Four per Cent. Stock.—The measure passed in the
last Session for reducing the interest on the 4 per
cent. stock, has produced a saving to the public of
about 750,000*l.* a year.   But the condition which
was attached to the operation of making the new $3\frac{1}{2}$
per cent. stock, that was given instead of the 4 per
cent. stock, irredeemable for ten years, seems to have
been quite unnecessary, and it may prove to be one
productive of a serious loss ; for if the funds should
rise before ten years expire, so that the 3 per cents.
should be at par, the opportunity may be retarded for
a considerable time of making a further reduction of
interest to the amount of 750,000*l.* a year, by paying
off the new $3\frac{1}{2}$ per cent. stock.

* Fourth Report, Committee of Finance.

A practice has very unwisely been allowed to grow up, of suffering the Government to make bargains for loans, reductions of dividends, renewing charters, and other important matters of finance, without previously applying to Parliament for authority to do these things. This practice should be abolished, not only as being inconsistent with every sound principle of Parliamentary control over ministers, but as one which experience has proved on many occasions to be productive of great public injury.

Chapter XV.

COLONIES.

THERE is no part of the public expenditure which admits of reformation more than that which is incurred upon the Colonies; and if the business of reducing it were undertaken on proper principles, it ought not to be attended with any very great difficulty.

No parliamentary documents show what the whole expense is that is paid by English taxes on account of the Colonies. It is generally estimated that from two to three millions are paid for the Army, Navy, and various Civil charges*; but, in addition to this, the public pay full two millions more for sugar and timber than they ought to pay, in consequence of the increased prices occasioned by the protection given to the colonists by the higher duties imposed on these articles when imported from foreign countries.

A Letter from the Treasury to the Secretary of State for the Colonies, dated the 24th March, 1827, fully explains the want of order, economy, and control, which has existed with regard to this important branch of administration †. This Letter states, that the collective expenditure of five of our Colonies has exceeded, on an account of ten and more years, the colonial revenues applicable to the discharge of it, so

* In No. 54 of the Anti-Slavery Reporter, there is a statement of the expenses incurred on the West India Colonies alone, making them amount to 1,996,186*l.*—p. 179.

† Papers Com. Fin.

as to have constituted a deficiency of 2,524,000*l.*;
that of this sum, 2,425,000*l.* has been paid, partly by
bills on the Treasury, by advances to the Agents of
the Colonies, and by the discharge of debts to the
East India Company; that the greater part of this
expenditure has been incurred without any previous
communication with the Treasury; and that the
Treasury has been uninformed, not only of the measures which, from time to time, have led to extraordinary expenses in these Colonies, but even of the
state of the ordinary revenues, and of the permanent
charges upon them. The Letter further states the
great inconvenience to which such an imperfect
administration of so important a branch of the public
expenditure is obviously liable, and the decided
opinion of the Treasury, that some alteration is
urgently required in the system on which the financial
arrangements of the Colonies have hitherto been
conducted.

If anything were wanted to confirm the accuracy
of the statements which have already been made as
to the profusion, neglect, and mismanagement, with
which the public money has been wasted, this Treasury Letter most completely supplies it. This Letter
places beyond all doubt the fact, that our expenditure
has reached its present amount, not by providing for
what the necessity of the public service has required,
but by sheer extravagance, arising from allowing the
different departments to have their own way in
spending whatever money they pleased.

When we see one department giving a lecture of
this kind to another, and making public how matters
have been going on amongst them, the inference
arising from the argument of the probability that

great retrenchment is practicable, is converted into a certain conclusion.

The past extravagance of our expenditure on the Colonies renders it highly probable, that if a wise system of management were introduced, a considerable reduction in the charge on the public purse would be the consequence. With respect to financial arrangements, the system of applying the revenues of the Colonies in paying exorbitant salaries, building Governors' houses, making canals, and roads, and improving in various other ways the estates of the colonial proprietors, should be abolished; for the effect of spending them in this manner is a deficiency of means for paying the expenses of the civil government of the Colonies, and the voting annually by the House of Commons of large sums of money out of the English taxes for virtually defraying these local expenses. In addition to this, the control of the Treasury over the Colonial Department should be insisted upon, and fully established. Monthly accounts should be laid before the Treasury, of the revenue and expenditure of each foreign possession; a Colonial budget should be stated to the House of Commons every session by the Chancellor of the Exchequer, and all Colonial expenses should be voted on a distinct estimate. The official establishments in the Colonies should be revised, and reduced to what is merely necessary; excessive salaries should be diminished, and none but efficient officers should be appointed. All restrictions on colonial trade should be taken off, and then each colony should be made to defray the expense of its defence.

With regard to the commerce of the Colonies, all that is wanted, is to give effect to the principle on which the colonial laws of 1822 and 1825 were enacted. The speeches with which these laws were introduced to Parliament by Lord Goderich and Mr. Huskisson proved and established the policy of free trade, and of putting an end to the old colonial monopoly ; and this principle the British legislature adopted in the most complete manner, as the future principle of colonial trade, by unanimously passing these laws.

But the trial that has been made of them shows that, in point of fact, they have had no kind of effect in making the trade of the Colonies more free than it was before. The House of Assembly of Jamaica has recently said, ' By the Colonial system, established by England for her own aggrandisement, British shipping, and British seamen, are exclusively employed in our commerce ; no article of European growth or manufacture can be purchased unless imported from the mother country, which obtains the benefit of the carrying trade for our supply, and double freights, the Colonies being burthened with the increase of charge. The whole of our produce is, by the same system, sent in British shipping to the markets of the mother country.' The truth is, that the principle of free trade, on which the act of 1825 was founded, has been completely inoperative in consequence of the clauses for imposing duties on foreign goods, according to the proviso in Mr. Huskisson's speech, on proposing this act, that ' the importation of foreign goods into the Colonies should be made subject to such moderate duties as may be found sufficient for the fair protection of British productions of a like nature.' The duties by this act are so high, that England still enjoys all the advantages of the old monopoly with respect to supplying the Colonies with her productions. The failure, therefore, which was foretold in 1825, of the attempt to establish a free colonial trade, and at the same time give protection to British manufactures, has come to pass; and it is now clear that these two things are quite incompatible, and that there is only a choice between two alternatives,—a choice between absolute freedom, and absolute prohibition.

What ought now to be done, in order to promote, in a certain and effectual manner, the interests both of the Colonies and the British public, is to amend the law of 1825, so as to make it, by repealing all the restrictions of the old system which that law continued, what it was avowedly intended by the legislature to be, namely, a law to give a perfect freedom of trade to the Colonies, and thus get rid, *in toto*, of the colonial monopoly.

The principal restriction arises from the duties just now referred to on foreign goods; these should be reduced, so as no longer to be duties for giving protection to British manufactures, but only for obtaining revenue. As the Colonies form so small a portion of the market for British goods, the admission of foreign competition would scarcely be perceived at home. It would, therefore, be a groundless exaggeration to say, that the British manufacturer would sustain injury from the removal of all restrictions on the intercourse of the Colonies with foreigners.

In the states of North and South America, where trade is free with all nations, the great mass of imports are received from Great Britain, because the British goods are cheaper than others; and the same reason would operate in securing to the British manufacturers the principal supply of the Colonies when all protection was removed.

By the existing law of navigation, the interests of the West India planters are severely obstructed in several ways. A foreign ship is prevented from importing into the Colonies any goods, except they are the produce of the country to which the ship belongs. This cannot fail to operate as an injurious restriction, and, therefore, it ought to be repealed. The idea of such a regulation being of any advantage to the British navy is absurd. By repealing it, the Colonies would be placed on the same footing as the East India Company's territories. Lord Goderich said, in proposing the Act of 1822 to the House of Commons, ' If we look to the dominions of England in the Eastern hemisphere, we shall find the restrictive system has been entirely and systematically abandoned. The whole of the East India Company's territories have never been shackled with the peculiar restrictions of the navigation laws ; and who will say,' said his Lordship, ' that the interests of commerce or of navigation have suffered ? or rather, who will deny that they have been materially benefited by the freedom they have enjoyed * ? ' Mr. Marryat, speaking on the same occasion, said, ' ships under any flag upon the face of the globe had free access to the ports of our East Indian territories, to bring commodities of every description, and to take away theirs in return. They could buy everything where they could buy cheapest, and sell everything where they could sell dearest †.'

The interests of the planters are further injured by

* Parliamentary Debates, vol. vi., p. 1416.
† Ib. vol. vii., p. 604.

the navigation law, by the restrictions imposed upon the exporting of colonial produce in foreign ships. The freight of sugar by British ships from the Colonies to the United Kingdom is five shillings the cwt.; while the freight of sugar from Cuba or the Brazils in foreign vessels, to the Continent of Europe, is three shillings and ninepence*.

But the foregoing are not the only instances in which the interests of the planters have been interfered with under the pretext of upholding the navy of England, but in reality for the purpose of promoting the interests of the shipowners. For instance, by the act of 1825, the following table of duties was enacted for the express purpose of giving to British ships the trade of supplying the West India Colonies with food and lumber:—

Table of Duties, by 6 Geo. IV., c. 114, on certain Articles of Provisions, and of Wood and Lumber, not being of the growth, production, or manufacture of the United Kingdom, nor of any British Possession, imported or brought into the British Possessions on the Continent of South America, or in the West Indies, the Bahama and Bermuda Islands included, viz.

Provisions, viz.	£.	s.	d.
Wheat, the bushel	0	1	0
Wheat Flour, the barrel	0	5	0
Bread or Biscuit, the cwt.	0	1	6
Flour or Meal, not of Wheat, the barrel	0	2	6
Peas, Beans, Rye, Calavances, Oats, Barley, Indian Corn, the bushel	0	0	7
Rice, the 100lbs. nett weight	0	2	6
Live Stock	10 per cent.		

---

* These prices of freight, and the several other facts hereinafter stated concerning the Colonial trade and revenue, are taken from documents of unquestionable authority, which will shortly be laid before the public.

Lumber, viz.	£.	s.	d.
Shingles, not being more than twelve inches in length, the 1000	0	7	0
being more than twelve inches in length, the 1000	0	14	0
Staves and Headings, viz.			
Red Oak, the 1000	0	15	0
White Oak, the 1000	0	12	6
Wood Hoops, the 1000	0	5	3
White, Yellow, and Pitch Pine Lumber, the 1000 feet of one inch thick . . .	1	1	0
Other Wood and Lumber, the 1000 feet of one inch thick	1	8	0
Fish, beef, pork, prohibited.			

The annual revenue collected as the produce of these and the other duties imposed by the Act of 1825 amounts to about 75,000*l.*, and the charges of collection to 68,000*l.* ! ! !

The effect of the foregoing duties in raising the prices of the food and lumber which the planters are under the necessity of importing, in order to carry on the cultivation of their estates, is made evident by the following statement, which shows what the prices are in the United States and in Europe, and what they are in Canada and in the United Kingdom:—

	£.	s.	d.
Herrings (Danish) at the Island of St. Thomas, the barrel	1	0	0
Herrings (British) in the Colonies, the barrel .	1	11	0
Mess Beef, in Hamburg . . do. . .	3	0	0
in United Kingdom do. .	4	0	0
Pork, in Hamburg . . . do . .	2	6	0
in United Kingdom . do. .	3	5	0
Red Oak Staves, in United States, per 1000 .	4	0	0
at Quebec . do. . .	7	8	4
White Oak Staves, United States do. .	6	10	2
at Quebec do. . .	10	6	2

		£.	s.	d.
Flour, in United States .	the barrel .	1	1	0
Quebec . . . do. .		1	5	5
Shingles, United States .	per 1000 .	0	14	0
Canada . . . do. .		0	18	0

No law, perhaps, that was ever made is so entirely at variance in its enactments with the principle on which it was proposed and professedly framed as the Colonial Act of 1825 ; and no more conclusive proof can be produced, than that which this act presents, of the errors which have been committed by those persons who either praise or blame the author of it (the late Mr. Huskisson), for having established free trade. The special provisions of this statute for keeping up the remnant of the navigation laws, for imposing the duties just described, and also duties on foreign manufactures, for giving protection, first, to the ship-owners ; secondly, to the proprietors of estates in Canada; thirdly, to the herring fisheries; and, fourthly, to the provision trade of Ireland, place it in the rank of the most impolitic and objectionable of the old laws for encouraging trade by legislative interference and restriction.

It is absolutely necessary that these enactments should be repealed, as the only true and direct mode of giving relief to the planters, and as the first step for such a reform of the whole colonial system as shall in the end diminish the burdens of the British public, with respect to the great expense now incurred in the civil government and defence of the Colonies.

The incomes of the owners of estates in the Colonies being derived from profits on their capital, and not from rent, the policy of doing what has just been recommended for giving relief to the planters, must be evident to every one ; for it is essentially necessary that the prices of the articles requisite for feeding and clothing the slaves, and of all other articles which are of the nature of materials for cultivating the land, and manufacturing sugar, rum, &c., should be kept down, so that the cost of production may be as low as possible. All the restrictions and duties on food, clothing, lumber, &c., are positive taxes on labour, and cannot be justified by any right of Irish, Scotch, or Canadian landowners, or of British shipowners, to claim protection for their particular interests.

If the planters of our Colonies are ever to carry on a successful competition with foreigners in supplying foreign countries with sugar, it is absolutely necessary that these restrictions on food, lumber, &c., should be done away, or that they should be countervailed by continuing to tax the people of England by high duties on foreign sugar. Our present system is the height of absurdity; first to raise the cost of producing sugar by taxing labour in the Colonies, and then to countervail the consequences of it by giving a bounty on exporting sugar, and imposing protecting duties on East Indian and foreign sugars: that is, by taxing the British public with increased prices of sugar, to repay the taxes levied on food and lumber in the West Indies.

The duty of 8l. 8s. a cwt. on refined sugar imported into England, operates as a prohibition of refining in the Colonies for the supply of the British market; and the bounty on refined sugar, exported from the United Kingdom, prevents any refining in the Colonies for foreign markets. If these impediments were removed, the business of refining sugar in the Colonies might be carried on to great advantage, for sugar could be refined there at one-third of the expense it costs in England. This circumstance, together with the diminished expense of freight for carrying refined sugar, would admit of the price of refined sugar being reduced, so as to increase the consumption of it in England, and to secure to it a market abroad. Mr. Bryan Edwards says, that the great progress which was formerly made in the improvement of the French Colonies was chiefly owing their being allowed to carry on the business of refining sugar.

In order to extend the market for all the different productions of the Colonies, and at the same time do what would be extremely beneficial to the public at large, particularly to the shipping interest, every article of the growth, produce, or manufacture of the Colonies should be admitted into the United Kingdom free of duty, except sugar, rum, and coffee, in the same way that the productions of Ireland are admitted into Great Britain. As a number of the West Indian productions are articles of raw materials of manufactures and trades, such a measure would be of the greatest advantage to them.

If all these measures were adopted which have just been suggested, then the principle of the law of 1825 would have full operation. There would be no obstruction in the way of the colonists turning their skill, industry, and capital to the best advantage in any manner they pleased. Instead of continually looking to Government and Parliament for relief from their distresses, they would either find out how to realize a fair profit in their present pursuits, or withdraw their capital, and place it where it could be turned to a better account.

But the benefit of these measures would not be confined to the colonists ; it would extend itself in various ways to the public at large.   In the first place, as the granting of a really free trade to the Colonies would be an abandonment of that part of the old colonial monopoly which secured to England the supplying of the colonies with her productions, the grounds would be laid for taking away from the Colonies the monopoly which they have of supplying the United Kingdom with sugar, and other productions.   So long as England forces the Colonies to resort to her for what they have to buy, they are entitled to demand that they should be allowed exclusively to supply England with colonial products ; but when we shall relieve them from all vexatious restraints, and allow them to resort to all the markets of the world, they will no longer have any claim to the monopoly of the British market.   When the merchants and manufacturers of England shall be deprived of the monopoly of the Colony market, we should be bound, in justice to the public, to deprive the colonists of the monopoly of the British market. It has always been admitted by the ablest defenders of the monopoly system, that one part of it could not be supported independently of the rest ; that the two branches of the monopoly must stand or fall together. Lord Sheffield says, ' The British dominions are as much entitled to the monopoly of the markets of the British West Indies, as the latter are entitled to those of the former ; and whenever that monopoly is given up, it will be the highest absurdity not to open all the British ports to foreign raw sugar [*].'

* Edinburgh Review, vol. xlii., p. 301.
The member of a city, the third in rank for its trade with the

Another most important benefit that the public at
large may derive from a really free colonial trade, is
the payment by the Colonies of the expense incurred
in supporting armies and fleets to defend them. One
of the witnesses examined before the Committee of
Finance, whose public situation made the evidence
given by him of the highest authority on this point,
said, that ' attempts have been made in all the West-
India islands to induce them to contribute to the expenses of the establishments ; and they have always
represented that their means of doing so were crippled by the commercial arrangements of the mother
country: they have said, " If you will let us trade as
we like, and collect our own custom duties, and so on,
we will do it*." '

This willingness to contribute towards the defence
of the Colonies on these conditions is declared by all
who are interested in them. The means, therefore, of
effecting a very great retrenchment in our present
expenditure is entirely in the hands of the legislature,
at no greater trouble than that of now doing what it
was the declared intention of the law of 1825 to do,
namely, establish, sincerely and thoroughly, a free
colonial trade.

If the bill brought in by the late Administration, to
increase the duties now payable on food and lumber
imported into the West Indies, shall pass into a law,

West Indies, expressed himself on this subject as follows, in the
session of 1829 :—' Let the trade on the part of foreign countries
with the West-India islands be opened upon payment of 5 per
cent. duty on all articles imported there, and then, and not till
then, would he consent to a reduction of the protecting duties on
East-India and foreign sugars.' (May 25, 1829.—Mr. Bright.)

* Evidence of Lord Palmerston, p. 146.

it will add a new obstacle in the way of colonial reform. This bill shows that if the late ministers had continued in office, all the distress suffered by the planters, and all the burdens borne by the public for the Colonies, would have continued just as they now exist. The conduct of the new ministers, with respect to adopting or abandoning this measure, will be a test how far they are more capable than their predecessors of wisely directing the financial and commercial affairs of the Colonies.

Another great benefit that will be gained by wholly getting rid of the old monopoly system, will be the removing of all difficulties in the way of forming a correct judgment upon the advantages of Colonies. The prevailing opinion, that large profits are obtained through the monopoly, has always confused the question. This opinion has been held to be so completely beyond all doubt, that the great value of Colonies has been considered as not admitting of dispute; and sufficient pains have not been taken to trace by facts in what way they are valuable. Had such an examination been properly gone into, it would have been found that neither the British public nor the Colonies have ever been benefited by the monopoly; and it would also have appeared that the possession of Colonies affords no advantages which could not be obtained by commercial intercourse with independent States.

There are only three ways that Colonies can be of any advantage, 1st, in furnishing a military force; 2d. in supplying the parent state with a revenue; 3d. in affording commercial advantages.

1. Instead of furnishing a military force, the Colonies are always a great drain upon the military

resources of the country, particularly in war, when they occupy a large portion of the army and fleet in their defence.　In the last war, while our own shores were threatened with invasion from Boulogne and Brest, our means of defence were greatly crippled by the number of troops and ships we were obliged to keep in the Colonies.

2. With respect to revenue, we have declared, by the Act of the 18 Geo. III., that we will not levy any taxes or duties in the Colonies except for their use.

3. As to commercial advantages, if the colonial trade were quite free, our commercial relations with the Colonies would resemble the intercourse we carry on with independent countries ; and, therefore, whatever advantages we can derive from them are embraced in two questions—1st. Whether our commerce with them is more beneficial than with independent countries ?　2d. Whether the capital employed in them is more beneficially employed than if employed in the United Kingdom?

With respect to the first question, it is one easily solved, because, where the employment of capital is free, the nett profit that may be obtained by the employment of it in commerce with independent countries, will always be as great as if it were employed in the colonial trade.　The trade we carry on with the United States proves this.

With respect to the second question, it is necessary to trace the operations of capital when employed in the Colonies, and when employed at home.　In the West India islands it feeds and clothes slaves ; it pays British agents, clerks, and managers ; it employs ships and sailors ; and although the gross profit upon it seems, in prosperous times, to be very high, when all the charges and risks are considered, and also the effects of competition, the nett profit is not greater than it is on capital employed at home. In point of fact, the free competition of capital makes it impossible it should be greater.

When capital is employed in the United Kingdom —for instance, on manufactures—it pays wages to English workmen, instead of buying clothes and food for slaves; it employs agents, clerks, and managers; it employs ships and sailors to import raw materials, and to export the finished goods; and the rate of nett profit on it, for the reason just given, is full as high as that on capital employed in the Colonies. The incomes derived by West India proprietors from profits on their capital are spent like incomes derived from rent, and add nothing to the national wealth; but the profits made on capital employed in trades at home are added to capital, and thus promote the constant accumulation of it. It is clear, therefore, that, on the whole, the public derives no commercial advantage from the Colonies, which it might not have without them.

They do not even afford any advantage, as some persons suppose, by enlarging the field for the employment of capital. The capital which supplies commodities for the Colonies would still prepare commodities if the Colonies ceased to purchase them; and these commodities would find consumers—for every country contains within itself a market for all it can produce. There is, therefore, no advantage derived, under freedom of competition, from that part of the trade with a Colony which consists in supplying it with goods, since no more is gained by it than such ordinary profits of stock as would be gained if no such trade existed *.

There are still means enough for employing capital with profit at home; if new means were wanted, they would be more effectually obtained by removing restrictions on trade and revising the taxes, than by increasing the productions of the Colonies.

This general reasoning, which the free principles of trade suggest, in refutation of the imaginary advantages of Colonies, is completely borne out by the experience of facts. The history of the Colonies for many years is that of a series of loss, and of the destruction of capital; and if to the many millions of private capital which have been thus wasted, were added some hundred millions that have been raised by British taxes, and spent on account of the Colonies, the total loss to the British public of wealth, which the Colonies have occasioned, would appear to be quite enormous.

The only conditions on which it can be wise and politic for us to continue to keep colonial possessions are, that the number of them should be greatly reduced ; and that those which we retain should contribute the whole expense incurred in their government and defence. Even with such conditions, no advantage would be gained, now or at any other time, by the public at large, unless the planters should prosper and accumulate wealth, and thus add to the general stock of public wealth. It is in order to secure this object, that the public is particularly interested in giving to the Colonies the full benefit of that perfect system of free trade, which everything connected

* Mill's Principles of Political Economy, p. 70.

with colonial reform and retrenchment shows to be wise and politic.

Dr. Chalmers, in referring to the peace of 1763, says, ' The true objection to this peace was, not that we had retained too little, but that we had retained too much ;' namely, Canada, Louisiana, Florida, Grenada, Tobago, St. Vincent, Dominica, and Senegal. ' Millions,' he adds, ' of productive capital were withdrawn from the agriculture, manufactures, and trade of Great Britain, to cultivate the ceded islands in the other hemisphere: domestic occupations were obstructed, and circulation stopped, in proportion to the stock withdrawn, to the industry enfeebled, and to the ardour turned to less salutary objects*.'

In settling the conditions of the last treaty of peace, it was most unwise to retain so many of the conquered Colonies. Trinidad, Demerara, Essequibo, and Tobago, were but little advanced in cultivation : a large transfer of capital was necessary for their cultivation, and there was little or no local revenue belonging to them.

At the close of the war, the East India Company was anxious to be allowed to have the Island of Ceylon, and it is not too late to give it up to them ; but, as large sums of public money have been expended since the war in adding to its value, the Company should repay a part of them, as the condition of becoming masters of this island.

As the Cape of Good Hope and the Mauritius are of no use, except for the defence of the East India Company's possessions, the Company ought to be called on to defray all the expense of their military

* Estimate, pp. 142, 143.

protection ; and it is to be hoped that the opportunity which the expiration of the Charter of the Company will offer, will lead to an arrangement which will secure all these objects.

When peace was made in 1814, the English government wished to let Austria have the Ionian Islands ; but France would not agree to this arrangement, and, in consequence, they were placed under the exclusive protection of Great Britain, by a treaty executed at Paris in November, 1815.

Four thousand troops composed the garrisons of these islands, in 1828, with a very numerous and extravagantly paid staff. Every kind of profusion has been carried on in creating civil employments with excessive salaries. The revenue of the islands, which is raised by a very injudicious system of taxation, amounts to about 140,000*l.* But instead of its being applied, as it was promised it should be, when these islands were taken under British protection, in paying the troops and the expenses of the Civil government, it has been squandered on salaries, and every kind of local expense that the Lord President and the Secretary of State of the Colonies have thought fit to patronise, without—as the letter of the Secretary of the Treasury before referred to states —any previous communication with the Treasury.

As there is now an established government in Greece, why should this country continue to burden itself with these islands ? No reason of public policy can be urged to show they are of any kind of benefit to this country. If the opportunity of relieving the public from the great expense which these islands lead to be not now taken advantage of, it will prove that our financial affairs are still managed by the old rule of listening to interested individuals and their representations of fallacious notions of what the true interests of the country require, and not by a correct understanding of what those interests really are.

The settlement of Sierra Leone and the military posts on the west coast of Africa should be given up. The public derives no benefit from these possessions, either in a commercial or military point of view; and with respect to the slave trade, the use they are of in contributing to put it down is so questionable, as not to justify the waste of money and of human life which they occasion.

With respect to Canada, (including our other possessions on the continent of North America,) no case can be made out to show that we should not have every commercial advantage we are supposed now to have, if it were made an independent State. Neither our manufactures, foreign commerce, nor shipping, would be injured by such a measure. On the other hand, what has the nation lost by Canada? Fifty or sixty millions have already been expended; the annual charge on the British treasury is full 600,000*l.* a year; and we learn from the Second Report of the Committee of Finance, that a plan of fortifying Canada has been for two or three years in progress, which is to cost 3,000,000*l.*

While the condition of the British West Indian colonies is one of continued distress, and with respect to their Civil government and defence, a most severe burden on the finances of the mother country, the Spanish colony of Cuba, under a more successful management, of which freedom of trade is a main principle, is flourishing, and even a source of revenue to Spain. That this is the case will appear by the following quotations taken from a recent description of this colony, drawn up from Humboldt's Political and Statistical Account of Cuba :—' Fortunately the liberalized system of trade in Cuba has furnished means for more effectually aiding the mother country . . . Havanna now ranks among the first commercial ports in the world . . : A considerable number of the small proprietors cultivate their properties without the aid of slaves.   Men thus habituated to the climate— many of them natives—form an admirable supply of militia, and accordingly we find that they are organized throughout the island into mounted militia, there called *monteros ;* and in the towns they form, as well as the free coloured people, regiments of foot militia.'

. . . ' Humboldt states a remarkable fact, as to the extraordinary consumption in the island of foreign merchandise, which he determines by the excess of the quantities imported over that which is re-exported . . . The increase of agriculture and commerce has been productive of a proportional increase of revenue; this M. Humboldt states as high as one million sterling.'

' We know that after meeting all the ordinary and extraordinary disbursements, including the maintenance of very large military and naval forces, which have been successively equipped since 1810, there has been a large surplus revenue applicable to local purposes, or to the more general objects of Spain *.'

These facts form a complete illustration founded on experience of the soundness of the reasons for the plan of colonial reform which has been suggested in this chapter.

* Foreign Quarterly Review, vol. iii., p. 400.

Chapter XVI.

IRELAND.

The principal reductions which may be made in Ireland have already been mentioned. Ireland, hitherto so heavy a burden to England, will now become, if her affairs be not strangely mismanaged, a source of great financial support. Industry, and the accumulation of wealth, must have been greatly obstructed by the continued agitation of all parts of that country previous to the settling of the Catholic Question. Mr. Malthus remarks, with great force, and in terms which render his observation peculiarly applicable to Ireland, that ' among the primary and most important causes which influence the wealth of nations, must be placed those which come under the head of politics and morals. Security of property, without a certain degree of which there will be no encouragement to individual industry, depends mainly upon the political constitution of a country, the excellence of its laws, and the manner in which they are administered ; and those habits which are the most favourable to regular exertions, as well as to the general rectitude of character, and are consequently most favourable to the production and maintenance of wealth, depend chiefly upon the same causes, combined with moral and religious [instruction*.' But the law which deprived several millions of Catholics in Ireland of their civil

* Principles of Political Economy, p. 344.

rights, established that hostility to laws of all kinds
which occasioned general discontent, and that series
of outrages and insurrections which kept the whole
country in a state of constant alarm and agitation.
It placed society under such circumstances as did not
admit of the existence of security of property in that
complete degree which is essentially indispensable,
in order that industry and capital should have their
proper effects in bringing into use the natural resources of the country, and augmenting its annual
productions ; under such circumstances as did not
admit of the forming of those habits among the
people which are the most favourable to regular
exertions and general rectitude of character, and
consequently most favourable to the production and
maintenance of wealth.

Ireland is not a poor country, and her people un-
employed, because she has not had opportunities of
being a rich and industrious country ; but because her
habits have been such, that these opportunities have
been thrown away.   During thirteen years, from 1802
to 1816, the demand for all her productions was so
great, and the prices of them so high, with relation
to the cost of production, that had it not been for the
defects in her political and moral condition, she must
have become a very rich and flourishing country.
Had she possessed the same free and tolerant laws,
and the same habits, as England, Scotland, Holland,
Switzerland, and the United States, an immense accumulation of wealth would have been secured before
the fall of prices which took place subsequent to
1816.

Now, however, that the main evil is removed, security of property will be established by every sect

being free from all restraint, and feeling interested in coming forward to promote the due administration of the laws ; this will draw forth the capital, which, under all disadvantages, exists in Ireland to a very considerable amount, and lead to a rapid progress in adding to it. As the markets of England are open to all Irish productions, and as, at the same time, the cost of production is low in Ireland, the rate of profit must be high ; and therefore accumulation, with improved habits, will be very rapid.

All the duties, commercial restrictions, and vexatious Custom-house regulations, which for several years after the Union continued to fetter the intercourse between Ireland and England, having been removed, the foundations are established for rendering the settling of the Catholic Question as completely successful in promoting the prosperity of Ireland, as the most zealous advocates of it have ever anticipated*.

---

* In the year 1821, a motion was made in the House of Commons by the Author of this work, for a Committee to inquire into the commercial intercourse between Great Britain and Ireland ; when he proposed the following measures : 1. The repeal of the Union protecting duties. 2. The repeal of the countervailing duties. 3. The placing the trade on the footing of a coasting trade. 4. The reduction of port charges. 5. The assimilation of the currency of Ireland to that of Great Britain*. Commissioners were appointed to inquire into these measures, and on their recommendation they have all been adopted. It is worthy of remark, that the great value of giving to Ireland the full benefit of the English markets, which these measures accomplished, is never noticed in the speeches and writings of those persons who, of late, have taken the lead as advocates of the interests of Ireland. This, perhaps, may be, in some degree, attributed to negligence on their part, in not having deeply studied the causes which contribute to the increase of the individual

* See Hansard's Debates, vol. v., p. 459.

Accounts are given in the Appendix which place the fact beyond all doubt, of the great progress that Ireland has made since the Union in agriculture, manufactures, and commerce *.

It may still, however, be a long time before the condition of the labouring class will become much better than it now is, notwithstanding a great increase of capital and of employment may take place. What the Rev. Mr. Howlett says concerning the labouring class of England, in his pamphlet on the poor laws, published in 1788, seems to be applicable to the present state of that class in Ireland. He describes the labourers of England as suffering greatly

comforts and the general wealth of nations. But as the discussing of questions of political economy in Ireland seems to have taken the place of the discussing of the Catholic Question, it is not likely that this defect will be of long continuance. Every speech at public meetings, every pamphlet and every newspaper, abounds with observations on the several matters which belong to the science of political economy ; such as the employment of labour, wages, population, the accumulation of capital, profits, demand and supply, production, consumption of articles of luxury, pecuniary remittances, and all things connected with the improvement of agriculture, manufactures, and commerce. The effect of this change in the habits of the well-informed portion of society in Ireland, is already visible in the evidence given by the witnesses from Ireland, before the Poor Law Committee of last session. This evidence is very superior to that given by the same class of witnesses before any former Committee, and for the most part in strict accordance with the principles of the most approved writers on political economy. There can, therefore, be no doubt, that the energy and natural ability with which the subjects just mentioned will continue to be discussed, will gradually lead to the more severe studying, in Ireland, of the science of political economy, and, in the end, to the general application of it to all matters of domestic policy in that country.

* See Appendix, No. VIII.

in the last century from wages not keeping pace with the price of food; the country, he observes, was advancing, but the population outstripped the demand. He says, ' there may be a constant and greatly-increasing demand for labour, and yet such may be the increase of people, and such the abridgement and facilitation of labour itself, that the price of it may make very slow, if any advances at all. This, in a great measure, seems to have been the case with us. So great has been the increase of our people, that the price of the workmanship has been little advanced, there being generally hands in abundance to perform it, and the master having, as it were, the choice of whom he should employ.'

The nett revenue now paid by Ireland is 3,700,000*l.*, but to this should be added about 300,000*l.* for duties paid in England, as foreign articles exported from thence to Ireland, making the actual revenue about 4,000,000*l.* If the population of Ireland be taken at 8,000,000, the amount paid by each individual will, on an average, be 10*s.* The revenue paid in Great Britain is at the rate of 60*s.* a head. If the improvement of Ireland shall so far increase its wealth as to make the revenue, received from the same taxes as those which now exist, amount to one-third of what is paid in Great Britain, the contribution of Ireland to the general revenue of the United Kingdom will be greater than it now is by a sum equal to her whole present revenue.

CHAPTER XVII.

SUMMARY OF RETRENCHMENT.

HAVING now gone through the principal heads of the public expenditure, it remains only to make a summary of the reductions which have been suggested.

As the only object of this publication is to show the expediency of reducing certain taxes, and the practicability of making retrenchment, the manner and time of carrying these measures into operation is left for others to settle. It is by no means intended or expected that all that has been proposed, under the conviction of the benefit which would be conferred on the public, should or could be immediately adopted. What is stated, therefore, as practicable in the way of retrenchment, is not to be taken as the proposing of a plan for carrying into effect any hasty or crude reform, but merely as the result of a careful consideration of all the facts of the case.

The following are the reductions of expense which have been suggested in the preceding pages.

I. Linen Bounties, 200,000*l.** Management of Debt, 270,000*l.* Lord Lieutenant of Ireland, 100,000*l.* Irish Miscellaneous Services, 150,000*l.* Slave Trade, 350,000*l.*†

* The Bounties on Fisheries ceased last April. The Bounty on Sugar exported is considered, by many very intelligent persons, to cost the country at least 100,000*l.* a year.

† The Bounty was reduced in the last session to 5*l.* for each Slave captured.

II. Under the collection of revenue, the greater part of 7 or 800,000*l.* a year, which is expended in attempting to suppress smuggling, would be saved by the proposed reduction of taxes; other expenses might be considerably reduced, so as further to save at least half a million a year; and if the system of drawbacks were abolished, half a million more would probably be saved.

III. What might be saved under the heads of the Management of the Expenditure and Civil Government, would amount to several hundred thousand pounds a year, if salaries were reduced, and the mode of conducting business revised and methodized.

IV. With respect to the military and naval expenditure, if no greater force were kept up either for the army, ordnance, or navy, than is really necessary; if the whole system of our military management of the Colonies were reformed; and if the half-pay and pensions were examined and put on a proper footing, 12 or 13,000,000*l.* a year, instead of 16,000,000*l.*, would be sufficient for this branch of the public expenditure. There are no other means but by saving here, or by laying on a property tax, of largely reducing the taxes.

V. If one million a year were applied in converting perpetual annuities into annuities for ninety-nine years, as a fixed plan of a Sinking Fund, a considerable redemption of debt would be secured, and two millions might be reduced of the present Sinking Fund—supposing the revenue so productive as to yield a surplus of 3,000,000*l.*

VI. If the measures proposed for reforming the Civil Government, finances, and trade of the Colonies, were adopted, the whole of the expense now incurred upon the Civil Government of them, in consequence of the deficiency of the colonial revenues, might be saved.

In drawing up the foregoing general estimate of what reductions might be made in the public expenditure, it has not been intended to insist that positive proof has been produced of the practicability of effecting them ; all that has been attempted in these pages, is to establish a case of presumptive proof, by reasoning on probabilities founded on those facts which are within the observation of every one—to show that no circumstances exist to justify the present expensive peace establishment, and to show the practicability of making the proposed reductions. Such a case as this has certainly been made out ; and few, therefore, should hesitate to believe that the Prime Minister of this country, if, acting in every instance with a pure spirit of public virtue and real economy, he should employ the great powers his office confers on him with competent skill, unceasing perseverance, and determined courage in carrying on in every direction the work of retrenchment, would not be able to accomplish all the reductions of expense and other reformations which have been suggested. It is easy to foresee, that unless he fairly make an attempt to accomplish them on a very large scale indeed, the public will be disappointed and dissatisfied, and value as nothing subordinate schemes for effecting trifling improvements.

Chapter XVIII.

NEW TAXES.

Although no retrenchment of expense has been proposed in the foregoing statement, for which reasons of greater or less force have not been given, still as the several reductions could not be brought into operation for some time, it would not be right to depend on them only for the means of making good the revenue that would be lost by repealing taxes. The proper principle on which the proposed reduction of taxation and expenditure should be conducted is, that the securing of a sufficiency of revenue should never be a matter of doubt ; and, therefore, it is particularly desirable that whenever a measure be taken for reducing taxes on a large scale, there should, at the same time, not only be other measures for reducing expense, but also a new tax or taxes of such a nature as to make quite certain of receiving full as much revenue as will make good all that is wanted for the public service.

In selecting a new tax of such a kind as will produce sufficient revenue to allow a very large reduction of taxes to take place, there seems to be but one opinion with respect to what tax that ought to be. Persons who hold the most opposite doctrines on the subject of our financial, commercial, and agricultural difficulties, in suggesting remedies, have made an Income Tax a part of them. Such a tax, if fixed at about one and a half or two per cent., would probably yield 3,000,000*l.* a year ; for though ten per cent. in 1814 yielded not quite 14,000,000*l.*, it is reasonable to assume that the progress of national wealth in the United Kingdom since that year would render a tax of two per cent. as productive as just stated. Although the rent of land may have been diminished, the rents now received from houses built since the peace, and the dividends from money invested in docks, canals, railways, &c., must have added very considerably to the national income.

If taxes were reduced, and monopolies and protections abolished in the way they ought to be, those who would have to pay an Income Tax would not pay much more out of their incomes than they now pay for high prices arising from existing taxation and monopoly.

Mr. Huskisson, in the last session (March 18, 1830), made the following observations, when speaking of an income tax.

' Now, Sir, I come to another question, and I am well aware that, in arriving at it, I am treading upon tender ground. I am well aware how many prejudices I shall have to encounter, and how many views of interest, erroneous views I shall call them, I shall have to contend with. But I feel so strongly that the situation of the country requires that I should state honestly and fairly, as an independent Member of Parliament, those views and opinions which I have long entertained, that I should be unworthy of the situation which I occupy, if I allowed myself to be deterred from stating, in respect to them, that which I believe to be the truth. I must say that after the best consideration which I have been able to bestow upon the subject, I still entertain strong

doubts, whether, after all this remission of taxation
(to the amount of 3,800,000*l.*), there will not still
remain a necessity of affording relief to those now
unfructifying capitals which are so immediately and
essentially the support of our productive industry.
If this shall be found to be hereafter the case, such
relief can only be administered by transferring the
burden from that class whose capital is employed in
promoting the active industry of the country, to that
class of incomes which is not derived from manufactures and commerce, and which is not so immediately
conducive to the maintenance and promotion of that
industry*.'

What has been said in the foregoing pages concerning the means of making good the revenue
which would be lost by reducing taxes, namely,—1.
by increased consumption; 2. by retrenchment, and
3. by an Income Tax; makes it clear that it is practicable to carry into effect a great part of the reform
of taxation which has been proposed. If an Income
Tax were imposed, and if, at the same time, government make those retrenchments which it has the
power of making without any difficulty, a reduction
of some millions of taxes might be attempted in the
first year; and if the business of retrenchment were
steadily and vigorously persevered in, a farther reduction of one or two millions of taxes might be effected
in each subsequent year, till the whole plan of reform
would be carried into execution†.

* Mirror of Parliament, Sess. 1830, p. 885.
† That there are other ways of imposing new taxes, appears
from the following extract taken from the pamphlet of Mr.
Humphreys. 'We have seen, that the stamp duties charged
on real and personal estates, though about equal in amount,

If, in addition to this reform of the taxes, all
monopolies and protections were abolished, the condition of every class of society, with respect to pecuniary impositions for the public service, would be
greatly improved. There would be less money, to
the amount of at least twenty millions a year, paid for
taxes and for protecting prices ; the prices of all
things would be greatly reduced ; the cost of production would be considerably diminished in manufactures ; the rate of profit on capital would be raised ;
the employment of capital and labour would be
greatly extended ; the interests of agriculture, manufactures, and foreign commerce, would be strength-

affect totally different transactions regarding them. Thus, on
the one hand, land is not charged with any duties on the following occurrences :—1. Settlements ; 2. Devises ; 3. Succession on intestacy, although personalty is charged to the
amount of nearly 2,000,000*l.* under these different articles. On
the other hand, personal estate, or at least the most important
part of it in this country—namely, the Public Funds, Bank and
East India stock,—is not charged with any duties on sale,
while these form an item among taxes on land amounting, after
making allowances for mortgages, to about 1,800,000*l.* Let,
then, each of the foregoing classes of real and personal property
be charged with the stamp duties from which it is at present
free, but which are borne by the other of them, and an additional revenue will be produced of about 3,500,000*l.* collected at
the smallest expense with a machinery already established, and
either included on the transaction, as on sales, or paid with
alacrity by those who at the same instant succeed to the property.'

Mr. Humphreys further says, that some of the scales of duties
on sales of land and mortgages require a more equitable adjustment ; that the duties on probates and wills should be gra-
duated by an equal per centage ; and that corporations aggregate need some special provision to subject them to a charge
corresponding to a succession tax of whatever description.
—Pp. 12, 13.

ened and advanced ; the accumulating force of acquiring new national wealth would be increased, and, if peace should continue, the sources of taxation would be so enlarged, that the practicability would be established of carrying on new wars without adding to the debt, and wholly by war taxes.   In this way all financial difficulty would be got rid of.

Chapter XIX.

THE NATIONAL DEBT.

The Fourth Report of the Committee of Finance contains the following account of the amount of the Funded Debt:—

Capital of Debt unredeemed	£777,476,890
Long Annuities	1,331,458
Imperial and Exchequer Annuities	67,718
Life Annuities	617,537
Annuity payable to the Bank	585,740*

As the great amount of the debt has produced a very general opinion that England cannot embark in new wars without destroying her trade and manufactures, and without so exhausting the resources of taxation as to incur the calamity of national bankruptcy, it is important to make some remarks on the funding system, by which the debt has been created, and to trace its effects on the industry, wealth, and power of the state.

It is now, while we are at peace, that it is proper to make those investigations which are necessary to enable us to form correct opinions respecting the injury which the debt has already occasioned ; and respecting the probable injury which will be the result of making additions to it. This opportunity ought not to be neglected for considering these questions, and for digesting and maturing those measures which, after a full examination of the financial circumstances of the nation, may appear most fit to be adopted.

* 4th Rep. Com. Fin. 1828; App. No. 17, p. 124.

But before going into this subject, a few remarks will be made to explain what the extent of the evil is which the debt has produced.

After the capital of individuals gets into the hands of Government in the shape of a loan, it is immediately paid away in purchasing stores, provisions, or in providing the instruments and materials of war; —that is, on perishable commodities. So that, at the end of a year, or at most a few months more, ' it is turned away from serving in the function of capital to serve in that of revenue, and is spent and wasted without even the hope of any future reproduction*.'

If the capital which, from time to time, has been contributed to loans, had not been so applied, it would still be in existence, and it would have been employed in carrying on some trade, with the ordinary rate of profit; so that it would, every year, have been augmented. The debt, therefore, has not only diminished the wealth of the nation, by the actual amount of the capital subscribed to it, but by the amount also of the accumulation of new capital, which would have followed from the lost capital being productively employed.

This is the great evil which has arisen from the funding system; and had it not been for the wonderful energies of the country in accumulating new capital to replace the immense amount that has been extinguished, poverty and ruin must have been the result†.

---

* Wealth of Nations, vol. iv. p. 30. Mr. M'Culloch's edition.

† ' The increased exertion and parsimony which were produced by the taxes during the war, make it extremely doubtful whether the capital of the country would have been materially greater than it is, had the general tranquillity been maintained from 1793 to the present time.'—See Wealth of Nations, vol. ii., p. 120, note of the Editor.

The next circumstance to be noticed, as arising from the debt, is the taxation which becomes indispensable, in order to provide the interest payable upon it.

Mr. Ricardo, in his work on The Principles of Political Economy, makes the following remarks upon the expediency of maintaining, in this respect, the credit and character of the nation. He says, ' Justice and good faith demand that the interest of the national debt should continue to be paid, and that those who have advanced their capitals for the general benefit, should not be required to forego their equitable claims on the plea of expediency. But, independently of this consideration, it is by no means certain that political utility would gain anything by the sacrifice of political integrity ; it does by no means follow, that the party exonerated from the payment of the interest of the national debt, would employ it more productively than those to whom indisputably it is due. By cancelling the national debt, one man's income might be raised from 1000*l.* to 1500*l.*, but another man's would be lowered from 1500*l.* to 1000*l.* These two men's income now amount to 2500*l.*,—they would amount to no more.' Mr. Ricardo further says, ' It is error and delusion to suppose, that a real national difficulty could be removed, by shifting it from the shoulders of one class of the community, who justly ought to bear it, to the shoulders of another class, who, upon every principle of equity, ought to bear no more than their share*.'

The annual charge for the debt is 28,372,142*l.*†
The raising of this sum by taxes has quite a different

---

* 3d Edition, p. 285.
† 4th Rep. Com. Fin., App. No. 17, p. 125.

effect upon the national wealth from that which has
been explained to be the effect of loans.   In the case
of taxes laid on for paying interest, instead of capital
being contributed, which is spent and lost, a portion
of the revenue or income of one set of persons is
taken, and paid over to another set, in the shape of
dividends.   There is, therefore, no positive diminution
of the national wealth occasioned by this operation;
and the paying of 28,000,000l. a year in dividends
is, in point of fact, a transfer of so much money from
the pockets of one part of the public into the pockets
of another part of it; so, on the other hand, no public
benefit would be derived by a forcible reduction of the
dividends.   And if the taxes for paying the dividends
did not fall on the materials of industry, on manufactures, or on food, the principal injury they would
occasion would consist in the expense and vexation
attending the collecting of them.   As a large amount,
however, of the existing taxes is of this description,
the debt is justly considered as a heavy burden on the
industry of the country.

If the facility with which money may be obtained
were the only circumstance to be attended to, there is
no question that the borrowing system is the best.
But other considerations should not be overlooked.
Those who are the advocates of this system seem not
to have taken any very comprehensive view of its different bearings and incidents.   They ought, however,
to extend their observations to the remote effects of
it, and trace its permanent and ultimate influence.
Our present situation, in consequence of the extent to
which taxation has been carried, for providing the
interest of the debt, ought to remove all doubts concerning its destructive character; for we certainly are

less able than we ought to be to resist whatever attacks may be made on our freedom and independence, as well as to interfere with decisive effect in defence of the liberties of others*.

On the other hand, the public derives some advantage from the debt, for it serves to promote the accumulation of capital by affording, with very little trouble or expense, the opportunity of investing money in stock with the certainty of receiving the interest upon it on a fixed day, and with the power of getting immediate possession of the principal whenever it may be wanted; but a fourth or a fifth part of our debt would be quite large enough for this purpose.

Although the immense efforts that have been successfully made in the last forty years to extend industry and increase production, particularly by the use of machinery, have in a great measure counteracted the evils of the funding system—in the long run, if the expenses of future wars be provided by loans, and if each war add some hundred of millions to the debt, and some ten or fifteen millions of permanent taxes to those we now have, no new efforts to extend industry and production will be able to counteract the effects of the kind of taxes which will, under such circumstances, be imposed. There must be a limit somewhere to taxation, beyond which, if it be carried, national decay will follow; and surely a debt of nearly 800,000,000*l.*, requiring 28,000,000*l.* of taxes for interest, must have brought the country a long way in the course of approximating to that limit.

* See note, Wealth of Nations, vol. iv., p. 561, &c.

CHAPTER XX.

FUTURE WAR EXPENDITURE.

SEEING what the amount of the debt is, or rather of the taxes for paying the interest on it, and what the consequences will be of new loans, the only conclusion to be come to on the whole case is, that the security and stability of the British empire depend on so managing the finances, that the whole expense of future wars may be provided for by war taxes.

In order to accomplish this, the principal measure to be adopted is to reduce the peace establishment; for if three, four, or more millions were reduced, these would be so many available millions in the possession of the public as resources for war expenditure.

With respect to the practicability of providing for war expenditure, by war taxes, if the reforms with respect to taxation and retrenchment, which have been proposed, were only in part adopted, the country would certainly be in a state to pay, within the year, all the expenses of a war conducted with proper economy.

The great expense which has been incurred, during the peace, upon the Army, Navy, and Ordnance, and the efficient manner in which the money has been applied in placing these services in a high state of preparation for war, should enable us to go to war without a very great additional expense.

There is now expended about 16,000,000*l.* annually on the Army, Navy, and Ordnance, of which

11,000,000*l.* is effective expenditure. In looking back to the annual expenditure in the last war, it appears that in 1798, when our fleets and armies were very numerous, and actively employed, the war expenditure may be taken at 23,000,000*l.* If, then, 30,000,000*l.* should be the annual expenditure in a new war, 19,000,000*l.* would be wanting in addition to the 11,000,000*l.* now expended.

As the Property Tax, and the half of the Assessed Taxes which have been repealed, yielded a revenue of 18,000,000*l.*, if no more than 19,000,000*l.* were required in addition to our present expenditure, there ought to be no difficulty in raising it ; for a Property-Tax of ten per cent., throughout the United Kingdom, should now yield a much larger revenue than it did in 1815, in consequence of the increased wealth of the nation since that time, notwithstanding the reduction of rents which has taken place.

If an Income Tax of ten per cent. should not produce sufficient revenue for all the war expenditure, it would be much better to make it twelve, or even fifteen per cent., than to raise money by loans, or to re-impose the high assessed taxes which were levied last war; for these would interfere with trade and industry much more than a higher rate of Income Tax.

As an Income Tax would chiefly fall on rent, tithes, interest money, and dividends, the large revenue which it would yield, from the moment it was imposed, would not be accompanied by any shock to industry ; it would produce no interruption to the usual operations of manufactures and trade ; it would not diminish the amount of capital employed on them, nor of the wages paid to the workmen ; nor would it have any influence in raising the prices of goods ;

and, consequently, it could not much diminish the market for them.   There is not, in point of fact, any foundation for the opinion which some persons are known to maintain, that the laying on of a large amount of war taxes would produce an enormous derangement of industry, and that war taxation would throw the country into more difficulty than loans. The heavy war taxes of 1798 produced no such derangement or difficulty.

But, in order to carry into effect a plan for avoiding the necessity of having recourse to loans in a new war, with any chance of success, some preparation is indispensable while we are in a state of peace. In the first place, a moderate Income Tax should be imposed, as has already been suggested, as a foundation to raise, in the first year of war, a full year's produce at an increased per centage; for, if no preparation be made, when war shall happen everything will be in confusion, and all money matters under great embarrassment.   There will be no time for deliberation; everything will be done in a hurry; every kind of expedient will be adopted that promises the means of overcoming the difficulty of the moment; and as the raising of money by loans will appear to divest the war of its chief privations and hardships, this will be, in all probability, under such circumstances, the course adopted.

Another indispensable measure of preparation for conducting the finances during war without loans, is the getting rid of the greater part of the unfunded debt.

The amount of Exchequer Bills issued and unprovided for is about 25,000,000*l.*

The only advantage the public derives from having

so much of its debt due upon Exchequer Bills, consists in the interest on them being lower than the interest would be on the same sum, if converted into stock. The annual saving may be estimated at 300,000*l*. But against this advantage, the following disadvantages are to be set:—

1. Whenever public or commercial credit receives a shock, Exchequer Bills come to a discount, and payments may be made in them to Government for taxes, or other purposes, just at the time when the revenue is most likely to be deficient. In the week ending September 4, 1830, the premium fell from 70*s*. to 50*s*., and it is now (Dec. 1830) at from 17*s*. to 19*s*.

2. The existence of a large unfunded debt at the commencement of a war, would deprive the Government of the advantage of being able to raise money on Exchequer Bills until the war taxes should become productive ; or, in case of a loan being unavoidable, it would take from the Government the only resource by which combinations of loan-contractors can be defeated.

3. As the Government deal chiefly with the Bank of England in disposing of Exchequer Bills, the capital of the Bank is vested in them to a very large amount, instead of being employed in discounts, and thus kept at the command of the Bank, so as to be available whenever a run may take place for gold. As long as this is the case, the currency is not settled or safe, nor the public free from being exposed to the evil of a renewed suspension of cash payments.

For these reasons, therefore, the loss in interest which would be incurred by funding the greater part of the unfunded debt, would be amply compensated by doing away with these very great disadvantages, which are the consequences of it, and which expose the country to suffer much larger losses.

The experience of what took place with respect to loans and war-taxes in the last war, affords the strongest reasons for inducing Parliament to come to a determination to carry the principle of war-taxes to the utmost limit in a new war, sooner than raise money by loans.

A Treasury Account that was laid before the Committee of Finance, contains the facts on which this policy may be justified *. In this account there is a column, No. 3, which shews what the expenditure was in each year from 1792 to 1816, exclusive of any charge for Sinking Fund on the debt as it existed in 1792; and also exclusive of every charge on any debt contracted subsequent to 1792. So that this expenditure is what would have taken place as the expenditure of the war, if, in 1793, the Sinking Fund had been discontinued, and if no loans had been made subsequent to 1792.

Another column of this account, No. 4, has the nett revenue yielded by taxes that was paid into the Treasury in each year from 1792 to 1816.

This account shows, by a comparison of the total expenditure during the wars of 1793 and 1803, (exclusive of interest on loans borrowed subsequently to 1792, and of payments on account of the Sinking Fund,) with the total revenue paid into the Exchequer, that the excess of expenditure was no more than 172,000,000*l.*, although 509,000,000*l.* in money were borrowed†—so that the difference between 172

* See Appendix, No. IV.
† Dr. Hamilton, p. 246, 3d ed.

and 509 millions was expended in paying the interest
on the loans raised subsequently to 1792, and in
paying the Sinking Fund ; both which drains of treasure would have been prevented if war-taxes had
been imposed in 1793.

The great sums of revenue raised by war-taxes
during the war, place it almost beyond a doubt, that
if an Income Tax of five per cent. had been imposed
at the commencement of it, and if its rate per cent.
had been increased, and if such other war-taxes had
been laid on as were actually laid on, according as
the expenses of the war increased, the whole expenditure of the wars of 1793 and 1803 might have been
provided in this way without having recourse to loans.

The average war expenses for the first five years of
the war was about 20,000,000l. When, however, it
appears that the ordinary taxes, with an Income Tax
of five per cent., and other war-taxes, produced, in
1799, 19,700,000l. more than the total peace expenditure of 1790*, it is evident that the whole of this
excess might have been obtained by war-taxes.

* According to the Report of a Committee of the House of
Commons on the Public Income and Expenditure in 1791, the
following was the amount of the Expenditure in 1790 :—

Interest and Charges of the Debt . .	£10,317,972
Unfunded Debt	260,000
Civil List	898,000
Other Charges on the Consolidated Fund . .	105,385
Navy	2,000,000
Army, including Militia	1,844,153
Ordnance	375,000
Miscellaneous Services	168,668
	15,969,178
The nett Revenue paid into the Exchequer in } 1799 (See Appendix, No. IV.) was . }	35,602,544
	£19,633,366

With respect to the war of 1803, it can be made appear by the account in the Appendix, that the revenue actually paid into the Exchequer only fell short by 23,000,000*l.* of the whole expenditure of 808,500,000*l.* in that war *.

The great mistake committed by Mr. Pitt, was postponing, till 1798, the plan of war taxes. The paying of the whole expense of the war by this plan, by that time became a much more difficult task to accomplish than it was in 1793 ; because, in the interval of five years between 1792 and 1798, 110 millions (in money) had been borrowed, and taxes to the amount of 5,700,000*l.*† had been laid on and permanently mortgaged for paying the interest on this new debt ‡.

What has now been stated with respect to preparing for going to war, shows that, if preparations for war are not to be confined to soldiers and sailors, but extended to matters of finance, and the means of paying for armies and fleets, no time should be lost in adopting the following measures :—

1st. Such a revision and reform of taxes, and of commercial regulations, as shall remove all existing obstructions in the way of the extension of industry, and of the accumulation of national wealth ; so that the sources of war taxes may be increased as much as possible.

2ndly. Such a revision and reform of the public expenditure as shall carry a strict and rigid principle of retrenchment into every part of it, and reduce the peace establishment to the lowest point consistent with the public service.

---

* See Appendix, No. IV. Columns No. 3 and 4.

† Dr. Hamilton, 3d ed. p. 320.   ‡ Ib. p. 246.

3rdly. The imposing of an Income-tax of $1\frac{1}{2}$ or 2 per cent., in order that one of 10 or 12 per cent. may be brought into full operation the moment a war becomes inevitable.

4thly. The funding of at least two-thirds of the unfunded debt, according as opportunities for doing so, without injury to public credit, present themselves.

These are all measures obviously necessary to allow the natural capacity of the nation to meet, in the most effectual manner, whatever difficulties may occur. The adopting of them cannot but be attended with every kind of advantage in peace, as well as in war; and the postponing of them will be nothing short of exposing the British Empire to the most formidable difficulties, and the greatest disasters.

Chapter XXI.

LOANS IN NOMINAL CAPITAL.

The loans raised prior to the war of 1793 were obtained for the most part on stock of the same amount as the sums lent, occasionally with a small bonus arising from profits of lotteries, or of a small terminable annuity *. But, in 1793, Mr. Pitt introduced two alterations in the plan of borrowing: 1st, That of borrowing in a nominal capital. 2dly, That of receiving biddings for loans from loan-contractors. Since that time nearly all loans have been made in 3 per cent. stock. These changes have proved very injurious, in consequence of their having prevented the public from taking advantage of the fall of interest on money in diminishing the charge on the national debt.

If it were the duty of a finance minister to raise loans at the lowest possible interest for which money could be procured, he would be right in borrowing in a 3 per cent. stock, or even in one of a lower price. But other circumstances of serious importance should be attended to; for experience has fully established the fact, that whatever may, on the one hand, be gained by borrowing at the lowest rate of interest at the time of making a loan, will, on the other, fall very far short of compensating the public for the loss which will follow, from not having the power to pay off the principal in peace, when the rate of

* Dr. Hamilton, p. 245, 3d edition.

interest shall fall.   It is now evident, that the gain
which arose from savings of interest during the war,
is but very small in comparison with what the loss
has been from not being able to take advantage of
the fall in the interest of money since the peace.   If
the millions of money which were borrowed between
1792 and 1816 had been borrowed in stock bearing
5, 6, or 7 per cent. according to the rate which the
circumstances of the time of borrowing made unavoidable, the public would have since been able to
reduce the charge 1, 2, or 3 per cent. on the amount
of the sums borrowed, in consequence of the reduced
rate of interest on money.

It has been usual to suppose that the higher rate of
interest which the 5 per cent. stock bore above that of
the 3 per cent. stock, during the war, was a justification for raising loans in the latter stock: but a reference
to the actual prices of these stocks, from 1792 to
1803, will show that the annual average excess of
interest on 5 per cent. stock was no more than
12s. 6d. per cent.* ; and as the largeness of the sum

3 per Cent.		Interest.			5 per Cent.		Interest.			Difference.	
		£.	s.	d.			£.	s.	d.		s.	d.
*1793 .	72	3	17	11	.	. 106	4	14	0	.	. 16	1
1794 .	70	4	5	8	.	. 101	4	18	11	.	. 13	3
1795 .	63	4	15	2	.	. 97	5	2	11	.	. 7	9
1796 .	69	4	6	11	.	. 100	5	0	0	.	. 13	1
1797 .	54	5	11	1	.	. 81	6	3	4	.	. 12	3
1798 .	48	6	5	0	.	. 69	7	4	0	.	. 19	0
1799 .	53	5	13	2	.	. 81	6	3	4	.	. 10	2
1800 .	61	4	18	2	.	. 90	5	11	1	.	. 12	11
1801 .	60	5	0	0	.	. 93	5	7	4	.	. 7	4
1802 .	68	4	8	2	.	98	5	1	10	.	. 13	8

10)125   6

12   6

The

of which any particular stock consists, has a considerable effect in bringing down the value of it, in consequence of the greater quantity of it that will be in the market for sale, had the loans been all made in this stock, this exceeding of interest would certainly have been still less.

The case in which the disadvantage of borrowing in a nominal capital at a low rate of interest is the most striking, is when funds can be provided for paying off the loans so borrowed; and to show this, it is necessary only to refer to the loan made in 1798, when 34,000,000*l.* of 3 per cent. stock were given for 17,000,000*l.* in money: for if this loan was now to be redeemed, it would be necessary to pay 82*l.* for every 50*l.* which was actually received. The debt created between 1775 and 1816, amounted in money to 417,851,817*l.* The capital that was funded amounted to 589,086,226*l.* Supposing, therefore, the 3 per cent. stock were to be at par, and that this debt were then to be redeemed, the public would sustain a loss of 171,234,449*l.* *

Although the system of borrowing on an advance of capital at a low nominal interest is now universally allowed to be wrong, an opinion prevails that Government could not obtain loans of large amount in any other way; but if the motives which induce persons to lend money are examined, there will appear to be no foundation for this opinion.

The prices of the 3 and 5 per cent. stocks are those in the first week of January in each year, and have been taken from a Table in Sir John Sinclair's History of the Revenue, vol. ii., p. 28. The rates of interest have been taken from Fairman on Stocks.

* Dr. Hamilton, p. 246, 3d edition.

When private individuals are the parties, four things are requisite in order to effect a loan. 1st. A party wishing to borrow. 2d. The solvency of the party. 3d. A readiness to pay the market rate of interest; and, 4th. A party possessed of money, by which he seeks to obtain a revenue by this rate of interest being secured to him. When these four circumstances occur, a loan takes place as a matter of course, because it is for the mutual benefit of both parties that it should take place.

When Government is the borrowing party, as the question of solvency is at once settled, as the security given for the loan can at all times be converted into money, and as the interest is always something more than the market rate, Government, instead of being compelled to borrow in this or that stock, ought to be able to choose its own arrangement for carrying into effect what is the real object of the lenders, though not that of the contractors, namely, the obtaining of good and well-secured interest for their money.

Although this conclusion is so self-evident, it is practically true, that for some reason or other the loan-contractors have had their own way, in having nearly all modern loans made in low 3 per cent. stock. The reason given by persons who have experience in these matters, is, that the taste of the public is for lending in a low-priced stock, and that the loan-contractors are governed by it; but this is not a true statement of the case, for the loan-contractors are governed by what is for their own peculiar benefit in making a loan, and not by the taste or interest of the subscribers to it, whom they represent; and it will be found, upon looking deeper into the matter, that the trammels in which Government has been placed are owing to the change which was made by Mr. Pitt, in 1793, in the manner of raising loans, by which loan-contractors were first made parties to the business.

The manner of transacting loans prior to 1793 was by open subscription at the Bank of England. Terms were proposed by Government, and these were arranged so as to afford the subscribers a small additional rate of interest above the market rate ; and the subscription was generally filled in a short time [*].

In 1793, Mr. Pitt introduced the plan which has since been regularly acted upon ; namely, that of the Chancellor of the Exchequer fixing the funds in which the loan is to be made, and giving public intimation that he is ready, on a certain day, to receive offers, and assign the loan, to the party who may be willing to propose the lowest terms. The consequence of this course of proceeding has necessarily been, that one individual, or one banking or mercantile firm, has become the representative of a body of subscribers willing to take the loan on certain conditions, arranged among themselves ; but the individuals making the offers have had not only the interests of the subscribers to their lists to attend to, but their own special interests as contractors : these have sprung up from their subscribing large sums, with, however, no intention of paying them, but wholly with the view of making a profit by selling their new stock immediately after they are declared to have got the loan.

Under these circumstances, it becomes the interest of the contractors to deal in 3 per cent. stock in preference to any other, because, in consequence of its

* Dr. Hamilton, p. 64, 1st edition.

large amount in the Bank-books, it is always more marketable; and hence it is, that, whatever may be the competition among these contractors, with respect to the rate of interest for which they are willing to make a loan, there is always a combination among them, founded on their mutual interests, to force Government to make it in a low-priced stock.

This scheme of raising loans by dealing with loan-contractors, adopted by Mr. Pitt in 1793, was the result of the ingenious reasoning of great monied men, plausibly impressed upon him to lead him into a plan for securing to themselves great gains ; and it is an additional instance of their ingenuity in advancing their own interests at the expense of the public, to say that, in requiring loans to be made in 3 per cent. stock, they are governed by the taste of the public for lending their money in a low-priced stock. The truth is, that those who are willing to lend their money to Government have no other object but to obtain a good rate of interest; and that, if they were allowed to subscribe to loans as formerly, the Government would be able, as formerly, to obtain loans on favourable terms, as to the rate of interest, for stock of the same denomination as that of the money actually lent.

This conclusion is borne out by the experience of the effects of the old mode of transacting loans ; for, notwithstanding they were almost all made from 1735 to the end of the American war, in real capital, the rate of interest seldom exceeded that which the price of the funds indicated as the market rate of money.

The loans raised in the seven years' war amounted to 53,000,000l., and the capital that was funded amounted to 54,230,000*l*.* The loans raised in the American war amounted to 91,763,842*l*., and the capital that was funded amounted to 115,267,993*l*.†

The history of the finances of this country since 1793, presents several instances of enormous loss, occasioned by mismanagement. A great many millions have been wasted in the following ways :— First, by the Sinking Fund of Mr. Pitt ; secondly, by raising loans in nominal capital; thirdly, by the Dead Weight Loan ; fourthly, by bad bargains for funding Exchequer Bills ; and, fifthly, by the Life Annuity scheme. No country has ever paid more dearly for the ignorance of its legislators in those things which are taught by the science of political economy ; for it is to pure ignorance, and not to any improper motives, that this immense loss of public property is to be attributed. Fortunately the force of common sense is contributing to the rapid extension of this science, in defiance of all the attempts of interested or prejudiced individuals to decry it ; and we may look forward to great practical relief from existing burdens and obstructions in finance and trade as the certain effect of its progress.

* Dr. Hamilton, p. 169, 1st edition.
† p. 246, 3d edition.

Chapter XXII.

TERMINABLE ANNUITIES.

The making of loans in Terminable Annuities has this great advantage over all other plans, that the extinction of each loan is secured for a very moderate annual charge. By this plan, time does that necessarily for the public, which, if left to Sinking Fund Schemes, might possibly never be done.

Although this plan of borrowing is accompanied with a higher rate of annual charge on the sum borrowed, than is necessary when borrowing in a perpetual annuity, this may be made very light by granting the annuity for a long period. The following extract, from Dr. Price's work on Annuities, fully explains the advantage of borrowing in Terminable Annuities, over the practice he refers to, as commonly adopted: 'It is obvious that accumulating debt so rapidly, and mortgaging posterity for eternity, in order to pay the interest of it, must, in the end, prove destructive. Rather than go on in this way, it is absolutely necessary that no money should be borrowed, except in annuities which are to terminate within a given period. Were this practised, there would be a limit beyond which the national debt could not be increased, and time would do that necessarily for the public, which, if trusted to the conductors of its affairs, would never be done. I am sensible, indeed, that the present burdens of the state would, in this case, be increased, in consequence of

the greater present interest which would be necessary
to be given for money; but I do not consider this as
an objection of any weight: for let an annuity be for
one hundred years, such an annuity is, to the present
views of man, nearly the same with an annuity for
ever; and it is also nearly the same in calculation;
its value at four per cent. being twenty-four and a
half years' purchase; and therefore, only half a year's
purchase less than the value of a perpetual annuity.
Supposing, therefore, the public able to borrow money at four per cent. on annuities for ever, it ought
not to give above 1s. 7d. per cent. more for money
borrowed for one hundred years.   But should it be
obliged to give a quarter, or a half per cent. more,
the additional burden derived from hence would not
be such as could be very sensibly felt, and the advantages arising from the necessary annihilation of the
public debt by time, would abundantly overbalance
them *.'

If all the loans which have been raised since the
beginning of the war of 1739, had been borrowed in
annuities for ninety-nine years, in eight years from
this time the extinction of them would commence,
and in eighty-four years the whole debt incurred, up
to 1815, would be extinguished; more need not be
said to prove the expediency of borrowing in Terminable Annuities.

The objection that is made to raising money by
this plan is the same as that made to borrowing in
stocks of real capital, namely, a supposed unwilling-
ness on the part of the public to lend money in any
but a low-priced perpetual stock.   This has been
shown to be an objection resting on no solid founda-

* Dr. Price on Annuities, vol. i., p. 273.

tion; and it is quite certain that if Government wished to raise loans on Terminable Annuities, it would be sure of obtaining them (after, perhaps, some difficulty in counteracting the schemes and combinations which old loan-contractors would at first enter into to thwart it) by having an open subscription, and offering a proper rate of interest, and by not being checked by the failure of the first attempts.

The mere statement of the operation of the act of 1829, for enabling the Commissioners of the Sinking Fund to give in exchange Terminable Annuities for money or Stock, proves the correctness of these observations.   From the 23d of Nov. 1829 to Dec. 18, 1830, the progress of the Terminable Annuities has been as follows:—

For Annuities for Terms of Years.

	£.	s.	d.
Money actually paid . . .	1,856,435	13	6
Money value of stock transferred	8,183,589	9	2
	£10,040,025	2	8

For Life Annuities.

	£.	s.	d.
Money taken	380,162	10	3
Money value of stock . .	432,957	10	11
	813,120	1	2
Add as above .	10,040,025	2	8
Total . .	£10,853,145	3	10

It is by making a proper use of Terminable Annuities, that the most easy and, at the same time, the most effectual means can be secured of redeeming a considerable part of the debt; and, therefore, if any

Sinking Fund be kept up, the whole of it should be applied in commuting some of the annuities for ever, of which the debt consists, into Long Annuities*.

With respect to getting rid of the present great amount of unfunded debt, nothing would be more for the public advantage than paying it off gradually by giving Long Annuities for Exchequer Bills, instead of funding them in 3 per cent. stock.

---

* See the Speeches of the Author in 1823, in the House of Commons, for an explanation of the operation of terminable annuities in redeeming debt.—Hansard's Debates, vol. viii., pp. 536, 548; and see Appendix, No. V.

Chapter XXIII.

ACCUMULATION OF CAPITAL.

THE power possessed by this country, and at all times in full activity, of annually accumulating several millions of new capital, is that peculiar property which has brought it, in defiance of all kinds of difficulties, to its present state of abundant wealth, and which will probably lead to such a further increase of wealth, as will make what now seem to be circumstances of depression and decline, when looked back upon some years hence, appear to be nothing more than groundless and frivolous apprehensions.

It has been shown in the preceding pages, 1st. That it was this power of accumulation which carried the country successfully through the financial efforts of the last war. 2dly. That since the war it has been greatly extended. 3dly. That, by adding to the national wealth, it has greatly lightened the pressure of taxation. And 4thly. It has been shown, that by taking proper measures for removing all obstructions in the way of its further extension, and for promoting its extension, the country will be in such a condition, as to wealth, that provision may be made by war taxes for the whole expenses of future wars.

Although a great many circumstances have been pointed out in considerable detail, that are great obstructions in the way of the accumulation of capital: such as the taxes on materials, on manufactures, and

on food; the protecting system, and the excessive
taxes on some principal articles of consumption;
there are, besides, other parts of our commercial
system, which are extremely injurious in diminishing
the employment of capital and labour, and which
ought to be removed: for instance, the protection
given to the shipping interest*; the usury laws; the
monopoly of the East India Company; the Bank
monopoly; and the prohibition of the exportation of
machinery.

Each of these measures prevents the capital, labour, and skill of the nation, from being as productive as they would be, if they could be freely employed.   But the manner in which this effect is
occasioned has been so fully explained in numerous
works which have recently been published, that it
would be merely to repeat what they contain to say

* The shipping interest is protected in the following ways.

1. By prohibiting the use of foreign-built ships, 6 Geo. IV.
c. 110, § 2 and 25; and by preventing any ship from continuing
to enjoy the privilege of a British ship, after the same shall have
been repaired in a foreign country, if the repairs exceed the sum
of 20l. a ton.   6 Geo. IV. c. 189, § 6.

2. By a duty of 4l. 15s. a cwt. on foreign-dressed hemp, and
a duty of only 4s. 8d. on undressed hemp.

3. By preventing more than 50,000 tons of coals, culm, and
cinders, from being brought to London by inland navigation.
45 Geo. III. c. 128.

4. By a duty of 2l. 15s. a load on European timber, and a
duty of 10s. a load on American timber.

5. By a duty of 8l. 8s. a cwt. on refined sugar when imported.

6. By duties on food and lumber imported from the United
States into the West Indies.

7. By preventing a considerable number of articles from being
imported, called enumerated goods, except in British vessels, and
by those provisions in the navigation laws which allow none but
British vessels in the Coasting and Colonial trades.

more upon the subject*. The vast importance of getting rid of every kind of impediment in the way of the accumulation of capital, points out the expediency of losing no opportunity of removing all these obstructions.

A review of all that has been suggested to be done, to place the finances and industry of the country on a proper footing, exhibits the consolatory fact, that it may be effected without any difficulty beyond that of having to contend against the importunities of those persons who are interested in the monopoly and regulating system ; for there is nothing wrong which may not be set right by the mere repeal of some erroneous legislative enactment, and, therefore, all that is wanted is to undo what has been badly done.

The statements in these pages which show what has been the quantity of foreign manufactures imported since 1825, the supposed era of free trade ; what the state is of the colonial trade, and what the existing restrictions are on shipping and navigation, when coupled with the actual state of the banking trade, of the trade with India, and of the usury laws; place beyond all doubt the fact that nothing can be more utterly groundless than the common notion that the changes, in 1825, of our commercial laws, established free trade. The arguments and conclusions, there-

* See the following works—Bentham on Usury, the Edinburgh Review, vol. xxvii., p. 339, and the Report of the Committee of the House of Commons on the Usury Laws.—'Free Trade and Colonization in India.'—'The Chinese Monopoly Examined,' by Mr. Crawford.'—The Reports of the Committee of the House of Commons, Session 1830.—' Observations on Paper Money, &c.,' by Sir Henry Parnell, Bart.—Report of Select Committee of the House of Commons on the Exportation of Machinery, Session 1825.

fore, of those persons who so confidently maintain
that the nation has been ruined by free trade, are quite
worthless, and the evils which exist must be traced to
some other cause. Those individuals who so much
fear a system of free trade, instead of assuming it to
be wrong, should attempt to refute the arguments
which are advanced to show that free trade affords
the most extensive employment of capital and labour,
and thus contributes to the greatest possible amount
of annual productions, and to the most rapid accumulation of national wealth. The advocates of it desire
to have its merits decided by the practical utility of
the principle, as illustrated by experience ; and they
fearlessly refer to the facts belonging to every branch
of trade, and to all experience, for the confirmation of
the soundness of their doctrines.

If once men were allowed to take their own way,
they would very soon, to the great advantage of
society, undeceive the world of the error of restricting
trade, and show that the passage of merchandise from
one state to another ought to be as free as air and
water. Every country should be as a general and
common fair for the sale of goods, and the individual
or nation which makes the best commodity should
find the greatest advantage. The distance and expense
of carriage are sufficient reasons for any nation's pre-
ferring its own goods to those of others, and when
these obstacles cease, the stranger is preferable to
our own countryman, otherwise domestic trade is
injured instead of being favoured. For these reasons,
trade claims liberty instead of those protections by
which it has been discouraged.

Happily, the time, if not yet arrived, is rapidly
approaching, when the desire to reduce the principles

of trade to a system of legislative superintendence, will be placed in the rank of other gone-by illusions. The removal of obstacles is all that is required of the legislature for the success of trade. It asks nothing from Government but equal protection to all subjects, the discouragement of monopoly, and a fixed standard of money. Restraints, regulation, inspection, have no success. All that is wanted is to let loose from commercial restriction, protection, and monopoly, the means the country has within itself by force of individual exertion of protecting and promoting its interests, to secure its future career in all kinds of public prosperity.

APPENDIX.

APPENDIX.

No. I.

ARTICLES,

Being Materials of Manufactures, Buildings, Ship-Building, &c. &c.

An Account of the Net Produce of the CUSTOMS DUTIES *in the United Kingdom, as stated in the Finance Accounts for the Year 1827, on each of the following Articles; and showing the Rate of Duty on each Article :—*

ARTICLES.	Net Produce in the United Kingd.			RATES OF DUTY.
Year 1827:	*l.*	*s.*	*d.*	
Annotto	1,977	16	10	Flag Annotto, 2*d.* per lb.
				Other sorts, 1*s.* per lb.
Antimony, crude	697	15	9	15*s.* per cwt.
Argol	1,123	2	6	Of British Possessions, 1*s.* per cwt.
				Of other places, 2*s.* per cwt.
Ashes, Pearl and Pot.........	5,777	13	2	Of British Possessions, free.
				Of other places, 6*s.* per cwt.
Barilla and Alkali	79,419	9	11	If not containing a greater proportion of mineral alkali than 20 per centum,
				Until the 6th Jan. 1829,.. 8*l.* 10*s.* per ton.
				From 5th Jan. 1829, to
				6th Jan. 1830......... 6*l.* 10*s.* per ton.
				From and after 5th Jan. 1830..5*l.* per ton.
				If containing a greater proportion of alkali than 20 per cent., higher rates of duty, in proportion to the amount of excess.
Bark, Oak, and Corktree	29,138	4	4	8*d.* per cwt.
Brimstone	5,243	8	1	Rough, 6*d.* per cwt.
				Refined, 6*s.* per cwt.
				In flour, 9*s.* 9*d.* per cwt.
Borax 2,737		2	3	Refined, 6*d.* per lb.
				Unrefined, 3*d.* per lb.
Bristles.....................	25,868	19	9	Dressed, 1*s.* per lb.
				Rough and in the tufts, and not sorted, 2¼*d.* per lb.
				Sorted, or arranged in colours, and not entirely rough and in tufts, 3¼*d.* per lb.
Cochineal	4,162	13	11	Of British Possessions, 2*d.* per lb.
				Of other places, 6*d.* per lb.
Cork	20,390	5	3	8*s.* per cwt.

ARTICLES.	Net Produce in the United Kingd.	RATES OF DUTY.
	l. s. d.	
Dye and Hardwoods, viz:		
Boxwood......................	2,179 1 9	Of British Possessions, 1*l.* per ton.
		Of other places, 5*l.* per ton.
Brazil and Zebra Wood	634 17 7	Brazil Wood, 5*l.* per ton.
		Zebra Wood, 2*l.* per ton.
Braziletto or Jamaica Wood	100 14 5	16*s.* 8*d.* per ton.
Camwood	479 18 8	15*s.* per ton.
Cedar Wood	4,498 6 2	Of British Possessions, 10*s.* per ton.
		Of other places, 2*l.* 10*s.* per ton.
Ebony	169 19 9	Of any British Possession, and imported directly from thence, 15*s.* per ton.
		Otherwise imported, 10*l.* per ton.
		Green Ebony, of and from any British Possession, 3*s.* per ton.
Fustic	821 14 5	From any British Possession, 3*s.* per ton.
		From other places, 4*s.* 6*d.* per ton.
Lignum Vitæ	648 8 6	Of British Possessions, 10*s.* per ton.
		Of other places, 2*l.* per ton.
Logwood	1,441 8 3	From any British Possession, 3*s.* per ton.
		From other places, 4*s.* 6*d.* per ton.
Mahogany	68,729 19 4	Of Bermuda or the Bahama Islands, and imported direct from thence, or imported direct from the Bay of Honduras, in a British ship cleared out from the port of Belize, 2*l.* 10*s.*
		From Jamaica, 4*l.* per ton.
		Otherwise imported, 7*l.* 10*s.* per ton.
Nicaragua Wood..............	1,423 7 2	15*s.* per ton.
Red or Guinea Wood	3 1 4	15*s.* per ton.
Barwood	74 3 7	7*s.* per ton.
Saunders, Red...................	97 9 5	12*s.* per ton.
Rosewood......................	7,276 5 4	10*s.* per ton.
Elephants' Teeth................	3,257 12 9	1*l.* per cwt.
Feathers for Beds	5,523 17 8	2*l.* 4*s.* per cwt.
Flax and Tow, and Codilla of Hemp and Flax..............	8,974 4 0	1*d.* per cwt.
Furs..........................	21,276 9 0	Badger, 1*s.* 6*d.* each.
		Bear, from any British Possession in America 2*s.* 6*d.* each.
		—— from other places, 4*s.* 6*d.* each.
		Beaver, from any British Possession in America, 4*d.* each.
		—— from other places, 8*d.* each.
		Cat, from any British Possession in America, 3*d.* each.
		—— from other places, 6*d.* each.
		Coney, 1*s.* per 100.
		Ermine, 8*d.* each.
		Fisher, from any British Possession in America, 6*d.* each.
		—— from other places, 1*s.* each.
		Fitch, 3*s.* 2*d.* per dozen.
		Fox, from any British Possession in America, 4*d.* each.
		—— from other places, 8*d.* each.
		Hare, 1*s.* per 100.
		Leopard, 9*s.* 6*d.* each.
		Lion, 6*s.* each.
		Martin, from any British Possession in America, 3*d.* each.
		—— from other places, 6*d.* each.
		Mink, from any British Possession in America, 2*d.* each.
		—— from other places, 4*d.* each.
		—— dressed, 2*s.* each.

ARTICLES.	Net Produce in the United Kingd.			RATES OF DUTY.
	l.	*s.*	*d.*	
Furs,—*(continued)*.				Mole, 6*d.* per doz.
				Musquash, 1*s.* per 100.
				Nutria, 12*s.* 6*d.* per 100.
				Otter, from any British Possession in America, 1*s.* each.
				—— from other places, 1*s.* 6*d.* each.
				Ounce, 7*s.* 6*d.* each.
				Panther, 9*s.* 6*d.* each.
				Raccoon, from any British Possession in America, 1*d.* each.
				—— from other places, 2*d.* each.
				Sable, 8*s.* 4*d.* each.
				Squirrel, undressed, 11*s.* 6*d.* per 100.
				—— tawed, 17*s.* 6*d.* per 100.
				—— tails 20*l.* per centum ad valorem.
				Swan, 1*s.* each.
				Tiger, 9*s.* 6*d.*
				Weasel, 4*s.* 9*d.* per 100.
				Wolf, from any British Possession in America, 1*s.* each.
				—— from other places, 2*s.* each.
				—— tawed, 17*s.* 6*d.*
				Wolvarine, from any British Possession in America, 6*d.* each.
				—— from other places, 1*s.* each.
				Unenumerated, undressed, 20*l.* per cent. ad valorem.
Galls	864	5	9	—— dressed, 75*l.* per cent. ad valorem.
Gums, viz.				5*s.* per cwt.
Animi and Copal	2,930	14	2	Rough, and in no way cleaned, 5*d.* per lb.
				Scraped, or in any way cleaned, 6*d.* per lb.
Arabic........................	9,075	1	8	From any British Possession, 6*s.* per cwt.
				From other places, 12*s.* per cwt.
Guaiacum	673	17	3	From any British Possession, 3*d.* per lb.
				From other places, 1*s.* 10*d.* per lb.
Lac, of all sorts	5,102	2	1	Cake-lac and Lac-lake, 10*l.* per cent. ad val.
				Lac-dye, Seed-lac, and Stick-lac, 5*l.* per cent. ad valorem.
				Shell-lac, 20*l.* per cent. ad valorem.
Senegal	4,601	6	8	From any British Possession, 6*s.* per cwt.
				From other places, 12*s.* per cwt.
Tragacanth..................	1,055	12	0	1*s.* per lb.
Hair, Horse........	3,199	0	6	6*d.* per cwt. after 10 August 1828.
—— Human....................	2,749	8	5	1*s.* per lb.
—— of all other sorts	922	6	3	Camels, of any British Possession, free.
				—— of other places, 1*d.* per lb.
				Cow, Ox, or Elk, 2*s.* 6*d.* per cwt.
				Goats, of any British Possession, free.
				—— of any other place, 1*d.* per lb.
				Unenumerated, 5*l.* per cent. ad valorem.
Hemp	104,473	2	9	Dressed, 4*l.* 15*s.* per cwt.
				Undressed, of any British Possession, or of New Zealand, free.
				—— of any other place, 4*s.* 8*d.* per cwt.
Hides, not tanned or dressed	26,104	18	5	Dry, of any British Possession, 2*s.* 4*d.* per cwt.
				—— of other places, 4*s.* 8*d.* per cwt.
				Wet, of any British Possession, 1*s.* 2*d.* per cwt.
				—— of other places, 2*s.* 4*d.* per cwt.
				Of the West Coast of Africa, not exceeding 14lbs. each, 2*s.* 4*d.* per cwt.
—— tanned	2,219	3	0	Horse, Ox, or Cow, tanned, and not otherwise dressed, of any British Possession, 3*d.* per lb.

ARTICLES.	Net Produce in the United Kingd.	RATES OF DUTY.
	l. s. d.	
Hides, tanned,—*(continued)*.		Horse, of other places, 6*d.* per lb.
		—— cut or trimmed, of any British Possession, 4½ per lb.
		—— of other places, 9*d.* per lb.
		Losh Hides, 1*s.* 8*d.* per lb.
		Muscovy or Russia, 15*s.* each.
Horns, Horn-tips, and pieces of Horns........................	814 10 9	2*s.* 4*d.* per cwt.
Indigo...........................	31,378 12 8	Of any British Possession, 3*d.* per lb.
		Of other places, 4*d.* per lb.
Iron, in bars, or unwrought	21,431 0 1	Of any British Possession, 3*d.* per ton.
—— of other sorts	805 5 5	Of other places, 1*l.* 10*s.* per ton.
		In rods, or drawn or hammered, less than ¾ inch square, 5*s.* per cwt.
		Cast, 10*l.* per centum, ad valorem.
		Hoops, 1*l.* 3*s.* 9*d.* per cwt.
		Old, 12*s.* per ton.
		Ore, 5*s.* per ton.
		Pig, of any British Possession, 1*s.* 3*d.* per ton.
		—— of other places, 10*s.* per ton.
		Wire, 1*l.* per cwt.
		Wrought, unenumerated, 20*l.* per centum ad valorem.
Isinglass........................	3,752 4 3	Of any British Possession, 15*s.* 10*d.* per cwt.
		Of other places, 2*l.* 7*s.* 6*d.* per cwt.
Juniper Berries.................	4,220 1 2	11*s.* 1*d.* per cwt.
Lead, Pig	32 12 3	2*l.* per ton.
——, Black	1,302 12 6	4*s.* per cwt.
Madder and Madder-root......	29,817 0 3	Madder, 6*s.* per cwt.
		Madder-root, 1*s.* 6*d.* per cwt.
Mother-of-Pearl Shells..........	502 10 9	5*l.* per centum, ad valorem.
Oil, Olive	35,767 7 5	8*l.* 8*s.* per tun.
—— Palm	12,239 11 3	2*s.* 6*d.* per cwt.
—— Train, Spermaceti & Blubber	5,934 5 9	Of British fishing, 1*s.* per ton.
		Of Foreign fishing, 26*l.* 12*s.* per ton.
—— Oker.......................	823 1 10	6*s.* 9*d.* per cwt.
Orchal and Orchelia............	685 7 1	3*s.* per cwt.
Paper	913 5 0	Brown Paper, 3*d.* per lb.
		Unenumerated Paper, 9*d.* per lb.
Pitch...........................	1,289 9 8	Of any British Possession, 9*d.* per cwt.
		Of other places, 10*d.* per cwt.
Platting of Chip and Straw	3,394 16 7	Of Bast Cane, Chip, or Horsehair, 1*l.* per lb.
		Of Straw, 17*s.* per lb.
Quicksilver.....................	4,970 3 6	6*d.* per lb.
Rags, &c. for making Paper......	2,026 11 9	5*s.* per ton.
Saltpetre.......................	4,017 8 9	6*d.* per cwt.
Seeds of all sorts (including Buck Wheat)...............	166,604 10 2	Acorns, 1*s.* per bushel.
		Aniseed, 3*l.* per cwt.
		Buck Wheat, 14*s.* per quarter until 15th July, 1828, from which date this article became subject to the Scale of Duties fixed by Act 9 Geo. IV. c. 60, as Corn.
		Burnet, 1*l.* per cwt.
		Canary, 3*l.* per cwt.
		Caraway, 1*l.* 10*s.* per cwt.
		Carrot, 9*d.* per lb.
		Clover, Lucerne, Trefoil, and Grass Seeds of all sorts, 1*l.* per cwt.
		Coriander, 15*s.* per cwt.
		Cummin, 1*l.* per cwt.
		Fennel, 9*d.* per lb.
		Fenugreek, 9*s.* 6*d.* per cwt.
		Flax and Linseed, 1*s.* per quarter.

ARTICLES.	Net Produce in the United Kingd.	RATES OF DUTY.
	l. s. d.	
Seeds of all sorts,—*(continued)*.		Forest and Garden, unenumerated, 6*d.* per lb
		Hemp, of any British Possession, 1*s.* per qr.
		—— of other places, 2*l.* per quarter.
		Leek and Onion, 1*s.* 6*d.* per lb.
		Millet, 11*s.* 6*d.* per cwt.
		Mustard, 8*s.* per bushel.
		Parsley, 1*d.* per lb.
		Peas for seed, 7*s.* 6*d.* per bushel.
		Piony, 6*d.* per lb.
		Quince, 3*s.* per lb.
		Rape, 10*s.* per last.
		Tares, 10*s.* per quarter.
		Worm, 1*s.* 6*d.* per lb.
		Unenumerated, 30*l.* per centum, ad valorem.
Shumac......................	3,515 17 2	1*s.* per cwt.
Silk, raw, waste, knubs, & husks	15,608 2 7	1*d.* per lb.
—— thrown	112,768 2 6	Not dyed, viz. Organzine and Crape, 5*s.* per lb.
		Not dyed, viz. Tram, 3*s.* per lb.
		Singles, 2*s.* per lb.
		Dyed, viz. Organzine and Crape, 6*s.* 8*d.* per lb.
		—————— Singles or Tram, 4*s.* per lb.
Skins, not being Furs..........	21,034 16 6	Calf and Kid, undressed, of any British Possession :—
		Dry, 2*s.* 4*d.* per cwt.
		Wet, 1*s.* 2*d.* per cwt.
		Of other places :
		Dry, 4*s.* 8*d.* per cwt.
		Wet, 2*s.* 4*d.* per cwt.
		Calf, tanned, and not otherwise dressed, 9*d.* per lb.
		—————————, cut or trimmed, 1*s.* 2*d.* per lb.
		——, tawed, curried, or in any way dressed, 1*s.* per lb.
		Deer, of any British Possession in America, 1*s.* per 100.
		——, of other Places, 2*d.* each.
		——, Indian, half dressed, 8*d.* each.
		——, undressed or shaved, 4*d.* each.
		Dog, 10*d.* per dozen.
		Dogfish, 5*s.* 2*d.* per dozen.
		Elk, 1*s.* each.
		Goat, 2*s.* 10*d.* per dozen.
		——, tanned, 2*l.* per dozen.
		Kid, 1*s.* 6*d.* per 100.
		——, dressed, 10*s.* per 100.
		——, dressed and dyed, or coloured, 15*s.* per 100.
		Lamb, 1*s.* 6*d.* per 100.
		———, tanned or tawed, 10*s.* per 100.
		———, tanned or tawed, and dyed or coloured, 15*s.* per 100.
		———, dressed in oil, 4*l.* per 100.
		Seal, of British taking, and direct from Newfoundland, 1*d.* each.
		——, of Foreign taking, 1*s.* each.
		——, otherwise imported, 3*d.* each.
		Sheep, 1*s.* per dozen.
		———, tanned or tawed, 2*l.* per 100.
		———, dressed in oil, 4*l.* per 100.
		Unenumerated, undressed, 20*l.* per cent., ad valorem.
		——————, tanned, &c. 75*l.* per cent., ad valorem.

ARTICLES.	Net Produce in the United Kingd.	RATES OF DUTY.
	l. s. d.	
Smalts	12,517 15 2	6*d.* per lb.
Soap, hard and soft	1,506 11 5	Of any British Possession in the East Indies: Hard, 1*l.* 8*s.* per cwt. Soft, 1*l.* 3*s.* per cwt. Of other places: Hard, 4*l.* 10*s.* per cwt. Soft, 3*l.* 11*s.* 3*d.* per cwt.
Spelter	3,190 8 0	10*s.* per cwt.
Stones, viz. Marble blocks	845 2 7	1*s.* per solid foot.
Tallow	188,557 15 3	From any British Possession not in Europe, 1*s.* per cwt. From other places, 3*s.* 2*d.* per cwt.
Tar	9,505 9 4	Of any British Possession, 12*s.* per last. Of other places, 15*s.* per last.

		Of the British Possessions in America, and imported directly from thence.			Otherwise imported.		
Timber, viz.			*l.*	*s.*	*d.*	*l.*	*s.*	*d.*
Balks and Ufers 1,096 4 0		Under 5 inches square, and under 24 feet long, per 120	3	5	0	18	2	7
		———— and 24 feet long, and upwards, per 120	4	17	6	27	0	0
Battens and Batten Ends 111,013 6 7		Five ins. square, or upwards, as Fir Timber :— Battens, 6 and not exceeding 16 feet long, and not above 2¾ inches thick, per 120	1	0	0	10	0	0
		———— exceeding 16, and not exceeding 21 feet long, and not above 2¾ inches thick, per 120	1	3	0	11	10	0
		———— exceeding 21 and not exceeding 45 feet long, or if exceeding 2¾ inches thick, per 120	2	0	0	20	0	0
		———— exceeding 45 feet long, or 2¾ inches thick, per 120	2	0	0	6 0 0 & 2*l.* 10*s.* per load.		
		Batten Ends, under 6 feet long, and not exceeding 2¾ ins. thick, per 120	0	7	6	3	0	0
		———— and exceeding 2¾ in. thick, per 120	0	15	0	6	0	0
Boards, Clap and Pipe 834 4 3		Clap Boards, per 120	0	12	4	6	2	0
		Pipe Boards, above 5¼ and not above 8 feet long, and under 8 inches square, per 120	0	19	6	9	3	0
		———— exceeding 8 feet long, and under 8 inches square, per 120	0	19	6	18	6	0
Boards, Paling, not above 1½ in. thick 352 8 2		Not exceeding 7 feet long, per 120 ..	0	5	0	2	0	0
		Exceeding 7 and not exceeding 12 feet long, per 120	0	10	0	4	0	0
Deals 634,737 18 7		Six and not above 16 feet long, and not exceeding 3¼ in. thick, per 120	2	0	0	19	0	0
		Above 16 and not above 21 feet long, and not exceeding 3¼ inches thick, per 120	2	10	0	22	0	0
		Above 21 and not above 45 feet long, and not above 3¼ in. thick, per 120	0	0	0	44	0	0
		Above 45 feet long, or above 3¾ inches thick, per 120	0	0	0	6 0 0 & 2*l.* 10*s.* per load.		

RATES OF DUTY.

ARTICLES.	Net Produce in the United Kingd. (l. s. d.)	Rate of Duty description	Of the British Possessions in America, and imported directly from thence. (l. s. d.)	Otherwise imported. (l. s. d.)
Timber, Deals,—(continued).		Six and not above 21 feet long, and exceeding 3¼ inches thick, per 120	4 0 0	—
		Exceeding 21 feet long, and not exceeding 4 inches thick, per 120....	5 0 0	—
		Exceeding 21 feet long, and not exceeding 4 inches thick, per 120 ...	10 0 0	—
		For the mines : 8 and not above 10 feet long, and not exceeding 1½ inches thick, per 120	0 0 0	8 2 6
Deal Ends, under 6 feet long	32,820 18 4	Under 6 feet long, and not exceeding 3¼ inches thick, per 120	0 15 0	6 0 0
		—— and exceeding 3¼ inches thick, per 120 ....ç................	1 10 0	12 0 0
Firewood............	2,913 5 5	The fathom, 6 ft. wide and 6 ft. high	0 0 10	0 16 0
Fir Quarters	3,520 14 2	Under 5 inches square, and under 24 feet long, per 120	3 5 0	18 2 7
		—— and 24 feet long, or upwards, per 120......................	4 17 6	27 0 0
		5 inches square, or upwards, as Fir Timber :		
Handspikes	660 15 0	Under 7 feet long, per 120..........	0 2 6	2 0 0
		7 feet long, or upwards, per 120	0 5 0	4 0 0
Knees of Oak.......	1,262 16 4	Under 5 inches square, per 120	0 2 0	0 10 0
		5 and under 8 inches square, per 120	0 15 0	4 0 0
		8 in. square, or upwards, per load ..	0 5 0	1 6 0
Lathwood..........	35,821 8 7	Under 5 feet long, per fathom......	0 15 0	4 5 0
		5 and under 8 feet long, ditto	1 5 0	6 16 0
		8 and under 12 feet long, ditto	1 5 0	10 4 0
		12 feet long, or upwards, ditto......	1 5 0	13 12 0
Masts and Spars....	21,464 16 7	Masts, Yards, and Bowsprits, viz. :		
		6 and under 8 in. in diameter, each	0 1 6	0 8 0
		8 and under 12 in. in diameter, each	0 4 0	1 2 0
		12 in. in diam., or upwards, per load	0 10 0	2 15 0
		Spars under 4 in. in diameter, and under 22 feet long, per 120.......	0 9 0	2 8 0
		—— & 22 ft. long or upwds., pr 120	0 16 0	4 5 0
		—— 4 & under 6 in. in diam., pr 120	1 15 0	9 0 0
Oak Plank..........	22,752 12 3	2 inches thick, or upwards, per load	0 15 0	4 0 0
Oars................	1,222 2 6	Per 120	0 19 6	14 19 3
Staves	50,139 5 11	Not exceeding 36 in. long, per 120..	0 2 0	1 3 0
		Above 36, and not exceeding 50 in. long, per 120	0 4 0	2 0
		Above 50, and not exceeding 60 in. long, per 120	0 6 0	3 0 0
		Above 60, and not exceeding 72 in. long, per 120...................	0 8 0	4 4 0
		Above 72 inches long, per 120......	0 10 0	4 16 0
		N.B.—Staves of the British Possessions in America, not exceeding 1½ in. thick, are chargeable with one-third part only of the above rates.		
Fir Timber, 8 inches square or upwards	575,452 4 4	Per load	0 10 0	2 15 0
Oak Timber, ditto..	30,102 9 11	Per load	0 10 0	2 15 0
Unenumerated Timber, ditto..........	7,880 0 7	Per load	0 5 0	1 8 0
Wainscot Logs, do.	13,270 14 1	Per load	0 12 0	2 15 0
Teakwood	8,690 17 4	Of any British Possession in Africa, 10s. per load. For ship-building—of the East Indies, New South Wales and Dependencies, or New Zealand—free. Otherwise imported, 1l. 10s. per load.		

ARTICLES.	Net Produce in the United Kingd.			RATES OF DUTY.
	l.	*s.*	*d.*	
Tortoiseshell, unmanufactured ..	1,673	3	0	From any British Possession, 6*d.* per lb. From other places, 2*s.* per lb.
Turmeric.........................	867	8	6	From any British Possession, 2*s.* 4*d.* per cwt. From other places, 10*s.* per cwt.
Turpentine, common............	65,566	18	1	Not of greater value than 12*s.* per cwt. 4*s.* 4*d.* per cwt.
Valonia.........................	7,058	9	4	1*s.* 6*d.* per cwt.
Verdigris	4,414	6	0	2*s.* per lb.
Vermilion.......................	299	9	4	1*s.* per lb.
Wax, Bees......................	12,596	3	4	From any British Possession, unbleached, 10*s.* per cwt. ——————— bleached, 1*l.* per cwt. From other places, unmanufactured, 3*l.* 6*s.* 6*d.* per cwt. White or manufactured, 6*l.* 3*s* 6*d.* per cwt.
Whalefins.......................	769	14	8	Of British fishing, 1*l.* per ton. Of Foreign fishing, 95*l.* per ton.
Wool, Cotton	332,355	11	11	From any British Possession, 4*d.* per cwt. From other places, 6*l.* per cent. ad valorem.
Wool, Sheep and Lambs	106,286	4	2	Of any British Possession, free. Of other places, not of the value of 1*s.* per lb., ¼*d.* per lb. ——————— of the value of 1*s.* per lb. and upwards, 1*d.* per lb. Red wool, 6*d.* per lb.
Yarn, Linen, raw...............	1,668	13	6	1*s.* per cwt.
——Mohair and Camels........	222	17	9	1*d.* per lb.
Zaffre	990	2	9	1*d.* per lb.
Acid, Boracic..................	516	7	8	4*d.* per lb.
Alum	9	9	6	17*s.* 6*d.* per cwt.
——Rock	53	4	7	11*s.* 8*d.* per cwt.
Amber, rough..................	35	7	1	1*s.* 8*d.* per lb.
Aquafortis......................				14*s.* 3*d.* per cwt.
Arsenic, white..................	156	12	9	14*s.* 3*d.* per cwt.
—— of other sorts	281	3	8	18*s.* 8*d.* per cwt.
Ashes, Soap, Weed, or Wood......	861	18	5	1*s.* 8*d.* per cwt.
Asphaltum	496	5	3	Of any British Possession, 5*d.* per lb. Of other places, 10*d.* per lb.
Bark, Extract of, for tanning	0	10	9	3*s.* per cwt.
—— not enumerated, for tanning or dyeing.....................	170	4	5	Of any British Possession, 10*l.* per cent., ad valorem. Of other places, 20*l.* per cent. ad valorem.
Basket Rods	3	16	1	3*s.* 2*d.* per bundle.
Bell-metal......................	8	10	8	1*l.* per cwt.
Bricks..........................	540	0	5	1*l.* 2*s.* 6*d.* per 1000.
Bulrushes	960	19	9	12*s.* per load of 63 bundles.
Chalk, unmanufactured............	1	11	0	20*l.* per cent. ad valorem.
Coals..........................	0	6	11	2*l.* per ton.
Cobalt.........................	287	8	4	3*d.* per lb.
Copper Ore	5	3	1	Of the British Possessions within the limits of the East India Company's Charter, 1*s.* per cwt. Of other places, 12*s.* per cwt.
—— old, for remanufacture	389	15	2	Of the British Possessions within the said limits, 9*s.* 2*d.* per cwt. Of other places, 15*s.* per cwt.
—— unwrought	0	18	9	Of the British Possessions within the said limits, 9*s.* 2*d.* per cwt. Of other places, 1*l.* 7*s.* per cwt.
Copperas, blue or green.................				5*s.* per cwt.
—— white.................	351	8	10	12*s.* per cwt.

ARTICLES.	Net Produce in the United Kingd.	RATES OF DUTY.
	l. s. d.	
Coral, in fragments	6 5 6	1*s.* per lb.
—— whole, unpolished............	2 17 1	5*s.* 6*d.* per lb.
Crystal, rough	89 13 0	20*l.* per cent. ad valorem.
Down	142 14 10	1*s.* 3*d.* per lb.
Dye and Hard woods, viz. :		
Beef-wood from N.S.W................		5*s.* per ton.
Cocus-wood	6 5 10	Of any British Possession, 3*s.* per ton.
Olive-wood	0 8 6	Of any British Possession, 12*s.* 4*d.* per ton.
		Of other places, 8*l.* 9*s.* 6*d.* per ton.
Sapan-wood	14 5 1	15*s.* per ton.
Emery stones	1,096 19 1	2*s.* per cwt.
Enamel	0 12 7	7*s.* 2*d.* per lb.
Glue	174 0 11	12*s.* per cwt.
Gypsum..........................	7 6 4	From any British Possession, 1*s.* 3*d.* per ton.
		Of other places, 1*l.* 11*s.* 8*d.* per ton.
Heath for Brushes		9*s.* 2*d.* per cwt.
Jet	0 2 0	2*s.* per lb.
Lamp-black	3 14 10	3*l.* 6*s.* 6*d.* per cwt.
Latten, black		8*s.* per cwt.
—— shaven		12*s.* per cwt.
Lead, Chromate of		2*s.* per lb.
—— Ore......................	538 3 8	1*l.* 5*s.* per ton.
—— Red.......................	2 9 7	6*s.* per cwt.
—— White	19 7 3	7*s.* per cwt.
Leaf Gold	0 8 1	3*s.* per 100 leaves.
—— Metal, not Gold..............	823 10 7	3*d.* per packet of 250 leaves.
Milboards	0 17 8	3*l.* 8*s.* 2*d.* per cwt.
Moss Rock, for Dyers' use.........	153 17 7	15*s.* per ton.
Nitre; viz. Cubic Nitre.................		6*d.* per cwt.
Nuts, Castor		From any British Possession, 6*d.* per cwt.
		From other places, 2*d.* per lb.
Oakum	490 19 9	4*s.* 9*d.* per cwt.
Oil of Cocoa Nut.................	497 9 10	2*s.* 6*d.* per cwt.
—— of Rapeseed, Linseed, & Hempseed	16 10 2	39*l.* 18*s.* per ton.
—— of Turpentine	0 8 0	8*d.* per lb.
—— of Vitrol		6*d.* per lb.
Ore, not otherwise enumerated	593 12 5	20*l.* per centum ad valorem.
Orpiment		1*l.* 8*s.* 6*d.* per cwt.
Orsedew	36 8 11	6*d.* per lb.
Parchment	0 10 0	10*s.* per dozen sheets.
Pasteboards	1 9 10	3*l.* 8*s.* 2*d.* per cwt.
Plaster of Paris	16 2 9	1*s.* per cwt.
Platina		1*s.* per oz.
—— Ore of	28 12 10	5*l.* per centum, ad valorem.
Polishing Rushes	2 13 0	20*l.* per centum, ad valorem.
Pumice Stones	290 13 6	1*l.* 13*s.* 4*d.* per ton.
Rosin.............................	8 2 3	Of the British Possessions, 3*s.* 2*d.* per cwt.
		Of other places, 4*s.* 9*d.* per cwt.
Saccharum Saturni		10*d.* per lb.
Sal Ammoniac......................		3*d.* per lb.
Scaleboards		3*l.* 8*s.* 2*d.* per cwt.
Seahorse Teeth	77 1 1	3*l.* 4*s.* per cwt.
Stones, Flint, for potters		2*s.* 6*d.* per ton.
—— for lithography	115 10 9	3*s.* per cwt.
Tarras	81 6 3	1*s.* 3*d.* per bushel.
Teasles	115 3 7	1*s.* per 1000.
Terra Japonica	6 15 4	3*s.* per cwt.
—— Sienna.....................	758 8 10	1*l.* 11*s.* 8*d.* per cwt.
—— Umbra	455 6 1	12*s.* per cwt.
Tiles.............................	8 18 2	Dutch tiles, 15*l.* per centum, ad valorem.
		Other sorts, 50*l.* per ditto ditto.
Timber, Anchor Stocks	33 12 2	Of the British Possessions in America, 10*d.* each.

ARTICLES.	Net Produce in the United Kingd.	RATES OF DUTY.
	l. s. d.	
Timber, Anchor Stocks,—*(continued).*		Of other parts, 8s. 4d. each.
Tin 1 11 3		2l. 10s. per cwt.
Varnish, unenumerated 1,895 6 8		30l. per centum ad valorem.
Vellum		7s. 2d. per skin.
Weld 20 8 7		1s. per cwt.
Woad 31 0 8		3s. per cwt.
Wool, Beaver		1s. 7d. per lb.
		Cut and combed, 4s. 9d. per lb.
——— Coney 143 3 8		2d. per lb.
——— Hares...................... 3 0 5		2d. per lb.
Yarn, Cable 0 5 9		10s. 9d. per cwt.
——— Worsted 0 18 3		6d. per lb.
		Note.—The rates of duty affixed to the various articles in this Return are those to which they are subject in Great Britain. The same rates are chargeable in Ireland in every instance, except in the case of certain descriptions of Wood; namely, Deals and Battens, the duties on which are, in Ireland, regulated by a different scale from that established in Great Britain.
Coals and Culm, coastways.... 838,508 8 5		Coals brought coastways into any port in England .. per ton .. 4s. per chaldron 6s. ——— into any port in Wales, per ton, 1s. 8d. ——— into any port in Ireland, per ton 1s. 7¼d.
Slates, coastways................39,271 1 8		If delivered by tale, various rates, from 6s. to 35s. 6d. per 1000, in proportion to the size thereof. If delivered by weight, viz.: Queen, or size rag and slab slates, 13s. per ton. Imperial or milled slates, 15s. 6d. per ton. Block slates and Westmorland rag slates, 14s. 6d. per ton. Slates not otherwise enumerated, 25l. per cent. ad valorem. Scotch slates, 7s. 6d. per 1000, or at the option of the importer, the duties above mentioned.
	4,153,070 5 9	

Inspector General's Office,⎫
  Custom House, London,⎬   **WILLIAM IRVING,**
  14 April, 1829.   ⎭

                    Inspector General of Imports and Exports.

ARTICLES,

Being Materials of Manufactures, Building, &c.

An Account of the Net Produce of the EXCISE DUTIES *in the United Kingdom, as stated in the Finance Accounts for the year* 1827, *on each of the following Articles, being Materials of Manufactures, Building, &c., showing the Rate of Duty on each Article.*

ARTICLES.	Net Produce.	RATES OF DUTY.
	l. s. d.	*s. d.*
Bricks and Tiles	368,533 14 4½	Bricks, common ....per 1000 5 10
		———— large................ „ 10 0
		———— polished .... „ 12 10
		———— ditto, exceeding 10 inches long
		and 5 wide, as paving tiles.
		Tiles, plain ....per 1000 5 8
		———— pan or ridge........... „ 12 10
		———— paving (small).........per 100 2 5
		———— ditto (large) .... „ 4 10
		———— all other ....per 1000 4 10
Hides and Skins*	386,039 19 7½	
Soap.........................	1,199,409 18 0½	Hard Soap .... per lb. 0 8
		Soft Soap .... „ 0 1¾
Starch........................	84,897 4 6	Starch........................ „ 0 8½
	2,038,885 16 6½	

Abstract of the Net Produce of the CUSTOMS *and* EXCISE DUTIES *in the United Kingdom, in the year* 1827, *upon various Articles specified in the two preceding Accounts, being Materials of Manufactures, Buildings, Ship-Building, &c.*

	l. s. d.
Customs	4,153,070 5 9
Excise	2,038,885 16 6½
	6,191,956 2 3½

Excise-Office, London,   }   J. EWBANK,
17th February, 1829.   }   General Accountant.

* Duty repealed Session 1830.

APPENDIX.—No. II.

An Account of the Quantities of the following Articles which have paid the DUTIES *of* CUSTOMS *and* EXCISE, *for Home Consumption; and the total of both; also, the total Net Amount of Revenue received on each Article, in each Year, from the Year* 1789 *to the Year* 1830 :—

TOBACCO in Great Britain and Ireland;
FOREIGN WINES in Great Britain and Ireland;
FOREIGN SPIRITS in Great Britain;
SUGAR in Great Britain;
SUGAR in Ireland;
TEA in Great Britain;
COFFEE in Great Britain; and
GLASS in Great Britain.

Also,

Similar Accounts of SPIRITS made in Ireland and Scotland, since the Year 1820.

| TOBACCO. | | | | |
| GREAT BRITAIN. | | | IRELAND. | |
Years.	Quantities retained for Home Consumption.	Net Revenue of Customs and Excise.	Quantities entered for Home Consumption.	Net Revenue of Customs and Excise.
	lbs.	l. s. d.	lbs.	l. s. d.
1789	8,152,185	408,037 4 1	2,765,441	120,704 8 4
1790	8,960,224	512,383 7 1	2,900,437	133,195 18 10
1791	9,340,875	585,966 9 1	2,549,043	117,420 0 2
1792	8,979,221	582,096 7 7	1,767,581	80,693 4 5
1793	8,617,967	547,217 14 4	5,568,857	125,844 17 1
1794	9,723,536	606,262 12 10	9,426,211	193,158 10 7
1795	10,972,368	659,969 3 4	7,874,409	215,719 9 0
1796	10,047,643	755,451 15 1	6,045,790	186,759 19 0
1797	9,822,439	813,027 16 2	8,445,555	267,721 16 4
1798	10,286,741	867,302 14 0	4,894,121	215,317 12 7
1799	10,993,113	799,369 14 2	5,876,172	288,023 4 9
1800	11,796,415	987,110 8 8	6,737,275	327,916 9 0
1801	10,514,998	923,855 3 5	6,389,754	285,482 6 4
1802	12,121,278	928,678 9 1	6,327,542	309,738 9 2
1803	12,589,570	1,028,563 16 1	5,278,511	265,944 3 4
1804	12,254,494	1,060,319 18 0	5,783,487	314,007 5 8
1805	12,656,471	1,088,821 4 5	4,158,794	302,316 8 1
1806	12,435,035	1,185,830 14 1	5,082,186	359,867 6 4
1807	12,432,994	1,336,542 17 9	4,531,049	315,417 4 3
1808	12,876,119	1,448,296 3 7	5,847,416	403,973 3 8
1809	13,054,870	1,325,154 5 7	6,497,662	451,278 19 11
1810	14,106,193	1,599,376 18 9	6,221,646	444,198 5 0
1811	14,923,243	1,701,848 8 2	6,453,024	552,082 9 9
1812	15,043,533	1,679,912 2 2	5,896,702	697,897 9 11
1813	13,648,245	Customs Records destroyed.	5,944,817	746,006 5 2
1814	10,503,917	1,581,694 12 9	4,869,304	653,708 12 11
1815	13,207,192	1,764,487 7 10	4,748,205	740,279 13 1
1816	12,815,808	2,035,109 2 8	4,732,085	750,510 7 6
1817	13,593,089	2,158,500 3 11	4,778,469	757,316 8 3
1818	13,688,437	2,173,866 19 2	4,194,041	664,183 9 1
1819	12,911,285	2,285,045 2 10	3,466,852	614,969 5 7
1820	13,016,562	2,610,972 7 9	2,582,498	516,446 2 6
1821	12,983,198	2,600,415 7 8	2,614,954	522,168 6 9
1822	12,970,566	2,599,155 15 1	3,309,072	664,016 7 4
1823	13,418,554	2,695,009 15 1	3,546,126	730,507 12 8
1824	13,083,094	2,627,955 12 6	3,749,732	750,589 5 4
1825	14,510,555	2,530,617 6 3	4,160,049	728,288 13 11
1826	13,784,370	2,077,875 14 7	3,898,647	580,893 11 0
1827	14,704,655	2,223,340 18 4	4,041,172	603,037 18 9
1828	14,540,368	2,198,142 18 2	4,013,915	595,683 4 3
1829	14,760,618	2,236,365 12 5	4,125,146	613,340 15 6

WINE.—GREAT BRITAIN.

Years.	QUANTITIES retained for Home Consumption.			NET REVENUE of CUSTOMS and EXCISE.		
	French.	Other sorts.	Total.	French.	Other sorts.	Total.
	Wine Gall.	Wine Galls.	Wine Galls.	*l.* *s.* *d.*	*l.* *s.* *d.*	*l.* *s.* *d.*
1789	234,299	5,580,366	5,814,665	36,549 10 8	684,969 8 7	721,518 19 3
1790	264,334	6,245,983	6,492,317	41,352 16 8	779,209 10 10	820,562 7 4
1791	250,839	7,407,437	7,658,276	43,417 0 8	873,351 19 9	916,769 0 5
1792	303,727	7,778,522	8,082,249	59,693 16 5	959,951 6 7	1,019,645 3 0
1793	256,160	6,634,750	6,890,910	30,308 6 8	660,377 18 6	690,686 5 2
1794	99,118	6,700,102	6,799,220	14,487 13 6	780,536 5 6	795,023 19 0
1795	118,587	6,808,534	6,927,121	55,579 4 11	1,375,143 10 2	1,430,722 15 1
1796	50,881	5,681,502	5,732,383	25,253 13 5	1,134,270 6 2	1,159,523 19 7
1797	Excess of Expts. 4,874 galls.	3,975,775	3,970,901	36,282 16 4	1,347,432 16 4	1,383,665 12 8
1798	45,367	4,715,290	4,760,657	33,247 0 11	1,339,414 5 8	1,372,661 6 7
1799	51,126	4,726,505	4,777,631	31,316 6 4	1,661,510 5 8	1,692,826 12 0
1800	83,471	7,645,400	7,728,871	42,341 16 5	1,924,871 12 0	1,967,213 8 5
1801	141,693	6,864,617	7,006,310	84,686 13 0	1,908,310 16 11	1,992,997 9 11
1802	129,280	6,226,469	6,355,749	61,514 17 2	1,870,358 2 7	1,931,872 19 9
1803	192,136	7,989,330	8,181,466	72,103 13 4	2,069,252 19 5	2,141,356 12 9
1804	21,804	4,818,915	4,840,719	34,423 7 4	1,779,899 18 1	1,814,323 5 5
1805	63,986	4,501,565	4,565,551	81,386 1 0	1,922,480 7 4	2,003,866 8 4
1806	156,002	5,780,233	5,936,235	94,813 3 5	2,225,615 8 3	2,320,428 11 8
1807	160,114	5,762,223	5,922,337	88,139 3 7	2,245,058 15 2	2,334,197 18 9
1808	186,944	6,221,590	6,408,534	126,936 11 1	2,226,800 8 0	2,353,736 12 1
1809	125,266	5,682,821	5,806,067	The net receipt of Duty on French and other descriptions of Wine cannot be separately stated for these years, in consequence of the destruction of the Customs Records by Fire.		2,361,118 18 3
1810	190,917	6,614,359	6,805,276			2,513,615 16 3
1811	63,221	5,797,653	5,860,874			2,169,871 6 3
1812	77,312	5,059,178	5,136,490			1,911,352 19 11
1813	186,747	4,531,921	4,718,568			Customs Records destroyd.
1814	36,880	4,904,783	4,941,663	73,185 5 3	1,959,655 14 1	2,032,840 19 4
1815	301,024	5,667,411	5,968,435	122,662 1 5	1,972,637 16 7	2,095,299 18 0
1816	126,625	4,294,182	4,420,807	76,046 15 0	1,534,252 10 8	1,610,299 5 8
1817	147,671	5,466,951	5,614,622	87,475 9 11	1,936,244 18 3	2,023,720 8 2
1818	266,424	5,873,066	6,139,490	155,370 0 10	2,086,010 1 9	2,241,380 2 7
1819	215,846	4,762,754	4,978,600	126,667 6 11	1,675,429 15 0	1,802,097 1 11
1820	182,175	4,837,785	5,019,960	106,892 11 1	1,711,503 10 4	1,818,396 2 5
1821	165,791	4,850,778	5,016,569	97,486 17 5	1,700,004 10 5	1,797,491 7 10
1822	177,758	4,797,401	4,975,159	104,425 1 5	1,689,588 9 9	1,794,013 11 2
1823	183,296	5,108,114	5,291,410	106,982 11 1	1,900,484 2 2	1,907,466 13 3
1824	204,901	5,274,831	5,479,732	117,202 1 8	1,850,751 12 2	1,967,953 13 10
1825	534,015	8,121,978	8,655,993	166,184 6 8	1,648,869 1 9	1,815,053 8 5
				Allowances for Stock in hand..		794,009 4 6
1826	356,846	6,023,968	6,450,814	107,292 14 2	1,162,825 7 4	1,270,118 1 6
1827	340,471	6,921,639	7,262,110	102,509 16 6	1,324,040 15 3	1,426,550 11 9
1828	451,361	7,129,264	7,580,625	136,024 9 9	1,370,098 5 7	1,506,122 15 4
1829	.. ..	.. .. ..	5,428,743 Imp. Mea.	.. .. ..	.. .. ..	1,292,463 0 0

WINE.—IRELAND.

Years.	QUANTITIES retained for Home CONSUMPTION.			NET REVENUE (CUSTOMS.)		
	French.	Other sorts.	Total.	French.	Other sorts.	Total.
	Wine Gall.	Wine Galls.	Wine Galls.	l. s. d.	l. s. d.	l. s. d.
1789	483,210	853,043	1,336,253	61,437 14 8	68,749 13 8	130,187 8 4
1790	496,034	932,895	1,428,929	63,056 1 7	75,533 11 0	138,589 12 7
1791	478,263	952,009	1,430,272	60,602 16 9	77,407 10 11	138,010 7 9
1792	443,266	896,534	1,339,800	56,540 12 6	72,569 13 0	129,110 5 6
1793	195,050	846,882	1,041,932	24,917 1 2	69,589 17 6	94,506 18 8
1794	145,799	1,228,630	1,374,429	18,614 7 4	99,224 14 11	117,839 2 3
1795	549,915	2,409,089	2,959,004	69,807 4 4	194,358 1 2	264,165 5 6
1796	64,808	1,134,321	1,199,129	10,584 5 0	118,144 4 6	128,728 9 6
1797	13,185	299,027	312,212	2,684 6 10	38,623 16 3	41,308 3 1
1798	25,930	1,532,335	1,558,265	4,679 13 7	179,809 18 11	184,489 12 6
1799	199,113	2,389,053	2,588,166	38,231 13 0	304,963 0 1	343,194 13 1
1800	12,821	1,012,011	1,024,832	5,005 5 6	152,589 7 6	157,594 13 0
1801	72,350	1,173,392	1,245,742	16,874 17 10	175,789 0 6	192,663 18 4
1802	173,452	2,006,898	2,180,350	41,696 10 8	306,503 4 1	348,199 14 9
1803	130,465	1,559,826	1,690,291	32,345 18 4	250,226 1 10	282,572 0 2
1804	123,393	1,585,117	1,708,510	31,037 16 11	296,094 16 11	327,132 13 10
1805	61,682	920,008	981,690	24,785 4 6	227,142 14 9	251,927 19 3
1806	56,551	997,428	1,053,979	21,225 3 11	232,877 3 9	254,102 7 8
1807	80,130	1,523,148	1,603,278	29,970 13 2	365,718 9 2	395,689 2 4
1808	44,226	1,145,490	1,189,716	13,894 0 9	280,842 14 0	294,736 14 9
1809	88,369	1,176,557	1,264,926	39,282 8 1	285,607 2 4	324,889 10 5
1810	64,107	956,168	1,020,275	22,958 1 0	250,013 11 7	272,971 12 7
1811	7,834	886,958	894,792	4,242 18 1	258,893 10 4	263,136 8 5
1812	100,862	792,084	892,946	45,226 8 7	232,838 18 9	278,065 7 4
1813	48,694	711,310	760,004	25,313 12 11	228,451 8 7	253,765 1 6
1814	20,294	615,843	636,137	13,070 15 11	221,665 11 4	234,736 7 3
1815	40,893	689,458	730,351	31,515 15 11	261,575 15 4	293,091 11 3
1816	22,874	416,728	439,602	13,569 6 7	153,588 15 5	167,158 2 0
1817	25,840	545,756	571,596	15,018 4 4	185,873 7 7½	200,891 11 11½
1818	45,913	596,293	642,206	26,019 19 4	199,915 11 6½	225,935 10 10½
1819	42,488	547,366	589,854	24,061 14 7	179,200 5 0	203,261 19 7
1820	12,721	495,780	508,501	7,485 18 5	161,935 7 0½	169,421 5 5½
1821	28,206	596,495	624,701	16 407 18 11	192,598 12 1	209,006 11 0
1822	25,780	543,258	569,038	14,772 4 3	174,095 16 3½	188,868 0 6½
1823	25,402	521,816	547,218	14,684 4 8	166,080 12 3½	180,764 16 11½
1824	24,022	540,507	564,529	13,779 5 3	171,379 6 1	185,158 11 4
1825	95,507	858,303	953,810	20,413 1 1¾	120,242 5 11½	140,655 7 1½
1826	65,601	766,985	822,586	16,507 13 7	138,653 18 11½	155,161 12 6½
1827	33,076	896,543	929,619	10,092 9 10	163,944 6 9½	174,036 16 7½
1828	55,596	947,628	1,003,224	16,771 5 1	177,157 5 8	193,928 10 9
1829	.. ..	.. ..	795,909 Imp. Mea.	.. .. ..	.. .. ..	181,149 1 2

BRANDY AND GENEVA IN GREAT BRITAIN.					
Years.	Quantities retained for Home Consumption.	Net Revenue of Customs and Excise.	Years.	Quantities retained for Home Consumption.	Net Revenue of Customs and Excise.
	Imperial Galls.	*l. s. d.*		Imperial Galls.	*l. s. d.*
1789	1,668,855	514,651 0 9	1810	1,788,379	1,791,768 2 4
1790	1,854,504	558,824 1 7	1811	1,107,889	1,066,605 11 7
1791	1,624,515	511,545 3 3	1812	187,413	235,106 16 0
1792	1,654,018	572,667 4 5	1813	239,208	302,766 1 4
1793	1,298,230	463,874 17 11	1814	310,841	412,534 18 4
1794	1,389,768	503,303 5 3	1815	847,052	953,204 15 8
1795	791,338	308,351 7 3	1816	761,035	859,272 0 11
1796	1,030,990	483,685 16 9	1817	739,500	835,572 0 4
1797	1,391,489	661,020 16 11	1818	644,837	727,089 19 3
1798	1,267,649	651,416 0 2	1819	889,945	1,004,868 13 3
1799	1,349,046	714,555 5 6	1820	947,931	1,071,179 11 11
1800	1,810,515	974,449 7 11	1821	1,004,073	1,135,293 12 9
1801	2,192,546	1,246,946 0 10	1822	1,090,277	1,232,397 19 7
1802	2,338,947	1,311,163 0 8	1823	1,165,888	1,318,923 19 7
1803	2,302,979	1,300,013 12 4	1824	1,316,320	1,488,293 14 11
1804	1,338,863	1,108,480 18 4	1825	1,405,036	1,584,231 13 5
1805	1,659,168	1,390,065 7 3	1826	1,540,322	1,712,052 12 5
1806	2,033,161	1,720,491 7 0	1827	1,363,977	1,528,706 4 3
1807	1,833,940	1,622,963 7 3	1828	1,370,966	1,539,226 13 3
1808	2,298,897	2,244,828 10 6	1829	1,336,751	1,500,412 14 8
1809	976,843	1,052,304 8 5			

SUGAR.

	GREAT BRITAIN.			IRELAND.	
Years.	Quantities retained for Home Consumption.	Net Revenue of Customs.		Quantities entered for Home Consumption.	Revenue of Customs.
	Cwt.	*l.* *s.* *d.*		Cwt.	Gross Revenue.
					l. *s.* *d.*
1789	1,547,109	862,632 11 11		191,748	125,431 6 1
1790	1,536,292	908,954 17 4		211,977	136,125 1 3
1791	1,403,211	1,074,903 16 5		214,168	139,443 5 5
1792	1,361,592	1,012,533 12 1		161,302	120,616 1 0
1793	1,677,097	1,316,502 14 3		196,371	148,790 6 4
1794	1,489,392	1,031,492 4 2		209,642	159,359 13 5
1795	1,336,230	949,961 16 1		227,978	171,666 12 10
1796	1,554,062	1,225,213 7 5		182,668	137,179 18 3
1797	1,273,722	1,299,744 0 7		231,233	204,464 19 8
1798	1,476,552	1,794,990 15 9		228,838	180,008 16 9
1799	2,772,538	2,321,935 16 5		263,603	233,203 5 6
1800	1,506,921	1,835,112 11 1		355,662	327,028 13 7
					Net Revenue.
1801	2,773,795	2,782,232 18 1		298,069	283,930 0 7
1802	2,250,311	2,210,801 6 11		329,150	394,261 15 5
1803	1,492,565	1,551,457 17 11		286,907	295,842 18 11
1804	2,144,369	2,458,124 18 3		313,710	381,753 10 7
1805	2,076,103	2,439,795 1 10		295,724	397,617 9 4
1806	2,801,747	3,097,590 3 6		267,805	373,039 11 4
1807	2,277,665	3,150,753 6 3		369,598	525,583 1 5
1808	2,842,813	4,177,916 3 4		437,867	582,494 19 3
				Quantities retained for Home ditto.	
1809	2,504,507	3,273,995 2 3		406,826	550,641 1 2
1810	3,489,312	3,117,330 12 9		280,253	394,185 4 5
1811	3,226,757	3,339,218 4 3		420,093	578,945 12 6
1812	2,604,019	3,939,939 17 2		445,035	629,167 5 2
1813	2,209,063	3,447,560 4 5		385,250	570,420 5 7
1814	1,997,999	3,276,513 6 5		326,052	491,010 16 6
1815	1,888,965	2,957,403 2 4		322,334	496,930 17 4
1816	2,228,156	3,166,851 18 0		301,775	445,341 9 10
1817	2,960,794	3,967,154 5 0		338,147	466,771 19 5
1818	1,457,707	2,331,472 3 5		269,189	419,634 19 6
1819	2,474,738	3,507,844 11 0		346,162	488,699 6 4
1820	2,581,256	3,477,770 11 4		320,608	447,617 5 1
1821	2,676,274	3,660,567 6 7		380,608	528,391 12 4
1822	2,618,490	3,579,412 12 1		370,567	481,031 11 4
1823	2,842,676	4,022,782 4 1		386,315	384,623 2 2
1824	2,957,261	4,223,240 18 5		410,163	418,704 4 0
1825	2,655,959	3,756,654 0 1		423,889	420,001 2 9
1826	3,255,075	4,518,690 15 9		318,915	432,307 11 1
1827	3,021,191	4,213,623 6 7		319,736	431,568 19 5
1828	3,205,843	4,576,287 13 4		315,576	426,008 16 9
1829	3,211,535	4,452,793 18 11		328,286	443,448 11 5

	TEA,—GREAT BRITAIN.		COFFEE,—GREAT BRITAIN.	
Years.	Quantities retained for Home Consumption.	Net Revenue of Customs and Excise.	Quantities retained for Home Consumption.	Net Revenue of Customs and Excise.
	lbs.	l. s. d.	lbs.	l. s. d.
1789	14,534,601	562,038 14 5	930,141	46,286 17 11
1790	14,693,299	547,230 4 8	973,110	50,799 7 4
1791	15,096,840	607,430 8 4	1,047,276	57,659 5 11
1792	15,822,045	616,775 6 9	946,666	48,825 6 2
1793	15,244,931	609,846 5 6	1,070,438	67,357 11 9
1794	16,647,963	628,081 6 5	969,512	74,430 4 6
1795	18,304,232	695,108 5 9	1,054,588	65,788 3 7
1796	18,009,922	877,042 13 0	396,593	30,048 6 11
1797	16,368,041	1,028,060 9 7	687,001	92,469 3 11
1798	19,566,934	1,111,898 9 1	697,487	78,966 6 9
1799	10,906,510	1,176,861 9 9	682,432	74,001 2 2
1800	20,358,702	1,152,262 0 0	826,590	142,867 11 5
1801	20,237,753	1,287,808 2 6	750,861	106,076 2 7
1802	21,848,245	1,450,252 7 9	829,435	72,188 2 3
1803	21,647,922	1,757,257 18 4	905,532	72,093 15 8
1804	18,501,904	2,348,004 4 8	1,061,327	151,388 0 11
1805	21,025,380	2,925,298 17 9	1,201,736	120,172 18 7
1806	20,355,038	3,098,428 13 2	1,157,014	152,759 6 9
1807	19,239,312	3,043,224 11 3	1,170,164	161,245 11 4
1808	20,859,929	3,370,610 0 10	1,069,691	229,738 16 8
1809	19,869,134	3,130,616 14 9	9,251,837	245,896 8 4
1810	19,093,244	3,212,430 1 1	5,308,096	175,567 1 4
1811	20,702,809	3,249,294 0 9	6,390,122	212,890 12 10
1812	20,018,251	3,258,793 2 9	8,118,734	255,184 7 1
1813	20,443,226	{ Customs Records destroyed. }	8,788,601	{ Customs Records destroyed. }
1814	19,224,154	3,428,236 3 4	6,324,267	213,513 18 4
1815	22,378,345	3,526,590 18 3	6,117,311	258,762 18 3
1816	20,246,144	3,956,719 0 5	7,557,471	290,834 0 11
1817	20,822,936	3,003,650 18 7	8,688,726	298,540 5 1
1818	22,660,177	3,362,588 10 1	7,967,857	250,106 4 10
1819	22,631,467	3,256,433 12 10	7,429,352	292,154 8 10
1820	22,452,050	3,123,449 17 0	6,896,286	340,223 6 7
1821	22,892,912	3,275,642 17 6	7,327,283	371,252 5 6
1822	23,911,884	3,434,292 19 10	7,404,204	374,596 19 7
1823	23,762,470	3,407,983 1 8	8,209,245	416,324 3 9
1824	23,784,338	3,420,205 11 11	7,993,040	407,544 4 8
1825	24,830,015	3,527,944 4 11	10,766,112	807,204 14 2
1826	25,238,067	3,291,813 19 5	12,724,139	824,667 11 1
1827	26,043,223	3,263,206 19 3	14,974,378	384,994 18 2
1828	*26,790,481	3,177,179 8 0	16,522,423	435,369 3 7
1829	29,495,199	3,321,722 0 0	18,906,373	484,975 10 8

* All Tea is included shipped to Ireland for consumption in that country, subsequently to the passing of the Act 9 Geo. IV., c. 44.

GLASS.—GREAT BRITAIN.

Years.	QUANTITIES of GLASS retained for Home Consumption.							Net Revenue of Customs and Excise.		
	Flint and Plate.		Broad.	Crown, or German Sheet.	Common Bottle Glass.	Plate, &c. imported.				
	Cwts.	Cwts.	Cwts.	Cwts.	Cwts.	Cwts.	Feet.	l.	s.	d.
1789	48,245	....	24,194	81,403	185,296	1,114	13,502	159,448	4	0
1790	44,527	....	21,302	81,285	215,034	1,270	11,375	160,057	11	1
1791	45,990	....	21,924	76,185	242,684	1,871	15,095	163,911	15	0
1792	51,410	....	22,214	75,610	238,127	1,358	28,004	167,966	10	6
1793	55,267	....	21,519	80,225	250,192	1,642	20,736	177,407	19	8
1794	67,615	....	20,607	83,940	227,476	2,593	223	178,958	6	0
1795	49,218	....	21,694	47,881	205,330	3,327	2,010	183,749	8	0
1796	49,166	....	26,254	53,538	165,065	2,081	10,076	176,944	8	5
1797	48,463	....	25,971	58,235	147,865	1,640	4,598	174,092	2	2
1798	49,938	....	20,621	50,790	105,096	1,313	409	156,380	6	2
1799	55,987	....	19,690	41,571	132,475	1,867	51	164,659	16	9
1800	61,748	....	19,874	55,821	159,334	2,235	1,958	188,240	3	3
1801	57,663	....	19,381	61,389	187,096	2,775	752	195,414	5	7
1802	59,483	....	20,948	67,401	199,939	2,850	267	209,740	18	2
1803	69,764	....	16,626	81,501	239,297	2,402	3,454	241,856	10	4
1804	62,656	....	12,741	68,678	223,174	1,927	567	219,979	11	8
1805	64,311	....	16,701	97,096	215,094	2,556	....	285,937	3	9
1806	59,027	....	16,224	84,949	183,832	1,561	....	316,059	1	7
1807	61,587	....	10,855	83,512	252,332	131	....	327,077	7	6
1808	64,682	....	12,145	89,544	283,498	149	....	325,565	19	7
1809	66,815	....	11,151	91,938	263,390	88	....	349,590	16	9
1810	68,872	....	9,176	69,252	252,872	120	....	318,831	19	9
1811	70,301	....	9,646	86,338	253,983	128	....	360,989	10	6
1812	60,248	....	7,010	91,881	260,664	48	....	364,686	11	11
	Flint.	Plate.								
1813	28,902	10,542	7,013	68,824	159,217	85	12	509,623	7	9
1814	32,503	9,139	8,609	60,170	139,746	110	8	425,235	2	11
1815	34,903	7,021	8,453	59,584	160,175	256	....	408,820	3	4
1816	25,959	3,641	6,140	55,502	155,595	167	....	325,963	14	0
1817	27,827	3,426	8,374	73,259	113,095	178	....	419,886	7	2
1818	33,948	7,647	8,319	83,986	200,011	223	....	548,309	10	7
1819	33,314	7,555	8,250	84,006	235,975	199	....	558,216	16	11
1820	29,437	8,822	7,782	70,253	167,208	202	....	469,609	6	11
1821	28,717	9,761	8,036	76,887	133,550	203	....	481,652	12	3
1822	28,892	9,661	8,353	83,799	149,754	294	....	506,987	6	0
1823	3,443	11,776	9,172	87,153	184,672	271	....	544,920	13	0
1824	32,568	13,564	9,300	104,489	229,134	277	....	645,172	9	6
1825	35,164	15,168	8,386	118,217	248,616	307	54	669,786	4	2
1826	45,262	12,523	8,118	98,380	248,103	341	588	622,216	7	10
1827	45,058	14,335	7,611	99,711	218,033	531	362	615,056	1	0
1828	51,063	17,071	6,956	90,603	224,864	750	1,092	602,632	6	4
1829	49,001	14,299	6,869	97,134	209,862	....	1,763	666,520	15	11

An Account of the QUANTITIES *of* SPIRITS *made in* IRELAND *and* SCOTLAND, *which have paid the Duties of Excise for Home Consumption ; stating the Rate of Duty paid; and also the Net Amount of Revenue received in each Year, since the Year* 1820.

Years.	IRELAND.		
	Number of Gallons.	Rate per Gallon.	Net Amount of Revenue.
	Imperial Measure.		*l.* *s.* *d.*
1821	2,649,170	5*s.* 6*d.* per Irish Gallon.	912,288 7 5
1822	2,326,367	. . Ditto . .	797,518 13 3
1823	3,348,505	Ditto . . From 10th October 1813, 2*s.* per English Wine Gallon.	634,460 7 2
1824	6,690,315	. . Ditto . .	771,690 16 0
1825	9,262,744	. . Ditto . .	1,084,191 6 5
1826	6,837,408	2*s.* 10*d.* per Imperial Gallon.	964,509 10 8
1827	8,260,919	. . Ditto . .	1,122,096 14 11
1828	9,937,903	. . Ditto . .	1,395,721 12 10
	SCOTLAND.		
1821	2,229,435	5*s.* 6*d.* per English Wine Gallon.	727,650 19 7
1822	2,079,556	. . Ditto . .	691,136 6 6
1823	2,232,728	Ditto . . From 10th October, 1823, 2*s.* per English Wine Gallon.	536,654 17 8
1824	4,350,301	. . Ditto . .	520,624 18 4
1825	5,981,550	. . Ditto . .	682,848 11 1
1826	3,988,788	2*s.* 10*d.* per Imperial Gallon.	563,263 4 0
1827	4,752,199	. . Ditto . .	672,441 6 6
1828	5,716,180	. . Ditto . .	809,559 6 7

APPENDIX.—No. III.

PROTECTING DUTIES.

TABLE I.

A LIST *of* ARTICLES, *of British Manufacture, not exposed to injury from Foreign competition, and of the Duties now charged upon similar Foreign Manufactures :—*

	l.	*s.*	*d.*
Brass manufacture ....per cent.....	30	0	0
Copper ditto ....do..	30	0	0
Cotton ditto ....do.........	10	0	0
Earthenware ....do.......	15	0	0
Glass (crown)..do.......	8	6	8
—— (German sheet) ....do.......	10	0	0
Hats (felt) ....each......	0	10	6
—— (chip, cane) ....dozen, from 1*l.* to 2	16	0	
—— (straw) ....ditto 3*l.* 8*s.* to 6	16	0	
Japanned ware..per cent......	20	0	0
Iron (wrought)......................................do.......	20	0	0
Lace ....do.......	30	0	0
Pewter manufacture ....do.......	20	0	0
Steel ditto..do.......	20	0	0
Tin ditto..do.......	20	0	0
Tobacco manufacture................................per lb......	0	9	6
Woollen manufacture................................per cent....	15	0	0

TABLE II.

A LIST *of* ARTICLES, *of British Manufacture, erroneously supposed to be liable to injury from Foreign competition, and of the Duties on similar Foreign Manufactures :—*

Books, being Editions printed prior to the Year 1801 ...per cwt.....	1	0	0
———, printed since 1801.................................do.......	5	0	0
———, if first composed, or written or printed in the United Kingdom, prohibited by 6 George IV. c. 107, § 52; except Books not reprinted in the United Kingdom, within Twenty Years, and Books not for sale..			
Candles, Tallow ....per cwt.....	3	3	4
————, Wax ....per lb.....	0	2	6

		l.	s.	d.
China Ware	per cent	15	0	0
Glass (Plate)	per foot, from 6s. to	0	11	0
Gloves, Men's	per dozen pair	0	5	0
——, Women's	do	0	4	0
Jewellery	per cent	20	0	0
Leather Manufactures	do	30	0	0
Linen ditto (on average)	do	40	0	0
Paper (stained)	per square yard	0	1	0
—— (waste or other)	per lb	0	0	9
—— (made of old rope)	do	0	0	3
Plate of Gold	per oz	3	16	9
—— of Silver	do	0	4	6
Silk Manufacture	per cent	30	0	0
Sugar (refined)	do	8	8	0
Spirits	per gallon	1	2	6
Watches	per cent	25	0	0

TABLE III.

A LIST *of* ARTICLES *of British Manufacture, of minor importance, and of the Duties on similar Foreign Manufactures* :—

		l.	s.	d.
Baskets	per cent	20	0	0
Blacking	per cwt	3	12	0
Boxes	per cent	20	0	0
Brocade of Gold and Silver	do	30	0	0
Buttons	do	20	0	0
Cables	per cwt	0	10	0
Candlewick	do	4	8	8
Cards (playing)	per dozen packs	4	0	0
Casks (empty)	per cent	50	0	0
Gunpowder	per cwt	3	0	0
Corks (ready made)	per lb	3	7	0
Embroidery and Needle-work	per cent	30	0	0
Furs, dressed	do	75	0	0
Haberdashery and Apparel	do	20	0	0
Instruments of Science	do	20	0	0
———— Music	do	20	0	0
Matting	do	20	0	0
Mattresses	do	20	0	0
Models	do	5	0	0
Parchment	per dozen skins	0	10	0
Pasteboard	per cwt	3	8	2
Pencils	per cent	30	0	0
Pens	do	30	0	0
Sealing-wax	do	30	0	0
Tiles	do	15	0	0
Manufactures of Hair or Goat's Wool, wholly or partly made up	do	30	0	0

	l.	s.	d.
Manufactures of Linen, made up ....per cent...	40	0	0
Ditto of Cotton or Woollen ....`....`...............do......	20	0	0
All goods being in part or wholly manufactured, and not being described in the Schedule of the Customs Duty, Act of 6 Geo. IV. c. 3 ....do.......	20	0	0

TABLE IV.

A LIST *of* ARTICLES, *being of English Manufacture, serving as prepared Materials for other Manufactures; and of the Duties on similar Foreign Manufactures :—*

	l.	s.	d.
Aquafortis ....per cwt.....	0	14	3
Copperas, White ....do.....	0	12	0
Cordage ....do.....	0	10	9
Glue ....do.......	0	12	0
Hemp, dressed.......................................do.....	4	15	0
Hides, tanned ....per lb.....	0	1	9
Ink, Printers' ....per cwt....	1	1	0
Mercury, prepared................................per cent....	30	0	0
Mill Boards ....per cwt....	3	8	2
Platting of Bast, Chip, Cane, or Horse-Hair ....per lb.....	1	0	0
Ditto of Straw ....do.......	0	17	0
Pots of Stone.......................................per cent....	30	0	0
Skins (Calf), tanned ....per lb.....	0	1	0
—— (Sheep), ditto ....per 100 skins..	2	0	0
—— Kid), ditto.....................................do.......	0	15	0
Soap, hard ....per cwt....	4	13	0
——, soft ....do.......	3	11	3
Thread ....the dozen lbs..	0	15	0
Thrown Silk ....per lb.....	0	7	6
Twine...per cwt....	1	11	0
Varnish ....per cent....	30	0	0
Verjuice ....per ton....	73	12	9
Verdigris ....per lb.....	0	2	0
Vinegar, or Acetous Acid..............................per ton....	18	18	0
Wire, Brass, or Copper ....per cwt...	2	10	0
Ditto, gilt or plated ....do........	25	0	0

APPENDIX.—No. IV.

An Account of the EXPENDITURE *during the* WARS *of* 1793 *and* 1803, *exclusive of the* INTEREST *on the* DEBT *contracted subsequent to* 1792, *and of the* REVENUE *Paid into the* EXCHEQUER.

An Account of the TOTAL CHARGE *on the* UNREDEEMED FUNDED DEBT, *and on the* UNFUNDED DEBT, *(exclusive of Sinking Fund, and of the Charge upon all Loans raised since 1792,) as it stood on the 5th Jan. 1793, and on the 5th Jan. in each subsequent year to the 5th Jan. 1816, making deductions for Annuities that fell in, in that period:—The Total Public Expenditure in the Year ending 5th Jan. 1793, and in each subsequent Year to the 5th Jan. 1816, exclusive of the Sinking Fund on the Debt due the 5th Jan. 1793, and of the Charge for any Debt, Funded or Unfunded, that was contracted subsequent to the 5th Jan. 1793:—also, The Total Net Revenue paid into the Exchequer in the year 1793, and in each subsequent year to the 5th Jan. 1816; showing the Excess, if any, of the Expenditure, or the Excess, if any, of Revenue over the Expenditure, together with the Total of Expenditure over Revenue.*

Years ending 5th January	(1) Charge of the Unredeemed Funded Debt, and on the Unfunded Debt, (exclusive of Sinking Fund, and of the charge upon all Loans raised since 1792,) as it stood on 5th Jan. 1793, and on the 5th Jan. in each subsequent Year to 5th Jan. 1816, making deductions for the Annuities that fell in in that period.	(2) Total Public Expenditure in the Year ending 5th Jan. 1793, and in each subsequent Year to the 5th Jan. 1816, exclusive of the Sinking Fund on the Debt due on the 5th Jan. 1793, and of the Charge of any Debt, Funded or Unfunded, that was contracted subsequent to the 5th Jan. 1793.	(3) TOTAL COLUMNS No. 1. and No. 2.	(4) TOTAL NET REVENUE Paid into the Exchequer in the Year 1793, and in each subsequent year to 5th January, 1816.	(5) THE EXCESS, if any, of EXPENDITURE, in Column 3, over the Revenue in Column 4.	(6) THE EXCESS, if any, of REVENUE in Column 4. over the Expenditure in Column 3.
1793	9,624,088 8 5¼	7,670,108 5 2	17,294,196 13 7¼	19,258,814 6 4¼	....	1,964,617 12 9
1794	9,623,441 5 8¾	14,759,206 15 11½	24,382,648 1 8¼	19,845,705 10 4	4,536,942 11 4¼	
1795	9,622,237 8 2	19,702,489 2 11½	29,324,726 11 1½	20,193,074 4 6½	9,131,652 6 7	
1796	9,620,466 3 1	34,300,764 17 4	43,921,231 0 5	29,883,520 13 0¾	24,037,710 7 4¼	
1797	9,618,550 15 0	45,814,275 8 11¾	55,432,826 3 11¾	21,454,728 4 5¼	33,978,097 19 6½	
1798	9,614,818 10 11½	36,202,873 13 11½	45,817,692 4 11	23,126,940 7 1	22,690,751 17 10	
1799	9,613,055 15 4½	33,279,071 18 5¾	42,892,127 13 10¼	31,035,363 2 4¼	11,856,764 11 6	
1800	9,611,668 10 8¾	38,166,697 19 7½	47,778,366 10 4½	35,602,444 8 11¼	12,175,922 1 5	
1801	9,609,884 13 5	39,074,449 13 11½	48,684,334 7 4½	34,145,584 4 1	14,538,750 3 3½	
1802	9,607,659 0 8	40,690,486 9 6¾	50,298,145 10 2¾	34,113,146 18 4¾	16,184,998 11 10	
1803	9,606,509 16 8	29,610,471 2 3¼	39,216,980 18 11¼	36,368,149 14 5	2,848,831 4 6¼	
1804	9,581,270 13 1¾	28,289,364 9 0¼	37,870,635 2 2	38,609,392 8 6	....	738,757 6 4
1805	9,580,272 3 1½	37,876,084 9 4½	47,456,356 12 6	46,176,492 19 8	1,279,863 12 10	
1806	9,548,920 6 3¼	44,765,873 0 10¾	54,314,793 7 2	50,897,706 5 10¼	3,417,087 1 3¾	
1807	9,538,508 1 7¼	45,485,499 7 0	55,024,007 8 7¼	55,796,086 8 2	....	772,078 19 6¾
1808	9,524,724 1 5½	43,970,956 9 8	53,495,680 11 1½	59,339,321 19 4¼	....	6,843,641 8 2¾
1809	9,104,238 8 7	49,821,335 7 0	58,925,573 15 7	62,498,191 9 7¾	....	3,572,617 14 0¾
1810	9,103,379 7 3	52,274,730 5 0½	61,378,109 12 3½	63,719,400 18 11	....	2,341,291 6 7½
1811	9,102,580 17 2½	52,551,395 4 3½	61,653,976 1 6	67,144,542 18 4¼	....	5,490,566 16 10¼
1812	9,101,931 10 11½	58,646,377 8 3½	67,748,308 19 2¾	65,173,545 12 8¾	2,574,763 6 6	
1813	9,101,399 7 7½	60,604,064 7 7½	69,705,463 15 3	65,037,850 1 7	4,667,613 13 8	
1814	9,100,154 8 1	77,406,919 8 6	86,507,073 16 7	68,743,363 6 3	17,758,710 10 4	
1815	9,098,917 16 4¼	76,227,766 13 10	85,326,684 15 2¼	71,134,503 2 2½	14,192,181 12 10¾	
1816	9,098,046 6 10¼	60,559,275 15 11½	69,657,322 2 9¾	72,210,512 15 7¼	....	2,553,090 12 9½
	226,356,723 16 8¾	1,027,750,537 19 9	1,254,107,261 16 5¾	1,081,513,382 0 10	195,870,641 12 11¼	23,276,761 17 2½
			Deduct Excess of Revenue..........		23,276,761 17 2½	
			Excess of Expenditure over Revenue.		172,593,879 15 7¾	

Whitehall, Treasury Chambers,
5th May, 1828.

GEO. R. DAWSON.

APPENDIX.—No. V.

National Debt Office, 12th *April* 1828.

RETURN *to an Order of the Honourable the Select Committee of the House of Commons on Finance; requiring Answers to the following Questions.*

QUESTION.

First.—If three per cent. Stock should be at such prices as to yield Interest at the rate of three and a half and four per cent. respectively; and if the sum of One Million a-year were applied in converting three per cent. Stock into Annuities for 35, 40, 45, 50, 55, 60, 65, 70, 75, 80, 85 and 90 years, how much Stock could be so converted, supposing the said sum of One Million to be divided into twelve equal parts, and each part into one of the beforementioned Annuities?

ANSWER.

	When the interest of money, payable half-yearly, is at the rate of	
	3½ per cent.	4 per cent.
The Annuity		
for 35 years should be converted for Stock....	L6,578,578	8,332,106
40	8,351,089	10,765,109
45	10,459,391	13,730,925
50	12,967,100	17,346,239
55	15,949,881	21,753,287
60	19,497,733	27,125,453
65	23,717,705	33,674,094
70	28,737,046	41,656,850
75	34,707,455	41,397,786
80	41,808,823	63,249,744
85	50,255,510	77,709,403
90	60,302,377	95,335,644
	L313,332,688	L462,066,640

QUESTION.

Second.—How large an amount of three per cent. Stock ought to be converted into a terminable Annuity of 30, 40, or 50 years, on payment of a bonus of One Million Sterling, when Stocks are at such prices as to yield interest at the rate of 3, 4, and 5 per cent respectively?

ANSWER.

And when the Stocks yield interest at the rate of		When the Annuity terminates in		
		30 years.	40 years.	50 years.
3 per cent.	The said Bonus should afford a	2,443,220	3,290,663	4,432,046
4 per cent.	conversion of the adjoining	4,374,708	6,500,596	9,659,523
5 per cent.	capitals in 3 per cents.	7,332,963	12,015,946	19,689,527

J. FINLAYSON,
Actuary of the National Debt.

APPENDIX.—No. VI.

PENSIONS ON CIVIL LIST: ENGLAND.

NAME.	Date of Grant.	Amount.
Arnold, James R.	20 July, 1793	£181 19 0
Aspenwall, Marg. C.	8 Aug. 1804	40 8 6
Attwood, Isabella	1 March, 1811	23 17 6
Auckland, George J. Baron	21 July, 1814	300 7 3
Audley, G. J. Baron	17 March, 1821	462 15 7
Arbuthnot, Harriet	5 Jan. 1823	938 10 0
Arnolfi, William F.	14 Jan. 1824	81 19 0
Bradshaw, Lawrence	,,	83 2 5
Bradshaw, Augustus H.	,,	88 2 5
Brudenell, Augusta	21 March, 1769	101 4 8
Barlow, Sophia	28 Jan. 1778	37 18 6
Brooksbank, Ann	4 March, 1783	155 2 0
Birt, Elizabeth	10 Nov. 1794	93 17 8
Biron de Goutant, J. and Charlotte S.	6 July, 1803	159 19 8
Brudenell, Augusta	28 Jan. 1805	101 4 8
Batt, John Thomas	24 July, 1806	600 8 9
Brereton, Mary	17 Sept. 1806	40 8 6
Berens, Catherine	,,	81 19 0
Bouverie, Frances C.	,,	81 19 0
Bisset, Christian M	4 Dec. 1806	100 8 5
Blackwood, Sir Henry, bart.	25 April, 1809	233 5 0
Bentinck, Lady Jemima Helen	10 Nov. 1809	233 5 0
Ball, Catherine	29 Sept. 1812	100 8 5
Bower, Jane	26 June, 1813	100 13 5
Bentinck, Antionette W. J.	28 Jan. 1814	100 8 5
Bearcroft, Susannah	16 April, 1814	87 1 6
Bearcroft, Frances	,,	87 1 6
Burrand, Dame Han.	27 Nov. 1815	400 15 9
Blackwood, Sir Hen. bart.	21 June, 1816	66 0 4
Barlow, Sophia	13 Oct. 1819	100 8 5
Birch, William	,,	100 8 5
Bacon, Henrietta S.	1 Dec. 1820	100 8 5
Bouverie, Hon. Arabella Edward	15 Dec. 1821	300 7 3
Baker, Sir Robert	14 Jan. 1822	500 6 1
Beddingfield, John	13 March, 1822	250 7 5
Beaufort, Louisa C.	15 April, 1822	81 19 0
Bathurst, Charlotte	10 Feb. 1823	600 8 9
Barnard, Edward	6 Sept. 1823	400 5 9
Braine, Mary	1 April, 1824	50 7 2
Bathurst, Charlotte	7 Jan. 1825	200 6 7
Bankhead, P. Mary	8 Oct. 1825	350 7 5
Boys, Jane Hartley	1 April, 1826	100 8 5
Bathurst, Mary	5 June, 1826	250 7 5
Bathurst, Charles	5 Aug. 1826	350 8 6
Brown, Thomas Henry	,,	200 6 7

NAME.	Date of Grant.	Amount.
Brodrick, Mary	10 Feb. 1827	£200 6 7
Brooksbank, Elizabeth, Isabella, and Elizabeth Hermoine	2 April 1827	300 7 3
Beaumont, Anne S.	6 Feb. 1829	40 8 6
Browne, Sir Henry	26 Aug. 1829	200 6 7
Bathurst, Charlotte	31 Dec. 1829	100 13 5
Cockburn, Dame Augusta Ann	,,	538 17 0
Clarke, Frances	3 Feb. 1779	81 19 0
Cary, Lavinia Matilda	,,	81 19 0
Cary, Amelia Sophia	,,	81 19 0
Christie, Ann	14 June, 1783	24 14 8
Calvert, Diana Ann	21 June, 1786	21 16 1
Christie, Ann	16 April, 1794	14 4 9
Cooke, Eliza	20 July, 1793	135 5 5
Cumberland, Lady A.	1 July 1794	311 10 0
Cathcart, Elizabeth, Baroness	16 Oct. 1798	389 9 0
Cockburn, Marianna	29 May 1800	115 19 6
Clare, Dowager Lady, and Lady Fitzgibbon	10 March, 1803	780 2 0
Campbell, Eliza M.	16 Sept. 1805	389 9 0
Clarkson, Elizabeth C.	30 Jan. 1806	40 8 6
Courtenay, Elizabeth	17 Sept 1806	76 19 0
Clarina, Penelope, Baroness	11 March, 1813	233 5 0
Clive, Mary Ann	13 March, 1815	81 19 0
Cort, Caroline	21 June, 1817	19 7 7
Cort, Catherine	,,	19 7 7
Coke, Elizabeth A.	31 Jan. 1818	81 19 0
Cameron, Lady Marg.	22 Dec. 1819	500 6 1
Campbell, Catherine	1 Aug. 1820	24 14 11
Cooke, Frances	27 Jan. 1821	200 6 7
Cooke, Mary	,,	200 6 7
Copinger, Catherine, widow	28 Jan. 1822	81 19 0
Cumming, Ann, spinster	,,	200 6 7
Cockburn, Dame M.	20 May, 1825	680 1 8
Cockburn, Augusta Harriet Mary	7 April, 1827	200 6 7
Croker, Rosamond	21 Aug. 1827	300 7 3
Courtenay, Ann	29 Sept. 1827	200 7 3
Congreve, Dame Isa.	26 Aug. 1829	311 10 0
Dorchester, Lady M.	16 Jan. 1764	115 19 6
Dundas, William, Jas. F., and John B.	23 Aug. 1804	36 15 0
Dickson, Jane	10 Feb. 1806	81 19 0
Dickson, Caroline E.	,,	81 19 0
Dickson, Louisa Sarah	,,	81 19 0

NAME.	Date of Grant.	Amount.
Douglas, Therese M. and De Bailleul, L.	5 May, 1806	*L*233 5 0
Dundas, Dame Char.	15 Jan. 1812	780 2 0
De Vries, Elizabeth	24 June, 1813	80 11 0
De Haeckel, J. P. and Ann Ernestine	6 July, 1813	200 6 7
Drummond, Mary D.	1 July, 1818	203 10 4
Douglas, Dame Ann	1 Aug. 1820	300 7 3
Dwight, S., widow	2 Dec. 1820	50 7 2
Drake, Frances Horatio Nelson	1 April, 1824	100 13 5
Drake, C. Digby M.	,,	100 13 5
De Roos, Lady G. F.	25 Aug. 1824	200 6 7
Durell, Patty, spinster,	8 Oct. 1825	100 13 5
Dean, Mary Beelby and Catherine L.	19 March, 1830	300 7 3
Ewart, John	10 Nov. 1794	93 17 8
Eyre, Juliana M.	29 May, 1800	115 19 6
Erskine, Louisa	1 Feb. 1801	233 5 0
Ernst, Charlotte	14 Oct. 1801	76 19 0
Ditto .	28 Aug. 1811	37 18 6
Emmerick, Hester S.	10 Sept. 1813	40 8 6
Edwards, Dame L. F.	8 March 1817	150 5 8
Eden, Emily .	1 July, 1818	203 19 4
Eden, F. Harriet	25 Jan. 1819	203 19 4
Erskine, Hon. Hamp.	30 Sept. 1824	50 7 2
Erskine, Hon. Frances	,,	50 7 2
Erskine, Hon. Agnes	,,	50 7 2
Flint, Jane, Charles Wm., Wm. and Ann	9 Oct. 1793	53 15 4
Francis, Frances	,,	48 15 0
Frances, Elizabeth	,,	48 15 0
Fallowfield, Ernest, Catherine, Louisa, Jas., Emelia, and William .	9 July, 1795	45 6 9
Fraser, Charlotte, M. A., Charles H. and Jane A. W.	3 April, 1799	389 9 0
Farrar, Ann S. and Lister Mary	17 July, 1771	311 10 0
Fitzgerald, Lord R.	12 March, 1801	624 0 0
Fox, E. B., widow	4 Dec. 1806	938 10 0
Fuller, Caroline	5 Dec. 1812	50 7 2
Fuller, Louisa	,,	50 7 2
Fuller, Isabella .	,,	50 7 2
Fielding, Martha	7 Feb. 1821	100 8 5
Fitzroy, Lady Mary	7 Feb. 1821	200 6 7
Farmer, Sir G. R., bt.	10 July, 1822	185 14 0
Freewin, Rebecca	25 Aug. 1824	100 13 5
Francillon, Sarah	14 Oct. 1825	21 16 1
Fitz Clarence, George	26 Aug. 1829	500 6 1
Fitz Clarence, Adol.	14 Nov. 1829	500 6 1
Godfrey, Edward Lee	,,	7 12 11
Gordon, Albina E.	1 July, 1794	76 19 0
Gwynne, G. Maria	29 May, 1800	115 19 6
Grattan, Lucia C.	10 March, 1803	32 4 0
Grattan, Caroline C.	,,	32 4 0
Grattan, Frances C.	,,	32 4 0
Goddard, Isabella	6 May, 1812	662 18 7
Grey, Elizabeth M.	1 July, 1820	81 19 0
Grey, Anna Maria	,,	81 19 0
Gordon, George H.	,,	155 2 0
Gwyn, Mary .	2 March, 1821	400 15 9
Grange, Mary G.	15 Dec. 1821	50 7 2
Goddard, Louisa	7 Jan. 1825	40 8 6

NAME.	Date of Grant.	Amount.
Griesbach, Caroline Amelia .	31 March, 1826	*L*50 7 2
Griesbach, Eliz. Ann	,,	50 7 2
Griesbach, F. Mary	,,	50 7 2
Gifford, R. F. Lord	26 March, 1827	800 8 2
Holdsworth, Eliza.	27 June, 1789	233 5 0
Hamilton, Sir C. bt.	11 June, 1790	155 2 0
Halifax, Gertrude	2 Sept. 1793	48 15 0
Halifax, Charlotte	,,	48 15 0
Halifax, Marianne	,,	48 15 0
Halifax, Caroline	,,	48 15 0
Halifax, Catherine	,,	48 15 0
Halifax, Elizabeth	,,	48 15 0
Herries, Isabella M.	17 April, 1799	115 19 6
Hereford, H. F. Vis.	29 May, 1800	115 19 6
Hewgill, Elizabeth	14 March, 1801	233 5 0
Heckeren, Anna M.	,,	68 1 2
Heathcote, Antoinette	30 Nov. 1802	233 5 0
Hammond, George	21 Feb. 1806	150 5 8
Hammond, Edmund	,,	150 5 8
Hammond, Margaret	,,	150 5 8
Hammond, Wm. A.	,,	150 5 8
Hope, Elizab. S.	21 April, 1806	100 13 5
Hereford, H. F. Vis.	17 Sept. 1806	467 12 0
Herries, Isabella M.	2 Dec. 1814	115 19 6
Hargrave, Harriet	27 Nov. 1817	50 7 2
Hayter, Elizabeth and Sophia .	16 Feb. 1818	101 4 8
Haldane, Maria	31 July, 1819	200 6 7
Hervey, Dame L.	30 June, 1826	300 7 3
Hume, Elizabeth	5 Aug. 1826	200 6 7
Humphrey, Louisa	5 April, 1827	150 5 8
Hawker, Dorothea, Julia and Mary	15 Dec. 1827	300 7 3
Harrison, Ann .	23 May, 1828	400 15 9
Hyde, Geo. Hooten	14 Aug. 1829	48 15 0
Huntingdon. Earl of	26 Aug. 1829	400 15 9
Hastings, Selina A. L.	,,	50 7 2
Hastings, Arabella G.	,,	50 7 2
Hastings, Louisa .	,,	40 8 6
Hastings, Edward P. R. H	,,	40 8 6
Hastings, Richd. G. H.	,,	40 8 6
Jeans, Rev. Thomas	16 July, 1780	178 17 0
Jennings, Ann	1 July, 1801	252 14 4
Jennings, Robert, John ,,		151 1 11
Johnstone, Mary	28 Aug. 1811	40 8 6
Jeffrey, Lucia	30 April, 1816	200 6 7
Jackson, Laura H.	,,	100 13 5
Jackson, Charles	,,	100 13 5
Johnston, E. John	9 Feb. 1827	400 15 9
Kilshaw, Rev. Richd.	,,	93 16 6
King, H. M. widow	5 June, 1792	431 10 9
Knollis, Lt.-gen. W.	21 Sept. 1814	400 15 9
Knight, E. Cornelia	31 Dec. 1814	300 7 3
Kuper, Rev. William	19 Oct. 1816	400 15 9
Lock, F. Augusta	18 March, 1811	81 19 0
Lushington, Dame Fanny Maria	27 Nov. 1813	350 8 6
Leigh, George, and Mary his wife	6 Sept. 1819	700 6 11
Lennox, S. G., Lady	21 Dec. 1819	150 5 8
Lavie, Dame Mary	15 April, 1822	155 2 0
Leach, W. Elford	14 Aug. 1822	100 13 5
Leeves, Edward	18 June, 1828	200 6 7
Lloyd, Mary Harriett	26 Aug. 1829	200 6 7

NAME.	Date of Grant.	Amount.
M'Leane, Jane .	10 Nov. 1785	L.115 19 6
Ditto .	28 Sept. 1786	115 19 6
Molleson, Eleanor	20 July, 1793	233 5 0
Mudge, Thomas	13 Jan. 1798	100 13 5
Minto, Earl of .	2 April, 1800	938 10 0
Montfort, Henry, Lord	8 Oct. 1800	407 12 0
Miller, Ann .	12 March, 1801	100 13 5
Montfort, H. Lord	10 March, 1803	155 2 0
Mallet, Ann, Baroness de .	1 June, 1803	100 13 5
Murray, Char. Ann	3 Dec. 1803	300 0 8
Magra, Emily Eliza	9 Aug. 1805	194 2 6
Magra, Harriett .	,,	194 2 6
M'Donogh, Harriet	7 Nov. 1805	100 13 5
Marsden, Elizabeth and Maria .	4 Dec. 1806	300 7 3
Morell, Frances	14 Sept. 1808	81 19 0
Milnes, Sir Robert Shore, bart. .	14 March, 1809	557 9 10
Moore, James .	24 July, 1809	780 2 0
M'Gowan, Ann	1 March, 1811	155 2 0
Moore, Elizabeth	27 Sept. 1811	155 2 0
Mornington, Ann, Count. Dowg. of	20 July, 1813	600 8 9
Massey, Hon. Emily	25 Feb. 1815	115 19 6
Muirson, Harriet	22 Nov. 1815	40 8 6
Muirson, Mary Ann Sansbury .	,,	40 8 6
Muirson, Clara	,,	40 8 6
Maccarmick, Catherine Dorothea	31 Jan. 1816	82 11 5
Maccarmick, Leonora	,,	82 11 5
Mitford, Letitia	31 Jan. 1818	100 13 5
M'Creight, Sarah	21 May, 1821	100 13 5
Murray, Hon. Deb.	15 Dec. 1821	200 6 7
Muskerry, Sarah, Baroness	6 June, 1825	233 5 0
Mellish, Amelia .	8 Oct. 1825	100 13 5
Mellish, Eleonora	,,	50 7 2
Mellish, Elizabeth .	,,	50 7 2
Mellish, Wilhelmina	,,	50 7 2
Mends, Eliza .	,,	50 7 2
Mends, Harriet A.	,,	50 7 2
Mends, Alice Sarah	,,	50 7 2
Mountain, Eliza M. W. . .	1 April, 1826	300 7 3
Mitchell, Martha M.	29 April, 1826	50 7 2
M'Cullock, Jane	12 May, 1826	100 13 5
Montgomery, Marian Emily .	30 June, 1826	40 8 6
Montgomery, Matilda	,,	40 8 6
Montgomery, Isabella Eliza .	,,	40 8 6
Mulgrave, Sophia, Countess of .	26 Aug. 1829	800 8 2
Noel, Maria .	27 June, 1789	81 19 0
Nepean, Margaret	2 Nov. 1792	501 16 6
Nott, Charlotte Georgina Augusta	2 Oct. 1799	115 19 6
Nedderberg, Sara Hendrika	14 March, 1801	68 1 2
Newcastle, Ann M. Duchess Dow. of,	10 March, 1803	780 2 0
Napier, Louisa M.	23 Nov. 1805	251 18 6
Nicolay, Augusta G. Louisa .	26 Oct. 1813	100 13 5

NAME.	Date of Grant.	Amount.
Nicolay, Maria Georgiana, widow .	16 Sept. 1818	L.250 7 5
Onslow, George W.	2 June, 1778	81 19 0
Onslow, Arthur .	,,	81 19 0
O'Hara, Jemima	27 Aug. 1773	81 19 0
O'Brien, Margaretta Madelena, widow	16 Feb. 1818	155 2 0
Paul, Frances Richmond .	,,	22 13 6
Ponsonby, Sarah	2 July, 1788	37 18 6
Perrott, Dame M. J.	7 Sept. 1789	48 15 0
Pye, Martha, widow	8 Dec. 1813	60 7 9
Pelham, Hon. Catherine, widow	16 Sept. 1818	233 5 0
Pent, Maria .	1 July, 1820	155 2 0
Popham, Mary Riggs	18 Jan. 1820	50 7 2
Page, Mary Harriet	1 Aug. 1820	60 7 9
Page Ann	,,	60 7 9
Page, Emma Rose	,,	60 7 9
Page, Elizabeth	,,	60 7 9
Price, John .	17 Aug. 1821	200 6 7
Ponsonby, Sarah	14 Jan. 1822	47 5 2
Pearce, Elizabeth	21 Feb. 1822	150 5 3
Proctor, A., widow	10 July, 1822	50 7 2
Pritchard, Anastasia Benedict F. .	9 Dec. 1822	50 7 2
Portmore, Thomas C. Earl of .	15 April, 1825	233 5 0
Pack, Arthur John	5 July, 1825	100 13 5
Pack, Denis William	,,	100 13 5
Pack, Elizabeth .	,,	100 13 5
Pack, Elizabeth C.	,,	100 13 5
Papendiech, Augusta Amelia A. .	16 April, 1827	100 8 5
Planta, Barbara U.	21 Aug. 1827	200 6 7
Ponsonby, Sarah	26 Aug. 1829	200 6 7
Pennell, Rosamond Hester Elizabeth	19 March, 1830	100 13 5
Rochford, Earl of	10 Feb. 1782	780 1 0
Randall, Susannah (now Lemyn), Martha (now Bowen), and Elizabeth (now Moore) .	19 March, 1792	40 8 6
Rose, Theodora .	9 Feb. 1785	233 5 0
Robinson, Catherine Gertrude	9 Oct. 1793	467 12 0
Rees, Mary .	2 May, 1798	12 1 0
Routh, Abigail .	30 Nov. 1802	81 19 0
Rooke, Dame Harriet Sophia .	14 Sept. 1808	233 5 0
Rodney, Hon. Ann	1 Sept. 1812	76 19 0
Raynsford, Mary	5 Dec. 1812	50 7 2
Raynsford, Louisa	,,	50 7 2
Radstock, Cornelia Jacoba, Baroness	25 Nov. 1814	389 9 0
Rook, Jane Elizabeth	16 April, 1816	60 7 9
Rook, Mary Hannah	,,	60 7 9
Rothes, Charlotte Julia, Dowager Count. of	21 June, 1817	155 2 0
Rogers, Elizabeth	1 July, 1818	40 8 6
Rogers, Hon. Ann, additional	16 Sept. 1818	76 19 0
Russell, Lucy, widow	1 Aug. 1820	18 0 0
Roby, Harriet Ann	30 July, 1821	43 13 3
Rose, Charlotte, wid.	6 Sept. 1823	194 2 6

NAME.	Date of Grant.	Amount.	NAME.	Date of Grant.	Amount.
Richardson, Fanny,			Taylor, Ann .	1 March, 1811	L.15 9 0
Elizabeth & Sarah	31 May, 1824	L.101 19 8	Trefusis, Barbara	28 Sept. 1812	81 19 0
Rennie, Margaret	28 Oct. 1825	40 8 6	Tyrconnel, John De-		
Rumbold, Emily	5 Aug. 1826	115 19 6	laval, Earl of	9 March, 1813	600 8 9
Rumbold, Car. Eliza	,,	115 19 6	Taylor, Maj.-gen. Sir		
St. John, Henry	12 Aug. 1780	101 4 8	Herbert .	30 April, 1819	933 10 0
Sunduis, Christopher	4 July, 1790	81 19 0	Treasure, E., widow	1 July, 1820	100 13 5
Shaw, Mary .	10 Nov. 1794	93 17 8	Tyndale, William	1 Aug. 1820	200 6 7
Swinburne, Mary	16 Oct. 1800	48 15 0	Torrens, Dame Sarah	,,	624 0 0
Stephenson, Hon.			Tildesley, Anna S.	31 May, 1825	61 4 11
Jane .	1 June, 1803	100 8 5	Van de Spiegle,		
Shee, Dame Eliz. M.	2 Dec. 1803	334 15 9	Adolph W.	14 March, 1801	68 1 2
Strangford, Maria,			Van de Spiegle, Maria		
Dowg. Viscountess	9 May, 1804	233 5 0	Adriana .	,,	68 1 2
Stanhope, Caroline	28 Jan. 1805	155 2 0	Vassar, Mary, widow	27 June, 1821	50 7 2
Southey, Robert	31 March, 1807	155 2 0	Webber, Mary	21 June, 1786	21 16 1
Selwyn, Charlotte	14 Aug. 1807	81 19 0	Willis, John .	29 Jan. 1791	559 6 10
Selwyn, Albinia F.	,,	81 19 0	Wraxall, Jane	20 July, 1793	311 10 0
Selwyn, Mary Louisa	,,	81 19 0	Walsingham, Lord,		
Selwyn, Hen. Eliz.	,,	81 19 0	and De Grey, Thos.	27 July, 1794	933 10 0
Smith, Isabella	28 Aug. 1811	40 8 6	Wilmot, Sarah Ann		
Smith, Lady Ann C.	12 Oct. 1812	600 8 9	Eardley, widow	14 Sept. 1797	311 10 0
Smith, Dame Car-			Wellington, Charlotte		
terette	16 March, 1813	155 2 0	Henrietta M.	29 May, 1800	115 19 6
Sterky, Rev. Alex.	19 Oct. 1816	400 15 9	Wickham, Eleanor M.	1 June, 1803	526 6 5
Sheridan, R. Brins.	2 March, 1818	57 1 6	Wilkins, Catherine		
Sheridan, Helen S.	,,	57 1 6	Eliza Marianne	29 May, 1800	115 19 6
Sheridan, Caroline E. S.	,,	57 1 6	Williams, Mary	17 Sept. 1806	40 8 6
Sheridan, Jane Geor.	,,	57 1 6	Winning, Henrietta	14 Sept. 1808	233 5 0
Sheridan, Francis C.	,,	57 1 6	Windus, Ann .	1 March, 1811	48 15 0
Sheridan, Charles K.	,,	57 1 6	Waldron, Jane .	22 Oct. 1812	40 8 6
Seymour, Sophia A.	1 July, 1818	81 19 0	Whitehouse, Eliz.	28 Aug. 1813	50 7 2
Sherwood, Susan	31 Oct. 1819	15 9 0	Wharton, Hen. widow	28 Dec. 1813	501 17 0
Sherwood, Rebecca	,,	15 9 0	Wolfe, Ann .	16 Sept. 1818	40 8 6
Sherwood, Ann	,,	15 9 0	Welsh, Mary Ann	1 July, 1819	50 7 2
Sherwood, Elizabeth	,,	15 9 0	Wynyard, Lady M.	30 June, 1819	467 12 0
Smithers, Joseph	1 Aug. 1820	15 9 0	Wills, Judith Eliz.	1 Aug. 1820	50 7 2
Shepherd, George		40 8 6	Wills, Mary ,	,,	50 7 2
Stables, Ann, widow	17 April, 1821	200 6 7	Wragg, John .	,,	26 8 11
Stuart, Sir S. H., bt.	14 May, 1822	200 6 7	Wilcox, Elizabeth D.	27 Jan. 1821	100 13 5
Shaw, Lieut.-col. M.	24 April, 1824	500 6 1	Wright, Phillis, wid.	2 March, 1821	30 2 3
Stoddart, Jane Car.	26 April, 1824	65 4 0	Whittingham, Maria		
Scott, Anne Lindsay	8 Oct. 1825	250 7 5	Magdalena .	14 June, 1822	400 15 9
Stepney, Dame Cathe-			Whitaker, Lucy, wid.	6 Sept. 1823	40 8 6
rine, widow .	28 Feb. 1826	200 6 7	Wiseman, Harriet	31 May, 1825	100 13 5
Scott, Sir D. D. bart.	7 April, 1827	300 7 3	Willimott, Mary	31 May, 1827	100 13 5
Spearman, A. A. and			Watson, Sir F. B.	21 Aug. 1827	933 10 0
Margaret Young	22 Dec. 1827	120 15 10	Wright, Alex. James	15 Nov. 1827	50 7 2
Thistlethwayte, Caro-			Wright, Alfred C. J.	,,	25 4 3
line .	28 Jan. 1778	40 8 6	Wright, Victorine Ca-		
Tinling, Frances	21 June, 1796	21 16 1	roline M. T. .	,,	25 4 3
Trimlestown, Ann,			Woodger, Thomas	18 Jan. 1828	50 7 2
Baroness Dowager	1 June, 1803	155 2 0	Yonge, Dame Ann	5 Dec. 1812	300 7 3
Ditto	1 Sept. 1810	100 13 5			
			TOTAL		L.70,010 11 0

In those Pensions where the date of the grant is not given, the exact date cannot be ascertained; those Pensions were all however granted previous to 1784.

PENSIONS ON IRISH CIVIL LIST.

NAME.	Date of Grant.	Amount.
Annesley, Richard, Widow and Children of . .	6 April, 1753	L.132 16 4
Ada'r, Robt. Diana and Elizabeth	24 June, 1772	445 19 4
Aylmer, Lord, and H. F. W. Aylmer	24 Feb. 1783	356 8 8
Ashworth, Robert	18 April, 1787	1,072 14 8
Ashworth, Henrietta	,,	266 18 4
Ashworth, F. .	,,	266 18 4
Ashworth, C. .	,,	177 11 8
Adair, George .	23 Dec. 1790	88 1 0
Annesley, Richard	17 Sept. 1792	88 1 0
Annesley, Elizabeth	,,	88 1 0
Allen, Viscountess	20 July, 1799	266 18 4
Ditto .	23 Oct. 1800	88 1 0
Aylmer, Lucy .	16 July, 1814	43 18 4
Allan, Viscount	15 Sept. 1821	266 18 4
Anderson, Dame Car.	13 Feb. 1823	88 1 0
Archer, Sophia .	1 March, 1827	47 12 8
Armstrong, Eleanor	28 Sept. 1829	23 10 4
Barton, James .	1 Jan. 1777	5 5 0
Burleigh,Rich. Mayne, Frances and Anne	4 Feb. 1782	88 1 0
Benson, Mary .	12 Oct. 1785	177 11 8
Bookey, Tho. Truelock	4 Feb. 1786	35 2 0
Bookey, Wm. Truelock	ditto	35 2 0
Bagot, Jane .	12 March, 1792	90 19 4
Bowen, Car. Cordelia, and Maria .	21 March, 1792	88 1 0
Bourchier, Mary .	29 June, 1792	88 1 0
Bruce, George Walker	,,	35 2 0
Beckford, Elinor	14 March, 1794	61 16 4
Burgh, Ann .	,,	177 11 8
Burgh, Elizabeth .	,,	266 18 4
Burgh, Catherine	,,	222 3 0
Blaquiere, Sir J.	17 March, 1794	1,072 14 8
Borough, Sir R. bart.	31 Dec, 1794	177 11 8
Bellew, William .	20 July, 1799	266 18 4
Ditto .	26 Nov. 1801	132 16 4
Burgh, Ann .	,,	177 11 8
Blaquiere, J. Baron De	8 Dec. 1802	893 13 0
Brown, Bridget .	8 July, 1811	88 1 0
Ditto .	24 Oct. 1815	43 18 4
Brennan, Anne Hel.	8 July, 1811	21 13 0
Blake, Honoria .	24 June, 1812	43 18 4
Blake, John .	,,	43 18 4
Blake, Henry James	,,	43 18 4
Bellew, William	15 June, 1813	132 16 4
Burnside, Thomas	26 March, 1814	88 1 0
Baker, Lady E. M.	6 Dec. 1814	445 19 4
Benning, Eliza .	30 Nov. 1815	43 18 4
Bruce, Sir S. bart.	13 Oct. 1817	177 11 8
Babington, Eli a F.	16 Sept. 1818	43 18 4
Battley, Arabella	17 July, 1820	43 18 4
Brandon, W. Baron	29 July, 1820	266 18 4
Ditto .	28 Nov. 1820	266 18 4
Blake, Margaret .	,,	88 1 0
Blundell, Elizabeth	,,	43 18 4
Beaufort, Mary .	2 Sept. 1821	70 15 4
Browne, Sarah .	24 March, 1823	L.43 18 4
Browne, James .	,,	43 18 4
Burrowes, Mary Ann and Eliza .	10 March, 1825	35 2 0
Baskerville, Ellen	3 Oct. 1826	37 18 8
Bowles, Chs. Oldfield and Eliz. his wife	17 Feb. 1827	192 5 8
Brownrigg, Ann	1 March, 1827	95 10 0
Browne, Frederick	14 Feb. 1828	47 12 8
Browne, Ellen .	,,	47 12 8
Cavendish, James	14 April, 1788	132 16 4
Cuthbertson, Olivia	9 Nov. 1791	42 15 4
Cuthbertson, Juliana	,,	42 15 4
Cuthbertson, Cath.	,,	42 15 4
Cary, Charlotte	29 June, 1792	52 17 4
Cavan, Earl of .	7 June, 1796	266 18 4
Cavendish, Theod.	14 June, 1797	43 18 4
Crosbie, Elizabeth	18 June, 1798	222 3 0
Cockayne, Barbara	20 June, 1798	222 3 0
Campbell, Dugald, & Catherine his wife	18 Feb. 1806	266 18 8
Clarina, P. Baroness	23 May, 1810	177 11 8
Crosbie, Margaret	24 June, 1812	43 18 4
Crofton, Frances	,,	43 18 4
Copinger, Jane L.	15 June, 1813	88 1 0
Crofton, George .	,,	43 18 4
Campbell, C. Elinor,	16 July, 1814	66 5 8
Corneille, C. Sophia	3 April, 1816	132 16 4
Crofton, Hon. Caro.	24 Oct. 1817	141 15 8
Cartwright, Sarah	16 Sept. 1818	21 13 0
Cartwright, Anne	,,	21 13 0
Cartwright, Elinor	,,	21 13 0
Cartwright, Eliza	,,	21 13 0
Clarke, Eliz. Martin, James & Harriet	22 April, 1819	35 2 0
Connor, E. Executors of	4 May,1819	177 11 8
Chamberlaine, Lucy	26 Jan. 1820	266 18 4
Cameron, Jane .	28 Nov. 1820	43 18 4
Crawford, Jane .	21 Sept. 1821	43 18 4
Cox, Letitia E. .	24 May, 1823	70 15 4
Corneille, Eliz. .	31 Jan. 1826	88 1 0
Clutterbuck, Eliza, Jane, Eliza and Alicia	5 Dec. 1828	28 7 4
Campbell, Dame Pamela Adel. Fel. Hen.	28 Sept. 1829	47 12 8
Curtis, Elizabeth	22 June, 1830	20 12 0
Dyson, Jeremiah, Representatives of	27 Jan. 1770	893 13 0
Daly, Richard, Representative of	6 Nov. 1797	88 1 0
Duhigg, Mary Ann	24 Oct. 1815	66 5 8
Dickson, Jane .	9 Sept. 1816	88 1 0
Dickson, Caroline E.	,,	88 1 0
Dickson, Louisa Sarah	,,	88 1 0
Dillon, Lady Maria	17 July, 1820	43 18 4
Dempsey, Mary .	,,	21 13 0
Elliot, Elizabeth	17 March, 1794	132 16 4
Errol, Countess D. of	15 Feb. 1809	88 1 0
Ellison, Florinda	8 July, 1811	21 13 0
Ellison, Susan .	,,	21 13 0

NAME.	Date of Grant.	Amount.
Ellison, Phœbe .	8 July, 1811	L.21 13 0
Erck, Jane Martha	15 June, 1813	88 1 0
Ellison, Catherine	14 Feb. 1828	95 10 0
Francis, Isabella F.	20 Dec. 1780	132 16 4
Ditto .	17 March, 1794	132 16 4
Forsayeth, Charlte.	23 March, 1796	43 18 4
Fitter, Jane .	29 Aug. 1796	43 18 4
Fox, Anne .	14 June, 1797	88 1 0
Fortescue, Jane .	3 Feb. 1804	266 18 4
Fetherston, Eliza, Catherine, Sarah, Isabella, Maria and Octavia .	18 Feb. 1806	266 18 4
Faulkner, Anne .	28 Aug. 1807	356 8 8
Fisher, Lucy .	15 June, 1813	132 16 4
Fisher, Charles F. ,,		88 1 0
Freemantle, Georgiana ,,		43 18 4
Freemantle, Albinia ,,		43 18 4
Freemantle, Frances A. ,,		43 18 4
Finucane, Emma	6 Sept. 1814	88 1 0
Flint, Sir Charles, & Dame Anna Maria	17 Oct. 1815	266 18 4
Foules, Dame Mar.	20 March, 1816	132 16 4
Fox, Anne	9 Sept. 1816	266 18 4
Farina, Margaret	17 July, 1820	21 13 0
Fitzbum, Madame	10 March, 1825	43 18 4
Fitzgibbon, Thomas	3 March, 1826	70 15 4
Fabian, Robert C.	14 Feb. 1828	111 12 8
Figg, Fanny .	28 Sept. 1829	47 12 8
Gordon, Jane	22 Oct. 1772	43 18 4
Guydickens, Frances	23 Dec. 1793	231 1 8
Green, Alice .	23 May, 1810	43 18 4
Ditto .	15 June, 1813	43 18 4
Gore, Sophia Jane	24 Aug. 1813	88 1 0
Gregory, William, & Lady Ann .	23 Sept. 1814	445 19 4
Godfrey, Letitia	1 March, 1816	21 13 0
Gilholy, Maria	28 Nov. 1820	21 13 0
Griffith, Walter H.	19 April, 1821	17 7 0
Griffith, Anne ,,		17 7 0
Griffith, Mary Eliz. ,,		17 7 0
Griffith, Henry Allen ,,		17 7 0
Griffith, George ,,		17 7 0
Griffith, Charlotte	10 Sept. 1821	17 7 0
Griffith, Wm. Downes ,,		17 7 0
Griffith, Charles J. ,,		17 7 0
Griffith, Arthur Hill ,,		17 7 0
Griffith, Harriet Sarah ,,		17 7 0
Going, Joanna	10 Dec. 1821	88 1 0
Ditto .	2 Aug. 1823	88 1 0
Gifford, Robert Francis, Baron	27 June, 1827	204 0 6
Gosset, Elizabeth L. & Gertrude Mary	5 Dec, 1828	192 5 8
Gosset, Ralph Allen	17 Feb. 1829	95 10 0
Gore, John .	28 Sept. 1829	47 12 8
Going, Francis Anne	22 June, 1830	47 12 8
Hooper, Charles, and P. Martin, Representatives of	15 Dec. 1726	177 11 8
Hall, John .	1 Jan. 1777	5 5 0
Henderson, John ,,		5 5 0
Hasler, Sarah	20 Dec. 1780	132 16 4
Hamilton, Arab.	19 March, 1785	177 11 8
Hyland, Thomas	9 Jan. 1787	43 18 4
Houghton, Penelope	10 Oct. 1787	88 1 0

NAME.	Date of Grant.	Amount.
Hamilton, John, deceased, Children of	20 Oct. 1787	L.445 19 4
Hernon, Sarah .	8 Aug. 1789	61 16 4
Hernon, Elizabeth ,,		61 16 4
Heatley, Mary .	24 Sept. 1790	177 11 8
Hamilton, Henry	10 March, 1795	186 10 8
Ditto .	16 July, 1795	123 17 0
Hamilton, Jane	10 March, 1795	88 1 0
Ditto .	16 July, 1795	43 18 4
Hamilton, Sack. R.	10 March, 1795	88 1 0
Hamilton, Arabella, Elizabeth, Mary & Isabella .	16 March, 1796	445 19 4
Hume, Hannah	29 Aug. 1796	88 1 0
Hamilton, Anne	16 July, 1814	43 18 4
Handfield, Catherine	6 Sept. 1814	88 1 0
Handfield, Anne Mar. ,,		88 1 0
Handfield, Eliza ,,		88 1 0
Handfield, Jane Isa. ,,		88 1 0
Handfield, Mary	3 April, 1816	88 1 0
Handfield, Julia Lucy ,,		88 1 0
Handfield, Sarah ,,		88 1 0
Hume, Eliza Grace	1 March, 1816	66 5 8
Hore, Elizabeth	13 Oct. 1817	132 16 4
Holmes, Margaret	16 Sept. 1818	26 2 8
Ditto .	17 July, 1820	17 7 0
Headfort, March. of	21 Sept. 1821	88 1 0
Hargrove, Frances, & Frances Eliza, Jane and George .	14 May, 1823	17 7 0
Hayman, Anne	25 Oct. 1823	266 18 4
Hare, Louisa . ,,		52 17 4
Hunter, Sir Richard	14 Jan. 1826	177 11 8
Ditto .	17 Feb. 1827	111 0 4
Hart, John .	15 Dec. 1828	114 18 0
Hutchinson, David Wilkinson .	22 June, 1830	95 10 0
Hutchinson, Eliza ,,		47 12 0
Joncourt, Isaac Stephen Lewis De	30 Oct. 1784	177 11 8
Jebb, Elizabeth	20 Oct. 1792	66 5 8
Jebb, Ross, . ,,'		66 5 8
Jebb, Elizabeth . ,,		32 17 0
Jebb, Mary . ,,		32 17 0
Jebb, Margaret . ,,		32 17 0
Johnston, Sir William, bart.	14 March, 1794	714 11 8
Jarnac, Madame de	19 March, 1794	177 11 8
Joddrell, Augusta ,,		177 11 8
Jackson, Sophia	23 March, 1796	35 2 0
Innes, Susannah	8 July, 1811	43 18 4
Jenkins, Harriet ,,		21 13 0
Johnson, C. Maria	24 June, 1812	88 1 0
Johnson, Anna Helena ,,		88 1 0
Johnstone, Edwin	13 Feb. 1823	177 11 8
Jephson, Henrietta	14 Feb. 1828	23 7 4
Jephson, Isabella	28 Sept. 1828	23 7 4
Juxon, Eliza	28 Sept. 1829	23 10 4
Kelly, James .	1 Jan. 1777	5 5 0
Kennedy, Anne	18 July, 1781	88 1 0
Knox, John .	9 June, 1800	585 10 0
Knox, Mary Anne	24 Nov. 1801	177 11 8
Knox, John .	8 Dec. 1802	177 11 9
Kirwan, Wilhelmina	23 Jan. 1807	266 18 4
King, Elizabeth	14 Dec. 1809	43 18 4
King, Margt. & Soph.	22 Feb. 1810	43 18 4

NAME.	Date of Grant.	Amount.
Keating, Oliver	18 Nov. 1818	L43 18 4
Keating, John	,,	43 18 4
Keating, Harriet	,,	43 18 4
Kinsale, Lord	13 Feb. 1823	356 8 8
Kent, Elizabeth	10 March, 1825	35 2 0
Kennedy, Elizabeth, Susannah, Sarah and Ellen	14 Jan. 1826	88 1 0
Kingsland, Viscount	10 Oct. 1826	192 5 3
Lennox, Lady L. M.	24 May, 1764	445 19 4
Lyndon, Helena	4 Oct. 1766	172 19 4
Leatherland, Thomas	1 Jan. 1777	5 5 0
Langrishe, Hannah	17 March, 1794	266 18 4
Ditto	,,	177 11 8
Lally Tollendal, Count de	19 March, 1794	266 18 4
Langrishe, Anne	29 Aug. 1796	177 11 8
Loftus, Arthur	20 June, 1798	43 18 4
Lysaght, Eliza. H.	23 May, 1810	43 18 4
Lynch, Martin F.	24 June, 1812	132 16 4
Lloyd, Mary, Anne Emma	8 April, 1815	266 18 4
Lyndon, Anne	24 Oct, 1815	21 13 0
Lloyd, Emma	3 April, 1816	177 11 8
Lloyd, Charles	21 June, 1816	43 18 4
Lambart, Florinda and Catherine	16 Sept. 1818	177 11 8
Lambart, Catherine	28 Nov. 1820	88 1 0
Lloyd, Emma	8 March, 1821	88 1 0
Lysaght, Sophia	10 Dec. 1821	43 18 4
Lefann, Elizabeth	25 Oct. 1823	88 1 0
Lynch, Jane	9 Feb. 1824	48 8 0
Lynch, Emily	,,	48 8 0
Lynch, Maria	10 March, 1825	35 2 0
Lefanu, Elizabeth and Elizabeth	17 Feb. 1827	47 12 8
Laffan, Sir Joseph de Courcey	5 Dec. 1828	192 5 8
La Touche, Lady C.	28 Sept. 1829	95 10 0
Molesworth, Elizabeth	15 Jan. 1756	61 16 4
Masters, John	1 Jan. 1777	5 5 0
Moore, Jane	16 Aug. 1785	177 11 8
Meares, Sarah	23 Dec. 1790	177 11 8
May, Sir G. S., bart.	18 Sept. 1792	88 1 0
Mountjoy, Lord, Representatives of	8 Oct. 1794	177 11 8
Ditto	,,	183 2 4
Mosse, Lewis	4 Jan. 1795	88 1 0
Marlay, Elizabeth	20 June, 1798	88 1 0
Murphy, Michael	23 Oct. 1800	88 1 0
Marsden, Alexander	3 Feb. 1804	356 8 8
M'Kenna, Theob.	20 March, 1805	266 18 4
Marsden, Elizabeth	18 Feb. 1806	266 18 4
Marsden, Alexander	27 Jan. 1807	266 18 4
Milnes, Sir R. S. and Dame Charlotte	2 Jan. 1809	445 19 4
Murray, Sarah	23 May, 1810	43 18 4
Milbank, Alice	8 July, 1811	30 12 4
Montgomery, Sir George, bart.	10 Dec. 1813	356 8 8
Molesworth, Mary	1 March, 1816	88 1 0
Ditto	3 March, 1826	88 1 0
Melville, Michael L.	18 Nov. 1818	21 13 0
Melville, Henry Crost	,,	21 13 0
Melville, Mary Anne	,,	21 13 0
Melville, Frances	,,	21 13 0
Molesworth, Visc.	16 Sept. 1818	L177 11
Ditto	29 July, 1820	177 11 8
Mitford, Letitia	17 July, 1820	43 18 4
Ditto	21 Sept. 1821	43 18 4
Mountmorres, Visc.	28 Nov. 1820	43 18 4
Moore, John	13 Feb. 1820	88 1 0
Marley, Elizabeth	10 March, 1825	39 8 8
Ditto	3 March, 1826	48 8 0
Mountmorres, Vis.	10 March, 1825	177 11 8
Marshall, Frances	3 March, 1826	88 1 0
Montgomery, Lady	13 April, 1826	146 5 0
Mountmorres, Visc.	,,	88 1 0
Maturin, Harriet	,,	43 18 4
Montgomery, Lady, and Marian Emily	17 Feb. 1827	92 12 0
Macleod, Lady Ara.	28 Sept. 1829	47 12 8
Morris, Theodosia	,,	47 12 8
Newburgh, Mary E.	4 Feb. 1782	177 11 8
Nesbitt, Henry	18 Aug. 1786	66 5 8
North, Elizabeth	9 Jan. 1787	52 17 4
Newenham, Thomas	29 June, 1792	177 11 8
Newenham, Robert O'Callaghan	,,	88 1 0
Ditto	19 March, 1794	177 11 8
Neal, Mary	28 Sept. 1829	23 10 4
O'Reilly, Myles J.	24 June, 1812	222 3 0
O'Dwyer, Cath.	1 March, 1816	92 10 8
O'Dwyer, Marcella	,,	57 6 8
O'Dwyer, Jane	,,	57 6 8
Ormsby, Margaret	17 July, 1820	88 1 0
O'Connell, Louisa	10 Dec. 1821	21 13 0
O'Connell Alicia	,,	21 13 0
O'Reilly, Christopher	28 Sept. 1829	47 12 8
O'Driscoll, Dorothea	,,	47 12 8
Pennefather, John	31 Oct. 1771	26 2 8
Pennefather, William	,,	26 2 8
Pennefather, Mary	,,	26 2 8
Pennefather, Catherine	,,	26 2 8
Pennefather, Margaret	,,	26 2 8
Pickford, Jacob D.	7 June, 1776	222 3 0
Pringle, Margaret	25 Nov. 1785	88 1 0
Purcell, Toby	23 Dec. 1790	70 15 4
Pickard, Eliza and Jane	,,	60 3 8
Penrose, Jane	6 Sept. 1793	43 18 4
Parks, William	8 Oct. 1794	321 7 4
Ponsonby, Sarah	2 Oct. 1809	88 11 0
Preston, Frances	23 May, 1810	88 1 0
Ponsonby, Sarah	,,	43 18 4
Pilsworth, Abigail	8 July, 1811	43 18 4
Parsons, Mary	15 June, 1813	177 11 8
Paine, Mary	10 Oct. 1814	61 16 4
Pilot, Judith H.	17 July, 1820	43 18 4
Phillott, Dame F.	28 Nov. 1820	88 1 0
Paine, Anne Jane	10 Dec. 1821	17 7 0
Percival, Harriet	,,	43 18 4
Proctor, Anne J.	10 March, 1825	21 13 0
Pack, Catherine A.	3 March, 1826	43 18 4
Price, Lucinda	1 March, 1827	51 10 4
Rodney, John	7 April, 1781	88 1 0
Rodney, Jane	,,	88 1 0
Rodney, Anne	,,	88 1 0
Rodney, Sarah	,,	88 1 0
Ridge, Catherine	5 Oct. 1785	29 2 8
Ridge, Sarah	,,	29 2 8
Ridge, Anne,	,,	29 2 8
Richardson, Ursula	23 Dec. 1790	172 19 4

NAME.	Date of Grant.	Amount.	NAME.	Date of Grant.	Amount.
Roberts, Jonath. B.	17 March, 179	L4132 16 4	Stack, Mary	14 Feb. 1828	L18 13 4
Roberts, Charlotte and Mary	31 Dec. 1794	132 16 4	Spray, Mary	,,	57 6 8
Roche, Dame Mary	29 July, 1797	177 11 8	Shawe, Mary, Catherine and Anne	28 Sept. 1829	95 10 0
Ditto	23 Nov. 1801	266 18 4	Turner, Sarah	24 Nov. 1774	42 15 4
Rounds, Jane	8 July, 1811	88 1 0	Thompson, Robert	23 Dec. 1790	88 1 0
Radcliffe, Maria	24 Oct. 1815	70 15 4	Trail, Rev. Anth.	17 March, 1794	132 16 4
Russell, Elinor	1 March, 1816	52 17 4	Trail, Clarissa	24 April, 1809	356 8 8
Ready, John	3 April, 1816	177 11 8	Tisdale, Mary	14 Dec. 1809	88 1 0
Ready, Charles	13 Oct. 1817	177 11 8	Tyrconnel, Earl of	15 June, 1813	445 19 4
Rich, Sir George	,,	132 16 4	Taylor, Sarah	10 Oct. 1814	52 17 4
Roscommon, Countess of	,,	88 1 0	Tracy, Elizabeth	4 Nov. 1814	66 5 8
Renny, Mary Jane	17 July, 1820	88 1 0	Tighe, George W.	17 Oct. 1815	356 8 8
Renny, Elizabeth A.	28 Nov. 1820	88 1 0	Taylor, Thomas	24 Oct. 1815	43 18 4
Renny, Isabella F.	27 Nov. 1821	88 1 0	Trimbleston, Anna, Baroness	25 Ott. 1823	26 2 8
Ram, Abel and Elizabeth	1 March, 1827	95 10 0	Tomlins, Sir Thomas E. and Dame Elizabeth	10 March, 1825	177 11 8
Roscommon, Earl of	28 Sept. 1829	192 5 8	Tighe, Charlotte	5 Dec. 1828	47 12 8
Strangford, Viscount, Daughters of	28 Sept. 1764	222 3 0	Udney, Martha	23 Oct. 1816	445 19 4
Sneyd, Elizabeth, and Eliza. her daughter	22 Jan. 1776	445 19 4	Usher, Alicia, Frances, Marg, and Sarah	1 March, 1827	95 10 0
Sterling, Edward	20 Dec. 1780	177 11 8	Vernon, Harriet	15 July, 1763	88 1 0
Sneyd, Hannah	19 Feb. 1781	266 18 4	Vernon, Caroline	,,	88 1 0
Swan, Maria	31 Oct. 1771	43 18 4	Vernon, Elizabeth	,,	88 1 0
Stuart, Jane	6 Feb. 1784	172 19 4	Vallancey, Mary	17 Dec. 1770	66 5 8
Shaw, Robert, representative of	24 Aug. 1786	714 11 8	Vallancey, Frances P.	,,	66 5 8
Smith, Sarah	10 Oct. 1787	35 2 0	Vallancey, Catherine	23 Dec. 1790	132 16 4
Stewart, Frances	23 Dec. 1790	88 1 0	Vernon, Harcourt and Charles	24 Oct. 1815	66 5 8
Stratford, Hannah	8 June, 1793	43 18 4	Vallancey, Fanny	16 Sept. 1818	21 13 0
Symes, William	12 Nov. 1794	52 17 4	Ditto	17 July, 1820	21 13 0
Strangford, Lord	2 Jan. 1797	88 1 0	Vallancey, Isabella	24 March, 1823	61 16 4
Steward, Elizabeth	29 July, 1797	114 18 0	Vernon, Sir Charles	25 Oct. 1823	266 18 4
Stanley, Jane	20 July, 1799	356 8 8	Whitelocke, George	1 June, 1765	177 11 8
Stannus, Caroline	23 Oct. 1800	88 1 0	Wren, Constantia M.	6 Feb. 1784	61 16 4
Sneyd, Anne	23 Aug. 1807	356 8 8	Warren, Mary	10 Oct. 1787	88 1 0
Strangford, Dowager Viscountess	2 Oct. 1809	266 18 4	Warren, Anne	,,	43 18 4
Smyth, Barbara	8 July, 1811	26 2 8	Warren, Sarah	,,	43 18 4
Smyth, Harriet	,,	26 2 8	Warren, Rebecca	,,	43 18 4
Straton, Lady Emily	15 June, 1813	177 11 8	Ward, George	29 June, 1792	52 17 4
Sealy, Catherine	,,	43 18 4	Winder, Barbara A., Jane A., and Rachael A.	29 Aug. 1796	88 1 0
Stewart, Frances	16 July, 1814	66 5 8	Webster, Caroline	20 June, 1798	64 1 4
Stock, Mary	27 Dec. 1814	88 1 0	Ditto	18 June, 1798	26 2 8
Standish, Frances D.	24 Oct. 1815	66 5 8	Wynne, Robert	20 March, 1805	266 18 4
Standish, Olivia	,,	66 5 8	Wilson, Christian	8 July, 1811	43 18 4
Slow, Anne	13 Oct. 1817	43 18 4	Whitelaw, Elinor	15 June, 1813	177 11 8
Slow, Caroline	,,	43 18 4	Wynne, Robert	29 Oct. 1811	177 11 8
Sewell, Hon. Harriet	10 Dec. 1821	88 1 0	Warre, Sarah	18 Nov. 1818	26 2 8
Steward, Catherine U.	25 Oct. 1823	266 18 4	Wade, Mary	21 Sept. 1821	43 18 4
Shaw, Meyrick	10 March, 1825	499 14 0	Westmeath, Emily, Marchioness of	26 Jan. 1829	386 5 4
Sharkey, Richard F.	13 April, 1826	88 1 0	Wade, Mary	28 Sept. 1829	57 6 8
Smythe, Hon. G. A. F. S.	14 Feb. 1828	104 4 0	Yates, Mary	14 March, 1794	177 11 8
Stanhope, Hannah M., and Charles Russell	,,	95 10 0	Young, Anne	8 Feb. 1804	445 19 4
St. George, Hannah M. and Mary Jane	,,	144 0 0	Yates, Jane	10 Oct. 1814	61 16 4
Stack, Annabella	,,	37 18 8			
Stack, Annabella	,,	18 13 4	Total		L.53,921 4 10

PENSIONS OUT OF THE HEREDITARY REVENUE IN SCOTLAND.

NAME.	Date of Grant.	Amount.
Aston, Walter Hutcheson Lord .	27 Jan. 1801	L.97 0 0
Arburthnot, Catharine	22 Oct. 1804	138 5 0
Arburthnot, Jane .	,,	138 5 0
Anderson, Sarah and Helen .	22 Nov. 1806	72 12 6
Anstruther, C. Lucy,	19 May, 1809	276 10 0
Buchanan, Elizabeth	30 Aug. 1786	97 0 0
Balmain, Isabella .	21 Oct. 1790	49 10 0
Burnet, Lamont .	20 Oct. 1804	39 10 0
Burnet, Christian .	,,	39 10 0
Burnet, Helen .	,,	39 10 0
Baillie, Elizabeth .	22 Oct 1804	39 10 0
Baillie, Jean .	,,	39 10 0
Baillie, Mrs. Menzies	,,	49 10 0
Brown, Jean .	,,	58 0 0
Bruce, Mary .	,,	97 0 0
Balmain, Isabella	30 Sept. 1805	49 10 0
Baillie, Ann .	23 Oct. 1806	24 14 0
Bartlet, Mary .	22 Nov. 1806	49 10 0
Baillie, Ann .	16 Feb. 1808	49 10 0
Blair, Isabella C. Mrs.	7 Oct. 1811	276 10 0
Blair, Isabella .	,,	138 5 0
Blair, Cornelia .	,,	138 5 0
Blair, William	,,	92 0 0
Ditto, additional .	5 Dec. 1812	92 0 0
Boswell, Euphemia	,,	49 10 0
Burnet, Deborah	,,	92 0 0
Blair, Ann .	12 June 1815	49 10 0
Blair, Janet .	,,	49 10 0
Bower, Jean .	27 Dec. 1816	100 6 6
Bruce, Mary .	24 June 1820	49 10 0
Black, Jean .	30 Aug. 1823	49 10 0
Black, Mary Ann	,,	49 10 0
Bodan, Barbara .	28 Sept. 1825	24 14 0
Bodan, Eliza .	,,	24 14 0
Burnet, Deborah	14 April 1826	92 0 0
Buchanan, Lady Janet	12 Oct. 1827	138 5 0
Buchanan, Susana	29 Nov. 1827	184 0 0
Cockburn, Jean .	8 Aug. 1789	184 0 0
Campbell, Mary	28 May, 1790	97 0 0
Colville, Ann .	1 July, 1790	97 0 0
Colville, Catherine	,,	97 0 0
Currie, Jean .	2 July, 1790	39 10 0
Cullen, Margaret and Robina	3 July, 1790	97 0 0
Cockburn, Fanny	14 Feb. 1791	97 0 0
Cockburn, Mary	14 March, 1791	97 0 0
Cockburn, Harriet	,,	97 0 0
Caithness, Jean, Countess of .	1 July, 1800	184 0 0
Campbell, Jean and Mary .	2 July, 1800	184 0 0
Campbell, Mary, John, and Amelia .	24 Oct. 1800	184 0 0
Cochrane, Lady Maria	,,	184 0 0
Chalmes, Catherine F.	1 July, 1801	97 0 0
Ciciaporci, Lucretia	,,	184 0 0
Caithness, Jean, Countess of .	2 July, 1802	92 0 0
Cleghorn, Hugh	28 Nov. 1803	138 5 0

NAME.	Date of Grant.	Amount.
Cunningham, Jean, Margery, and Lavinia	3 Jan. 1804	L.97 0 0
Christie, Margaret	22 Oct. 1804	24 14 0
Christie, Helen .	,,	24 14 0
Cleghorn, Hugh	,,	49 10 0
Cleghorn, Janet .	,,	49 10 0
Cleghorn, Rachel .	,,	49 10 0
Cleghorn, Jean .	,,	49 10 0
Clerk, Dame M. Dacre	,,	97 0 0
Campbell, Thomas	28 Oct. 1806	184 0 0
Campbell, Mary .	9 Feb. 1809	97 0 0
Campbell, Mary .	13 Sept. 1810	184 0 0
Christie, Elizabeth	23 Feb. 1814	49 10 0
Cooper, Helen .	19 June 1817	44 10 0
Chisholme, Margaret	18 Jan. 1819	72 12 6
Cranstown, Jas. E. Ld.	27 Nov. 1821	184 0 0
Craigie, Margaret	30 Aug. 1823	24 15 0
Campbell, Helen	25 Oct. 1824	97 0 0
Caithness, Francis Herriet, Countess of	28 Sept. 1825	276 10 0
Crawnstown, Lady	31 Aug. 1826	97 0 0
Dich, Ann .	20 Feb. 1778	97 0 0
Delzell, Henrietta, Helen, Agnes Brown, and Elizabeth .	8 July, 1790	184 0 0
Dundas, Lady Eliz. E.	14 Feb. 1801	276 10 0
Drysdale, Martha	28 Nov. 1803	49 10 0
Dyer, Martha Laetitia	10 May, 1804	97 0 0
Dalrymple, Margaret	22 Oct. 1804	49 10 0
Dalrymple, Helen	,,	49 10 0
Dalrymple, Elizabeth	,,	49 10 0
Davidson, Mary	22 Sept. 1806	49 10 0
Drummond, Clementina	,,	49 10 0
Duncan, Williamina	24 Mar. 1807	39 10 0
Dunmore, Helen Wilson, and Janet Napier	14 Mar. 1808	9 2 5
Douglas, Grace .	18 July, 1809	138 5 0
Davidson, Ann .	27 Sept. 1809	29 10 0
Davidson, Elizabeth	,,	29 10 0
Davidson, Mary	,,	29 10 6
Davidson, Jean	,,	29 10 0
Davidson, Joanna Wau.	,,	29 10 0
Drummond, Lady Am.	5 Dec. 1812	97 0 0
Downie, Jean .	14 June 1816	49 10 0
Douglas, Elizabeth	24 June 1820	276 10 0
Dalzell, Mary .	21 Nov. 1821	49 10 0
Dalzell, Alice .	,,	49 10 0
Drummond, the Rev. Charles Edward	26 Sept. 1822	97 0 0
Dalzell, Elizabeth	14 April, 1826	49 10 0
Dunmore, Janet Nap.	12 Nov. 1828	52 11 6
Erroll, Elizabeth Jemima, Countess of .	7 Feb. 1791	276 10 0
Elphinstone, Ann	24 June 1791	184 0 0
Erskine, Lady Louisa	5 Mar. 1801	276 10 0
Erroll, Elizabeth Jemima, Countess Dowag. of	18 Aug. 1803	276 10 0
Elphinstone, John Elphinstone Lord	23 Feb. 1814	138 5 0
Elphinstone, Elizabeth, Mackenzie and Keith	9 Nov. 1814	276 10 0

NAME.	Date of Grant.	Amount.	NAME.	Date of Grant.	Amount.
Elibank, Lady .	17 June 1818	L. 92 0 0	Hamilton, Henrietta	28 Nov. 1803	L. 97 0 0
Erskine, Erskine, wid.	22 Dec. 1818	276 10 0	Hamilton, Catharine	3 Jan. 1804	49 10 0
Erroll, Geo. Earl of	6 May, 1819	276 10 0	Halket, Mary & John	22 Oct. 1804	97 0 0
Erroll, Herriot, Countess			Hay, Mary Turner	24 May 1805	97 0 0
of . .	24 June 1820	276 10 0	Hay, Jane . .	,,	97 0 0
Elibank, Lady .	16 June 1821	92 0 0	Hay, Jane . .	19 Nov. 1805	97 0 0
Erskine, Euphemia	30 Aug. 1823	14 8 2	Hay, Isabella .	22 May 1806	97 0 0
Erskine, Helen .	,,	49 10 0	Hamilton, Ann .	16 Feb. 1808	97 0 0
Erskine, Marianne	,,	49 10 0	Hall, Mary Maxwell	21 Dec. 1812	97 0 0
Erskine, Jean .	,,	49 10 0	Honyman, Dame M.	23 Feb. 1814	138 5 0
Erskine, the Hon.			Honyman, Mary	12 June 1815	18 12 0
Margaret .	25 Oct. 1824	138 5 0	Honyman, Catherine	,,	37 0 0
Elibank, Alexander			Honyman, Margaret	,,	37 0 0
Murray Lord .	31 Aug. 1826	138 5 0	Honyman, Jemima	,,	37 0 0
Elphinstone, John E.			Hunt, Mary .	28 Sept. 1816	150 5 6
Lord . .	,,	138 5 0	Harley, or Colville,		
Forbes, Elizabeth	4 Sept. 1786	19 16 0	Elizabeth .	19 June 1817	14 14 0
Fergusson, Johanna	2 July, 1790	67 15 0	Hamilton, Marion	19 Nov. 1822	49 10 0
Fleming, Jean .	23 Aug. 1792	49 10 0	Hamilton, Amy .	,,	49 10 0
Fleming, Elizabeth	,,	49 10 0	Hamilton, Eleanora	,,	49 10 0
Fleming, Catherine	,,	49 10 0	Hay, Lady Fanny	31 Dec. 1822	97 0 0
Fowlis, Lady .	,,	97 0 0	Hay, Lady Mary	13 Dec. 1823	184 0 0
Fergusson, Isabella,			Hay, Lady Mary	27 Dec. 1824	92 0 0
Mary and Margaret	8 Mar. 1799	184 0 0	Hunter, Dr. John	6 June 1827	97 0 0
Fergusson, Elizabeth	26 Nov. 1805	97 0 0	Hepburne, Cath.	16 March 1829	184 0 0
Fullarton, Eliz. .	24 March, 1807	49 10 0	Irvine, Charles	13 March 1792	97 0 0
Fraser, William .	16 Oct. 1807	97 0 0	Imlach, Elspet	13 Sept. 1810	24 14 0
Farquharson, Margaret			Inglis Henry .	4 March 1825	24 14 0
Euphemia .	16 Feb. 1808	49 10 0	Kirkpatrick, Isab.	15 March 1782	49 10 0
Fordyce, Helen .	13 Sept. 1810	24 14 0	Kerr, Lady Sidney	16 June 1792	55 12 10
Fordyce, Jean .	,,	24 14 0	Kirkpatrick, Isabella	23 Aug. 1792	97 0 0
Falkland, Lucius Ben-			Kennedy, Margaret,		
tinck, Viscount .	14 June 1816	184 0 0	Ann, Barbara,		
Gordon, Margaret S.	26 Feb. 1783	49 10 0	Frances and Eleo.	3 Jan. 1804	110 10 0
Grant, Sophia Jane	23 Dec. 1784	49 10 0	Kennedy, Mary .	10 May 1804	49 10 0
Grant, Charlotte F.	,,	49 10 0	Kennedy, Janet .	,,	49 10 0
Grant, Catharine, Ann			Kennedy, Mary,		
and Heriot .	2 July 1790	97 0 0	widow . .	21 Aug. 1823	97 0 0
Gloag, Euphemia, Hen-			Kerr, Mary .	30 Nov. 1825	184 0 0
rietta and Martha	28 Nov. 1803	58 0 0	Kerr, Lady Mary	31 Aug. 1826	92 0 0
Gordon, Goodrich Ann	,,	97 0 0	Kirkcudbright, C. G.		
Goldie, Magdalene .	22 Oct. 1804	97 0 0	M., Baron .	19 Nov. 1828	184 0 0
Gillon, Catherine .	30 Sept. 1805	97 0 0	Livingstone, Lady	7 Sept. 1791	97 0 0
Gillon, Elizabeth	,,	97 0 0	Livingstone, Ann and		
Gray, Lady MaryAnn	20 Dec. 1806	97 0 0	Elizabeth .	1 Oct. 1791	97 0 0
Gillies, Dr. John	5 July 1813	184 0 0	Leslia, Eugenia .	9 Oct. 1792	58 0 0
Graham, Isabella, Mary			Linley, or Stavely,		
Cathcart, E. Georgi-			Henrietta .	7 Aug. 1798	37 2 6
ana, Margaret, Cath-			Loch, Margaret .	1 July 1801	53 2 6
erine, Roberta and Ca-			Loch, Frances .	,,	53 2 6
roline Æ. M'Kay	14 June 1816	276 10 0	Leslie, Lady Charlotte	3 Jan. 1804	97 0 0
Gray, Mary . .	,,	184 0 0	Leitch, Isabel .	19 Nov. 1805	138 5 0
Gilmour, Kennedy	11 Sept. 1817	49 10 0	Leith, Mary .	22 Sept. 1806	97 0 0
Gordon, Sir G. bt.	16 June 1821	138 5 0	Legertwood, Jean and		
Grant, Ann, widow	28 Sept. 1825	49 10 0	Barbara .	16 Feb. 1808	97 0 0
Gifford, Robert, Lord,			Law Jean .	12 Aug 1809	97 0 0
Children of the late	17 Aug. 1827	198 16 0	Laing, Margaret	12 June 1815	24 14 0
Grant, Ann, widow	31 Oct. 1827	49 10 0	Lapslie, Margaret L.	22 Oct. 1825	24 14 0
Hamilton, or Irvine,			Lapslie, Gloriana .	,,	24 14 0
Grizle .	4 May 1789	49 10 0	Muir, William .	15 Nov. 1777	276 10 0
Haldane, Euphemia	1 Oct. 1791	63 17 0	Mercer, Jean .	24 Sept. 1787	39 10 0
Home, Alex. Earl of	23 Aug. 1792	276 10 0	Mackenzie, Mrs. Henry	1 Oct. 1791	97 0 0
Hay, Dorothea Judith	19 May 1800	97 0 0	Mackenzie, Margaret and		
Hay, Lewis . .	,,	97 0 0	Mary	,,	97 0 0
Hay, Elizabeth .	,,	97 0 0	Moncrieffe, Douglas	19 June 1793	184 0 0

NAME.	Date of Grant.	Amount.		
Maxwell, Elizabeth	18 July 1793	L.72	15	0
Murray, Lady Virginia	7 Aug. 1798	184	0	0
Mackenzie, Hope and Helen	1 July 1801	97	0	0
Macdonald, Mary	2 July 1802	97	0	0
Maclean, Ann	,,	39	10	0
Maclean, Sibella	,,	39	10	0
Murray, George	24 Dec. 1802	97	0	0
Murray, Mary	,,	97	0	0
Murray, Eliz. Ann	,,	97	0	0
Murray, Emily	3 Jan. 1804	72	12	6
Mackay, Ann	,,	184	0	0
Mackay, Louisa	22 Oct. 1804	97	0	0
Maclaurin, Eliza	,,	97	0	0
Maxton, Marion	,,	97	0	0
Murray, Catherine S.	,,	97	0	0
Macfarlane, Margaret	1 Nov. 1806	97	0	0
Maclean, Maria	24 March 1807	49	10	0
Moodie, James	,,	97	0	0
Maxwell, Susan	16 Feb. 1808	29	10	0
Maclauria, Colin	16 Nov. 1808	97	0	0
Macdougall, Margt.	18 July 1809	101	5	0
Mackenzie, Henrietta Wharton	13 Sept. 1810	97	0	0
Macquarrie, Ann	,,	29	10	0
Macquarrie, Jean	,,	29	10	0
Mitchell, C. Forbes	17 June 1818	49	10	0
Macneill, Ann, widow	10 Nov. 1820	184	0	0
M'Cormick, Rachel	26 Nov. 1821	49	10	0
M'Cormick, Helen	,,	49	10	0
Mackay, Flora, widow	17 Sept. 1822	49	10	0
Maitland, Frances J.	21 Aug. 1823	49	10	0
Napier, Catherine Douglas & Maria	16 Feb. 1808	97	0	0
Napier, Caroline	17 June 1818	97	0	0
Napier, Sophia	,,	97	0	0
Nairne, Lord	17 Sept. 1822	184	0	0
Nairne, Caroline, Baroness	18 Feb. 1829	184	0	0
Orr, Martha	10 May 1804	49	10	0
Ogilvie, Jean	22 Oct. 1804	24	14	0
Ogilvie, Rebecca	,,	24	14	0
Outram, Margaret	13 Sept. 1810	97	0	0
Plummer, Mary and P. R. Macmurdo	1 July 1801	97	0	0
Palmer, Lady Madel.	17 Dec. 1801	184	0	0
Paul, Susan	28 Nov. 1803	6	18	9
Portmore, T. Earl of	25 Oct. 1824	276	10	0
Russell, Eleonora	3 July 1790	97	0	0
Robison, Rachel	7 Sept. 1791	92	0	0
Rose, Margaret	15 Nov. 1791	97	0	0
Robertson, Capt. Geo. Children of	21 March, 1792	97	0	0
Ruthven, Wilhelmina	1 July, 1801	230	5	0
Rose, Ann Fraser	24 Feb. 1803	92	0	0
Robison, Rachel	28 Nov. 1803	92	0	0
Reay, Eric Mackey, Baron	3 Jan. 1804	184	0	0
Robertson, Sarah	24 Sept. 1806	49	10	0
Read, or Potts, Cath.	23 Mar. 1807	97	0	0
Rollo, Isabella & Mary	24 Mar. 1807	184	0	0
Rose, Ann Fraser	16 Feb. 1808	47	0	0
Ross, or Baillie, Margaret	,,	97	0	0
Rose, Mary	16 Nov. 1808	97	0	0

NAME.	Date of Grant.	Amount.		
Ross, Anna Munro	13 Sept. 1810	L.29	10	0
Rothes, Charlotte J., Countess Dow. of	11 Sept. 1817	276	10	0
Rothes, G. W. E., Earl of	16 June, 1821	276	10	0
Stewart, Elizabeth	12 Sept. 1774	49	10	0
Sinclair, Elizabeth	30 Dec. 1775	138	5	0
Sinclair, Chas. Lord	14 Aug. 1778	184	0	0
Sutherland, Eliz.	26 June, 1789	97	0	0
Stewart, Jean & Lillias	8 Aug. 1789	49	10	0
Sinclair, Lady Isabella	2 July, 1790	115	0	2
Sinclair, Ann	1 Oct. 1791	37	0	0
Sinclair, Catherine	,,	20	15	4
Stewart, or Crawford, Elizabeth	,,	97	0	0
Simpson, Charlotte	30 Dec. 1791	97	0	0
Sutherland, Louisa	,,	97	0	0
Stewart, Ann	31 March, 1792	49	10	0
Shaw, Agnes	16 Nov. 1792	49	10	0
Swinton, Marga., Mary, Isabel, Harriet, and Ann	4 July, 1800	276	10	0
Sommerville, Dr. Thos.	6 Oct. 1800	92	0	0
Sempill, Janet	1 July, 1801	97	0	0
Steel, Jessy	,,	58	0	0
Stewart, Lady Louisa	,,	97	0	0
Scott, Dame Harriet	2 July, 1802	184	0	0
Simpson, Marianne	,,	39	10	0
Salvison, Sarah	3 Jan. 1804	49	10	0
Stewart, Ann	22 Oct. 1804	49	10	0
Stewart, Grace	,,	49	10	0
Shaw, Hannah	28 Oct. 1806	69	2	0
Stewart, Lady Lucy	22 Nov. 1806	184	0	0
Smollet, Susan	16 Nov. 1806	97	0	6
Stodart, Ann	28 Aug. 1809	49	10	0
Stodart, Barbara	,,	49	10	0
Stodart, Jean	,,	49	10	0
Stodart, Mary	,,	49	10	0
Sherkin, Amelia	28 Sept. 1816	102	3	6
Sempill, Hon. Maria	21 Nov. 1821	49	10	0
Sempill, Hon. Sarah	,,	49	10	0
Sempill, Hugh, Lord	31 Aug. 1826	97	0	0
Scotland, Eliz. widow	20 Sept. 1826	49	10	0
Scott, Sir David, bart.	30 Oct. 1827	149	7	0
Strathmore, Marianne, Lady	19 Nov. 1828	230	0	0
Telfer, Jean & Cecilia	11 May, 1789	97	0	0
Taylor, Marion, widow	3 Oct. 1826	49	10	0
Williamson, Helen	21 March, 1792	97	0	0
Wylde, John	16 March, 1796	138	5	0
Wilson, Ann, Children of	11 July, 1797	276	10	0
Willoughby, Harriet	22 Nov. 1806	276	10	0
Williamson, Marrianne, B.	24 March, 1807	49	10	0
Walker, Agnes	23 Feb. 1814	9	16	0
Walker, Janet	,,	9	16	0
Walker, Jean	,,	9	16	0
Wardlaw, Sir Wm.	25 Oct. 1824	72	12	6
Young, Ann	13 Sept. 1810	9	16	0
Young, Janet	,,	9	16	0
Young, Margaret	,,	9	16	0
Total Pensions on the Scotch Pension List		L.31,252	3	8

ADDITIONAL PENSIONS ON THE CIVIL LIST, ENGLAND.

THE return of Pensions on the Civil List, presented on the 2d December *, contains all the Pensions granted up to the close of the reign of his late Majesty George the Fourth ; and the Civil List to be assigned to his present Majesty not having yet received the sanction of Parliament, the formal documents which are required previous to the payment of any of the Pensions granted by his present Majesty cannot yet be completed.

His Majesty has, however, been pleased to direct, through the First Lord of the Treasury, by communications addressed by his Grace to the Board of Treasury, and dated respectively, as will appear in the following return, that warrants should be prepared for granting the following Pensions on the Civil List.

NAME.				DATE.	NET AMOUNT.		
					L.	s.	d.
Lady Hill	.	.	.	5 April, 1830	467	12	0
Colonel D'Este	.	.	.	29 June, 1830	467	12	0
Miss D'Este	.	.	.	,,	467	12	0
Colonel Frederick Fitzclarence	.		.	,,	500	0	0
Mrs. Tierney	.	.	.	,,	400	0	0
Thomas Knox Holmes	.		.	16 Nov. 1830	500	0	0
Edward Drummond	.		.	,,	250	0	0
Algernon Greville	.	.	.	,,	250	0	0
Dame Mary Ray	.		.	20 Nov. 1830	660	0	0
					L. 3,962	16	0

The warrant for the Pension to Lady Hill was prepared and sent for signature in June last, and was returned to the Treasury after the death of the late king, among other warrants which had not received the royal signature.

In addition to the new Pensions stated in this return, directions have been given that upon the re-grant of the Pensions on the late Civil List, the Pension held by Colonel George Fitzclarence, of 500l. per annum net, should be made payable to Mary Fitzclarence his wife ; and that the Pension held by Sir Robert Taylor, of 938l. 10s. net, should now be granted to Sir H. Taylor and Lady Taylor, or the survivor.

Whitehall, Treasury Chambers, 7 December, 1830.

ADDITIONAL PENSIONS ON THE SCOTCH CIVIL LIST.]

*Chargeable on the Hereditary Revenue of Scotland, under the Act of
50 Geo.* III *, c.* 111.

NAME.				DATE.	NET AMOUNT.		
					L.	s.	d.
Lady Elibank	.	.	.	9 Oct. 1830	138	5	0
Frances Catherine Sandford	.		.	,,	97	0	0
Lady Charlotte Murray MacGregor				,,	97	0	0
Harriett H. Gordon	.	.	.	,,	97	0	0
Mrs. Brown	.	.	.	.	,,	97	0	0
Mary Cockburn	.	.	.	.	,,	49	10	0
Barbara Reid	.	.	.	.	,,	49	10	0
Captain George Drummond (De Melfont)				,,	97	0	0
Agnes Lindsay	.	.	.	,,	49	10	0
					L. 771	15	0

No Pensions have been granted upon the *Irish* Civil List since the accession of his present Majesty.

* Sess. Paper, No. 42.

APPENDIX.—No. VII.

An Account of all SALARIES, PENSIONS, PROFITS, PAY, FEES, and EMOLUMENTS held and enjoyed by all Persons, between 5th January, 1829, and 5th January, 1830, the Total Amount of which shall exceed 1000l.; specifying with each Name the Total Amount received by each Individual, and distinguishing the various sources from whence the same are derived.—

1. Civil Officers.
2. The Court of Chancery and other Judicial Officers.
3. Diplomatic and Consular Officers.
4. Naval Officers.
5. Military Officers returned by the Secretary at War.
6. Ordnance and Military Officers not included in the Secretary at War's Return.
7. Officers in the Colonies.
8. Officers in the House of Commons.

1. CIVIL OFFICERS.

SALARIES.

Earl of Aberdeen, Secretary of State for Foreign Affairs		L. 6000 0 0		
Lord Ashley, Commis. for Affairs of India		1500 0 0		
W. D. Adams, Commissioner of Woods		1200 0 0	. . Also 375l. per ann. as late Comptroller of the Lottery.	
Henry Arbuthnot, Commissioner of Audit		1200 0 0		
E. Arnaud, Collector of Customs at Liverpool		2200 0 0		
R. Aberdeen, Coll. Customs, Bridge Town, Barbadoes		1500 0 0		
T. Amyott, Registrar of Colonial Slaves		800 0 0	. Also 400l. per ann. Compensation allowance for loss of office as Secretary and Register of Records in Lower Canada.	
H. S. Alves, Sen. Clerk, India Bd. Office L. 900 0 0				
Ditto Master of the Mint, Scotland 390 0 0	—1290 0 0			
J. Angell, Chief Clerk, Ordnance Office		1162 17 6		
W. T. Aiton, Director-General of his Majesty's Gardens and Plantations		1000 0 0		
Earl Bathurst, President of the Council 2835 2 0				
Ditto Teller of the Exchequer 2700 0 0				
Ditto Clerk of the Crown 1105 18 10	—6641 0 10			
Stamp Brooksbank, Chief Clerk in the Treasury, and Auditor of Treasury Accounts		1650 0 0	. Salary to be hereafter 1450l. per annum.	
T. C. Brooksbank, Chief Clerk, Treasury 1200 0 0				
Ditto, Agent and Paymaster of Chelsea Out-Pensioners 750 0 0				
Ditto, Agent for the Bahamas 150 0 0				
Ditto, Commissioner of Lottery 150 0 0	—2250 0 0			
Charles Bourchier, Assistant Solicitor to the Treasury, in lieu of Bills 1500 0 0				
Ditto, Emoluments 400 0 0	—1900 0 0			
John Bidwell, First Senior Clerk and Superintendent of the Consular Department		1400 0 0		
J. Backhouse, Under Secretary of State 500 0 0				
Ditto, Receiver-General of Excise 1500 0 0	—2000 0 0	. . The salary is 2000l. but Mr. Backhouse only receives 500l. in consequence of his being Receiver Gen. of Excise.		
Thomas Bidwell, Chief Clerk in the Office of Secretary of State for Foreign Affairs 1250 0 0				
Ditto, Deputy Clerk of the Signet 95 6 6	—1345 6 6			

SALARIES.

James Bandinel, Senior Clerk in the Office of the Secretary of State for Foreign Affairs . . L. 1200 0 0

G. Baillie, Senior Clerk in the Office of the
Secretary of State for the Colonies . L. 739 1 4
Ditto, Agent for Sierra Leone and the Royal
African Corps . . 639 3 4—1378 4 8

R. Brown, Chief Examiner War Office . 1350 0 0
Ditto, Agent for Paying retired or officiating Chaplains . . . 250 0 0—1600 0 0 . . Also 273*l*. 15*s*. per

J. Buller, Clerk of the Council . . 2500 0 0 annum, half-pay as

G. Bankes, Secretary to India Board . 1452 6 7 Deputy Commissary
Ditto, Cursitor Baron Exchequer . 455 0 0—1907 6 7 General.

R. Byham, Secretary to the Board of Ordnance . 1400 0 0

J. H. Barnouin, Chief Clerk to Clerk of the Ordnance 1062 17 6

John Barrow, Second Secretary to the Admiralty . 1500 0 0

H. I. Bouverie, Commissioner of Customs . 1400 0 0

D. M. Binning, ,, ,, . 1400 0 0

Sir W. Boothby, Receiver Gen. of Customs 1500 0 0
Ditto, Agent for New Brunswick . 150 0 0
Ditto, Paymr. Band of Gent. Pensioners 230 0 0—1880 0 0

W. Barraud, Receiver of Duties, Customs 500 0 0
Emolumts. & Fees paid by individuals 660 0 0—1160 0 0

W. R. Brown, Cocket-writer, Customs, Salary 60 0 0
Fees paid by individuals 1028 0 0—1088 0 0

A. H. Brooking, Collector of Customs, Newfoundland 1400 0 0

J. W. Bowden, Commissioner of Stamps . 1012 0 0

R. Browne, Solic. Stamp Board (Ireland), in lieu of bills 2000 0 0

J. Blackburn, Distributor of Stamps for part of Lancashire . . . 1530 19 10

Edward Bates, Secretary to Board of Taxes 1539 9 0
Ditto, Husband of the 4½ per cent duties 400 0 0—1939 0 0

W. Bagott, Receiver General of Taxes . 1200 0 0

G. C. Bedford, Chief Clerk to Auditor of the Exchequer 1200 0 0

A. Bulley, Clerk of the Issues, Exchequer 750 0 0
Ditto, Assessor, Receiver and Clerk to Commissioners of 1s. 6d. duty . 252 4 4—1002 4 4

Robert Bingley, King's Assay Master, Mint . 1033 19 8

Hon. W. Bathurst, Deputy Teller, Exchequer . 1000 0 0

Timothy Brent, Sec. Board of Green Cloth 1185 0 0
Ditto, Secretary to the Lord Steward 124 14 0
Ditto, Groom and Clerk of the Robes . 155 0 0—1464 14 0

Sir John Beckett, Judge Advocate General . 2500 0 0

William Bowles, Comptroller-General Coast Guard 1000 0 0 . . Also 228*l*. 2*s*. 6*d*. per

The Hon. W. Cust, Commissioner of Customs . . 1400 0 0 annum half-pay, as

The Right Hon. T. P. Courtenay, Vice President Captain in the Navy.
Board of Trade . . 2000 0 0
Ditto, Agent for Cape of Good Hope . 600 0 0—2600 0 0

Marquis of Camden, Teller of his Majesty's Exchequer 2700 0 0

Right Hon. J. Calcraft, Paymaster Gen. of the Forces 2000 0 0

Right Hon. J. W. Croker, Secretary to the Admiralty 3000 0 0

Earl of Clarendon, Chief Justice in Eyre, Nth. of Trent 2250 0 0

Viscount Clifden, Clerk of the Privy Council, Ireland 1450 4 10

Marquis Conyngham, Lord Steward . . 2435 15 0 .˙. See also Military Return. Lord Conyngham received in 1829, 636*l*. 10*s*. Military Pay.

William Cotton, Chief Clerk in the Treasury . . 1400 0 0

Thomas Crafer, Principal Clerk Assis. to Secretaries, Treasury . . . 1100 0 0
Ditto, Paymaster of American Loyalists, and Examiner of American Claims 300 0 0—1400 0 0

John Calvert, Secretary to the Lord Chamberlain . 1676 10 6

Alexander Campbell, Commissioner of Excise . 1400 0 0

Morton Carr, Solicitor to Excise for Scotland, in lieu of all Bills . . 1500 0 0

Lieut.-Gen. Sir H. Campbell, Commissioner of Taxes 1000 0 0 . . See also Military Return. Gen. Campbell received also 1294*l*. 14*s*. 2*d*. military pay, 1829.

Sir W. H. Cooper, bart. and F. G. Cooper, Auditor of
Land Revenue for England,—Salary . 100 0 0
Emoluments 3971 12 11—4071 12 11

SALARIES.

C. G. Christmas, Deputy Auditor Land Rev. *L.* 80	0	0				
Ditto, Acting Auditor for Lincoln, Notting-ham, Derby, and Chester,—Salary . 280	0	0				
Emoluments 2193	0	6—2553	0	6		
J. H. Capper, Clerk for Criminal Business in the Home Department . . 670	0	0				
Ditto, Superintendent Convict Establish. 400	0	0—1070	0	0		
Rich. Cane, Sub-Agent to Chelsea Hospital, in Ireland 1200	0	0				
Ditto, Agent to Yeomanry . ditto 461	10	9				
Ditto, Agent to Police . ditto 461	10	9—2123	1	6		
E. H. Clark, Clerk of Warrants, Customs, Salary . . . 40	0	0				
Fees paid by individuals . . 2642	9	0—2682	9	0		
George Cooper, Assistant Surveyor, Customs, Salary . . . 400	0	0				
Fees paid by individuals . 693	0	0—1093	0	0		
S. M. Clogstone, Collector of Customs, Trinidad . 1500	0	0				
J. Chapman, Commissioner of Audit . . 1200	0	0				

Edw. Conner, Clerk, Chief Secretary's Office, Ireland   923   1   6

Also,
L. 91   8   4 per ann. as late Secret. Bd. of Gen. Officers;
159 18   4 per ann. for losses by the Union, and
177   7   8 per annum Pensions.
—————
428 14   4

Sir George Cockburn, Lord of the Admiralty	1000	0	0			
Lord Dunglass, Uunder Secretary of State 2000	0	0				
Chamberlain of Ettrick Forest . 300	0	0—2300	0	0		
John Dyer, Chief Clerk in the Admiralty .	1150	0	0			
R. B. Dean, Chairman of Board of Customs 2000	0	0				
Ditto, Clerk to Master in Chancery in Alienation Office . 50	0	0—2050	0	0		
John Dyer, Receiver of the Grand Receipt of Customs,—Salary . . 300	0	0				
Emoluments and Fees paid by individuals 1524	9	0—1824	2	0		
Hart Davis, Commissioner of Excise . 1400	0	0				
E. Dew, Examiner of Dry Goods, Customs, Salary . . . 400	0	0				
Fees paid by individuals . . 1741	6	0—2141	6	0		
Sir F. H. Doyle, Deputy Chair. Excise Board 1700	0	0				
Ditto, Deputy Lieutenant of the Tower 786	0	0—2486	0	0		
W. Knight Dehany, Solicitor to Excise, in lieu of Bills 2500	0	0				
E. Donne, Sol. to Commissioners of Hackney Coaches 1636	0	0				
H. Dawkins, Commissioner of Woods . . 1200	0	0				
G. R. Dawson, Secretary of the Treasury . . 3500	0	0				

Also,
L. 593 2 6 per ann. as Admiral, &
1037 5 0 per ann. as Major-Gen.
—————
1630 7 6 of Marines.

Lieut.-Col. Drinkwater, Comptroller of Army Accounts   1500   0   0   { . . Also 520*l.* 2s. 6d. per ann. as Lt.-Col. and Retired Com.-Gen. of Accounts.

J. E. Dorington, Parliamentary Agent to the English and Irish Departments of the Treasury . . 1100	0	0				
Lord Ellenborough, Pres. of India Board 5000	0	0				
Ditto, Chief Ck. Ct. of King's Bench Fees 9625	8	1—14625	8	1		
Lord Eliot, Lord of the Treasury . . 1220	0	0				
William Earnshaw, Assistant Solicitor of Customs 1500	0	0				
William Everett, Receiver-General of Taxes . 1200	0	0				
H. Ellis, Clerk of the Pells in the Exchequer . 1400	0	0				
J. Ebbs, Deputy Clerk of the Council and Keeper of the Council Chamber, Ireland 865	4	3				
& Clerk in Chief Secretary's Office, Ireland 184	12	3—1049	16	6		

{ . . Also, 290*l.* 5s. as Clerk of the Fees, House of Commons.

. . Also 65*l.* 19s. per ann. for loss by the Union.

SALARIES.

Right Hon. W. F. V. Fitzgerald. Treasurer of
the Navy . . . *L.* 3000 0 0
Ditto, President of the Board of Trade 2000 0 0—5000 0 0 Since resigned.
Edward Fauquier, Senior Clerk in the Trea. 849 4 0
Ditto, Super. of St. James's & Hyde Parks 207 16 0—1057 0 0
Sir W. Franklin, Prin. Inspector, Army Medical Board 1200 0 0
R. Fall, Assist. Surveyor, Customs, Salary 300 0 0
    Fees paid by individuals 1120 0 0—1420 0 0
Sir F. Freeling, Secretary to the Post-Office 1200 0 0
    Emoluments . . . 2965 6 4—4165 6 4
J. C. Freeling, Secretary to the Excise . 1500 0 0
Sir C. W. Flint, Resident Secretary, Irish.
    Office, London . . . 1550 0 0   { . Also a pension of
Ditto, Comptroller of Killibeggs* . 87 8 4—1637 8 4   266*l.* 13*s.* 10*d.* per an.
    * To be abolished

Right Hon. Sir W. H. Freemantle, Treasurer of his Majesty's Household . . . . 904 0 0   { . . Also 924*l.* 8*s.* per ann. for loss of the office of Joint Sol. in England for Irish Affairs, which office is abolished.

Duke of Gordon, Keeper of the Great Seal of Scotland 1850 0 0 *See* also Military Return.
Lord Grenville, Auditor of the Exchequer . 4000 0 0
Right Hon. H. Goulburn, Chancellor of Exchequer 5219 16 0
Right Hon. T. Grenville, Chief Justice, in Eyre, South of Trent 2316 0 0
James Grange, Senior Clerk in the Treasury . 1000 0 0 . . Also a Pension of 250*l.* per ann. on the 4½ per cent. Fund.

A. Gordon, Chief Clerk, Secretary of State's
  Office for the Colonies . *1500 0 0   { . . Also a compensation allowance of 572*l.*
    Agent for Demerary . . 400 0 0   11*s.* per ann. as naval officer, Trinidad.
    Agent for Lower Canada . 200 0 0—2100 0 0   * Salary to be reduced to 1250*l.* on vacancy.

C. Greville, Comptroller of Cash in Excise 600 0 0
  and Receiver Gen. of Taxes, Nottingham 600 0 0
Ditto, Secretary of the Island of Tobago 350 0 0—1550 0 0 . . Also an allowance of 500*l.* per ann. as late naval officer, Demerara
C. C. F. Greville, Clerk of the Council . 2000 0 0
Ditto, Secretary and Clerk of the Enrolments in the Island of Jamaica . *3000 0 0—5000 0 0 . . * Also included in the Return of "Officers in the Colonies."
Marquis of Graham, Commissioner for Affairs of India 1500 0 0
Right Hon. Lord F. L. Gower, Chief Sec. for Ireland 4323 10 5
W. Gregory, Under Secretary for Ireland 2075 4 0
Ditto, Keeper of Phœnix Park . 26 16 7—2102 0 7
D. M. Grant, Collector of Customs, Kingston, Jamaica 2500 0 0
Right Hon. J. C. Herries, Master of the Mint . 3000 0 0

Right Hon. Sir G. F. Hill, Vice Treasurer of Ireland 2000 0 0   { . . Also a pension of 2091*l.* 8*s.* 2*d.* as Clerk of the late Irish House of Commons.

Right Hon. H. Hobhouse, Keeper of State Papers and Secretary of the Latin Language . . . 811 4 2 . . Also a Pension of 1000*l.* per ann. as late Under Secretary of State.
William Harrison, Parliamentary Counsel to the Treasury . . . 1000 0 0
Ditto, Law Clerk, War Office . 400 0 0—1400 0 0
Thomas Hoblyn, Chief Clerk in the Treasury . 1400 0 0
R. W. Hay, Under Secretary of State for the Colonies 2000 0 0
J. Hicks, Senior Clerk in the Secretary of State's Office, Home Department . . . 1129 0 0
Lewis Hertslet, Librarian, Secretary of State's Office, (Foreign) . 700 0 0
Ditto, Superintendent and Comptroller of King's Messengers . . 450 0 0—1150 0 0 . . Also a Compensation Allowance of 300*l.* per
J. D. Hume, Joint Assistant Secretary, Board of Trade . 1500 0 0 ann. for loss of Fees in
Terrick Haultain, Accountant, Army Pay Office . 1200 0 0 the Customs.

SALARIES.

E. Finch Hatton, Inspector Gen. of Tea & Coffee, Excise L.292 10 0	. . Also a Retired Allowance of 600l. per ann. as late Commissioner of Stamps.
Hon. A. A. H. Hutchinson, Commissioner of Customs	1400 0 0
L. Howard, Computer of Wine and Plantation Duties, Customs, Salary . . 300 0 0	
Fees paid by individuals 1163 11 0—1463 11 0	
Thomas Holmes, Collector of Customs, Grenada . 1500 0 0	
G. Huskisson, ditto ditto St. Vincent 1500 0 0	
Hon. J. Hewett, Commissioner of Excise . 1400 0 0	
Thomas Harrison, ditto. 1400 0 0	
S. Higham, Sec. and Comptroller, National Debt Office 1300 0 0	
Sir Henry Hotham, Lord of the Admiralty . 1000 0 0	{ . . Also 593l. 2s. 6d. per ann. as Vice-Admiral
Lt.-Col. Sir W. Herries, Comptroller of Army Accounts 1500 0 0	{ . . Also a Pen. of 300l. per ann. for loss of leg
Lt.-Gen. Sir T. Hammond, Chief Equerry and Clerk Marshal to his Majesty . . . 1030 0 0	{ . . 593l. 2s. 6d. per ann. as Lieut.-General. See Military Return.
Sir Ever. Home, Serj.-Surgeon to the King 277 14 0	
Ditto, Surgeon to Chelsea Hospital . 546 3 0— 823 17 0	. . Also a retired Pay of 187l. 10s. per annum.
William Holmes, Treasurer of the Ordnance . 1565 0 0	
Sir H. Hardinge, Secretary at War . . 2480 0 0	. . Also a Pension of 300l. for wounds.
B. S. Jones, Assistant Secretary, India Board 1200 0 0	
Henry Jadis, Paymaster, Exchequer Bills 600 0 0	
Ditto, Clerk in India Board Office . 500 0 0—1100 0 0	
R. H. Jenkinson, Registrar of Excise . 400 5 0	
Ditto, Receiver of Stamps . 800 0 0	
Ditto, Lieutenant of Dover Castle . 168 0 0—1368 5 0	
E. Jesse, Dep. Surv. of the Royal Parks, &c. 400 0 0	
Ditto, Commissioner of Hackney Coaches 330 0 0	
Ditto, Gentleman of the Ewry (Household) 285 0 0—1015 0 0	
T. N. Jefferey, Coll. of Customs, Halifax, Nova Scotia 2000 0 0	
John Kirkland, Joint Receiver of Crown Rents in London and Middlesex . 500 0 0	
Ditto, Agent for Nova Scotia & Cape Breton 200 0 0	
Ditto, Gen. Agent for Recruiting Service 834 0 0—1534 0 0	
Sir A. B. King, his Majesty's Stationer, Ireland 335 4 0	. . Also 850l. 8s. per ann. as Printer to the late House of Commons, Ireland. The office of King's Stationer, Ireland, is abolished.
T. Lack, Assistant Secretary Board of Trade . 1500 0 0	
R. Lukin, First Clerk, War Office . 1400 0 0	
S. G. Lushington, Commissioner of Customs . 1400 0 0	
Hon. H. Legge, ditto . . . 1400 0 0	
Viscount Lowther, 1st Commissioner of Woods . 2000 0 0	
J. Lack, Clerk of Rates, Customs, Salary 1,000 0 0	
Fees paid by individuals 100 0 0—1100 0 0	
Duke of Leeds, Master of Horse to His Maj. 3350 0 0	
Ditto, Constable of Middleham Castle 46 10 6—3396 10 6	
W. Lee, Ck. of Ships Entries, Customs, Salary 800 0 0	
Fees paid by Individuals 416 0 0—1216 0 0	
Horatio Leggatt, Solicitor of Taxes, in lieu of Bills 1500 0 0	
F. S. Larpent, Chairman of the Board of Audit 1500 0 0	
H. F. Luttrell, Commissioner of Audit . 1200 0 0	
Sir E. S. Lees, Secretary and Clerk of a Road Post-office, Ireland . . . 1424 2 6	
T. O. Lees, Chief Clerk and Clerk of a Road Post-office, Ireland . . . 816 0 0	
Ditto, Searcher, Packer, & Gauger, Wexford 504 0 0—1320 0 0	
Peter Low, Commissioner of Inquiry, Ireland . 1200 0 0	
Hon. H. Legge, Deputy Comptroller of the Navy 1200 0 0	
Duke of Montrose, Lord Chamberlain of His Majesty's Household . 3053 2 4	
Ditto, Lord Justice General, Scotland 2000 0 0—5053 2 4	
Duke of Manchester, Postmaster-General . 2500 0 0	
Viscount Melville, First Lord of Admiralty 5000 0 0	
Ditto, Lord Keeper Privy Seal, Scotland 2675 0 0—7675 0 0	
Earl of Macclesfield, Captain of the Yeoman of the Guard (Household) 1341 16 0	

SALARIES.

Ld. Maryborough, Master of His Majesty's Buckhounds	L. 2606 15 0			
Sir George Murray, Secretary of State	6000 0 0	. . See also Military Return. Sir G. Murray received 1309*l.* 16*s.* 6*d.* military pay in 1829.
G. Maule, Solicitor of Treas. in lieu of Bills	2000 0 0	
Emoluments	850 0 0—2850 0 0	
W. T. Manning, Third Clerk to Clerk of Ships		
Entries, Salary	100 0 0	
Fees paid by individuals	1711 19 6—1811 19 6	
T. B. Mash, Comptroller of Accounts in the Lord		
Chamberlain's Department	1445 6 6	Including fees.
George Maynard, Computer of Duties on		
East India Calicoes (Customs) Salary	300 0 0	
Fees paid by individuals	1149 0 0—1449 0 0	
Sir J. Mortlock, Commissioner of Excise	1400 0 0	
P. W. Mayow, Assist. Solicitor of Excise in lieu of Bills	2000 0 0	
G. W. A. Montagu, Deputy Chairman, Board of Stamps	1412 0 0	
H. S. Montagu, Commissioner of Stamps	1012 0 0	
Robert Mitford, Chairman, Board of Taxes	1600 0 0	
Ditto, Agent for Scotland, and Herring		
Fishery	230 0 0—1830 0 0	
G. R. Minshull, Police Magistrate	800 0 0	. . Also an allowance of 300*l.* per annum, as late Receiver Gen. of Taxes.
Alex. Milne, Secretary to Commissioners of Woods, and		
to Commissioners for executing the Acts 4, Geo. 4, c.		
74, and 7 Geo. 4, c. 77	1650 0 0	
A. Mangin, First Clerk Chief Secretary's Office, Ireland	1074 0 8	
Edward Mitchell, Senior Clerk Vice Trea-		
surer's Office, Ireland	720 0 0	
Ditto, Computer of Off-reckonings	184 0 0— 904 0 0	. . Also a retired allowance of 507*l.* per ann., as late Clerk in the Irish Treasury.
Alexander Maclean, Receiver General of Scotland	2000 0 0	
B. Mitford, Commissioner of Inquiry, Ireland	1200 0 0	
H. Mackenzie, Comptroller of Taxes, Scotland	720 0 0	
Ditto, Clerk to King's Remembrancer, ditto	350 0 0—1070 0 0	
Hon. G. Murray, Principal Auditor Exchequer, Scotland	1200 0 0	. . Also 492*l.* 15*s.* per ann. as Major-Gen. See Military Return.
Duke of Northumberland, Lord Lieutenant of Ireland	23153 17 5	Salary now fixed at 20,000*l.* a year.
H. Noble, Senior Clerk in the office of the Secretary		. . Also a compensation, allowance of 379*l.* 6*s.* 4*d.* per ann., as Naval Officer, Newfoundland.
of State, Home Department	925 0 0	
Gilbert N. Neyle, Auditor of the Accounts of the		
Registrar of the High Court of Admiralty	500 0 0	. . Also a retired allowance of 600*l.* per ann. as late Commissioner of Stamps.
Earl O'Neill, Postmaster-General, Ireland	1384 12 4	
Sir John Osborn, Commissioner of Audit	1200 0 0	
J. W. Ogle, Cocket Writer, Customs, Salary	60 0 0	
Fees paid by individuals	1043 0 0—1103 0 0	
Wm. Oxenford, First Clerk to the Register		
of Debentures (Customs) Salary	120 0 0	
Fees paid by individuals	1070 0 0—1190 0 0	
A. O'Connor, Distributor of Stamps for Antrim	1076 0 0	
Rt. Hon. Sir Rt. Peel, Sec. of State, Home Department	6000 0 0	
J. Planta, Secretary of the Treasury	3500 0 0	
W. Y. Peel, Under Secretary of State, Home Depart.	2000 0 0	
S. M. Phillipps, Ditto ditto	2000 0 0	
T. H. Plaskett, Chief Clerk in ditto	1329 18 0	
R. Penn, Agent for Ceylon	800 0 0	. . Paid by the Colony; also a retired allowance of 750*l.* per ann. as late Clerk in Sec. of State's Office.
W. Palgrave, Collector of Customs, Dublin	1200 0 0	
Woodbine Parish, Commissioner of Excise	*1400 0 0	
William Plunkett, Ditto	*1400 0 0	. . Also 267*l.* 18*s.* 4*d.* per annum, for loss of the office of Auditor, &c. Kilmainham Hospital.

SALARIES.

Hon. B. Paget, Commissioner of Excise . . L.*1400 0 0 * These Salaries to be
Hon. W. H. Percy, Ditto . . . . *1400 0 0 reduced to 1200l. each as
              Collector of Customs, Quebec 1500 0 0 vacancies arise.
M. B. Peacock, Solicitor to the Post Office,
                   Salary . 300 0 0
                   Emoluments 1500 0 .0—1800 0 0
Spencer Perceval, Teller of the Exchequer 2700 0 0
Ditto, Clerk of the Ordnance . 1200 0 0—3900 0 0
Earl of Rossyln, Lord Privy Seal . . . 2193 6 2 .. Also Director of Chan-
C. C. Raper, Clerk in War Office . 800 0 0   cery Scotland, 1852l. 7s.
Ditto, Paymaster of Pensions to Widows   6d. and Colonel of 9th
  and Children of Foreign Officers 250 0 0—1050 0 0   Dragoons, 1415l. 2s. 2d.
J. S. Reynolds, Principal Assistant Clerk, Commissariat,   See Military Return.
  and Clerk of Securities, Treasury . . 1050 0 0
Henry Richmond, Commissioner of Customs,
                   Salary 1400 0 0
                   For loss of Fees 800 0 0—2200 0 0
W. T. Roe, Commissioner of Customs 1400 0 0
Ditto, Steward of the Savoy . 15 0 0—1415 0 0
C. Robinson, Collector of Customs, Demerara . 2000 0 0
W. H. Roberts, First Clerk and Clerk of Exitus and
  Receiver of Fees, Exchequer . . 1350 0 0
Hon. G. A. C. Stapylton, Chairman of Victualling Board 1200 0 0
Hon. J. H. K. Stewart, Assistant Secretary, Treasury 2500 0 0
Lord G. C. H. Somerset, Commissioner of the Treasury 1220 0 0
William Speer, Chief Clerk in the Treasury and Auditor
  of Treasury Accounts . . 1700 0 0
John Smith, First Clerk, Irish Department, Treasury 1000 0 0   Also a Pension of
A. Y. Spearman, Assist. Clerk and Superinten-   92l. 6s. 2d. per annum,
  dant of Parliamentary Accounts, and for   and another of 212l. 6s.
  making special payments . 875 0 0   2d. for loss of office in
Ditto, First Clerk, Civil List Audit Office 400 0 0—1275 0 0   Irish House of Com-
William Sargent, Principal Clerk of the Commissariat   mons, per Act 40 Geo. 3.
  Department, Treasury . . . 1500 0 0   The office to be abo-
H. T. Short, Senior Clerk, Secretary of State's   lished on vacancy.
  Office, Colonial . . 855 6 10
Ditto, Agent for Trinidad . 344 0 0—1199 6 10
P. Smith, Clerk, Secretary of State's Office,
  Colonial . . 726 12 4.
Ditto, Agent for Mauritius . 500 0 0—1226 12 4
James Stephen, Law Adviser, Colonial Department
  and Board of Trade, in lieu of Fees . . 1500 0 0
L. Sullivan, Deputy Secretary at War . . 2000 0 0
W. H. Spicer, Deputy Treasurer, Chelsea Hospital 1016 5 0
William Stace, Ordnance Storekeeper, Woolwich 680 0 0   Also a Pension of
William Spencer, Ordnance Storekeeper, Portsmouth 1002 7 6 365l. per annum for
George Smith, Secretary to the Navy Board 1200 0 0   good Services.
Hon. E. Stewart, Deputy Chairman of the Customs 1700 0 0
Culling C. Smith, Commissioner of Customs . 1400 0 0
A. G. Stapleton, Commissioner of Customs 1400 0 0
Ditto, Agent for Grenada . 172 0 0
Ditto, Clerk of the Signet . 300 0 0—1872 0 0
C. Scovell, Assistant Secretary Customs . . 1200 0 0
Lord G. Seymour, Chairman of the Excise Board 2000 0 0
M. A. Saurin, Solicitor to Excise, Ireland, in lieu of Bills 1500 0 0
J. Staniforth, Distributor of Stamps for part of Lancashire 1599 4 11
Benjamin Sayer, Comptroller of Accounts, Tax Office 1131 5 0
A. Stanhope, Comptroller of the Foreign-Office in the ·
  General Post Office; Emoluments paid by individuals 1915 17 3
D. Stow, Superintending President and Clerk
  of a Road, in General Post Office, Salary 530 0 0
      Emoluments paid by individuals 1110 0 0—1640 0 0
Sir R. Seppings, Surveyor of the Navy . . 1000 0 0 Also a pension of 400l.
B. C. Stephenson, Surveyor General of Works 1500 7 0
Ditto, Riding Forester, New Forest 452 11 0—1952 18. 0

SALARIES.

E. Saurin, Commissioner of Stamps			*L.* 1012	0	0	. . Also 57*l.* 14*s.* per ann. as Captain R.N.
F. W. Trench, Principal Storekeeper of the Ordnance			1200	0	0	
Horace Twiss, Under Secretary of State			2000	0	0	
Hon. C. R. Trefusis, Commissioner of Excise		.	1400	0	0	
T. Tanner, Assistant Clerk of Ship's Entries,						
Customs . Salary	300	0	0			
Fees paid by individuals	2932	0	0—3232	0	0	
John Thornton, Chairman of the Board of Stamps			2012	0	0	
George Talbot, Paymaster of His Majesty's						
Household .			800	0	0	
Ditto, Receiver General of Assessed Taxes	600	0	0—1400	0	0	
Thomas Thompson, Solicitor to the Post Office, Ireland			1437	2	0	
Sir T. E. Tomlins, Parliamentary Council to						
the Chief Secretary, Ireland	400	0	0			
Ditto, ditto, to Treasury .	500	0	0			
Ditto, For Compiling Index to Acts relating						
to Ireland	200	0	0—1100	0	0	. . Also a pension of 168*l.* 6*s.* 2*d.* per annum.
C. W. Thornton, Commissioner of Hackney						
Coaches	364	9	0			
Ditto, Lieutenant Governor of Hull	182	0	0			
Ditto, Aid de Camp to the King	182	10	0— 728	19	0	. . Also 200*l.* per ann. as retired Captain of
T. Venables, Clerk in Sec. of State's Office						Artillery, and a pen-
and Private Sec. to Secretary of State	912	14	8			sion of 391*l.* per ann.
Ditto, Receiver of the eight Police Offices	500	0	0			for good services.
Ditto, Receiver of Tenths	300	0	0—1712	14	8	
A. Van Spiegel, Senior Clerk in the Treasury			1000	0	0	. . Also a pension of
G. W. F. Villiers, Commissioner of Customs	.		1400	0	0	67*l.* 13*s.* per annum.
Duke of Wellington, First Lord of the Treasury			5000	0	0	. . *See* also Military
Marquis of Winchester, Groom of the Stole to His Maj.			2130	10	0	Return. The Duke of
Gilbert West, Senior Clerk in the Treasury, and for						Wellington also re-
making special payments			1100	0	0	ceived other emolu-
Edw. Walpole, Senior Clerk in the Treasury						ments amounting in
and Private Secretary to the Chancellor						1829 to 7873*l.* 15*s.* 5*d.*
of the Exchequer	900	0	0			
Ditto, For making out East India Accounts	300	0	0—1200	0	0	. . Also 984*l.* 4*s.* 4*d.* per
R. R. Wood, Sen. Clerk, Sec. State's Office	935	3	0			annum for loss of the
Ditto, Naval Officer, Grenada	200	0	0—1135	3	0	office of Vendu Master
T. Whitmore, Secretary to the Board of Customs			1700	0	0	at Malta.
J. G. Walford, Solicitor to the Board of Customs, in lieu						
of Bills .			2500	0	0	
Thomas Willimott, Coll. of Customs, Salary	1500	0	0			
For loss of Fees	900	0	0—2400	0	0	
R. Willimott, Distributor of Stamps, Excise	1000	0	0			
Ditto, Receiver-General Post Office .	800	0	0—1800	0	0	
William Willimott, Receiver of Wine and						
Plantation Duties, Customs, Salary .	300	0	0			
Emols. and Fees paid by individuals	1136	5	0—1436	5	0	
J. K. Walker, Cocket Writer, Customs, Salary	60	0	0			
Fees paid by individuals	991	0	0—1051	0	0	
J. C. Weston, Cocket Writer, Customs, Salary	60	0	0			
Fees paid by individuals	1808	0	0—1868	0	0	
Thomas Watson, First Clerk to Clerk of the						
Rates, Customs, Salary	300	0	0			
Fees paid by individuals	2814	3	6—3114	3	6	
R. J. Williams, First Clerk to Receiver of						
Customs Duties, Outwards, Salary .	300	0	0			
Fees paid by individuals	832	0	0—1132	0	0	
George Wyke, Collector of Customs, Antigua			2000	0	0	
Edward Wilkinson, Clerk of the Affidavits,						
Customs, Salary .	200	0	0			
Fees paid by individuals	1995	0	0—2195	0	0	
Collector of Customs, St. Johns, New Brunswick			1200	0	0	
John Wilkin, Inspector and Receiver, 1*s.* 6*d.*						
Duty			399	10	0	
Receiver of Crown Rents for Wales,						
Chester, and Monmouth			433	10	0— 833	0	0	. . Also a retired allow- ance of 400*l.* per ann. as late Clerk in Tax Office.

SALARIES.

R.Watts,Clk. of a Road, Gen.Post Office, Sal.£.380   0   0
    Emoluments paid by individuals   951 10   0—1131 10   0
J. Whishaw, Commissioner of Audit   .   .   1200   0   0
R. Plumer Ward, Auditor of the Civil List   .   .   1400   0   0   { . . Also a Pension of 500l. per ann. as late Clk. of the Ordnance.
Sir F. B. Watson, Master of His Majesty's Household   .   1158   0   0 . . Also a pension of 931l.
William Wynne, Commissioner of Inquiry, Ireland   1200   0   0 6s. 6d. pr. ann.,Civil List.
Isaac Wolley, Deputy Chairman, Victualling Board   .   1000   0   0 . . Also a pension of
Right Hon. Charles Yorke, Teller of the Exchequer   2700   0   0 250l. per annum for
M. Zachary, Cocket Writer, Customs, Salary   60   0   0   wounds.
    Fees paid by individuals 1638 16   0—1698 16   0

PENSIONS AND SUPERANNUATION ALLOWANCES.

Earl Amherst, Hereditary Pension on the Consolidated
  Fund, by Act of Parliament   .   .   3000   0   0
Lord Abercrombie, Hereditary Pension on Consolidated
  Fund, by Act of Parliament   .   .   .   2000   0   0
Earl of Athlone, Hereditary Pension on Consolidated
  Fund, Ireland, by Act of Parliament   .   2000   0   0
Earl of Abergavenny, Compensation allowance for loss
  of the Office of Inspect. of Prosecutions in the Customs   1545   0   0
Lord Bexley, Pension on the Consolidated Fund, as late
  Chancellor of the Exchequer   .   .   .   3000   0   0
Sir S. Bentham, Pension as late Civil Archi-
  tect and Surveyor of the Navy   .   1000   0   0
    Ditto for relinquishing an employ-
    ment in Russia, in 1797   .   500   0   0—1500   0   0
James Buller, Retired Allowance as late Commissioner
  of Customs   1100   0   0
Rev. G. Burraud, Compensation Allowance for Loss of
  the Office of Searcher in the Customs   .   1100   0   0
H. B. Beresford, Compensation Allowance for Loss of
  the Office of Joint Storekeeper (Customs)   .   2157 13   4
J. C. Beresford,   Ditto   ditto   ditto   2157 13   4
T. Burton, Retired Allowance as late Secretary to the
  Board of Excise   1500   0   0
Executors of Mrs. Burke, Pension on the 4½ per ct. Fund   2500   0   0
Lord Colchester, Hereditary Pension on the Consoli-
  dated Fund, by Act of Parliament   .   .   3000   0   0
Trustees for the Family of the late Mr. Canning, Pension
  on the Consolidated Fund by Act of Parliament   .   3000   0   0
Hon. Jane Carr (late Perceval) Pension on the Consoli-
  dated Fund, by Act of Parliament   .   .   2000   0   0
Earl Cowper, Hereditary Pension out of Excise Revenue   1600   0   0
J. Chapman, Retired Allowance as late Clerk in the
  Colonial Office   .   .   .   1100   0   0 . . Also 1427l. per ann. as Clerk of the Council at Trinidad.
Dugald Campbell, Retired Allowance as
  Register of Forfeitures, Ireland   .   276   0   0
    Ditto as Commissioner of Military
    Accounts, Ireland   .   .   367 10   4
    Pension on Irish List   .   .   266 18   4— 910   8   8 . . Also 130l. 17s. per annum, as Accountant to Board of General Officers, Ireland.
Jas. Corry, Late Sec. to Linen Board, Ireland 616   9 11
    Late Clerk of the Journals, Irish House
    of Lords, by Act of Parliament   .   609   4   8—1225   4   7
Geo. Delavaud, Retired Allowance as late Secretary of
  Customs   1500   0   0
R. Dawkius, Retired Allowance as Commissioner of
  Excise   1050   0   0
Viscount Duncan, Hereditary Pension on
  the Consolidated Fund, Great Britain, by
  Act of Parliament   .   .   2000   0   0
    Pension on the Consolidated Fund,
    Ireland   .   .   .   1000   0   0—3000   0   0

PENSIONS. &c.

Edw. Earl, Retired Allowance as late Commissioner of Customs	*L.* 1500	0	0	
John Edwards, Retired Allowance as late Solicitor of Excise	1292	6	2	
Lord Farnborough, Pension on the 4½ per cent. Fund	1500	0	0	
John Fullarton, Moiety of the Earl of Bath's Hereditary Pension out of the Excise Revenue . .	1200	0	0	
Duke of Grafton, Hereditary Pension out of Excise Revenue 7200 0 0				
Ditto, ditto Post Office ditto 4700 0 0—11900	0	0		
H. G. Grady, Compensation Allowance as late Counsel to Excise, Dublin, on abolition of the office .	1333	6	8	
George Harrison, Superannuation Allowance as late Assistant Secretary, Treasury . . .	2200	0	0	
J. Harrison, Compensation Allowance for loss of the Office of Port Surveyor, Customs, Dublin .	1207	0	0	
Lord Hood, Pension on the 4½ per cent. Fund .	1875	0	0	
Lord Hutchinson, Pension on the Consolidated Fund, by Act of Parliament	2000	0	0	
F. Leigh, Retired Allowance as late Collector of Excise	1384	12	4	
S. M. Leake, Retired Allowance as Comptroller of Army Accounts	2000	0	0	
Right Hon. S. R. Lushington, Pension on Consolidated Fund	1500	0	0	
Viscount Lake, Pension on ditto	2000	0	0	. Also 712*l.* 10*s.* per ann. as Lord of the Bed Chamber, and 456*l.* 5*s.* per ann. as Lieut.-Gen.
Duke of Marlborough, Hereditary Pension out of the Post Office Revenue	5000	0	0	
Duchess Dowager of Manchester, Compensation Allowance for loss of the Office of Collector of Customs outwards, held by the late Duke of Manchester .	2923	7	4	
William Marsden, Retired Allowance as late Secretary to the Admiralty	1500	0	0	
E. J. Mascall, Retired Allowance as late Coll. of Customs	1750	0	0	
Earl of Mayo, Pension as Chairman of the Committees of the late House of Lords, Ireland. Granted per Act 40 Geo. 3	1332	5	8	
J. & W. F. M'Clintock, Late Chief Serjeant at Arms, Ireland, per Act 40 Geo. 3	2545	6	2	
Earl Nelson, Pension on Consolidated Fund, by Act of Parliament	5000	0	0	
Lady Nelson, Ditto, ditto	2000	0	0	
John Penn, Hereditary Pension on Consolidated Fund	3900	0	0	
Hon. T Pakenham, Late Master General Ordnance, Ireland, per Act 40 Geo. 3	1107	14	0	
Ld. Rodney, Hereditary Pension on Consolidated Fund, by Act of Parliament	2923	1	6	
Earl of Roden, Late Auditor of the Exchequer, Ireland	2700	0	0	
Heir of the Duke of Schomberg, Hereditary Pension out of the Post Office Revenue	4000	0	0	
Viscount St. Vincent, Pension on Consolidated Fund .	3000	0	0	
Viscount Sidmouth, Ditto, ditto, as late Sec. of State	3000	0	0	
Sir John Sinclair, Compensation Allowance on abolition of the Office of Cashier of Excise, Edinburgh .	2000	0	0	
Lord H. Seymour, Compensation Allowance for loss of the Office of Craner and Wharfinger, Port of Dublin	1251	0	0	
Earl of Shannon, Late Clerk of the Pells, Ireland .	3133	0	0	
A. Tyton, Retired Allowance as late Solicitor to the Customs	1800	0	0	
T. N. Wittwer, Retired Allowance as late Accountant to the India Board	1150	0	0	. Also 300*l.* per ann. for investigating Accounts between the public and the East India Company.
G. Wilson, Retired Allowance as late Commissioner of Customs	1050	0	0	

2.—JUDICIAL OFFICERS.

THE LORD CHANCELLOR.

The Emoluments of the Lord Chancellor, from the 5th Jan. 1829 to the 5th Jan. 1830:—
Net Salary, 4829*l*. 5*s*.   Fees after deducting 2500*l*. paid to the Vice Chancellor,
and 450*l*. Land Tax, 5442*l*. 12*s*. 11*d*.   .   .   .   .   .   **L. 10271 17 11**

[This does not include the Fees received as Speaker of
the House of Lords.—*C.K. Murray, Secretary.*]

The Vice Chancellor, Sir L. Shadwell . . .	6000	0 0
Charles Knight Murray, Principal Secretary to the Lord Chancellor	1070	13 6
Francis Barlow, Secretary for Commissions of Bankrupt . .	2709	14 4
L. A. Lowdham, Secretary of Lunatics . . .	1301	18 10
W. H. J. Scott, Receiver of the Fines of the Court of Chancery .	240	14 8
W. H. J. Scott, Registrar of Affidavits . . .	1816	13 8
W. H. J. Scott, Clerk of the Letters Patent . .	553	14 11
H. Haines, Gentleman of the Chamber to the Lord Chancellor .	1755	0 0
Earl Bathurst, Clerk of the Crown Office in Chancery . .	1108	0 5
Mr. Thomas Thurlow, Patentee for the Execution of the Laws and Statutes concerning Bankrupts	8502	9 5
J. G. Seton, Keeper or Clerk of His Majesty's Hanaper . ,	1192	7 5
Thomas Thurlow, Prothonotary of the Court of Chancery .	97	10 0
H. J. Shepherd, Counsel to the Admiralty, &c., Commissioner of Bankrupts, Clerk of the Custodies, and Clerk of Presentations . .	1173	0 0
J. S. Harvey, Master in Ordinary, and Accountant General .	3184	9 7

MASTERS IN CHANCERY.

1. Francis Paul Stratford, Esq.	3948	2 3
Which is subject to a deduction of about 100*l*. for land tax and other matters.		
The Master's Chief Clerk, Henry Kensit . . .	1075	3 11
Which is subject to a deduction of about 120*l*. for expense of paper, writing, and other stationery.		
2. Samuel Compton Cox, Esq.	3994	2 11½
Chief Clerk to Samuel Compton Cox, Esq. . . .	1425	15 6
3. James Stephen, Esq.	3700	0 0
As the chief clerk's official emoluments altogether do not amount to 1000*l*., no return is made for him.		
4. J. E. Dowdesdale, Esq.	3896	17 6
Subject to a deduction of about 70*l*. per annum for land-tax and other disbursements.		
Chief Clerk to John Edmund Dowdesdale, Esq. . .	1426	10 1
5. F. Cross, Esq.	3799	19 3
Chief Clerk to Francis Cross, Esq.	1443	16 2
6. James Trower, Esq.	3510	14 6
Chief Clerk to James Trower, Esq.	1200	13 1
7. William Wingfield, Esq.	4161	17 8
Clerk to William Wingfield, Esq.	1476	19 0
8. James William Farrer, Esq.	3622	1 6½
Chief Clerk to James William Farrer, Esq. . .	1479	14 1
9. Sir Giffin Wilson	2586	6 2
Chief Clerk to Sir Giffin Wilson	1137	0 0
10. The Honourable Robert Henly Eden . . .	4644	0 10
Chief Clerk to the Honourable Robert Henly Eden . .	1650	0 0
Master of the Report Office	4589	11 10

REGISTRAR OF THE COURT OF CHANCERY.

	Salary.	Allowances.	Fees.	Total.
	L. s. d.	L. s. d.	L. s. d.	L. s. d.
Thomas Alexander Raynsford	550 0 0	110 0 0	4201 19 0	4861 19 0
Francis Benjamin Bedwell .	358 5 1	110 0 0	3409 12 10	3877 17 11
James Crismas Fry . .	000 0 0	110 0 0	4114 2 10	4224 2 10
Edward Dod Colville . .	91 10 0	77 10 0	2590 7 2	2759 7 2
William South . .	273 0 0	— — —	1301 19 · 6	1576 19 6
Joseph Collis . .	286 0 0	— — —	1161 13 10	1447 13 10
John Francis Le Cointe .	297 2 7	— — —	933 15 10	1230 18 5
Henry Edgworth Bicknell .	200 16 8	— — —	1421 7 5	1622 4 1

N.B. The above salaries and allowances are paid out of the suitors' fund.

SALARIES.

The Master of the Rolls . . . . . L. 7,000 0 0
Henry Gawler, Esq., the Chief Secretary to the Master of the Rolls . 1,487 15 0
John Kipling, Francis Vesey, Edward Vernon Utterson, William Turton, and
   Launcelot Baugh Allen, Esqrs., five of the Six Clerks of the Ct. of Chancery each 1,217 10 0
John Nursey Dancer, Esq., one of the Examiners of the Court of Chancery . 1,300 0 0

Sir Wm. Alexander, Chief Baron of the Court of Exchequer			L.7016 10 0	
John Henry Abbot, Marshal and Associate to the Chief Justice, King's Bench . .	2665 0 0			
Commissioner of Bankrupts	320 0 0	—2985	0 0	Derived from Fees.
Thomas Abbott, Clerk at Nisi Prius to the Chief Justice of the King's Bench . .			1000 1 6	Ditto.
James Abercromby, Lord Chief Baron of the Exchequer, Scotland . . .			4000 0 0	
Wm. Adam, Lord Chief Com. of Jury Court, Scotland			4000 0 0	
Sir John Bayley, Senior Puisne Judge of the Court of King's Bench . . .			5540 0 0	
Sir Wm. Bolland, one of the Barons of the Ct. of Exchq.			5516 10 0	
David Boyle, Lord Justice Clerk, Scotland			4000 0 0	
C. K. Bushe, Chief Justice of the King's Bench, Ireland			5076 18 8	
Charles Burton, third ditto ditto ditto			3692 6 4	
A. R. Blake, Chief Remembrancer of the Exchequer, Ireland . . .			2817 4 4	
Peter Burrows, Commissioner for the Relief of Insolvent Debtors, Ireland . .			2092 9 4	
Robert Craigie, Lord of Session, Scotland .			2000 0 0	
G. Cranstoun, ditto ditto .			2000 0 0	
James Clancey, Taxing Officer in Common Law Business, Ireland			1107 14 0	
Roderick Connor, Master in Chancery, Ireland .			3323 1 8	. . . He receives also
P. Dealtry, King's Clerk, Crown Office; Salary . . .	30 7 8			55*l*. 7*s*. 9*d*. per annum, as late Clerk in House
Ditto, Secondary, Clerk in Court, Clerk of the Affidavit, and Chief Usher, Court of King's Bench; Fees . .	1672 5 11	—1702	13 7	of Commons, Ireland.
Charles Dyneley, Deputy Register, Prerogative Court of Canterbury; from Fees . .			1193 15 4	
William Dundas, Lord Clerk, Register and Keeper of the Signet, Scotland .			3300 0 0	
Thomas Ellis, Master in Chancery, Ireland .			3323 1 8	
Josh. Farran, Clerk of the Pleas, Court of Exchequer, Ireland . . .			1384 12 4	
John Hay Forbes, Lord of Session, Scotland .			2000 0 0	
John Fullarton, ditto ditto .			2000 0 0	
Sir William Garrow, one of the Barons of the Court of Exchequer . .			5516 10 0	
Nathaniel Gostling, Deputy Register of the Prerogative Court of Canterbury; from Fees .			1317 13 0	
Adam Gillies, Lord of Session and Justiciary, Scotland . .	2600 0 0			
Ditto, Commissioner Jury Court, ditto	600 0 0	—3200	0 0	
William Hanmer, Clerk of Nisi Prius for the Northern and Norfolk Circuits .	580 6 0			
Ditto, Clerk of the Inner Treasury, Court of King's Bench . .	602 18 5	—1183	4 5	
William Hewitt, Clerk of the Papers, King's Bench Prison; from Fees, about .			1000 0 0	
Chas. Hope, Lord President, Court of Session, Scotland			4300 0 0	
Robert Hamilton, Principal Clerk of Session, Scotland . .	1000 0 0			
Ditto, Professor of Public Law .	230 14 0	—1230	14 0	
David Hume, one of the Barons Exchequer, Scotland			2000 0 0	
The Right Hon. Sir A. Hart, Lord High Chancellor of Ireland			9834 1 6	

SALARIES.

William Henn, Master in Chancery, Ireland	*L.* 3323	1	8			
R. Hamilton, Prothonotary King's Bench, Ireland	1384	12	4			
Rowley Heyland, Clerk of the Rules, ditto ditto	1107	14	0			
Sir Henry Jardine, King's Remembrancer Court of Exchequer, Scotland	1700	0	0			
W. Jones, Marshal of the King's Bench Prison; from Fees, about	2804	0	0			
Alexander Irvine, one of the Lords of Session, Scotland	2000	0	0			
I. Iggulden, Deputy Register Prerogative Court of Canterbury; from Fees, about	1200	0	0	.	. Mr. Iggulden only
Richard Jebb, 2d Justice King's Bench, Ireland	3730	17	4		received 778*l.* in 1829,
William Johnson, 3d Justice Common Pleas, Ireland	3692	6	4		but the annual amount
Lord Kenyon, Custos Brevium, Court of King's Bench; from Fees	2696	6	6		is as stated.
Hon. Thos. Kenyon, Filazer, Exigenter and Clerk of the Outlawries in the Court of King's Bench Fees 1254 9 0						
Compensation, per Act 6, Geo. 4 5463 7 0—6717	17	0			
Viscount Kilwarden, Public Register of Deeds, Ireland	1200	0	0	.	. He also received a
Henry Kemmis, Assist. Barrister, Kildare 369 4 8					Pension of 1200*l.* per
Ditto, Commissioner of Inquiry, Ireland 990 0 0—1359	4	8		annum from Consoli-
Josh. Littledale, Judge of the Court of King's Bench	5500	0	0		dated Fund, Ireland.
					(Since deceased, and
Thomas Le Blanc, Master of the Court of King's Bench 2000 0 0					Office regulated.)
Ditto, one of the Registrars for Middles. 582 4 3—2582	4	3		{	. . Emoluments from
					business performed
					for the Suitors.
Lord Loughborough, Clerk of the Chancery, Scotland	1135	17	6	.	. He also receives
John Lloyd, Commissioner for the Relief of Insolvent Debtors, Ireland	2062	3	4		419*l.* ¡15*s.* per ann. as Lieut.-Colonel.
David Monypenny, Lord of Session and Justiciary, Scotland 2600 0 0					
Ditto, Commissioner of the Jury Court, do. 600 0 0—3200	0	0			
Alex. Maconochie, Lord of Session and Justiciary, ditto 2600	0	0			
J. H. M'Kenzie, Lord of Session and Justiciary, ditto 2600 0 0					
Ditto, Commissioner of Jury Court, ditto 600 0 0—3200	0	0			
Sir J. W. Moncrieff, Bart., Lord of Sess. and Justic. do. 2600	0	0			
Sir William Miller, Lord of Session, ditto 2000	0	0			
J. W. Murray, Lord of Session, ditto 2000 0 0					
Ditto, Commissioner of the Jury Court, do. 600 0 0—2600	0	0			
Sir P. Murray, Bart. Baron of the Exchequer, ditto 2000	0	0			
James M'Clelland, Baron of the Exchequer, Ireland 3692	6	4			
Arthur Moore, 2d Justice Common Pleas, ditto 3692	6	4			
Sir W. M'Mahon, Master ef the Rolls, ditto 3969	4	0			
Sir John Nicholl, Judge of the Arches and Prerogative Courts of Canterbury, about 3350	0	0			
S. O'Grady, Chief Baron Exchequer, Ireland 4615	8	0			
James Parke, one of the Judges of the King's Bench 5500	0	0			
Lord Plunkett, Chief Justice Common Pleas, Ireland 4615	8	0			
R. Pennefather, Baron of the Exchequer, ditto 3692	6	4			
Hon. David Plunkett, Prothonotary Common Pleas, do. 1384	12	4			
Earl of Rosslyn, Director of Chancery, Scotland 1352	7	6	.	. Also Lord Privy Seal,
Richard Richards, Accountant General and one of the Masters of the Court of Exchequer 1863	4	7		2193*l.* 6*s.* 2*d.*; and Col. of 9th Dragoons,
Sir C. Robinson, Judge of the High Court of Admiralty 2402	0	0		1415*l.* 2*s.* 2*d.*
Adam Rolland, Principal Clerk of Session, Scotland 1000 0 0					
Ditto, Clerk to his Majesty's Processes, do. 40 0 0—1040	0	0			
James Clerk Rattray, Baron of the Exchequer, ditto 2000	0	0			
Sir William Rae, Bart., his Majesty's Advocate, ditto 2500	0	0			
John Radcliffe, Judge of the Prerogative Court, Ireland 3090	0	0			
Sir Walter Scott, Bart., Principal Clerk of Session, and Sheriff of the Shire of Selkirk, ditto 1600	0	0			
Charles Short, Clerk of the Rules and Orders of the Court of King's Bench 5172	13	1	.	. Derived from Fees.

SALARIES.

Sir W. C. Smith, Baron of the Exchequer, Ireland   *L.* 3692   6   4
J. W. Stockes, Taxing Officer Common Law Business, do.   1107 14   0

Sir James Scarlett, Attorney General   .   .   1737   6   1 { . . This Amount is not for the whole year ; Sir James Scarlett was appointed 2d June, 1829.

Sir E. B. Sugden, Solicitor General   .   .   1417   6   0 . . Ditto   ditto
Right Hon. Lord Tenterden, Lord Chief Justice of the
   Court of King's Bench   .   .   .   10000   0   0 . . This Salary was set-
Thos. Thomson, Principal Clerk of Session,   tled per Act 6, Geo. IV.,
   Scotland   .   .   .   1000   0   0   c. 82, in lieu of all Fees
   Ditto, Deputy Clerk Register, ditto   .   500   0   0—1500   0   0   and patronage of sale-
John S. Townshend, Master in Chancery, Ireland   3138   9   4   able offices.
R. Torrens, 4th Justice of the Common Pleas, Ireland   3692   6   4
Sir J. Vaughan, one of the Barons of Court of Exchequer 5516 10   0
T. B. Vandeleur, 4th Justice of the King's Bench, Ireland 3692 6   4
D. Williamson, Lord of Session, Scotland   .   2000   0   0
John Waters, Clerk to the Lord Chief Justice of the
   Court of King's Bench   .   .   .   2169 13   5 . . Arising from Fees.
Right Hon. Sir N. C. Tindal, Lord Chief Justice Court
   of Common Pleas   8000   0   0
Hon. Sir James Allan Park   .   .   .   5500   0   0
Hon. Sir Stephen Gaselee   .   .   .   5500   0   0
Hon. Sir John Bernard Bosanquet   .   .   5500   0   0
Thomas Hudson, George Watlington, and Henry B. Ray,
   Prothonotaries of the Court, each   .   .   2600   0   0
Keene Fitzgerald, Clerk of the Warrants, &c.   .   1252 14   8
W. R. H. Brown, Warden of the Fleet Prison   .   2000   0   0
Wm. Woodroffe, Associate to the Lord Chief Justice   1020   0   8

PENSIONS.

Viscount Avonmore, late Principal Registrar, Court of
   Chancery, Ireland   .   .   .   4199 19   0
Sir W. M'Leod Bannatyne, late Lord of Session, Scotld. 1500   0   0
Lord H. S. Conway and Lord R. S. Conway, late Protho-
   notaries of the Court of King's Bench, Ireland   .   7137   8   0 . . Office regulated.
Sir A. Campbell, late Lord of Session, Scotland   .   1950   0   0
John Clerk, late Lord of Session, ditto   .   1500   0   0
Charles Day, late Justice of the King's Bench, Ireland   2400   0   0
S. G. Daly, late Justice of ditto, ditto   .   2344 16   7
Francis Dwyer, late Six Clerk, Chancery, Ireland   1088 10   8
Earl Eldon, late Lord High Chancellor of Great Britain   4000   0   0
Sir Wm. Grant, late Master of the Rolls   .   3750   0   0
Sir Robert Graham, late Baron of the Exchequer   .   3500   0   0
Sir John Holroyd, late Judge of the King's Bench   .   3500   0   0
H. G. Heard, late Six Clerk Chancery, Ireland   .   1348 15   5
Robert Johnson, late Justice Common Pleas, Ireland   1107 14   0
Thomas Lord Manners, late Lord Chancellor of ditto   3692   6   4
Lord Norbury, late Chief Justice Common Pleas, ditto   3046   3   1
Viscount Northland and the Hon. V. Knox, late Protho-
   notaries of the Common Pleas, Ireland   .   7150   3   0 . . Office regulated.
William Robertson, late Lord of Session, Scotland   .   1500   0   0
Lord Redesdale, late Lord Chancellor of Ireland   .   3692   6   4 . . Since deceased.
Sir John Richardson, late Justice of the King's Bench   3500   0   0
Sir S. Shepherd, late Chief Baron Exchequer, Scotland   3000   0   0
Jones Stevelly, late Six Clerk Chancery, Ireland   .   1498 14   8
Marquis Wellesley and Richard Wellesley, late Chief
   Remembrancer Court of Exchequer, Ireland   .   5387 15   8 . . Office regulated.
Lord Wynford, late Chief Justice Common Pleas   .   3750   0   0

3.—DIPLOMATIC AND CONSULAR OFFICERS.

SALARIES.

Henry Unwin Addington, Minister at Frankfort to 10th Oct., and at Madrid from 10th Oct. * * L.	3802	0	0	
Arthur Aston, Secretary of Legation and Chargé d'Affaires at Rio de Janeiro . . .	1368	13	4	
Lord Bloomfield, Envoy Extraordinary and Minister Plenipotentiary at Sweden . . .	4900	0	0	. . Also 1003*l.* per ann.
Sir Charles Bagot, Ambassador to the Hague	11661	2	4	as Col. of Artillery.
Lord Burghersh, Envoy Extraordinary and Minister Plenipotentiary at Florence . . .	3900	0	0	
Peter Browne, Secy. of Legation and Chargé d'Affaires at Copenhagen . . .	1151	0	0	
George Bosanquet, Secretary of Legation and Chargé d'Affaires at Madrid . .	2260	0	0	

Sir Daniel Bayley, Consul General at St.
Petersburgh   .   .   .   *L.* 1000   0   0
                      Fees   .   13   0   0—1013   0   0

J. M. Brackenbury, Consul at Cadiz, Salary   800   0   0
                      Fees   .   416   0   0—1216   0   0

A. St. John Baker, Consul General at Washington   1600   0   0

John Barker, Consul Gen. in Egypt, Salary   1000   0   0
                      Fees   .   615   0   0—1615   0   0

Lord Cowley, Ambassador at Vienna . .	12000	0	0
Sir Stratford Canning, Ambassador at Constantinople (to 24th May)	4460	5	6
G. W. Chad, Minister at Colombia . .	2787	4	0
Thomas Cartwright, Secretary of Embassy, and for acting as Minister Plenipotentiary at the Hague .	1638	17	8
Patrick Campbell, Secretary of Legation and Chargé d'Affaires in Colombia . . .	3125	0	0

H. Canning, Con. Gen. Hamburgh, Salary   1500   0   0
                      Fees   .   336   0   0—1836   0   0

Sir H. Chamberlain, Bart., Consul at Rio (to 5th June)   1041   13   4

John Cartwright, Consul General at Constantinople   1600   0   0

Walter Cope, Consul at Guayaquil, Salary   1000   0   0
                      Fees   .   33   0   0—1033   0   0

Matt. Carter, Consul at Coquimbo, Salary   1250   0   0
                      Fees   .   4   0   0—1254   0   0

E. C. Disbrowe, Envoy Extraordinary and Minister Plenipotentiary at Stutgard . .	3300	0	0
E. J. Dawkins, Resident in Greece . .	2900	0	0
Charles Dashwood, Consul at Guatemala .	1500	0	0
Lord Erskine, Envoy Extraordinary and Minister Plenipotentiary at Munich . . .	4900	0	0
Right Hon. A. J. Foster, Envoy Extraordinary and Minister Plenipotentiary at Turin . . .	4249	0	0

John Falconer, Consul at Leghorn, Salary   800   0   0
                      Fees   344   0   0—1144   0   0

Sir R. Gordon, Ambassador at Constantinople, from 5th April	6000	0	0
Hord Heytesbury, Ambassador at St. Petersburgh .	12000	0	0
Henry Hayne, Commissary Judge at Rio Janeiro .	1326	18	0
Right Hon. W. Noel Hill, Envoy Extraordinary, &c. at Naples	6000	0	0
H. C. J. Hamilton, Secretary of Embassy at Paris .	1100	0	0
James Henderson, Consul General at Bogota .	2000	0	0

R. Hesketh, Consul at Maranham, Salary   1000   0   0
                      Fees   105   0   0—1105   0   0

T. S. Hood, Consul at Monte Video, Salary   1250   0   0
                      Fees   27   0   0—1277   0   0

George Jackson, Commissary Judge at Sierra Leone   2145   4   0

Patrick Kelly, Vice Consul at Lima, Salary   700   0   0
Allowance as Pro Consul   .   .   450   0   0
                      Fees   27   0   0—1177   0   0

SALARIES.

Sir H. Lushington, Consul General at Naples,
Salary . . . . L. 1200 0 0
Fees . . . . 150 0 0—1350 0 0
J. H. Lance, Commissary Judge at Surinam . 1500 0 0
D. R. Morier, Consul General at Paris, Salary 1600 0 0
Fees 274 0 0—1874 0 0
Hon. J. Meade, Consul General at Madrid,
Salary 1600 0 0
Fees . . . . . 13 0 0—1613 0 0
J. R. Matthews, Consul General at Lisbon,
Salary 1200 0 0
Fees . . . . . 170 0 0—1370 0 0
W. S. Macleay, Com. of Arbitration at the Havanna 1850 0 0
W. T. Money, Consul Gen. at Venice, Salary 1000 0 0
Fees 43 0 0—1043 0 0
M. M'Gregor, Consul at Panama, Salary 1250 0 0
Fees 127 0 0—1377 0 0
C. R. Nugent, Consul General in Chili . . 2500 0 0
C. T. O'Gorman, Consul General at Mexico . 2000 0 0
Hon. A. Percy, Minister Plenipotentiary at Berne . 2900 0 0
Lord Ponsonby, Envoy Extraordinary and Minister Ple-
nipotentiary at Rio de Janeiro . . 4681 6 8
R. Pakenham, Secretary of Legation in Mexico, and
Chargé d'Affaires ditto . . . 2825 0 0
W. Pennell, Consul at Bahia to 5th July, and at Rio
from 5th July 1350 0 0
John Parkinson, Consul at Pernambuco,
Salary 1200 0 0
Fees . . . . 551 0 0—1751 0 0
Sir R. Kerr Porter, Con. at Caracas, Salary 1250 0 0
Fees 11 0 0—1261 0 0
Woodbine Parish, Consul General and Chargé d'
Affairs at Buenos Ayres, Salary . 3595 0 0
Fees . 200 0 0—3795 0 0
Udny Passmore, Consul at Arequipa, Salary 1250 0 0
Fees 15 0 0—1265 0 0
C. M. Ricketts, Consul General at Lima . . 1600 0 0
Lord Stuart de Rothesay, Ambassador at Paris 11000 0 0
G. H. Seymour, Secretary of Legation Berlin, and
Secretary of Embassy Constantinople . 1909 13 11
C. M. St. George, Secretary of Legation and Chargé
d'Affaires at Turin 1401 0 0
James Stirling, Consul at Leghorn, Salary 800 0 0
Fees 261 0 0—1061 0 0
G. Salkeld, Consul at New Orleans, Salary 800 0 0
Fees 336 0 0—1136 0 0
Robert Sutherland, Consul at Maracaibo . 1250 0 0
E. W. H. Schenley, Consul in Haiti . . 1200 0 0
W. Smith, Commissioner of Arbitration at Sierra Leone 1831 3 0
Sir Brook Taylor, Envoy Extraordinary and Minister
Plenipotentiary at Berlin . . . 5164 10 9 . . Also 291*l.* 11*s.* 7*d*
Hon. W. Temple, Sec. of Embassy at St. Petersburgh 1100 0 0 per annum as Clerk of
William Turner, Secretary of Embassy at Constanti- the Signet.
nople to 1st September, and Envoy Extraordinary in
Colombia from 1st September . . 5074 9 7
Right. Hon. C. R. Vaughan, Envoy Extraordinary and
Minister Plenipotentiary at Washington . 6000 0 0
Right Hon. H. W. W. Wynn, Envoy Extraordinary and
Minister Plenipotentiary at Copenhagen . 4900 0 0
E. M. Ward, Minister Plenipotentiary at Dresden . 2601 14 8
E. Watts, Consul at Carthagena, Salary 1500 0 0
Fees 90 0 0—1590 0 0
T. S. Willimott, Vice Consul at Lima, and Allowance
as Pro Consul 1150 0 0

PENSIONS.

*(These Pensions are subject to deduction, on account of Land Tax,
1s. 6d. Duty, and Exchequer Fees.)*

Robert Adair, late Ambassador to the Ottoman Porte	L.	2300	0	0
Earl of Clancarty, late Ambassador to the Netherlands		2000	0	0
A. Cockburn, late Minister to Wurtemberg .	.	1700	0	0
Earl of Cathcart, late Ambassador at Petersburgh		1784	16	0 . . Also 1816l. 17s. 6d. as
H. Elliott, late Minister to the Two Sicilies	.	2000	0	0 Col. 2d Life Guards.
Earl of Elgin, late Ambassador to the Ottoman Porte		2000	0	0 . . Also 593l. 2s. 6d. per
B. Frere, late Minister to the Ottoman Porte	.	1200	0	0 ann. as Lieut.-Gen.
Right Hon. J. H. Frere, late Minister to Spain	.	1700	0	0
Lord Robert Fitzgerald, late Minister to Lisbon	.	1700	0	0
Sir J. Gambier, late Consul General in the Netherlands		1200	0	0
Lord Henley, late Envoy, &c. to Vienna	.	2000	0	0
G. Hammond, late Minister to United States	.	1200	0	0
L. Hervey, late Minister to Madrid .		1200	0	0
Daniel Hailes, late Envoy, &c. to different Courts		1127	0	0
Sir R. Liston, late Ambassador to the Ottoman Porte		2300	0	0
Sir Frederick Lamb, late Minister to Frankfort	.	1700	0	0
A. Merry, late Envoy, &c. to the United States	.	1700	0	0
J. Morier, late Minister to Mexico	. .	1100	0	0
J. P. Morier, late Minister to Saxony	.	1700	0	0
Sir Gore Ouseley, late Ambassador to Persia	.	2000	0	0
Sir A. Paget, late Ambassador to the Ottoman Porte		2000	0	0
Hon. H. Pierrepont, late Envoy, &c. to Stockholm	.	1200	0	0
Viscount Strangford, late Ambassador to Russia		2300	0	0
J. S. Smith, late Envoy, &c. to Stutgard	.	1200	0	0
J. Straton, late Minister to Sweden	.	1500	0	0
Lord St. Helens, late Ambassador to Russia	.	2300	0	0 . . Also 712l. 10s. per an.
Sir Edward Thornton, late Envoy, &c. to Portugal		2000	0	0 as Gentleman of the
Right Hon. W. Wickham, late Minister to Swiss Cantons		1200	0	0 Bedchamber.

4.—NAVAL OFFICERS.

PAY, ETC.

Vice-Admiral Sir H. Blackwood, Commander-in-Chief at the Nore	2555	0	0
Rear-Admiral T. Baker, Com.-in-Chief, South America	1545	0	0 . . Only in command a
Vice-Admiral Sir G. Cockburn, Vice-Admiral, and Maj.-General of Marines	1630	7	6 . . See also Civil Return.
Vice-Admiral Hon. C. E. Fleming, Commander-in-Chief, West Indies	2555	0	0
Vice-Admiral Sir P. Malcolm, Commander-in-Chief, Mediterranean	2555	0	0
Vice-Admiral Sir T. B. Martin, Comptroller of the Navy	2000	0	0
Admiral the Earl of Northesk, Real-Admiral of Great Britain, and Commander-in-Chief at Plymouth .	3290	4	3
Rear-Admiral Sir Cha. Ogle, Commander in Chief at Halifax and Newfoundland . . .	2190	0	0
Rear-Admiral Sir R. W. Otway, Commander-in-Chief, South America	1367	0	0 . . Only in command a
Rear-Admiral Sir E. W. C. R. Owen, Commander-in-Chief, East Indies . . .	2190	0	0 part of the year 1829.
Rear-Ad. Sir C. Paget, Commander-in-Chief, Ireland	2190	0	0
Hon. G. Poulett, Flag Captain of H. M. S. " Prince Regent"	799	19	2 . . He also receives 400l.
Ad. Sir R. Stopford, Commander-in-Chief at Portsmouth	2920	0	0 per annum, as late Receiver-Gen. of Taxes.
Vice-Admiral Sir James Saumarez, Vice-Admiral of Great Britain, and Admiral of the White . . 1230 15 8			
Ditto, Pension on Consolidated Fund, by Act of Parliament . . 1200 0 0—2435 15 8			

PAY, &c.

Captain Sir M. Seymour, Commissioner of the Naval
   Yard, Portsmouth   .   .   .   .   L. 1100 0 0

PENSIONS.

Admiral Lord Exmouth, Pension on Consolidated Fund,
   by Act of Parliament   .   .   .   2000 0 0 . . He also receives 766*l.*
Sir F. H. Hartwell, late Deputy Comptroller of the Navy 1164 12 6   10*s.* per annum as Ad-
Vice-Admiral Sir James Saumarez, Pension on Conso-   miral.
   lidated Fund, by Act of Parliament   .   .   . . See above.
Admiral Sir William Sydney Smith, Pen-
   sion on Consolidated Fund   . 1000 0 0
   Ditto, Pension on 4½ per Cent. Fund 1250 0 0—2250 0 0 . . He also receives 766*l.*
                                        10*s.* per annum as Ad-
                                        miral.

5.—MILITARY OFFICERS.

PENSIONS, &c.

Gen. Viscount Combermere, Col. 1st Life Guards, Pay
   and Emoluments   .   1800 0 0
   Ditto, Governor of Sheerness   .   200 0 0
   Ditto, Pension for Military Services by
   Act of Parliament   .   . 2000 0 0—4000 0 0
Gen. Earl Cathcart, Col. of 2d Life Guards, Pay and
   Emoluments   .   .   1816 17 6 . . Also Vice Admiral of
Lieut. Gen. Sir H. Fane, Col. of 1st Dra-   Scotland ; Emolu-
   goon Guards, Pay   .   .   987 9 6   ments from 10*l.* to 20*l.*
   Ditto, Surveyor General of Ordnance   960 16 0—1948 5 6   per annum, and Pen-
Gen. Loftus, Col. 2d Dragoon Guards, Pay   sion of 1784*l.* 16*s.* as late
   and Emoluments   .   1579 15 8   Ambassador.
   Ditto, Lieutenant of the Tower   . 745 16. 7—2325 12 3
Gen. Sir William Payne, Col. 3d Dragoon Guards, Pay
   and Emoluments   .   .   1424 3 8
Gen. Sir George Anson, Col. 4th Dragoon Guards, Pay   911 4 2 . . The Emolument from
Gen. the Hon. R. Taylor, Col. 6th Dragoon Guards,   Clothing not yet known.
   Pay and Emoluments   .   . 1578 10 4
Lieut. Gen. Sir R. Bolton, Col. 7th Dragoon Guards,
   Pay and Emoluments   .   . 1334 16 5 . . Also Equerry to the
Lieut. Gen. Lord R. E. H. Somerset, Col.   King, 750*l.* per annum.
   1st Regiment of Dragoons, Pay and
   Emoluments   -   .   1520 12 0
   Ditto, Lieut. Gen. of the Ordnance   659 6 9—2179 18 9
Gen. Sir James Steuart, Col. 2d Regiment of Dragoons   . . Return not yet rec.
Maj. Gen. Lord G. R. Beresford, Col. 3d Dragoons,   Also Comptroller of
   Regimental and Unattached Pay   .   425 15 0 { the Household, 903*l.*
                                          { 4*s.*
Gen. Francis Hugonin, Col. 4th Dragoons   .   . . . Accounts not yet re-
                                          ceived ; Regiment in
Lieut. Gen. Hon. Sir W. Lumley, Col. 6th   India.
   Dragoons, Pay   .   .   911 4 2 { Also Groom of the
   Ditto, for Wounds   .   .   400 0 0—1311 4 2 { Bedchamber, 366*l.* 4*s.*
Gen. the Marquis of Anglesey, Col. 7th Dragoons   . . Has not yet sent in
Gen. Sir B. Tarleton, Col. 8th Dragoons,   his Return.
   Pay and Emoluments   .   . 1243 8 7
   Ditto, Governor of Berwick   .   647 2 8   { Also Keeper of Privy
   Ditto, Pension for Wounds   .   300 0 0—2190 11 3 { Seal, 2193*l.* 6*s.* 2*d.,*
Gen. Earl of Rosslyn, Col. 9th Dragoons   .   1415 2 2¼ { and Director of
                                          { Chancery, Scotland,
Gen. Lord Wm. Bentinck, Col. 11th Hussars, Pay and   { 1852*l.* 17*s.* 6*d.*
   Emoluments   .   .   2511 11 9 . . Emoluments as Go-
Maj. Gen. Sir R. H. Vivian, Col. 12th Light   vernor of India not in-
   Dragoons, Staff and Regimental Pay   cluded. Also Clerk of
                                            the Pipe, 1131*l.* 1*s.* 2*d.*

PENSIONS, &c.

and Emoluments	L.2225 17 1		Also Equerry to the
Ditto, Pension for Wounds	350 0 0—2575 17 1		King, 750l.

Gen. Hon. H. G. Grey, Col. 13th Light Dragoons, Pay 1057 4 2 . . Clothing Emoluments
Lieut. Gen. Sir V. O. Vandeleur, Col. 14th not stated.
ditto, Pay and Emoluments . 1501 11 8
Ditto, Pension for Wounds . 350 0 0—1851 11 8
Maj. Gen. Sir Colquhoun Grant, Col. 15th
Light Dragoons, Pay and Emoluments . 1237 3 8
Maj. Gen. Sir John Elley, Col. 17th Light
Dragoons, Pay . . 580 18 2
Ditto, Governor of Galway . 343 18 8
Ditto, Pension for Wounds . 300 0 0—1229 16 10
Field Marshal The Duke of Wellington,
Col.1st Foot Guards, Pay and Emolu. 2695 0 0
Ditto, Col. in Chief of Rifle Brigade 238 15 5 Also First Lord of the
Ditto, Constable of the Tower . 950 0 0 Treasury, 5000l.,
Ditto, Pension from Consolidated Fund 4000 0 0—7873 15 5 Lord Warden of the
Cinque Ports, 295l.
13s. 7d.

Gen. George Duke of Gordon, Col. 1st Foot
Guards, Pay and Emoluments . 2325 12 6 Also Lord Keeper of
Ditto, Governor of Edinburgh Castle 1046 15 3—3472 7 9 the Great Seal of
Scotland, 1850l.
Gen. Rt. Hon. Sir W. Keppel, Col. 2d Foot, Pay and
Emoluments . . . . 876 2 11 . . Also Groom of the
Gen. Sir George Don, Col. 3d Foot, Pay and Bedchamber, 344l. 4s.
Emoluments . . 1318 4 10
Ditto, Lieut.-Gov. of Gibraltar, Govern-
ment and Local Pay and Revenues 4211 15 0—5529 19 10 . . Included also in Co-
Gen. John Earl of Chatham, Col. 4th Foot, Pay and lonial Return.
Emoluments . . . .
Ditto, Governor of Gibraltar . . . . Return not yet rec.
Gen. Sir Henry Johnson, Col. 5th Regiment of Foot
Ditto, Governor of Ross Castle . . . . Ditto.
Gen. Sir George Nugent, Col. 6th Foot, Pay 613 2 6
Ditto, Captain of St. Mawes . 102 5 10— 715 8 4 . . Clothing Emolu-
Gen. Sir Alured Clarke, Col. 7th Foot, Pay and Emo- ments not yet known.
luments . . 1153 10 4
Lieut. Gen. Henry Bayly, Col. 8th Foot,
Pay and Emoluments . . 1320 16 5
Ditto, Pension for Wounds . 350 0 0—1670 16 5 . Also Equerry to the
Gen. Sir Robert Brownrigg, Col. 9th Foot, King, 749l. 10s.
Pay and Emoluments . 1323 13 3
Ditto, Governor of Landguard Fort 339 1 6
Ditto, Pension from the Revenues of
Ceylon, as a reward for past services 1000 0 0—2662 14 9
Lieut. Gen. Sir John Lambart, Col. 10th Foot, Pay
and Emoluments . . 1224 3 11
Lieut. Gen. Hon. Robert Mead, Col. 12th
Foot, Pay and Emoluments . 1266 6 9
Ditto, Pension for Wounds . 400 0 0—1666 6 9
Gen. Edward Morrison, Col. 13th Foot, Pay 613 2 6 . . Clothing Emolu-
Ditto, Governor of Chester . 169 9 0— 782 3 3 ments not yet known.
Gen. Thomas Lord Lynedoch, Colonel 14th
Foot, Pay . . 613 2 6
Ditto, Governor of Dumbarton Castle 164 16 11 . . Ditto.
Ditto, Pension by Act of Parliament 2000 0 0—2777 19 5
Lieut. Gen. Sir Moore Disney, Col. 15th Foot, Pay
and Emoluments . 1272 8 10
Gen. Viscount Beresford, Col. 16th Foot,
Pay and Emoluments . . 1182 2 6
Ditto, Governor of Jersey . 1100 0 0
Ditto, Master General of the Ordnance 3175 18 4
Ditto, Capt. of Cadet Company 469 0 0
Ditto, Pension by Act of Parliament 2000 0 0—7927 0 10

PENSIONS, &c.

Gen. Josiah Champagne, Col. 17th Foot, Pay and Emoluments				1315	14	5
Gen. Earl Donoughmore, Col. 18th Foot,						
Pay and Emoluments	1258	6	4			
Ditto, Governor of Stirling Castle	857	5	8			
Ditto, Pension for Military Services	2000	0	0—4115	12	0	
Lieut. Gen. Sir Hilgrove Turner, Col. 19th Foot				.	.	. Return not yet rec.
Lieut. Gen. Sir W. Houston, Col. 20th Foot, Pay		613	2	6	. . Clothing Emolu-
Gen. James Lord Forbes, Col. 21st Foot, Pay and Emolu. 1174	17	6	ments not yet known.
Gen. Hon. Edward Finch, Col. 22d Foot, ditto	.	1231	5	1	Also Groom of the
Lieut. Gen. Sir J. W. Gordon, Col. 23d						Bedchamber, 366*l*. 4*s*.
Foot, ditto	1034	3	7			
Ditto, Quarter Master Gen.	1883	19	2—2918	2	9	
Maj. Gen. Sir James Lyon, Col. 24th Foot,						
Pay and Emoluments	1514	15	0			
Ditto, Staff Pay as Lieut. Gen. commanding Windward and Leeward Islands	1383	19	2			
Ditto, Governor of Barbadoes, Pay and Emoluments	3767	17	6			.
Ditto, Pension granted by Queen Charlotte 100	0	0—6766	11	8 . . Included also in Co-
Gen. Hon. Charles Fitzroy, Col. 25th Foot			.	.	lonial Return.
Lieut. Gen. Earl of Dalhousie, Col. 26th Foot			.	. . Return not yet rec.
Lieut. Gen. Hon. Sir G. L. Cole, Col. 27th Foot			.	. . Ditto.
Gen. Hon. Sir E. Paget, Col. 28th Foot,			.	. . Ditto.
Pay and Emoluments	1062	19	0			
Ditto, Gov. of the Royal Military College	1500	0	0			
Ditto, Pension for loss of a limb	400	0	0—2962	19	0	
Lieut. Gen. Rt. Hon. Sir J. Byng, Col. 29th						
Foot, Pay and Emoluments	793	2	6			
Ditto, Commanding in Ireland, Staff Pay and Emoluments	3,607	11	4—4400	13	10	
Lieut. Gen. Sir T. Bradford, Col. 30th Foot						
Pay and Emoluments	1311	5	5			
Ditto, Pension for Wounds	350	0	0—1661	5	5	
George H. Earl of Mulgrave, Col. 31st Foot			.	. . . Ditto.
Gen. Alexander Campbell, Col. 32d Foot,						
Pay and Emoluments			1351	10	1	
Gen. Lord C. H. Somerset, Col. 33d Foot, ditto	.	1054	19	2	
Lieut. Gen. Sir Thomas Brisbane, Col. 34th Foot, ditto	1095	12	6	
Lieut. Gen. Sir John Oswald, Col. 35th Foot, ditto	1287	7	0	
Lieut. Gen. Sir R. H. Sheaffe, Col. 36th Foot, ditto	.	. . Return not yet rec.
Gen. Sir Charles Green, Colonel 37th Foot, ditto	1123	9	4	
Gen. George J. Earl Ludlow, Colonel 38th						
Foot, Pay	613	2	6	.	. . Clothing Emolu. not
Ditto, Governor of Berwick	169	0	9		stated in his Return.
Ditto, Pension for loss of an Arm	400	0	0—1182	3	3	
Lieut. Gen. Sir George Airey, Col. 39th Foot			.	. . . Return not yet rec.
Lieut. Gen. Sir James Kempt, Col. 40th						
Foot, Pay and Emoluments	1020	7	6			
Ditto, Commander of Forces in Canada, Staff Pay and Emoluments	8143	4	6—9163	12	0	
Lieut. Gen. Hon. Sir E. Stopford, Col. 41st Foot, Pay	613	2	6 . . Emolu. for Clothing
Lieut. Gen. Right Hon. Sir G. Murray, Col.						not yet known.
42d Foot, Pay and Emoluments	1168	2	6			
Ditto, Governor of Fort George	141	14	0—1309	16	6 { Also Secretary of State, 6000*l*.
Lieut. Gen. George Browne, Col. 44th Foot, Pay	.	613	2	6 . . Clothing Emolu-
General the Earl of Cavan, Colonel 45th						ments not yet known.
Foot, Pay	613	2	6	.	. . Ditto.
Ditto, Governor of Calshot Castle	43	0	0			
Ditto, Pension	260	0	0— 916	2	6	
Gen. Henry Wyndward, Col. 46th Foot, Pay		613	2	6 ; ; Ditto.
Lieut. Gen. Hon. Sir Alexander Hope, Col.						
47th Foot, Pay and Emoluments	900	2	3			
Ditto, Lieut. Gov. of Chelsea Hospital	464	14	0			
Ditto, Pension for Wound	400	0	0—1764	16	3	

PENSIONS, &c.

Lieut. Gen. Sir Thomas Hislop, Col. 48th Foot, Pay and Emoluments . . .	L.1081 18 2		
Gen. Sir James Duff, Col. 50th Foot, ditto .	1234 15 3		
Maj. Gen. Sir B. D'Urban, Col. 51st Foot . . .			. . Return not received.
Lieut. Gen. Sir G. T. Walker, Col. 52d Foot . .			. . Ditto.
Gen. Right Hon. R. Lord Hill, Col. 53d Foot, ditto . . .	1358 4 6		
Ditto, General Commanding in Chief	3458 7 6		
Ditto, Governor of Hull . .	617 15 10		
Ditto, Pension granted by Parliament in 1814 . . .	2000 0 0	—7434 7 10	
Gen. Isaac Gascoyne, Col. 54th Foot, Pay .	613 7 6		. Clothing Emoluments not yet known.
Lieut. Gen. Sir William Henry Clinton, Col. 55th Foot, Pay and Emoluments .	1109 10 11		. During part of the year 1829, he was also
Lieut. Gen. Lord Aylmer, Col. 56th Foot, Pay and Emoluments . .	1208 3 3		in the receipt of pay as Lieut. Gen. of the Ord-
Ditto, Pension . . .	600 0 0	—1808 3 3	nance (amount not stated).
Lieut. Gen. Sir F. P. Robinson, Col. 59th Foot, Pay and Emoluments . . .	1171 19 9		
Gen. N. C. Burton, Col. 60th Foot (1st Bat.), ditto	1331 13 8		
Gen. Hon. Edmund Phipps, Col. 60th Foot (2d Bat.), ditto . .	782 14 6		
Ditto, Clerk of Deliveries of Ordnance	1018 5 0	—1800 19 6	
Gen. Right Hon. Sir G. Hewett, Col. 61st Foot, Pay and Emoluments . . .	1221 3 6		
Gen. Rt. Hon. Sir S. Hulse, Col. 62d Foot, do.	1136 10 10		. . Also Vice Chamberlain part of the year, and Master of
Ditto, Deputy Ranger of Windsor Park	545 1 4		the Household part of the year, having
Ditto, Governor of Chelsea Hospital .	739 3 4	—2420 15 6	received in the year 1088l. 19s. 4d. Since deceased.
Lieut. Gen. Wm. Dyott, Col. 63d Foot, Pay & Emolmts.	1245 17 5		
Lieut. Gen. Sir W. H. Pringle, Col. 64th Foot, ditto .	1245 13 8		
Gen. Thomas Grosvenor, Col. 65th Foot, ditto .	1241 7 2		
Maj. Gen. J. Macdonald, Col. 67th Foot, Pay	613 2 6		. . Clothing Emoluments
Ditto, Dep. Adjut. Gen. to the Forces	691 19 7	—1305 2 1	not stated.
Lieut. Gen. Sir H. Warde, Col. 68th Foot, & Emolts.	1170 17 4		
Lieut. Gen. Sir John Hamilton, Bart., Col. 69th Foot .			. . . Return not yet received.
Lieut. Gen. Lord Howard of Effingham, Col. 70th Foot, Pay and Emoluments . . .	1343 2 11		
Major Gen. Sir Colin Halkett, Col. 71st Foot .			. . Ditto.
Lieut. Gen. Sir J. Hope, Col. 72d Foot, Pay & Emolmts.	1158 14 6		
Major Gen. Sir F. Adam, Col. 73d Foot, Regimental and Unattached Pay .	434 0 0		. . Clothing Emoluments
Ditto, Staff Pay as Lieut. Gen. commanding in the Ionian Islands . .	1383 19 2		not known.
Ditto, Pension for wounds .	300 0 0	—2117 19 2	
Lieut. Gen. Hon. Sir C. Colville, Col. 74th Foot .			. . . Return not yet received.
Lieut. Gen. J. Dunlop, Col. 75th Foot, Pay & Emolmts.	1135 2 6		
Lieut. Gen. Christ. Chowne, Col. 76th Foot, ditto	1321 11 9		
Lieut. Gen. Sir G. Cooke, Col. 77th Foot, do.	1249 12 7		
Ditto, Pension for wounds .	350 0 0	—1599 12 7	
Lieut. Gen. Sir E. Barnes, Col. 78th Foot . .			. . . Ditto.
Lieut. Gen. Sir R. Fergusson, Col. 79th Foot, Pay .	612 2 6		. . Emoluments for
Lieut. Gen. Sir R. S. Donkin, Col. 80th Foot, Pay and Emoluments . . .	1412 3 9		Clothing not yet known.
Major Gen. Sir R. D. Jackson, Col. 81st Foot, Pay . .	613 16 9		
Ditto, Deputy Quarter Master General	691 19 7	—1305 16 4	
Gen. Henry Pigot, Col. 82d Foot, Pay & Emoluments	1073 8 4		
Lieut. Gen. Sir F. Maclean, Bart., Col. 84th Foot, Pay and Emoluments . . .	1286 14 2		
Lt. Gen. Sir H. Taylor, Col. 85th Foot, ditto	938 8 11		
Ditto, Adjutant General . .	1884 2 2	—2822 11 1	

PENSIONS, &c.

Gen. Francis Earl of Kilmorey, Col. 86th Foot, Pay and
Emoluments L.1220 6 9
Gen. Sir J. Doyle, Bart., Col. 87th Foot, do. 1228 14 5
  Ditto, Governor of Charlemont . 665 14 0—1894 8 5

Lt. Gen. Sir H. Campbell, Col. 88th Foot, Pay & Emol. 1292 14 2 { . . Also Commissioner of Taxes, 1000*l.*

Lieut. Gen. Sir Robert Macfarlane, Col. 89th Foot,
Pay . . . . 613 2 6 { . . Emoluments for Clothing not yet known.

Lieut. Gen. Sir Ralph Darling, Col. 90th Foot . . . Return not yet received.
Gen. Duncan Campbell, Col. 91st Foot, Pay and Emol. 1241 3 1
Lieut. Gen. Hon. A. Duff, Col. 92d Foot, ditto . 1307 12 0
Major Gen. Sir Hudson Lowe, Col. 93d Foot . . . . Ditto.
Major Gen. Sir John Keane, Col. 94th Foot,
  Regimental Pay . . 425 15 0
  Ditto, Unattached Pay, and Staff Pay in
    Jamaica . . . 1901 18 4
  Ditto, Pension for wounds . 350 0 0—2677 13 4
Major Gen. Sir J. Fuller, Col. 96th Foot, Pay
  and Emoluments . . 1119 14 6
  Ditto, President of the Consolidated Board
    of General Officers . 197 3 4—1316 17 10
Maj. Gen. Hon. Sir R. O'Callaghan, Col. 97th
  Foot, Regimental and Unattached Pay 494 1 11
  Ditto, Commanding Forces in North
    Britain, Staff Pay . 1183 7 1—1677 9 0
Lieut. Gen. Hall, Col. 99th Foot, Pay and Emoluments 1264 12 9

Maj. Gen. Sir A. Barnard, Col. Rifle Brigade, 1st Batt.
  Pay and Emoluments . . 1182 12 0 { . . Also Equerry to the King, 749*l.* 10s.

Maj. Gen. Sir T. S. Beckwith, Col. Rifle Brigade, 2d Batt. . . . . Return not yet received.
Major Gen. Sir P. Maitland, Col. 1st West In-
  dia Regiment . . . . .
  Ditto, Unattached Pay as late Captain
    Grenadier Guards . . 500 0 0
  Ditto, Staff Pay and Emoluments as Lieut.
    Governor of Nova Scotia and Governor
    of Anapolis . . 6093 18 9—6593 18 9 . . Also in Col. Return.
Gen. Francis Fuller, Col. 2d. West India Regiment . . . Return not yet received.
Maj. H. J. Ricketts, Royal African Corps, Pay 292 0 0
  Ditto, Lieut. Governor of Sierra Leone 2095 3 0—2387 3 0
Gen. Fred. Maitland, Col. Ceylon Rifle Regi-
  ment, Pay and Emoluments . 921 10 0
  Ditto, Lieut. Governor of Dominica . 366 6 0—1287 16 0
Maj. William Cox, Commanding Cape Mounted Rifle . . . . Ditto.
Maj. Thos. K. Burke (Lieut. Col.), Commanding New-
  foundland Veteran Company . . . . . Ditto.

Lieut. Gen. Marq. Conyngham, Unattached
  Pay as Lieut. Gen. . . 593 2 6 { * * The Fees on his Commission have reduced his Emoluments for the period.
  Ditto, Governor of Windsor* Castle, from
    24th Sept. 1829 . . 43 7 6 — 636 10 0 Also Lord Steward, 2435*l.* 15s.

Lieut. Gen. Sir W. Inglis, Governor of Cork . . . . Return not yet received.
Gen. Wm. Knollys, Unattached Pay as late
  Major of the 3d Foot Guards 800 0 0
  Ditto, Governor of Limerick . . 306 8 0
  Ditto, Pension . 399 13 8—1506 1 8
Gen. George V. Hart, Unattached Pay as Gen.
  Officer . . . 593 2 6
  Ditto, Gov. of Londonderry and Culmore 499 19 6—1093 2 0
Maj. Gen. Ld. Fitzroy Somerset, Unattached
  Pay as Major General . 500 0 0
  Ditto, Military Secretary to the General
    Commanding in Chief , 2000 0 3
  Ditto, Pension for wound . . 300 0 0—2300 0 0

PENSIONS, &c.

Lieut. Col. G. Desbrow, Capt. and Lieut. Col.
of Gren. Guards, Pay and Emoluments 494 15 7
Ditto, Assistant Military Secretary to the
General Commanding in Chief . . 600 0 0—1094 15 7
Maj. Maling, Capt. 2d West India Reg., Pay 243 16 5
Ditto, Assistant Military Secretary to the
General Commanding in Chief . 800 0 0—1048 16 5
Maj. Gen. Sir H. F. Bouverie, Commanding
Northern District, Staff Pay . 874 13 7
Ditto, Unattached Pay as Major in the
Coldstream Guards . 700 0 0—1574 13 7
Maj. Gen. Sir Colin Campbell, Commanding
South West District, Staff Pay . 691 19 7
Ditto, Unattached Pay as Major in the
Coldstream Guards . 500 0 0
Ditto, Governor of Portsmouth . . . 168 9 0—1360 0 4
Maj. Gen. Sir John Cameron, Commanding
Western District, Staff Pay . . 691 19 7
Ditto, Unattached Pay as Major . . 310 5 0
Ditto, Lieut. Gov. of Plymouth, Pay & Emol. 493 7 6
Ditto, Pension for injuries received in the
service . . . 800 0 0—1795 12 1
Maj. Gen. Sir Colin Halkett, Commanding at Jersey . . . . . Return not yet re-
Maj. Gen. J. Ross, Commanding at Guernsey   ceived.
and Alderney, Staff Pay as Colonel 560 2 6
Ditto, Pay and Emoluments as Lieut. Gov.
of Jersey . . . 627 10 0
Ditto, Unattached Pay as Lieut. Col. . 310 5 0
Ditto, Pens. for injuries received in Service 350 0 0—1847 17 6
Col. Sir A. Christie, Unattached Pay as Col.
of 1st Royal Veteran Battalion . 501 17 6
Ditto, Commandant of Chatham Depot . 726 16 2
Ditto, Pension for wounds . . : 600 0 0—1828 13 8
Col. Sir J. Douglas, Lieut. Col. of Portuguese
Army, Half Pay . . 200 15 0
Ditto, Dep. Quart. Mast. Gen. in Ireland 746 7 5
Ditto, Inspector of Army Clothing . 346 15 0
Ditto, Pension for loss of leg . . 350 0 0—1643 17 5
Maj. Gen. W. Thornton, Staff Pay as Major
General Northern District, Ireland . 868 17 6
Ditto, Unattached Pay as Lieut. Col. . 310 13 4—1170 10 10
Maj. Gen. Sir T. Arbuthnot, Staff, Western
District, Ireland . . 891 19 7
Ditto, Unattached Pay as Major General 310 5 0
Ditto, Pension for a wound . 300 0 0—1502 4 7
Maj. Gen. Sir G. R. Bingham, Staff, Southern
District, Ireland . . 891 19 7
Ditto, Unattached Pay as Lieut. Col. . 310 5 0—1202 4 7
Maj. Gen. Sir E. Blakeney, Staff, South-wes-
tern District, Ireland . 691 19 7
Ditto, Unattached Pay as Lieut. Col. . 310 5 0—1002 4 7
Maj. Gen. Hon. F. C. Ponsonby, Unattached
Pay as Inspecting Field Officer . 383 5 0
Ditto, Lieut. Gov. of Malta . 4000 0 0
Ditto, Pension for wounds . 300 0 0—4683 5 0   Return not yet re-
Maj. Gen. Sir John Colborne, Commanding in Canada . . .   ceived. See also Col.
Maj. Gen. Sir H. Douglas, Bart., Staff, Nova   Return, No. 7.
Scotia and New Brunswick . . 691 14 9½   . . See also Colonial
Ditto, Unattached Pay as Maj. Gen. . 292 0 0— 983 14 9½   Return.
Maj. Gen. Sir James Campbell, Staff at Gre-
nada, Staff Pay . 828 17 1
Ditto, Governor of Grenada, Pay and Emo-
luments . 2775 3 0   . . Ditto.
Ditto, Unattached Pay as Major General 310 5 0—4914 5 1   . . Ditto.
Maj. Gen. L. Grant, Staff at Trinidad . . . . . . Ditto.

PENSIONS, &c.

Maj. Gen. Nicolay, Staff at Dominica, Pay and Emoluments . . . 2795 18 3			
Ditto, Unattached Pay as Lieut. Col: . 419 15 0—3215 13 3			. . Included also in Colonial Return.
Maj. Gen. Sir P. Ross, Governor of Antigua, Pay and Emoluments . . .		4542 0 0	
Maj. Gen. N. Blackwell, Governor of Tobago, Home Salary and Colonial Emoluments 2910 0 0			. . Ditto.
Ditto, Unattached Pay as Major General 319 17 6—3229 17 6			
Col. Maxwell, Governor at St. Kitts, Pay and Emoluments		3822 10 0	{ . . Included also in { Colonial Return.
Col. F. Cockburn, Governor of Honduras .	— — —		. . Return not received.
Maj. Gen. Sir John Nicolls, on the Staff in India	— — —		. . Ditto.
Maj. Gen. Sir Sam. F. Whittingham, Ditto ditto .	— — —		. . Ditto.
Maj. Gen. Earl of Carnwarth, Ditto ditto .	— — —		✓. . Ditto.
Maj. Gen. Sir T. Pritzler, Ditto ditto .	— — —		. . Ditto.
Maj. Gen. Sir Lionel Smith, Ditto ditto	— — —		. . Ditto.
Lieut. Col. Churchill, Military Secretary at Ceylon	— — —		. . Ditto.
Col. G. Arthur, ditto Van Diemen's Land .	— — —		. . Ditto.
Sir Wm. Franklin, Principal Inspector Army Medical Department		1200 0 0	
Lt. Col. Ld. Loughborough, Unattached Pay as Lt. Col.		419 15 0	. . Also Clerk of the
Maj. Gen. Dalbiac, Unatt. Pay as Lieut. Col. 419 15 0			Chancery in Scotland,
Ditto, Staff Pay as Major General . 690 5 7—1110 0 7			1135*l.* 17*s.* 6*d.*
Col. Ld. Downes, Unatt. Pay as Lieut. Col. 200 15 0			
Ditto, Sec. to the Mast. Gen. of Ordnance 1200 0 0—1400 15 0			
Lieut. Gen. Earl of Elgin, Unatt. Pay as Lieut. General		593 2 6	{ . . Also a Pension as { late Foreign Ambas- { sador, 2000*l.*
Lieut. G. Sir T. Hammond, Unatt. Pay as Lieut. Gen.		593 2 6	. . Also 1030*l.* as Equerry
Lieut. Gen. Viscount Lake, Unattached Pay as Lieut. General . 456 5 0			and Clerk Marshall to His Majesty.
Pension from Consolidated Fund 2000 0 0—2456 5 0			
Maj. Gen. Hon. G. Murray, Unatt. Pay as Maj. Gen.		492 15 0	{ . . Also Principal Au- { ditor of the Excheq. { of Scotland, 1200*l.*

6.—ORDNANCE AND MILITARY OFFICERS

(Not included in the Return from the War Office.)

Col. C. Bingham, Col. Royal Artillery, and Fire Master Royal Laboratory . . .		731 17 6	{ . . Also a Pension of { 300*l.* per annum, for { wounds.
Maj. Gen. Sir A. Bryce, Col. Commandant Royal Engineers, and Dep. Inspect. Gen. of Fortifications		1875 5 0	. . Also a Pension of
Lieut. Gen. W. Cuppage, Col. Commandant Royal Art. and Inspect. of Royal Carriage Depart. Woolwich .		1430 7 6	182*l.* 10*s.* for good services.
Lieut. Col. F. Colby, Lt. Col. Roy. Engineers 384 15 5			
Ditto, Extra Pay for Survey of Gt. Britain 495 0 7			
Ditto, Superintendent of the Trigonometrical Survey, Ireland . . 500 0 0—1379 16 0			
Col. Percy Drummond, Col. Royal Artillery 602 5 0			
Ditto, Lieut. Gov. Military Acad. Woolwich 400 0 0—1002 5 0			
Col. W. Dixon, Col. Commandant Royal Artillery		1003 0 0	
Lieut. Col. Sir A. Dickson, Lieut. Col. Royal Horse Art. and Deputy Adj. Gen. Royal Art. . .		1350 10 0	. . Also a Pension of
Col. E. Durnford, Col. commanding Royal Engineers, Canada		1195 7 6	365*l.* per annum for good services.
Dep. Commissary Gen. Drake, in charge of the Commissariat, West Indies . . .		1317 0 10	
Dep. Com. Gen. Edwards, in charge of the Commissariat at Jamaica . . .		1040 4 0	
Col. Sir A. Fraser, Col. of the Royal Horse Artillery, and Director of the Royal Laboratory .		967 9 2	. . Also a Pension of
Maj. Gen. G. B. Fisher, Unattached General Officer and Commandant Woolwich Garrison . .		1247 1 8	182*l.* 10*s.* per annum, for good services.

PENSIONS, &c.

Lieut. Gen. W. Fyers, Col. commandant Royal Engineers, commanding in Ireland . .	2164	15	0	. . He also receives 415*l.* 17*s.* 8*d.* per ann. as late Dep. Barrackmaster, and 558*l.* per ann. as Commiss. of Board of Works, Ireland.
Lieut. Gen. Q. J. Freeman, Lieut. Gen. in the Army	593	2	6	
Col. Gardiner, Lieut. Col. and Deputy Adj. Gen. and Inspector of Clothing in Ireland . .	1044	5	0	
Lieut. Col. C. W. Holloway, Lieut. Colonel Royal Engineers, commanding at the Cape . .	897	5	10	. . Also a Pension of 200*l.* per annum for a wound.
Col. John Hussard, Col. commanding Royal Engineers, Ionian Islands	1195	7	6	
Col. John T. Jones, Lieut. Col. commanding Royal Engineers, Woolwich, and for inspecting Fortresses in the Netherlands . .	1170	5	7	. . Also a Pension of 300*l.* per annum for wounds.
Sir James M'Gregor, Director General Army Medical Board, and Physician to the Garrison at Portsmouth	2172	7	6	
Maj. T. Maling, Assistant Military Secretary to Commander-in-Chief, and Captain 2d West India Regt.	1043	16	5	
Lieut. Gen. Sir John Macleod, Colonel Commandant Horse Artillery, Director General of Artillery, and Master Gunner, St. James's Park . .	2782	7	6	
Gen. Gother Mann, Col. commanding Royal Engineers and Inspector General of Fortifications	2964	5	0	
Col. G. Nicholls, Col. commanding Royal Engineers, Nova Scotia	1195	7	6	
Maj. Gen. R. Pilkington, Unattached Maj. Gen. and commanding Royal Engineers, Gibraltar .	1742	7	6	
Dr. G. Renny, Director General of Hospitals, and Physician and Surgeon to Kilmainham Hospital .	1296	2	2	
Commissary Gen. Routh, in charge of the Commissariat in the Canadas	1862	4	7	
William Somerville, Physician to Chelsea Hospital	576	6	0	Also 600*l.* per annum as late Inspector Army Medical Department.
Maj. Gen. H. Shrapnell, Col. Commandant Royal Artillery	1003	0	0	Also a Pension of 1200*l.* per annum for inventions.
Lieut. Col. Sir C. F. Smith, Lieut. Col. commanding Royal Engineers, West Indies . .	1234	18	4	. . Also a Pension of 300*l.* per annum for a wound.
Lieut. Gen. John Smith, Col. Commandant Royal Artillery	1003	0	0	
Lieut. Gen. T. Seward, ditto, ditto .	1003	0	0	
Maj. Gen. J. F. S. Smith, Colonel Commandant Royal Artillery, commanding in Ireland .	1870	8	4	
Maj. Gen. Sir G. Wood, Maj. Gen., unattached .	590	1	8	. . Also a Pension of 456*l.* 5*s.* for good services.
Maj. Gen. G. Wulff, Col. Commandant Royal Artillery	1003	0	0	
Maj. Gen. W. Wilson, ditto, ditto .	1003	0	0	
Col. G. Whitmore, Colonel Royal Engineers, and Commanding Royal Engineers, Malta . .	1195	7	6	

7.—OFFICERS IN THE COLONIES.

Colony, Name, and Office.	Salary	Fees	Total	From what Source derived.
	£ s. d.	£ s. d.	£ s. d.	
Antigua, Sir Patrick Ross, Governor	4600 0 0	259 10 1	4859 10 1	Paid from Home .. 1850 0 0; Ditto Antigua ... 2900 0 0; Ditto, Montserrat. 250 0 0 — 4060 0 0
Thomas Lane, Public Secretary		1981 12 9		From the Colony.
Ditto, Registrar in Chancery		207 18 2	1469 10 11	
Barbadoes, Sir James Lyon, Governor	3866 13 4		3866 13 4	Paid from Home .. 1900 0 0; Ditto the Colony .. 2666 13 4 — 3866 13 4
Hon. P. C. Wyndham, Secretary and Clerk of the Council		1270 19 4		From the Colony.
Ditto, Remembrancer of the Court of Exchequer		not known		
Ditto, Clerk of the Court of Common Pleas		205 8 6—	1476 7 10	
Thomas Carter, Provost Marshall [To the principal and deputies.]		1500 0 0	1500 0 0	Ditto.
Dominica, Major General Nicolay, Governor	2400 0 0	165 18 3	2565 18 3	Paid from Home .. 1200 0 0; Ditto the Colony .. 1200 0 0 — 2400 0 0
St. Christopher, C. W. Maxwell, Esq., Governor	3490 0 0		3490 0 0	Salary from Home 1640 0 0; Ditto St. Kitt's .. 1500 0 0; Ditto St. Nevis .. 350 0 0 — 3490 0 0
St. Vincent, Sir Charles Brisbane, Governor [Receives also an allowance of 100*l*. currency, for house-rent.]	3522 4 5	266 13 5	3788 17 10	Paid from Home .. 1300 0 0; Ditto the Colony .. 2222 4 5 — 3522 4 5
Trinidad, Major General Grant, Governor	4000 0 0	1335 0 0	5335 0 0	From the Colony.
Jas. Chapman, Island Secretary and Clerk of the Council		1427 0 0	1427 0 0	Ditto.
Henry Gloster, Protector of Slaves	1300 0 0		1300 0 0	Ditto.
E. Murray, Registrar of Slaves	500 0 0	2153 10 9	2653 10 9	Ditto.
A. Warner, Chief Judge	2000 0 0	743 6 0	2743 6 0	Ditto.
G. Fitzwilliam, Deputy Vendue Master		1075 0 0	1075 0 0	Ditto.
A. Gomez, Assessor to the Governor	1500 0 0		1500 0 0	Ditto.
L. F. C. Johnston, Judge of Criminal Inquiry	1500 0 0		1500 0 0	Ditto.
H. Mackworth, Alguacil Mayor		2217 6 0	2217 6 0	Ditto.
F. N. West, Escribano to the Court of First Instance		1821 9 6	1821 9 6	Ditto.
J. Miller, Judicial Referee, and Liquidator and Partidor		1902 16 0	1902 16 0	Ditto.
Tobago, Major General Blackwell, Governor	3027 0 0		3027 0 0	Home Salary .. 1250 0 0; Colonial Ditto .. 1777 0 0 — 3027 0 0
Berbice, Henry Beard, Esq., Lieutenant Governor [Has likewise an allowance of 20*l*. per annum for stationery.]	4000 0 0		4000 0 0	From the Colony.
Charles Bird, Government and President's Secretary	214 0 0	621 0 0		
Ditto, Clerk in Secretary's Office	163 0 0			
Ditto, Private Secretary to Governor	163 0 0			

Colony, Name, and Office.	Salary.	Fees.	Total.	From what Source derived.
Ditto, Receiver of Petty Duties..........	157 6 6	12 0 0	1730 0 0	Ditto.
Deputy Protector of Slaves..............	318 0 0	......	2000 0 0	Out of Fees of Office.
Ditto, Registrar of Vice Admiralty	......	63 ..0	1017 0	From the Colony.
James Innes, Secretary and Registrar......	2000 0 0	......		
David Power, Protector of Slaves...........	1017 0 0	......		
M. S. Bennett, Fiscal...............	357 for House-rent 257	627 0 0 257 0 0	1241 0 0	Colonial Funds 2500 0 0
	5000 0 0 for House-rent 5000 Table Money.	857 0 0	5857 0 0	King's Chest 2500 0 0—5000 0 0
Demerara, Sir B. D'Urban, Lieutenant-Governor..........				From the Colony.
[Receives also allowance as a Major-General on the Staff.]				
W. J. D'Urban, Government Secretary......	214 0 0	1382 0 0	1596 0	From the Colony.
[Captain in the 25th Foot, and A. D. C. to the Lieutenant-Governor.]				
J. A. Sullivan, Colonial Secretary and Registrar .... For House	7050			
Ditto, King's Receiver ...... For House	178 501 71 0 0	7050 178 501 71 0—	7800 0 0	Ditto.
[To Principal and Deputies.]				
Charles Wray, President, Court of Justice	3000 0 0	430 0 0	3500 0	Salary from King's Chest 1500 0 0
Ditto, Judge, Vice-Admiralty	......	70 0 0		Ditto from Colonial Funds 1500 0 0—3000 0 0
R. J. Ritemeyer, Colonial Receiver........	......	......	1571 0 0	Colony.
[A per centage on the Revenues collected.]				
J. A. Goodman, Vendue Master	......	......	2986 0 0	Ditto.
[A per centage on Public Sales.]				
J. W. Young, Protector of Slaves........	2000 0 0	......	2000 0 0	From King's Chest 1500 0 0 Ditto Colony 500 0 0—2000 0 0
W. D. Farr, First Marshall........	......	5100 0 0	5100 0 0	From the Colony.
[To Principal and Deputies.]				
R. H. Muddle, Harbour Master...............	......	868 0 0	1019 0 0	From the Colony.
Ditto, Superintendent of Pilots....... [Captain, Half-Pay, R.N.]	157 0 0	......		
Charles Herbert, First Fiscal......... For House	2600 0 0 300 0 0	300 0 0 178 0 0	3978 0 0	From the Colony 2986 0 0; From King's Chest 514 0—2000 0 0; From the Colony 1671 0; From King's Chest 157 0
George Bagot, Second ditto.............	1228 0 0	......	1228 0 0	From King's Chest 1228 0—1228 0 0
Jamaica, Earl of Belmour, Governor	7000 0 0	......	7000 0 0	From the Colony.
Right Rev. W. Lipscombe, D.D., Bishop of Jamaica	4000 0 0	......	4000 0 0	Grant from Parliament.
Rev. E. Pope, Archdeacon, ...	2000 0 0	......	2000 0 0	Ditto.
C. C. F. Greville, Clerk of the Council, and Island Secre.	3000 0 0	......	3000 0 0	From the Colony.

Name and Office				Total	Source
J. A. Sullivan, Provost-Marshal..............	1590 0 0	....	....	1590 0 0	Ditto.
Sir M. H. Nepean, Clerk of Supreme Court......	1850 0 0	....	....	1850 0 0	Ditto.
Hon. P. C. Wyndham, Registrar in Chancery, and Clerk, of the Patents ....[To the Principal and Deputies.]	475 0 0	3574 0 0		4050 0 0	Salary from Colonial Funds.
Rev. J. P. Williams, Rector of St. Elizabeth.......	438 Glebe 89 0 0	640 0 0—		1147 0 0	From the Colony.
Sir W. Scarlett, Chief Justice.............. [The amount of the Chief Justice's salary is not stated in the Returns sent home.]				....	Ditto.
St. Lucia, Major-General D. Stewart, Governor......	2500 0 0			2500	Ditto.
J. Jeremie, Chief Justice	2000 0 0			2000	Ditto.
J. M. Stephen, Registrar of Slaves............ For Clerk and Stationery	500 0 0	380 0 0 108			
Ditto, Judge Surrogate of Vice-Admiralty Court......			60 0 0—	1046	Ditto.
Bahamas, Major-General Sir J. C. Smyth, Governor...... [If the Fees do not amount to 500*l.*, it is made up by Parliamentary Estimate, *under the head of "Contingencies,"* also pay of 479*l.* 1*s.* 3*d.* per annum as Major-General, and a Pension of 465*l.* for good Services.]	2150 0 0	500 0 0		2650	Colonial Funds . 650 0 0; Parliam. Estimate 800 0 0; 4½ per cent. Duties 700 0 0—2150 0 0
Samuel Nesbit, Secretary and Registrar	475 0 0	558 0 0			Parliamen. Estimate 150 0 0; Colonial Funds .... 325 0 0— 475 0 0
Ditto, Clerk of the Council..............	135 0 0	18 0 0—		1186 0 0	
Grenada, Major-General Campbell, Governor ...... [Receives likewise Military Allowances as Major-General.]	3502 0 0	341 0 0		3843 0 0	Paid from Home .. 1290 0 0; From the Colony.. 2222 0 0—3502 0 0
Oursley Rowley, Secretary, Registrar, and Clerk of Council	177 0 0	867 0 0		1044 0 0	From the Colony.
Malta, Major-General F. Ponsonby, Lieutenant-Governor .. [Receives also Military Allowances; likewise an allowance for Gardeners and Labourers in Gardens of St. Antonio, and in lieu of Forage, and in pay of Coachmen and Colesse Drivers.]	4000 0 0			4000	Ditto.
Sir F. Hankey, Chief Secretary	1500 0 0	88 7 0 Colesse Allow.		1588 7 0	Ditto.
Hon. S. Bathurst, Treasurer to Government..........	1000 0 0	83 7 0 Colesse Allow.		1083 7 0	Ditto.
Sir John Stoddart, Chief Justice	1500 0 0	7 13 2		1507 13 2	Ditto.
Gibraltar, Earl of Chatham, Governor.......... [Receives likewise Military Allowances, and is Colonel of the 4th Regiment of Foot.]	2800 0 0			2800 0 0	Ditto.
General Sir George Don, Lieutenant-Governor	365 0 0				
Ditto, General Commanding in Chief .... [Is Colonel of the 3d Regt. of Foot, and receives other Military Allowances.]	3500 0 0			3865 0 0	Ditto.
Colonel K. S. Chapman, Civil Secretary to Garrison, and Registrar of the Court of Appeal.............. [Receives also 479*l.* 1*s.* 3*d.* per annum, pay as Colonel in the Army, and a Pension of 400*l.* per annum for good Services.]	1200 0 0			1200 0 0	Ditto.
Sierra Leone, Lieutenant-Colonel Findlay, Lieut.-Governor...	2000 0 0			2000 0 0	Parliamentary Estimate.
W. Jeffcott, Chief Justice..............	1500 0 0			1500 0 0	Ditto.

Colony, Name, and Office.	Salary.	Fees.	Total.	From what Source derived.
Cape of Good Hope, General Sir G. L. Cole, Governor	7000 0 0	....	7000 0 0	From the Colony.
[Sir G. L. Cole is Colonel of the 27th Foot, and Governor of Gravesend and Tilbury Forts.]				
Lieutenant-Colonel John Bell, Secretary to Government..	2000 0 0	....	2000 0 0	Ditto.
Sir John Wild, Chief Justice..	2500 0 0	....	2500 0 0	Ditto.
W. Minzin, 1st Puisne Judge	1500 0 0	....	1500 0 0	Ditto.
W. W. Burton, 2d ditto..	1500 0 0	....	1500 0 0	Ditto.
George Kekwith, 3d ditto..	1500 0 0	....	1500 0 0	Ditto.
Anthony Oliphant, Attorney-General..	1500 0 0	....	1500 0 0	Ditto.
Upper Canada, Major-Gen. Sir J. Colborne, Lieut.-Governor..	3000 0 0	....	3000 0 0	Ditto.
[Receives also Pay as a Major-General on the Staff.]				
J. R. Robinson, Chief Justice..	1500 0 0	....	1960 0 0	Ditto.
Ditto, Spkr. of Legisl. Council, & Chairm. of Exec. Conu.	460 0 0			
K. J. Boulton, Attorney-General ..	300 0 0	550 0 0	1192 0 0	Ditto.
Ditto		342 0 0—		
[342l. is in lieu of Fees from Land Granting Department.]				
Sir W. Campbell..	....	....	1200 0 0	Ditto.
[Pension for length of Service.]				
Lower Canada, Lieut.-Gen. Sir J. Kempt, Governor-in-Chief..	4500 0 0	....	4500 0 0	Ditto.
[Receives also Pay and Allowance as Commander of the Forces, as Colonel of the 40th Regiment of Foot, and as Governor of Fort William.]				
Sir F. Burton, Lieutenant-Governor ..	1500 0 0	400 0 0	1500 0 0	Ditto.
[In lieu of a House.]				
Hon. C. J. Stewart, Bishop of Quebec..	2400 0 0	....	2800 0 0	Ditto.
Jonathan Sewell, Chief Justice, Quebec..	1500 0 0	....	2400 0 0	Ditto.
Ditto, Speaker of Legislative Council ..	900 0 0	....	1100 0 0	From the Colony.
James Reid, Chief Justice, Montreal..	1100 0 0	....	2100 0 0	Ditto.
James Stuart, Attorney-General..	300 0 0	1800 0 0	3700 0 0	By Parliam. Grant 2000 0 0 Local Revenue .... 1700 0 0 0—3700 0 0
Nova Scotia, Lieut.-Gen. Sir P. Maitland, Lieut.-Governor..	3700 0 0	....	3700 0 0	Parliamentary Grant.
Dr. Inglis, Bishop of Nova Scotia ..	2000 0 0	....	2000 0 0	Ditto.
[Receives also 150l. for travelling expenses.]				
J. S. Blowers, Chief Justice..	850 0 0	300 0 0	1150 0 0	Parliamentary Grant 250 0 0 Local Revenue .... 1100 0 0 0—1350 0 0
Sir Rupert George, Colonial Secretary..	250 0 0	1100 0 0	1350 0 0	From the Colony
New Brunswick, Sir Howard Douglas, Lieutenant-Governor ..	1500 0 0	1400 0 0	2900 0 0	From the Colony
[Receives likewise military allowances as Major-General.]				
John Saunders, Chief Justice ..	950 0 0	150 0 0	1100 0 0	Parliamentary Grant.
N. F. Odell, Colonial Secretary ..	250 0 0	800 0 0	1050 0 0	Ditto.
Thomas Baillie, Commissioner Crown Lands ..	900 0 0	700 0 0	1600 0 0	From the Colony.
Prince Edward Island, Lieut.-Colonel Ready, Lieut.-Governor	1000 0 0	60 0 0	1060 0 0	Parliamentary Grant,
[He likewise receives about 360l. yearly, by vote of the Colonial Legislature.]				
Newfoundland, Sir Thomas Cochrane, Governor ..	3000 0 0	....	3000 0 0	Ditto.
R. A. Tucker, Chief Justice ..	1200 0 0	....	1200 0 0	Ditto.

	£	s.	d.		£	s.	d.	£	s.	d.	Remarks
Bermuda, Sir H. Turner, Governor................	3035	0	0		200	0	0	3235	0	0	Parliamentary Grant 1500 0 0 Local Revenue .... 1535 0 0—3035 0 0
[Receives likewise the rations of a Major-General.]											
James C. Eaten, Chief Justice................	1000	0	0		20	0	0	1080	0	0	From the Colony.
R. Kennedy, Colonial Secretary	800	0	0		350	0	0	1150	0	0	Ditto.
New South Wales, Lieut.-General Darling, Governor-in-Chief	4200	0	0		...			4200	0	0	Ditto.
[Receives allowances as a Major-General on the Staff, and as Colonel of the 90th Reg. Foot.]											
Alexander M'Leay, Colonial Sec. and Registrar of Records	2000	0	0		...			...			
Ditto, Compensation for loss of Pension for past services in Transport Office	750	0	0		...			—2750	0	0	
Francis Forbes, Chief Justice	2000	0	0		...			2000	0	0	Ditto.
John Stephen, Assistant Judge	1500	0	0		...			1500	0	0	Ditto.
James Dowling, Assistant Judge	1500	0	0		...			1500	0	0	Ditto.
A. M. Baxter, Attorney-General	1400	0	0		...			1400	0	0	Ditto.
Venerable J. Broughton, Archdeacon	2000	0	0		...			2000	0	0	.. At present paid from the Colonial Revenue, but will eventually be defrayed out of the proceeds of Clergy and School Estates.
Van Diemen's Land, Colonel Arthur, Lieut.-Governor	2500	0	0		200	0	0	2500	0	0	From the Colony.
J. Burnett, Colonial Secretary	1200	0	0		for House-rent.			1400	0	0	Ditto.
J. L. Pedder, Chief Justice.........	1500	0	0		...			1500	0	0	Ditto.
Ceylon, Lieut.-General Sir Edward Barnes, Governor	10000	0	0		...			10000	0	0	Ditto.
[Receives likewise military allowances as commanding the Forces, and as Col. of 78th Foot.]											
Major General Sir H. Lowe, Second in Command	3808	0	0		...						
[Colonel of 984 Foot.]	691	19	7		...						
Hon. John Rodney, Chief Secretary to Government.	3200	0	0		...			3200	0	0	Ordinaries of the Army.
T. Eden, Deputy ditto and Secretary to the Councils	3000	0	0		...			3800	0	0	From the Colony.
Ditto, Superintendent of Charitable Establishments	180	0	0		...			2180	0	0	Ditto.
W. Granville, Vice Treasurer and Com. of Stamps	2000	0	0		...			2000	0	0	Ditto.
H. A. Marshall, Auditor and Accountant-General.	2000	0	0		...			2000	0	0	Ditto.
C. E. Layard, Civil and Military Paymaster General.	2000	0	0		...			2000	0	0	Ditto.
Dr. Forbes, Superintendent General of Vaccine Establish.	450	0	0		...						
Ditto, Deputy Inspector of Hospitals	820	2	0		...			1270	2	0	Ditto.
Hon. R. Boyd, Sole Commissioner of Rev. and Commerce	3000	0	0		...			3000	0	0	Ditto.
J. Walbeoff, Superintendent of Cinnamon Plantations	1500	0	0		...						
Ditto, Sitting Magistrates, Mahabadde	180	0	0		...			1680	2	0	Ditto.
P. Anstruther, Collector of Revenue, Colombo ...	750	0	0		*788	69	1	1680	2	0	Ditto.
L. Sansoni, ditto, and Customs, Galle ...	750	0	0		*275	1	6	1538	19	2¼	Ditto.
J. N. Mooyaart, ditto, ditto, Tangaile	750	0	0		*356	6	3	1025	1	6	Ditto.
H. R. Scott, ditto, ditto, Batticelau	750	0	0		*41	7	7				
Ditto, Provincial Judge, Batticelau	750	0	0		*93	7	4	1041	7	7	Ditto.
P. A. Dyke, Collector of Revenue & Customs, Trincomalee	500	0	0								
Ditto, Government Agent for Tambukaduoe,...	750	0	0		*123	3	7	1843	7	4	Ditto.
J. Price, Collector of Revenue and Customs, Jaffnapatam	750	0	0		*34	7	6	1173	3	7	Ditto.
J. W. Huskisson, ditto ditto Manar ...	750	0	0								
Ditto, Supervisor of Pearl Banks,...	200	0	0								
Ditto, Provincial Judge and Sitting Magistrate, Manar	200	0	0		...			1184	7	6	Ditto.

Colony, Name, and Office.	Salary.			Fees.			Total.			From what Source derived.
Ceylon, F. J. Templer, Collector of Revenue and Customs, Chilaw	750	0	0	*294	14	7½	1544	14	7½	From the Colony.
Ditto, Provincial Judge, Calpentyn	500	0	0							
[* The sums thus marked is a commission of 2½ per cent. on the net receipts of the year 1829.]										
Sir R. Otley, Chief Justice	4500	0	0	...			4500	0	0	Ditto.
Charles Marshall, Puisne Justice	2500	0	0	...			2500	0	0	Ditto.
W. Norris, Advocate Fiscal	1800	0	0	...			1800	0	0	Ditto.
J. Perring, ditto and Master in Equity	1200	0	0	...			1200	0	0	Ditto.
H. Pennell, Provincial Judge, Colombo	1600	0	0	...			1600	0	0	Ditto.
R. M. Sneyd, Judge of Provincial Court of Galle & Matura	1500	0	0	100	0	0	1600	0	0	Ditto.
				Contingencies.						
D. A. Blair, Prov. Judge and Sitting Magis. Trincomalee	1152	0	0	...			1152	0	0	Ditto.
P. Brownrigg, Provincial Judge, Jaffnapatam	1500	0	0	...			1500	0	0	Ditto.
Venerable J. M. S. Glennie, Archdeacon	2000	0	0	...			2000	0	0	Ditto.
Honourable and Rev. E. Finch, Senior Chaplain	800	0	0	—						
Ditto, Principal of Schools	270	0	0	...			1070	0	0	Ditto.
J. Downing, Judicial Commission, Kandyan Provinces	2000	0	0	...			2000	0	0	Ditto.
G. Turnour, Revenue ditto	1500	0	0	...			1500	0	0	Ditto.
Sir E. Carrington, Pension as a retired Chief Justice	1200	0	0	...			1200	0	0	Ditto.
Sir A. Johnstone, ditto ditto	1600	0	0	...			1600	0	0	Ditto.
Mauritius, Lieut.-General Sir C. Colville, Governor	8000	0	0	...			8000	0	0	Ditto.
F. E. S. Viret, Private Secretary to the Governor	400	0	0							
Ditto, Colonial A.D.C.	450	0	0							
Ditto, Chief Clerk, Civil Establishment	450	0	0	...			1270	0	0	Ditto.
Colonel Barry, Chief Secretary to Government	3000	0	0	150	0	0	3150	0	0	Ditto.
				for a House.						
N. S. Kelsey, Acting Auditor General	1006	0	0	...			1006	0	0	Ditto.
S. F. Ferris, Treasurer and Paymaster-General	2000	0	0	...			2000	0	0	Ditto.
E. A. Draper, Registrar of Slaves	1500	0	0	322	14	3	1822	14	3	Ditto.
John Finness, Chief Commissary of Police	1008	16	0	...			1008	16	0	Ditto.
R. M. Thomas, Protector of Slaves	1000	0	0	144	0	0	1144	0	0	Ditto.
				for a House.						
E. B. Blackburn, Chief Judge and Commissary of Justice, and Judge of Vice-Admiralty	3500	0	0	18	0	0	3518	0	0	Ditto.
E. F. Prior, Registrar of Court of First Instance	162	0	0	914	1	1	1076	1	1	Ditto.
J. N. Foisy, Procureur General	840	0	0							
Ditto, King's Attorney to Land Court	360	0	0	...			1200	0	0	Ditto.
Tangiers, Drummond Hay, Consul General	2000	0	0	...			2000	0	0	⎫
Algiers, R. W. St. John, ditto	2000	0	0	...			2000	0	0	⎬ From Funds voted by Parliament.
Tunis, Sir Thomas Reade, ditto	1800	0	0	...			1800	0	0	
Tripoli, H. Warrington, ditto	1800	0	0	...			1800	0	0	⎭
Honduras, Major-General Codd, Superintendent	1200	0	0	...			1200	0	0	From the Colony.

This Account is not prepared in all cases for the year 1829. In some instances the accounts for 1829 have not been received, and the last account received has therefore been adopted in those cases.

8.—OFFICERS OF THE HOUSE OF COMMONS.

		l.	*s.*	*d.*

The Right Honourable the Speaker:
Salary, as regulated by Act 30 Geo. III. c. 10   .   .   . 6000 0 0
John Henry Ley, Esq., Clerk of the House of Commons:
Salary, as regulated by Act 52 Geo. III. c. 11, paid out of the Fees belonging
to his Office 3500 0 0
Henry Seymour, Esq., Serjeant at Arms:
Salary, as regulated by Act 52 Geo. III. c. 11, paid out of the Fee
Fund L.2000 0 0
Allowance for a House   .   .   .   . 300 0 0—2300 0 0
John Rickman, Esq., Clerk Assistant:
Salary, as regulated by Act 52 Geo. III. c. 11, paid out of the Fee Fund   . 2500 0 0
(Mr. Rickman's Salary of 200*l.* a year, as Secretary to the Commis-
sioners of Highland Churches, ceased in Aug. 1830.)
William Ley, Esq., Second Clerk Assistant:
Salary, as regulated by Act 52 Geo. III. c. 11, paid out of the Fee Fund   . 2000 0 0
Sir Edward Stracey, Bart., one of the Four Clerks out of Doors attending Com-
mittees; and Clerk of Ingrossments:
Ingrossing Fees 342 3 3
Committee Fees   .   .   . 990 10 11
Salary as Committee Clerk   .   . 50 0 0—1382 14 2
John Bull, Esq., Clerk of the Journals and Papers:
Salary, 500*l.*, out of which 100*l.* is paid to his Assistant   . 400 0 0
Allowance of one-fourth on the Amount paid for copying Papers
in the Office, upon which Fees are paid   .   . 55 16 10
Paid by the Commissioners for regulating the Offices of the
House of Commons, for superintending the general Business
of the Journal Office, and the printing of the Sessional Papers,
in lieu of a charge for the Copy of Papers ordered to be printed,
the same being less than an average of such Copy Money for
the five years immediately preceding the year 1823, when this
arrangement was made by the Commissioners; paid out of
the Fee Fund 1000 0 0
Paid for superintending the compiling of the Journal; abstract-
ing the Petitions; examining the Proofs with the Minute Books;
and finally reading over the sheets preparatory to their being
sent to press 180 0 0
For delivering the printed Journals and Reports to Members;—
these last sums charged in the Journal Account   . 21 0 0—1656 16 10
Andrew Dickinson, Esq., Assistant Clerk of the Journals:
Salary allowed by the Treasury, paid out of the Salary of the
Clerk of the Journals   .   .   . 100 0 0
Paid by the Commissioners, out of the Fee Fund   . 2 8 0
For assisting in compiling the Votes; for nightly attendance;
and for making two Indexes, viz., one for the Table of the
House, and one for the Journal Office; charged in the Account
for printing the Votes of 1829   .   . 503 3 4
For compiling and examining the Journal, and making an Index
thereto; charged in the account for printing the Journal of 1829 639 7 0
Paid out of 400*l.* allowed by the Treasury to the Clerks in the
Offices of the Clerk of the Fees and Clerk of the Journals   . 60 0 0—1304 18 4

APPENDIX.—No. VIII.

1.—A STATEMENT, *showing the Annual Average Amount of the* IMPORTS *and* EXPORTS *of* Ireland, *for the Triennial periods terminating on 5th January,* 1790, 1800, 1810, 1820, *and* 1830 *respectively; distinguishing the Trade with* Great Britain *from the Trade with Foreign Parts.*

PERIODS.	Annual Average Amount of the Imports into Ireland,			Annual Average Amount of the Exports from Ireland.		
	From Great Britain.	From Foreign Parts.	Total.	To Great Britain.	To Foreign Parts.	Total.
Three Years ended	*l.*	*l.*	*l.*	*l.*	*l.*	*l.*
Mar. 25 1790	2,429,176	1,106,412	3,535,588	3,112,817	1,012,516	4,125,333
,, 1800	3,441,101	858,392	4,299,493	3,487,865	528,111	4,015,976
Jan. 5 1810	5,160,924	1,374,144	6,535,068	4,710,713	559,758	5,270,471
,, 1820	4,988,668	1,019,605	6,008,273	5,544,135	747,140	6,291,275
,, 1826	6,102,975	1,388,915	7,491,890	7,751,907	703,011	8,454,918
,, 1830	....	1,573,545	....	....	839,014	

Note.—In the Return here submitted, the Statement of Irish Commerce for the Triennial period terminating on 5th January, 1830, is necessarily confined to the trade carried on with foreign parts. The trade with Great Britain having, since the year 1825, been governed by Coasting Regulations, which deprive this department of the means of keeping any record of the interchange of goods between the two countries, except in so far as the article of corn is concerned.

With the view, however, of bringing down the comparison upon the aggregate Imports and Exports to the latest possible period, it has been thought advisable to introduce the averages of an additional term of three years, ending 5th January, 1826, the date at which the record of the Cross-Channel Trade was finally discontinued.

Inspector General's Office,
Custom House, London,
15th January, 1831.

WILLIAM IRVING,
Inspector General of Imports and Exports.

2.—A STATEMENT, *showing the Annual Average Quantities of the following Articles retained for Home Consumption in Ireland, in the Triennial periods terminating on the 5th of January,* 1790, 1800, 1810, 1820, *and* 1830 *respectively; viz.,* TEA, COFFEE, SUGAR, FLAX, SEED, COTTON YARN, COTTON WOOL, WOOLLEN *and* WORSTED YARN ; SILK, *Raw and Thrown;* IRON, *Unwrought;* TIMBER, DEALS, *and* COALS.

PERIODS.	ANNUAL AVERAGE QUANTITIES retained for HOME CONSUMPTION in IRELAND.							
	Tea.	Coffee.	SUGAR.			Flax Seed.	Cotton Yarn.	Cotton Wool.
			Raw.	Refined.	Total stated as Raw.			
Three Years ended	lbs.	lbs.	cwts.	cwts.	cwts.	Bush.	lbs.	lbs.
Mar. 25, 1790	1,732,374	44,370	199,255	9,913	216,106	339,745	68,717	1,351,680
,, 1800	2,773,070	73,262	226,934	8,405	241,224	327,691	557,720	1,166,106
Jan. 5, 1810	3,551,183	173,273	353,656	30,056	404,763	226,527	1,043,637	3,313,834
,, 1820	3,316,321	405,196	269,499	28,431	317,833	296,142	1,279,374	2,873,862
,, 1826	3,548,293	277,465	301,903	61,697	406,789	460,043	2,510,303	4,368,656
,, 1830	3,887,955	579,260	321,199	....	....	168,459	......	2,478,965
	Jan.5,1828							

	ANNUAL AVERAGE QUANTITIES—continued.					
	Woollen and Worsted Yarn.	Silk, Raw and Thrown.	Iron Unwrought.	Timber, (eight inches square and upwards.)	Deals and Deal Ends, and Battens, and Batten Ends.	Coals.
	lbs.	lbs.	Tons.	Loads.	Hundreds.	Tons.
Mar. 25, 1790	2,294	92,091	9,971	20,138	17,492	338,934
,, 1800	1,880	79,060	10,241	6,973	12,024	362,499
Jan. 5, 1810	287,652	77,632	15,758	15,304	8,726	491,374
,, 1820	608,452	73,005	14,566	33,858	7,691	675,910
,, 1826	632,750	25,983	18,838	55,575	9,417	711,876
,, 1830	......	3,190	871`	66,588	12,071	796,773

Note.—The view which this Statement affords of the average Consumption of the Triennial period, terminating on 5th January, 1830, is to a certain extent defective, inasmuch as the Coasting Regulations by which the Cross-Channel Trade has been governed since the year 1825, prevent the keeping of any record of goods imported duty free from Great Britain, either in the case of British Productions or of Foreign Merchandise, upon which duty has already been paid in a British Port; of the articles included in the present Account, those in respect to which the comparison is most affected by this circumstance, are, Refined Sugar, Flax Seed, Cotton Wool, Cotton Yarn, Woollen Yarn, Raw and Thrown Silk, and Unwrought Iron.

The consumption of Tea in Ireland cannot be ascertained for any annual period, later than the year ended 5th January, 1828, a regulation having been established in the course of the following year, which requires that Tea, destined for consumption in Ireland, shall be charged with Duty in Great Britain, previously to its delivery from the Warehouses.

To compensate as far as possible for the defect in the averages of the period ended 5th January, 1830, it has been thought proper to introduce those of the period ended 5th January, 1826, the date at which the Duty-free Importations from Great Britain ceased to be recorded.

Inspector-General's Office,
    Custom-House, London,   WILLIAM IRVING,
        15th Jan. 1831.   Inspector-General of Imports and Exports.

3.—A STATEMENT, *showing the Annual Average Quantities of the following*
1800, 1810, 1820, *and* 1830, *respectively; distinguishing the Exports to* Great
HORSES, BACON *and* HAMS, BEEF *and* PORK, BUTTER, WHEAT,
MANUFACTURES, LINEN YARN, COTTON MANUFACTURES.

Periods.	ANNUAL AVERAGE QUANTITIES . . .						
	Oxen.	Sheep.	Swine.	Horses.	Bacon and Hams.	Beef and Pork.	Butter.
Three Years ended	No.	No.	No.	No.	Cwts.	Barrels.	Cwts.
Mar. 25, 1790	19,319	......	5,636	2,063	17,026	88,583	198,149
,, 1800	14,105	871	4,033	692	41,948	229,179	215,100
Jan. 5, 1810	19,376	10,203	9,830	3,363	152,070	211,482	309,179
,, 1820	51,880	24,774	36,637	1,978	294,380	170,362	378,303
,, 1826	57,395	62,919	73,912	2,496	338,218	143,725	441,226
,, 1830	....	......	......	......	......	......	......

Periods.	ANNUAL AVERAGE QUANTITIES . . .						
	Oxen.	Sheep.	Swine.	Horses.	Bacon and Hams.	Beef and Pork.	Butter.
Mar. 25, 1790	138	....	49	211	3,960	138,981	120,900
,, 1800	73	....	3	64	314	48,897	65,549
Jan. 5, 1810	227	27	....	104	2,096	66,824	46,423
,, 1820	36	6	199	41	5,658	54,658	65,553
,, 1826	32	110	1	42	1,696	46,206	51,637
,, 1830	94	193	13	138	1,335	52,402	45,576

Periods.	ANNUAL AVERAGE QUANTITIES . . .						
	Oxen.	Sheep.	Swine.	Horses.	Bacon and Hams.	Beef and Pork.	Butter.
Mar. 25, 1790	19,457	....	5,685	2,274	20,986	227,564	319,049
,, 1800	14,178	871	4,086	756	42,262	278,076	280,649
Jan. 5, 1810	19,603	10,230	9,830	3,467	154,166	278,306	355,602
,, 1820	51,916	24,780	36,836	2,019	210,038	225,220	443,856
,, 1826	57,427	62,929	73,913	2,538	389,914	189,931	492,863
,, 1830	....	....	....	....	....	....	......

Note.—In the foregoing Return, the Exports to Great Britain for the Triennial period
terminating on the 5th January, 1830, are necessarily omitted, except in so far as they
consisted of Corn; other Articles, under the Coasting Regulations, by which the
Cross-Channel Trade has been governed since the year 1825, being exported without
specific entry at the Custom-House.   The

Inspector-General's Office,
Custom-House, London,
15th Jan. 1831.

Articles exported from Ireland *in the Triennial Periods ended 5th January,* 1790, Britain *from those to Foreign Countries; viz.,* OXEN, SHEEP, SWINE, *and* WHEAT FLOUR, OATS *and* OATMEAL, IRISH SPIRITS, LINEN

					Cotton Manufactures :	
Wheat and Wheat Flour.	Oats and Oatmeal.	Irish Spirits.	Linen Manufactures.	Linen Yarn.	Entered by the Yard.	Entered otherwise than by the Yard.

EXPORTED TO GREAT BRITAIN.

Quarters.	Quarters.	Imp. Galls.	Yards.	Cwt.	Yards.	Value. l. s. d.
41,616	285,015	3	30,410,840	29,197	. . . .	47 16 0
24,077	320,470	291	32,986,029	16,434	159	19 16 11
61,097	673,895	321,968	37,812,960	17,177	10	110 11 3
113,110	878,179	35,468	43,330,864	10,005	188,713	4,997 5 1
375,781	1,301,183	527,918	49,031,073	3,181	5,997,918	14,887 1 7
525,619	1,697,509	684,680				

EXPORTED TO FOREIGN PARTS.

70,640	27,978	161	3,780,914	. . . . . .	. . . .	8,213 18 0
1,573	3,559	2,083	3,126,340	27	8,988	9,494 5 1
1,495	3,543	1,921	2,938,927	2	77,486	20,203 9 2
3,337	7,265	50,570	4,934,847	. . . . . .	314,679	11,528 15 5
1,802	4,270	4,786	2,916,340	5	1,795,955	8,525 6 0
21	3,625	20,429	3,295,233	. . . . . .	4,163,212	3,296 16 2

EXPORTED TO ALL PARTS.

112,256	312,993	164	34,191,754	29,197	. . . .	8,261 14 0
25,650	304,029	2,374	36,112,369	16,461	9,147	9,514 2 0
62,592	677,438	323,889	40,751,887	17,179	77,496	20,314 0 5
116,447	885,444	86,038	48,265,711	10,070	503,392	16,526 5 7
377,583	1,305,453	531,907	51,947,413	3,186	7,793,873	23,412 8 8
525,640	1,701,134	705,109				

The Averages of the Triennial period ended 5th January, 1826, are inserted in addition to those of the periods mentioned in the Order of the Honourable House, for the purpose of showing the comparative amount of the Exports to Great Britain, at the latest date to which the record of those Exports extends.

WILLIAM IRVING,
Inspector-General of Imports and Exports.

4.—A STATEMENT, *showing the Annual Average Number and Tonnage of* VESSELS *entered Inwards and cleared Outwards, in the Ports of* Ireland, *in the Triennial Periods terminating on* 5th January 1790, 1800, 1810, 1820, *and* 1830, *respectively; distinguishing the Trade with* Great Britain *from the Trade with Foreign Parts.*

TRIENNIAL PERIODS. Terminating on 5th January.	ANNUAL AVERAGE NUMBER AND TONNAGE OF VESSELS ENTERED INWARDS.					
	From GREAT BRITAIN.		From FOREIGN PARTS.		From ALL PARTS.	
	Number.	Tonnage.	Number.	Tonnage.	Number.	Tonnage.
1790	The Entries Inwards from Great Britain and from Foreign Parts are not distinguished in the Records of this period.				7,243	622,013
1800	6,523	544,723	686	97,754	7,209	642,477
1810	7,744	674,425	653	90,233	8,397	764,658
1820	10,018	823,307	937	138,577	10,955	961,884
1830	12,329	1,153,937	1008	166,142	13,337	1,325,079

Note.—There being no record of the Number and Tonnage of Vessels Cleared Outwards, from the Ports of Ireland, for the first or second of the Triennial Periods included in the Order of the Honourable House, the foregoing Return is confined to the Vessels Entered Inwards.

Office of Register General of Shipping,
　Custom House, London,
　　15th January, 1831.

　　　　　　　　　　　JOHN COVEY,
　　　　　　　　　　　Register General of Shipping.

INDEX.

THE END.